*A Trappist
Meeting
Monks from Tibet*

A Trappist Meeting Monks from Tibet

Bernard de Give
Monk of Scourmont

Translated from the French
by Sister Catherine Barker, O.S.B.
of Chester Abbey

*With a Foreword by
His Holiness the Dalai Lama*

GRACEWING

First published in French in 2009 as
Un trappiste à la rencontre des moines du Tibet
by Les Indes savantes, 22 rue de l'Arcade, 75008 Paris

First published in English in 2010
Gracewing
2 Southern Avenue, Leominster
Herefordshire HR6 0QF

All rights reserved. No part of this publication may be reproduced, stored in a retrieval system, or transmitted in any form, or by any means, electronic, mechanical, photocopying, recording or otherwise, without the written permission of the publisher.

© 2009 Les Indes savantes
English translation © Gracewing Ltd

The right of Bernard de Give to be identified as the author of this work has been asserted in accordance with the Copyright, Designs and Patents Act 1988.

UK ISBN 978 085244 535 8

Typeset by
Action Publishing Technology Ltd, Gloucester GL1 5SR

Contents

Foreword	xv
Introduction: A Personal Testimony	1
Tibet's perils and opportunities	1
What is the origin of your interest in the East?	1
Many stages	2
Is it a valid experience?	3
Silence and dialogue	3
A reading guide	4
I. The protagonists in the meeting	4
II. The encounter	4
III. Theological reflections	4

PART ONE: THE PROTAGONISTS IN THE MEETING

Chapter I: The Subject of Religious Experience	9
The three levels of self	9
Interiority following John Tauler	10
The ground of the soul – essence or faculty?	11
On the bank of the Cardoner	13
Benedict's vision	13
Anattā in Buddhism	15
No personal self	17
The great spiritual currents of India	18
Chapter II: Tibetan Monasticism	25
The monasteries	25
The rule for religious	27
Eremitical life	29
The first contact, rather disconcerting in its nature	29

An unmistakable tone 30
Monks at prayer? 31
Prayer and personal relationship 31
A graduated path: Lam Rim 33
At the level of Mahāyāna 33
The practice of Guruyoga 34
General survey of the means 35
The symbolism of sexual union 36

Chapter III: Tibetan Nuns 40
A NEGLECTED GROUP: BUDDHIST NUNS 40
Tracing the historical roots 41
What woman proposes – or founder in spite of himself 42
Why leave the world? To what were they committing themselves? 43
The greatness and decline of feminine monasticism 44
In the land of the Rising Sun 45
In the tradition of Tibetan nuns 46
The state of monasticism in Tibet before the Chinese invasion of 1950 47
EXILE AND RENAISSANCE: TIBETAN NUNS IN INDIA 48
In the shadow of Tai Situ: Sherab Ling 48
Tilokpur, on the summit of the holy hill 49
In the atmosphere of the Gelugpa: McLeod Ganj 50
A recent evolution 53
The nuns of Spiti: new horizons 54
Provisional survey 54
VOWS AND OBSERVANCES 56
What is their motivation? 57
On the quest for full ordination, or the lure of the Chinese tradition 58
WESTERN NUNS ON THE TIBETAN WAY 60
Advantages and drawbacks 61
Prospects for the future 62

Chapter IV: Cistercian Spirituality 67
What is the purpose of this chapter? 67
The founding of Cîteaux 67
Cistercian observance 69
The expansion of Cîteaux 70

Contents vii

Attempts at reform	71
Rancé and the La Trappe reform	71
The epic of Augustin de Lestrange	72
Growth in fidelity	73
The return to the sources	74
SPIRITUALITY IN THE COURSE OF THEIR HISTORY	75
The period of origins	75
The spirituality of La Trappe	77
Towards a new equilibrium	78
Moving on from false images	79
A powerhouse of prayer?	80
Nearer to you, my God	81

PART TWO: THE MEETING

Chapter V: First Encounters (India)	87
MEETING OTHER RELIGIONS	87
PRELIMINARY STAGES OF DIALOGUE	89
Bangkok – Bangalore	89
Béthanie (Loppem) – Petersham	89
A TOUR OF MONASTIC INDIA	90
Chapter VI: Meetings in Europe	94
THE INTERRELIGIOUS MEETING AT PRAGLIA	94
The participants	95
The order of the day	95
The themes put forward	96
The second meeting at Praglia	96
The dialogue commission	97
TWO TIBETAN MONASTERIES IN SWITZERLAND	97
Rikon	97
At Mont-Pèlerin: Tharpa Chœling	98
Vevey and Rikon revisited	99
A BUDDHIST MONASTERY IN BURGUNDY	100
Kagyu-Ling	100
Over the course of the years	103
Is interreligious dialogue taking place?	104
A BUDDHIST RETREAT AT SAINTE-BAUME	105
A Mahāyānist retreat at the Viviers seminary	106
A great heart: Lama Thubten Yeshe	107

VISITING NON-CHRISTIAN MONASTERIES IN GREAT
BRITAIN 109
   In Wales: Penrhos 109
   Manjushri Institute, Ulverston 110
   A Vedānta Centre: Bourne End 112
TWO THERAVĀDA BUDDHIST CENTRES 113
   The Mahābodhi Society, London 113
   The Wimbledon Vihāra 114
A TIBETAN MONASTERY IN SCOTLAND: SAMYE LING 115
A MEETING BETWEEN CHRISTIAN AND BUDDHIST
MONKS IN HOLLAND: MAITREYA INSTITUUT, EMST
(25–27 August 1988) 118
   Some of the points raised 120
A GELUGPA PRESENCE IN THE TARN: A CENTRE AND
A MONASTERY AT LAVAUR 121
   Vajra Yoginī 121
   Nālandā monastery 122
UNDER SPANISH SKIES 124
   Barcelona – Madrid 124
   Kalu Rinpoche and the Rimé movement 126
   Panillo (Huesca) 127
TWO TIBETAN CENTRES IN BELGIUM 128
   Yeunten Ling, Tihange 128
   Brussels, rue Capouillet 130
CHRISTIAN-BUDDHIST ENCOUNTERS AT
KARMA-LING (SAVOY) 130
   Spirituality in daily life – Fourth Encounter (6–8 June 1987) 132
   God and Emptiness – Fifth Encounter (2–4 September 1988) 133
   A shared linguistic research project 135
   The Dalai Lama's visit to Karma-Ling, Saturday
     30 October 1993 136
EAST-WEST SPIRITUAL EXCHANGES WITH JAPANESE
ZEN MONKS 137
EXCHANGES WITH TIBETAN MONKS 138
   Intermonastic hospitality programme 138
THE DEVELOPMENT OF THE COMMISSION FOR
   MONASTIC INTERRELIGIOUS DIALOGUE 139
A DIALOGUE IN BOTH DIRECTIONS 141

Contents   ix

Chapter VII: At Home with the Lamas	147
A MOUNTAIN MONASTERY ON THE DARJEELING	
ROAD: SONADA	148
FIRST STAY IN NEPAL	151
RETURN TO INDIA	152
DHARAMSALA, OR TIBETAN CULTURE IN EXILE (1980)	153
Life at Dharamsala	154
A meeting with a young Indian	157
The influence of the hill: political, educational, social	
and religious	158
THE STAGES OF MY RETURN JOURNEY	159
By way of a conclusion	160
THE TIBETAN MONASTERIES OF KARNATAKA	
(SOUTH INDIA) (1983)	162
In Nepal	162
In Karnataka	163
Tibetan monasteries in India	164
Ganden	165
Drepung	168
Sera	170
Tantric College	172
RETURN TO NEPAL	173
Patna – Rājgir – Amritsar – Bangalore	174
DHARAMSALA AND HIMĀCHAL PRADESH (1983)	176
Settling in and companions	176
Sherab Ling – Bīr Settlement	177
Catholic presence	178
At a Hindu ashram	179
A dash of climatic information	180
Tashi Jong and its ritual dances	180
Rewālsar: its monasteries and hermits	183
An educational paradigm: the Tibetan Children's village	184
Holy Week	185
A provisional balance-sheet	185
Dharamsala, a centre for dialogue	186
Bön: an unappreciated tradition	188
Life at Dharamsala	188
From Delhi to Kathmandu	191
THIRD STAY IN NEPAL (1983)	192
Here the Buddha was born	193

The Pokhara site	194
The monasteries at Pokhara	195
BIHĀR, A MONASTIC COUNTRY	197
1. The University of Nālandā	197
2. The magic of Rājgir	199
3. Visiting the Jain nuns	199

Chapter VIII: More Recent Visits — 204
A MAJOR SPIRITUAL EXCHANGE:
CHRISTIAN AND BUDDHIST MONKS MEET IN INDIA
DHARAMSALA – ASIRVANAM: 15–29 NOVEMBER 1992 — 204

Eventful beginnings	205
The Lord's Day at Delhi	206
The ascent to Sherab Ling	207
The hospitality of the Tibetan nuns and the Nunnery of McLeod Ganj	208
A Kagyupa monastery in full expansion: Sherab Ling	211
Pilgrimage to Rewalsar	213
Tashi Jong and its ritual dances	215
The flourishing of gonpas in the Bīr Settlement	216
A momentous day at Dharamsala	217
Dharamsala–Delhi	219
Delhi–Bangalore–Asirvanam	219
Excursion to Mysore	220
A day of arrivals	221
THREE DAYS IN SESSION AT ASIRVANAM	222
1. Wednesday 25th November	222
High Mass	222
Opening Session	223
2. Thursday 26th November	223
Lecture on exegesis	223
The silk farm	224
Expositions by the Tibetan monks	224
3. Friday 27th November	224
On the Rule of Saint Benedict	224
Testimonies from the nuns	225
Celebration of Light	225
At the monasteries of Bylakuppe	225
The Benedictine monasteries of Bangalore	226

MADURAI	227
Minakshi Temple	227
Madurai Mission	227
Hindu temples in the neighbourhood of Madurai	228
An arduous journey	229
The return journey	229
A MONASTIC PILGRIMAGE TO TIBET (1994)	230
The participants	230
From Europe to Nepal	231
IN NEPAL	232
Kathmandu	232
Kopan	233
Bodnath	234
Pulahari	234
ON THE ROOF OF THE WORLD	235
LHASA	236
On the Barkor	236
The Jokhang	237
Tour of Lhasa	238
Drepung	239
Sera	240
Life at Lhasa	241
The Norbulinka	243
Ani Sangkhung	245
An expedition: Tsedang, Samye	246
The Potala	248
Tsurphu prohibited	249
Ganden	249
Ascent to the Nunnery of Chouk-seb	251
NEPAL REVISITED	252
Pharping and its temples	254
Patan, the old capital	255
Kopan once more	255
And Bodnath	256
RETURN VIA DELHI	256
Conclusion	257

PART THREE: THEOLOGICAL REFLECTIONS

Chapter IX: Introduction: Divergences and Convergences   263

OUR PROGRAMME   267
TRINITY AND TRIKĀYA   267
  1. The Christian Trinity   268
  2. The three Bodies of the Buddha   269
  3. The three conditions of the Body of Christ and the three Bodies of the Buddha   270
  4. The three divine Persons and the three Bodies of the Buddha   271
  5. Some difficult points   271

Chapter X: Mahāyāna Compassion and Christian Charity   274
  What is the question in hand?   274
  Mary's compassion   275
  Compassion of the faithful   275
  And in the presence of the Buddha?   276
  Buddhist benevolence   277
  Monsignor Lamotte's conclusion   278
  The Openness of the Mahāyāna   280
  The bodhisattva ideal   280
  A Buddhist without knowing it   282
  Jesus, the perfect bodhisattva   283
  Some classic works   283
  A double bodhicitta   285
  On the island of Hokkaidō   286

Chapter XI: The Philosophy of the Person and the No-Self of Christianity   290
  A word of introduction   290
    I. The person in Christianity   290
      Philosophical personalism   293
    II. Facing the no-self of Buddhism. Uncompromising replies: incompatibility   295
    III. Towards a conciliation   296
    IV. The no-self of Christianity   304

Chapter XII: Prospects for the Future, and What is at Stake   312

Concise Bibliography   314
Index of Names   316
Index of Places   320

The Dalai Lama,
photo copyright Karma Ling

THE DALAI LAMA

FOREWORD

Historically individuals and communities across the world have looked to their religion and culture as a source of basic values. In our present increasingly standardised world it is sad to see that the influence of religion on our lives has declined and there seems to be less concern for humane values. However, if human society loses such values as justice, compassion and honesty, we will face greater difficulties in the future.

Therefore, religions have an important role to play. Each has its own philosophy and there are similarities as well as differences among the various traditions. What is important is what is suitable for a particular person or group of people. All religions make the betterment of humanity their main concern. When we view different religions as essentially instruments for developing good human qualities such as compassion, tolerance, forgiveness and self-discipline, we can appreciate what they have in common.

The most significant obstruction to interreligious harmony today is lack of appreciation of the value of others' faith traditions. Until comparatively recently, communication between different cultures, even different communities, was slow or nonexistent. For this reason, sympathy for other faith traditions was not necessarily very important - except of course where members of different religions lived side by side. But this attitude is no longer viable. In today's increasingly complex and interdependent world, we are compelled to acknowledge the existence of other cultures, different ethnic groups, and, of course, other religious faiths. Whether we like it or not, most of us now experience this diversity on a daily basis.

One of the best ways to overcome ignorance and bring about understanding is engaging in dialogue with members of other faith traditions, which can take place in a number of different ways. Discussions among scholars that explore and appreciate where different faith traditions converge and perhaps more important where they differ are very valuable. On another level, it is very helpful when ordinary but practising followers of different religions meet to share their experiences.

Belgian Trappist monk Fr. Bernard de Give is a living example of the positive value of such an approach. For many years he has engaged particularly with Tibetan Buddhist scholars and ordinary practitioners alike in conversation and actively shared experiences with them. The result, I believe, has not been a compromise of faith for any involved, but rather a mutual enrichment. In this book Fr. Bernard tells many stories about the places he has visited, some in Europe, others in Asia and the wide variety of people he has met in his mission to appreciate the spiritual lives of others. His is an inspiring account of making firm friends and developing mutual respect, which I believe is essential if we are to make inter-religious harmony a reality.

October 16, 2009

Introduction:
A Personal Testimony

Quo coeli iussu
Go where heaven urges you
(*The de Give motto*)

Tibet's perils and opportunities

The invasion of Tibet by the Chinese Communists in 1950, followed by the voluntary exile, in 1959, of the Dalai Lama and of a significant number of Tibetans (there are 100,000 in India, 1,300 in Switzerland) overturned the political and cultural situation of a country which, after centuries of fierce isolation, suddenly saw itself catapulted outside its frontiers. This was simultaneously a disaster and an opportunity for this traditional culture which became accessible to Westerners, then seeking and eager for a spirituality which would correspond to their needs and to their anguish. As we are to discuss experience and dialogue, I may be permitted to give a personal testimony, since in these areas all abstract speculation seems vain and insubstantial.

Urging me to write a book on the subject, a Buddhist nun, French by birth and a fine philosopher too, had insisted: "State in your preface that this work, resting as it does upon the spiritual life, cannot be understood by anyone who has no experience of meditation. We do not make a simple comparison of abstract doctrines, useful though the knowledge of them may be."

What is the origin of your interest in the East?

The author of these pages, while having acquired a real sympathy for the Dharma and for its adherents, is not a Buddhist nor even a seeker. For a long period a member of the Society of Jesus, I was, in this capacity, a seminary professor for eight years, first in Sri Lanka and then in India. I had the opportunity to pursue Oriental studies for a year in Oxford, where I struck up a friendship with the young Chögyam Trungpa and the future Abbot (Bönpo) of Dolanji, Sangye Tenzin Jongdong.

Since becoming a Trappist in 1972, I have been happy in my vocation and, as a monk, enjoy meeting the monks of other religions: Hindu Swāmis, Jain ascetics, Buddhist monks and, particularly, Tibetan Lamas. At the end of 1977, a Benedictine and Cistercian commission for Monastic Interreligious Dialogue (D.I.M.) was set up, and it was with alacrity that I became involved with this from the beginning. We had the opportunity to take part, that same year and again in 1979, in interreligious meetings at Praglia, near Padua, bringing together again in fraternal dialogue qualified representatives of various non-Christian monastic orders. They appreciated these exchanges with us monks in the congenial atmosphere of a great Benedictine Abbey.

Many stages

Thanks to the openmindedness of the Abbot of our monastery, I was able to visit in person a good number of Tibetan centres in most of the countries of Western Europe: Switzerland, France, England, Scotland, Belgium, Spain, Holland ... I had the closest ties with Kagyu-Ling, in Burgundy, where I went each summer for ten years to follow a course in Tibetan.

In addition, a productive collaboration with the Karma-Ling Institute, in Savoy, gave rise most notably to the organising of Christian-Buddhist colloquia on themes of doctrine and spiritual life. These took place over five years, which provided continuity. In another connection, and something which is unusual for a Trappist, I was permitted to make three visits to India and to Nepal (1979, 1980, 1983) for language-study, and in order to become better acquainted with the everyday life of Tibetan monks. One venture, this time as part of a group, was the journey of November 1992, organised by D.I.M., the Indian Benedictine Federation and, on the Tibetan side, by one of the four Regents of the Karma Kagyu Order and the representatives of the Dalai Lama. At the time of writing, I had just returned, with several Catholic monks and nuns, from an impressive pilgrimage to Tibet, of which more will be said later. It took place from the 8th to the 29th July 1994. Thirty or so French Buddhists had responded to the invitation of the lamas of Plaige, in Saône-et-Loire.

Is it a valid experience?

Not in the narrow sense of a regular practice of the methods of Eastern meditation; I know them rather by hearsay and by their outward aspect. I have, I believe, heard enough said about them to be able to guess at their content and their impact. Besides, it is impossible to spend any length of time in so many Tibetan monasteries without attending their ceremonies and being struck by the atmosphere, in which all the senses are overwhelmed (by the riot of vivid colours, the resounding of trumpets, cymbals and conches, the fragrance of incense), in which the purpose is a calming of the soul (*shiné*) and discerning vision (*laktong*) towards Vacuity. Above all, it is the encounters with great spiritual men among the lamas which has made the most lasting impression on me.

Silence and dialogue

This is not the place to recall the doctrinal differences between our two religions, obvious and considerable as they are. There are frequent enough conferences and colloquia to go thoroughly into these. The overriding consideration for me (and I am not alone) is a very lively and undeniable feeling of encounter in depth. The most real self of the persons with whom one is speaking, particularly if these are monks, meets a sister soul (even if, in theory, there is no soul). Whether one speaks or remains silent, a dialogue is definitely taking place.

For this to be so, it is essential that one passes, according to the magnificent formula of Saint Augustine, *ab exterioribus ad interiora, ab inferioribus ad superiora*: "from outward things to inward, from lower to higher" *(Enarrationes in psalmos,* CXLV, 5): in short, to detach oneself from the corporeal world for the sake of the spiritual, for the immanence within us of the divinity and in order to become aware of its transcendence. A Hindu yogi, a deeply spiritual man, one day offered his autobiography to an Indian Carmelite Friar, with this dedication:

> *Find light within.*
> *Heart is God's Throne*[1]

A reading guide

This introduction sums up the message of this book, which will be ordered quite naturally around the theme of *encounter*. Now, an encounter, of its nature, implies the existence of at least two persons or two groups. The plan of the book stems from this: the protagonists of the encounter, the circumstances which made it possible for them to know each other and then the content of their dialogue. We originally considered giving this book the title *Encounter and Dialogue*. An encounter is essential, if one is not to repeat the all-too-frequent occurrence of the intellectual in his study, surrounded by volumes on Buddhist philosophy which he sets about criticising, but in whom one looks in vain for that inner resonance which can only come from a contact with living Buddhists. This point made plain, the plan of work will be as follows:

Part One: The Protagonists in the Meeting

1. The subject of the religious experience
2. Tibetan monasticism
3. Tibetan nuns
4. Cistercian spirituality

Part Two: The Encounter

1. First encounters (India)
2. Encounters in Europe
3. Living with lamas
4. More recent visits

Part Three: Theological reflections

1. Introduction: divergences and convergences
   Trinity and Trikāya

2. Mahāyāna compassion and Christian charity
3. Philosophy of the person and No-self in Christianity
4. Prospects for the future and what is at stake

It should not be matter for surprise that the character of the three parts of this book should differ. The first is intended as a general presentation of monasticisms brought face to face; it concerns history and spirituality. The second part, which constitutes the body of the work, gives the particulars of my personal encounters of these monks of the East. The last part, calling for the most reflection, embarks upon a more theoretical discussion of the philosophies to be compared. In any case, the work will retain, we hope, a genuine unity of inspiration. It was completed in October 1995. As for the visits to centres and monasteries, they will be described as I found them at the relevant period. There is no plan to update the descriptions.

One might well ask why the first part begins with a comparative study of the *subject*, or the meaning of the person. This is because the matter is absolutely basic. If one is to maintain a critical stance, it is essential to avoid confusion from the outset. Now this is one of the points on which Eastern religions differ most sharply from our Judaeo-Christian tradition. At the Abbey of Praglia, when I was saying, "I thank you" to a great Swāmi, who had come from Rishikesh, he looked directly at me and said, "Who is *I* ? And who is *you* ?"

This first chapter is, in short, no more than a sketch of the state of the question. We shall postpone until the third part of the book any effort to go to the heart of the matter, with the aim which serves as the guiding-thread of the enterprise: to try to discover, beyond the dogmas that separate us, a deeper intuition which unites us. Did not Jesus himself declare: "I tell you, many shall come from East and West and take their places at the banquet with Abraham, Isaac and Jacob, in the kingdom of heaven" (Matthew 8.11)?

I wish to put on record my gratitude to Dom Guerric Baudet, former Abbot of Scourmont, and to his successors, who allowed me to make these journeys, exceptional for a Trappist. I am especially grateful to our current Abbot, Dom Armand Veilleux, who made this edition possible and who took great care over the correct presentation of the work.

My thanks extend also to Sister Catherine Barker, a Benedictine nun of Chester Abbey, who was so careful in the work of translating the original French text into English. And to Mr Tom Longford, who kindly accepted this book for Gracewing Publishing.

Last but not least, we want to express our thankfulness to His Holiness the Dalai Lama, who sent to us such a kind Foreword to this book.

Note

[1] S. VALLAVARAJ, S. PILLAI, *J'ai rencontré le Christ chez les vrais yogis*. Nauwelaerts, Leuven-Paris, 1977, p. 24.

Part One

The Protagonists in the Meeting

Chapter I

The Subject of Religious Experience

> In my Father's House
> there are many dwelling places.
> (*John 14.2*)

The subject of spiritual experience ... This theme is one of such fundamental importance that one approaches it with trepidation. And as for incorporating everything which has been said about it by all the mystics of East and West, who could claim to have the necessary competence? The only options are to resort to a general survey or, alternatively, to try to detect the main trends. For experienced readers, this is no more than a reminder, but one which is not without usefulness. Our reading places us more often before discussions of the object of religious experience; here, instead, are different ways of considering the human subject which governs the different options of mysticism.

The three levels of "self"

A number of years ago, I was present at a lecture, given at Louvain by Father Yves Raguin on the approach to non-Christian religions. Not having recorded his text, I am unable to reproduce it here. However, I remember that he began in a very psychological fashion by making us aware of *three levels of "self"*. The following paragraphs sum up what he said.

> 1. The first observation of a person who has travelled a good deal: all the great cities of the world look alike. Neon signs, refrigerators, bus services, coca-cola ... (This reminds me of Father René Voillaume, arriving in Calcutta. I was showing him around and expected to hear

expressions of surprise, but all that he said was: "These great modern cities are all the same; you could say we were in New York, Tokyo, Paris ...").

2. However, if one takes the trouble to talk to people and find out how they think, it becomes clear that, under this "crust" of a wholly superficial uniformity, there is to be found, at the level of rational constructs, cultures, an astonishing diversity, indeed, seemingly irreducible oppositions: philosophies, nationalisms, political preferences, schools of art ...

3. This diversity, however, is not ultimate; the person who succeeds in penetrating more deeply to the heart of human nature, to its most secret hopes and desire, reaches bedrock, wrapped in mystery but more real than everything else. It is possible that, at this level, everyone is united, close and alike. It is there that God creates us in his own image, where he dwells and opens us to the infinite. It is home to the thirst for the true, to poetry and to mysticism. There is no place here for mental combat, for the sphere of secondary constructions in order to drink at the source.

In other words, we find ourselves within concentric spheres. The most distant is in constant contact with the sensory world. This is the animal in us, which falls into the realm of biology, medicine and mechanics. Sphere number two is the complex totality of all our faculties, with which philosophers such as Aristotle, as well as the psychologists and moralists, are concerned. But this is not the deep self, the kernel of our being, infinitely precious and our capacity for the Absolute.

I do not think I am mistaken in saying that it is there that one must place oneself in order to make any worthwhile approach to souls of another culture, age and religion. It is in this sense that I was delighted by a remark made by a young Englishman who had become a Buddhist novice in Oxford: "If everyone gave himself up to meditation, all the religions would meet".

Interiority following John Tauler

The spiritual author who seems to me to have best explained the matter is the 14th-century Dominican of the Rhineland, John Tauler.[1] Within the manifest unity of the human being, he distinguishes three orders within which life develops. "Man consists of three men who, nevertheless, make one whole. The first is the outer man, the sensitive animal. The second is the rational man. The third is the *Gemüt,* the higher part of man. All that, reunited makes one man only, even though there may be different wills within these three men, each willing according to his own fashion" (LXIV.4).[2] The distinction between the first two men, says Father Hugueny, between the life of feeling and that of reason, is a fact of everyday experience on which we do not need to dwell. It is concerning the third man, *the interior man,* that we need fuller explanations.

In our view, in relation to the text just quoted and in relation even to different passages in the same sermon where there is reference to *Gemüt,* this *Gemüt* would seem to be the entire interior man. However, it is but one element and is distinct from the *ground of the soul (der Grund der Seele,* sermon VI.5). "When the *Gemüt* is properly disposed, it is inclined to retire to the ground, where the heavenly soul rests above all the faculties." So the interior man is composed of two elements, the *ground* and the *Gemüt.* In the course of explaining the different names applied to the soul, Tauler tells us: "The soul is also called *mens* (the Augustinian term). My children, here is the ground in which the true image of the Blessed Trinity lies hidden, and this ground is so noble that no proper name can be given to it; sometimes it is called the *ground* of the soul, and sometimes the *apex*[3] of the soul, but it is no more possible to name it than it is possible to name God. Greatly blessed would that person be who could see how God lives in this ground. The closeness and the kinship which the soul, in this ground, has with God are so ineffably great one would not dare, indeed could not, say much about it (LVI. 5)."

Tauler does not go on to say, as Eckhart is blamed for having said, that the *mens,* the ground of the soul, is uncreated; however, it is something which is above all human concepts and which has the unutterable property of being that by which God unites himself to us, in the mysterious union which perfects the image of the blessed Trinity in us.

The ground of the soul – essence or faculty?

Here Father Hugueny, whose explanation we are following, wonders whether or not this ground is a special faculty. At first glance it would seem not to be one ... This distinction between the ground and the faculties is clearly set out in the following passage: *"In the midst of the silence, a mysterious word was spoken in me.* Where is the silence and the place where this word is spoken? It is in that which is the purest that the soul has to offer, in that which it has which is the noblest; it is in the ground, in short, in the essence of the soul. Here the soul performs no action and has no knowledge; it is unaware of any image, either of itself or of any creature. The soul carries out all its actions through its faculties: that which it knows, it knows by understanding; when it thinks of something, it does so by memory; if it is to love, it does so with the will. This is how it acts through the faculties and not through the essence. Each of its activities is always tied to some intermediate image, but in the essence there is no activity of any kind."[4] To judge from this passage, one would be justified in thinking that Tauler situates contemplation in the very essence of the soul. However, with him, as with Eckhart, the words *faculty* and *essence* do not have the same meaning as in the philosophical treatises to which we are accustomed.

This "something" which Eckhart is blamed for having said to be uncreated, and which he does tell us is an intellectual passivity distinct from the essence of the soul, is this very capacity for contemplation of which Tauler writes: "About this interior nobility, hidden in the ground of the soul, many learned men have written. One calls it a *spark* of the soul, another a *ground* or an *apex*, a third the *principle* of the soul.[5] Saint Albert the Great calls it an image in which the Blessed Trinity is represented and where it resides. This spark withdraws to the summits which are its true home, where the understanding cannot follow it, for it does not rest until it returns to the Ground from which it proceeds and where it was in its uncreated state (LXIV. 2)." If Tauler calls the Ground *a pure and simple substance of the soul*, it is somewhat after the manner of Albert the Great, in his wish to distinguish a faculty of contemplation: a divine passivity, closed against any action on the part of creatures, open to the immediate action of God, eager to receive it. Close by it, there is the *Gemüt*, an *innate will* which, at the higher level of contemplative union and after having drawn us towards God, gives us the full awareness of the mystical union. It is at this moment that the image of the Blessed Trinity comes to perfection in us.[6]

Let us leave Tauler[7] now and give ourselves a brief respite from such abstract considerations by making contact with men of flesh and blood whose experience shows how greatly mystical knowledge differs from the kind that is acquired through our discursive reasoning. In order to give no occasion for jealousy, I shall take what seem to me to be typical examples, from Saint Ignatius and Saint Benedict.

On the bank of the Cardoner

In his solitude at Manresa, the converted knight gave himself up to great austerities. He who would later call himself the Pilgrim reports how "God treated him in the same way as a schoolmaster treats a child he is teaching and, whether because of his roughness and his untrained mind, or because he had no one to teach him, or because of the firm will God had given him to serve him, he definitely considered, and has always believed, that *it was God* who treated him in this way. One day he went, out of devotion, to a church which was a little more than a mile away from Manresa, along the path which runs beside the river (the Cardoner). Continuing his devotions, he sat for a time, his face turned towards the river which flowed a little way below him. While he sat there, the eyes of his mind began to open. This was not a vision, but he knew and understood many things, as much concerning the spiritual life as matters of faith and of science, and this in such a light that everything appeared to him new. He received such light in his understanding that, when he recalled all the help that he had received from God, and all the things that he had learnt in the course of his life (down to the age of sixty-two), put together in one heap, this did not seem to him to equal what he received on this occasion. And all this happened in a manner which gave him such light in his understanding that he seemed to himself to be a different man and to have a different mind to that which he had previously."[8] When one considers that Ignatius was no romantic and weighed his words well ...

Benedict's vision

My example from the *Dialogues* of Saint Gregory the Great is extremely well known; Benedictines know it by heart. I should like them, nevertheless, to hear it anew, with the same freshness of soul and the same amazement with which Peter the deacon heard it for the first time. The event occurred, as you know, a short time before the death of this Father of monks.

> While the disciples were still asleep, the man of the Lord, Benedict, was already keeping watch, anticipating the hour of night prayer. Standing before his window, he was praying to the almighty Lord when suddenly, at that very hour of the night, he saw a light streaming which drove away the darkness and shone with such splendour that the light of day would be dim in comparison. While he gazed at it, something quite extraordinary happened: as he narrated this later, the whole world came together before his eyes, as though in a single ray of sunlight *(velut sub uno solis radio collectus)*.
> Peter (the deacon): This is something I cannot imagine, having never experienced anything of the kind. How could a single man possibly see the whole world?
> Gregory: Peter, bear in mind what I am about to tell you: for the person who sees the Creator *(animae videnti Creatorem)*, the entire creation is a tiny thing. However slight the glimpse he has had of the light of God, all that is created becomes too confined for him; for the light of interior contemplation extends the capacity of the soul *(mentis laxatur sinus)* and, as a result of its expanding in God, it is higher than the world. What can I say? The soul of the contemplative *(videntis anima)* transcends itself when it is carried away in the light of God above itself; and, in looking down from above, it understands how limited is that which she could not master when on the ground. This man could not have had such a vision except in the light of God. What is so amazing, then, if he saw the whole world gathered together before him, since he was lifted up outside the world, in the light of the mind *(in mentis lumine)*? When it is said that the world was gathered together before his eyes, it is not that the heavens and the earth were contracted, but the soul of the seer had expanded. Carried away in God, he could without difficulty see all that was below God. When the marvellous light blazed before the eyes of his body, his mind received a marvellous light which showed the soul of the seer, carried away towards things on high, how little was everything below.[9]

Although no claims to technical accuracy are made for this page from Saint Gregory, it will be remembered that, in his third homily on Ezekiel, he lays great emphasis on a pair of opposites which has become a classic: on one hand, *notitia*, which is intellectual knowledge, the fruit of meditation on the mysteries revealed by faith; on the other hand, wings, *volatus,* the ecstatic flying-off which raises us above ourselves[10] or, to return to Tauler on this point, a faculty of knowing, broad in a different way and deep in a different way from our discursive reason: *Mentis laxatur sinus ... Videntis animus est dilatatus.*

Anattā in Buddhism

However, you are eagerly waiting to hear about Eastern religions. We shall first consider Buddhism, as being the most difficult, and, in fact, I have to square the circle by explaining what constitutes the subject of religious experience in a religion which admits of no subject at all – nor, come to that, any object of metaphysical value. Western Christians are astonished at this and often ill-informed. To use a discerning remark by Caesar in his *Civil War: Quae volumus, ea credimus libenter; et quae sentimus ipsi, reliquos sentire speramus.* (*"We willingly believe that which corresponds to our desires and those feelings which we ourselves feel, we wish that others also should feel."*[11]) So Buddhists are supposed to be much closer to our own ideas than they are in actuality; so one wishes that they worship a personal God, or to believe that they express themselves badly when they assert that there is no such thing. In this connection I recall that, having attended all the meetings of the Buddhist Society in Oxford in 1963–1964, and, long and animated as they often were, I cannot remember the name of God being once mentioned. As for the personal self, it was discussed, for the purpose of answering questions from those in the audience who were completely at sea with a doctrine which refuses the self in any shape or form. But good intentions have a hard time of it, and we shall hear, for a long time to come, of Christians trying to persuade Buddhists that, for transmigration to take place, there must be someone who transmigrates, and that that one who attains the longed-for enlightenment must be a person, to which genuine Buddhists persist in responding in the negative. These are what have been justly called *the paradoxes of Buddhism.*[12] We may not, in the name of a false sympathy, pretend that these do not exist, for we should be condemning ourselves in advance to cruel disappointment.

By way of reminder, *the aim of Buddhism* is not in any sense the arrival at a union of love between man and God, since God does not enter into the case and because even the human body is understood in a different way (something which we will discuss later). But one endeavours, just as in Hinduism, to escape from an infernal cycle of reincarnations, since existence is suffering. To be convinced that the exclusion of a real subject is the authentic teaching of Buddhism, it should be sufficient to read, for example, the attractive little work which Chögyam Trungpa published under the title: *Cutting through Spiritual Materialism*.[13] This book is full of wisdom and insight. All the same, one will see all the way through it, on the grounds of cutting through any "spiritual materialism", a systematic demolition of anything offering support to the person. It is fundamentally anti-metaphysical; something which does not prevent this monk from saying excellent things concerning the façade of this world, or from urging a radical form of detachment.

I was at the Charterhouse at Parkminster, after a Buddhist monk had visited them, passing rapidly through the cloisters, the longest in the world, I believe, and where no one is to be seen, since the monks live as hermits. When I expressed a rather high regard for Buddhism, the Prior answered me: "What is an interior life without God?"

I feel obliged to warn the well-intentioned and the over-enthusiastic against ambiguities of language. This is not to say that a study of Sanskrit or Pāli is essential, highly useful though it might be, but what is called for is linguistic self-discipline. Such words as *liberation* or *salvation, enlightenment, awakening* or *faith,* have, in a Buddhist context, a very precise technical meaning, and the same applies to the word *incarnation* if one wishes to employ it, in Hinduism, for *avatāra*. Even such general and inoffensive terms as *truth, light, illumination, peace* or *good-will* assume, in the religions of Asia, a very different meaning from that which they have in Catholic theology, or even in the ordinary usage of Western philosophers. It is important to be aware of this and to take it into account; otherwise, one is easy game for every syncretism, whether inadvertent or intentional.

No personal self

It was with interest that I read Chögyam Trungpa's book: *Cutting through Spiritual Materialism*.¹⁴ This is pure Buddhism, even though the Lama gives evidence, in his frequently subtle analyses, of a thorough acquaintance with our depth psychologies. He appears to be particularly adept at unmasking the wiles of the *ego*. If there is any one lesson which he inculcates throughout these pages, it is "seeing things as they are". But notice should be taken, here: this is not a matter of *res uti sunt in se*, as in Saint Thomas Aquinas. In Buddhism, there is no *in se*, neither in things nor in man: no intelligible reality, only chains of phenomena which bind us to transmigration, or the succession of mental states, the origin of which has to be observed without conferring on them the dignity of a metaphysical self. "*Seeing things as they are*" aims, in this context, at freeing the invalids that we are from the multiple illusions or neuroses which this path is intended to cure, without having recourse, as a Christian would, to the help of God as Father. One often has the impression of dealing with the logic more of a psychotherapy than of a religion.

If one now turns to a more technical book, such as the work of Father Joseph Masson: *Bouddhisme, chemin de libération*,¹⁵ there will be presented the clearest texts on the impermanence (*anicca*) of every thing and also of man himself, owing to his composite nature. Not only is the human body impermanent, but it is nothing in itself but the accidental and impersonal union of the four primary elements. Similarly in the other, spiritual, elements of his existence, the *khandha*, man is impermanent and unstable.¹⁶ As for the human being in its totality, this is even less solid and unified than its constituent parts. The *Milinda-Pañha* compares man to a chariot. Just as this is composed artificially of different parts: wheels, axle, shafts, body ... none of which is really, and substantially, the chariot, the same is true of every man.

In addition to their impermanence, all beings are likewise insubstantial (*anattā*). The so-called man "is nowhere" and he is obliged to admit: "I am not a reality for anyone". This way of seeing things is fundamental in Buddhism: it is to be found everywhere and in every period of time. An ancient text says, and is quoted by a present-day author: "One says: 'a person', as a conventional designation, but not as an essential reality."¹⁷

"Destitution exists, but there are no destitute. There is no agent, nothing to be found but the action. A path exists, but there is no traveller."[18] Monsignor Lamotte sums up the Buddhist outlook in one short sentence: "I am nothing but a constantly renewed line of momentary phenomena."[19]

The modern catechism by Subhādra[20] states categorically:

> The Buddha considers erroneous the belief in an immortal soul. Buddhism does not teach the transmigration of a soul but, rather, the new formation of an individual in the material world of phenomena, by virtue of the will-to-live (*tanhā*) and of the moral character (*karma*).
> Q. – Is the ego identical with what is known as the soul?
> A. – No. The ego is not a lasting entity or an immaterial substance, but a given condition arising from the five elements.[21]

"The core of the message, it may be said with confidence, is the absolute renunciation of the idea of and the attachment to a personal self."[22]

The great spiritual currents of India

When the Jesuits specialising in Hinduism, and resident in India, published a series of studies on this religion, the title given to this work was: *The Quest for the Eternal*,[23] the eternal understood, of course, not as a person but as a neutral adjective. This corresponds to the Sanskrit *amritam, a state of soul* such as to endure for ever and to transcend death. It is this ideal which is found to underlie the many and varied exertions of the devout and of the ascetics of India. To cut a long story short, let us look at the way in which, each with its own particular emphasis, the different systems of Hinduism have this common base.

1. For the Jains and the yogis of *Sāṃkhya*,[24] the objective is the liberation of the individual soul, considered as an eternal monad, whose being was located, in its origin, outside time and space. This needs to be set free from all that is not eternal, that is to say, from the body, from the emotions and from discursive thought. The happiness of liberation, therefore, consists in a form of isolation (*kaivalyam*), the isolation and retreat of the soul into its own interior, which is of a timeless essence. Yoga, which was associated particularly with the *Sāṃkhya* school, was primarily a psychologi-

cal technique for discerning the immortality of one's own soul, by differentiating it simultaneously from the empirical ego and from the objective world. Like primitive Buddhism, *Sāṃkhya* is essentially an atheistic environment. Besides, whatever the school, the basic objective is for the soul to be set free from the grip of the world of phenomena and of the ego. For the Indian, this is the fundamental role of religion; the question of the existence and of the nature of God is, in short, of secondary importance. This is stated by Professor Zaehner in his fine work of synthesis: *At Sundry Times*.

2. The famous doctrine of *Advaita* is very well known in the West, Shankara being the absolute master. You will recall that this is a matter of the acknowledged identity of the profound self of a person, *ātman*, and the divine but impersonal substrata of the world, *brahman*.[25] The system is complex, and not lacking in subtlety, but it professes explicitly a quite thoroughgoing pantheism.

Oliver Lacombe, one of the most competent specialists in *Vedānta*, ends his preface to Father P. Johanns' work, *La pensée religieuse de l'Inde*, as follows: "'Unitive Way' is too weak an expression, from the viewpoint of the *Vedāntin*: it is for *identity*, in the strictest sense, with the universal Absolute for which he thirsts. This is a profound, monolithic and drastically unilateral metaphysic, notwithstanding the disposition for welcome and condescension which it shows for as long as its most fundamental intuition is not at stake. This is a spirituality of immanence which is, however, shaped by an ardent passion for divine purity and inviolability, safeguarded – to sum up – by the sacrifice of any finite reality."[26]

It will be noted that such an experience of immersion in the All, of fusion with the Infinite of the cosmos, of identification with the Self of the world, is not the sole prerogative of India. We are not referring to Father Le Saux, who was granted this profound experience of *Advaita* and was able, in moving terms, to give some idea of it, at the Congress of Bangalore,[27] to name one occasion. His dependence upon Hinduism is all too much in evidence. However, so as not to overlook that isolated individuals in the West may be the silent beneficiaries of such a "grace", suffice it to recall Master Eckhart, by whom the Hindus set great store.

There was also Plotinus, whose wonderful experience would merit study in this context. It is heartrending, in the closing pages of the *Enneads*, to sense the force of the conflict, as one might say, between, on the one hand, his Hellenic outlook in which there are no irrational and unforeseen occurences and, on the other, an invasion by a living Person, as his comparisons bear witness: a father, a spouse. Attention has even been drawn to a cosmic, indeed "oceanic" experience in Saint Bernard. But in his case, even more than in that of Eckhart, it is impossible to isolate such favours from the general context of his mystical life, which is completely penetrated by Christian personalism. What is peculiar to India is to have systematized this nature mysticism,[28] and attaching ultimate value to it, to prize it so highly as to find, in principle, the idea of its being surpassed quite unthinkable.

As Father Raguin rightly observed at Bangalore, "It can truthfully be said that, in Christianity too, the experience of the 'impersonal' in God does exist."[29] This experience of Nature, however, cannot be exclusive of God as person.

3. As for the various *bhakti* movements, that is to say, of loving devotion to a divine incarnation, I should not like to lessen the impact that these have on any religious sensitivity. This predisposition has given rise to some admirable prayers and outpourings which we encounter in the *Bhagavad-gītā*, in the wonderful Shaivite poets of South India, or in such engaging mystics as Kabīr, Tulsīdās, Tukārām or Caitanya. However, it must in all honesty be recognised that *this personal love is not ultimate,* that it gives way, as always in India, to a finality of absorption into the divine, by *identification*. This is fully evident in the most objective studies of the system of Rāmānuja,[30] the great theoretician of *bhakti*. His opposition to Shankara notwithstanding, the material world, souls and *Brahman*, for him were one and the same reality.[31]

At Bangalore, concluding his fine account of the religious poets of South India, Father M. Dhavamony was obliged to admit: "Not even the Shaivite theism which, amongst all the Hindu systems, is the closest to Judaeo-Christian theism, entirely escapes a kind of semi-pantheism."[32]

We Christians will always have a basic difficulty in grasping the nature of the self which undergoes spiritual experiences in the various forms of non-revealed religions. It is as well to tread warily, for it would be unwise to see in these Buddhist monks[33] or those Indian *sannyāsīs* Christians who do not know how to express themselves.

The preceding account is intended to be loyal. One does not have to conclude that a divergence in doctrine at so fundamental a level automatically excludes any form of dialogue. It is quite the contrary that we shall endeavour to show. But we must first of all inquire further into the nature of Tibetan Buddhism, and into the important place which monasticism occupies in it.

Notes

[1] This is not the place to give the history of trichotomy. We know that it is found explicitly in St. Paul. On this subject, see the excellent study of Father FESTUGIÈRE in *L'Idéal religieux des Grecs et l' Évangile*, Excursus B, pp. 196–220: *La division corps – âme – esprit de 1 Thessal. 5.23 et la philosophie grecque*. The author shows how general this tripartite division was amongst the Greeks. He also, however, draws attention to the modification made to it by Saint Paul, substituting, for the first term of the trinomial *nous-psyche-soma*, the word *pneuma*, in which one recognises a biblical influence. On the opposition between the psychic man and the pneumatic, see 1 Cor. 2. 13–14 and 1 Cor. 15.42–49. Leaving aside Plotinus, the trichotomy is to be found in authors such as Evagrius, Cassian and William of Saint Thierry (*Golden Letter*, nn. 287–289).

[2] *Sermons de Tauler*, translation by Hugueny, Théry and Corin , 3 volumes, Éditions de la Vie spirituelle, Paris, Desclée, 1927–1935. We are using the *Introduction théologique* by Father Hugueny, O.P., volume I, pp. 75–79.

[3] This most secret, and properly called divine, element of the soul is sometimes called *Burg, citadel* or *stronghold*. The "deepest centre" of the soul is found also in Saint John of the Cross. Cf. A. Roberts, *Collectanea Cisterciensia* 38 (1976), pp. 115–119.

[4] *Von der ewigen Geburt*. Sermon for the 1st Sunday after Christmas.

[5] J. ANCELET-HUSTACHE, *Maître Eckhart et la mystique rhénane*. Coll. Maîtres spirituels, Éd. du Seuil, 1956. His mysticism is clearly explained there (pp. 52–74); on the ground of the soul and the equivalent terms used in the history of Christian mysticism, see pp. 66–67.

[6] The tripartite division has been restored to its place of honour in our time by Thomas Merton, who showed it to be in agreement with the distinctions made in Hinduism. The empirical ego corresponds to the *ahamkāra* of *Sāṃkhya*, the "self-in-depth" to the Hindu *ātman*. Insofar as there exists an unconscious storehouse as C.G. Jung revealed it, this was already worked out by *Mahāyāna*

Buddhists under the name of *ālayavijñāna* ("consciousness – deepest stratum"). Father Heinrich DUMOULIN, S.J., in "A History of Zen Buddhism" (London, Faber and Faber, 1963), however, warns (pp. 279–280) against a simple identification of Zen *satori* with a liberation of the unconscious. While not allowing a metaphysical interpretation, the primordial energy exalted by *Tantra* Buddhism does have some points of contact with the *voluntas ut natura* of the Scholastics and the *Gemüt* of Tauler. See CHÖGYAM TRUNGPA, *Cutting through Spiritual Materiali*sm, (London, Robinson and Watkins, 1973, and Berkeley, Shambhala Publications, 1973). "This energy is the support of the primordial understanding which observes the phenomenal world. It gives their impetus alike to the enlightened and the confused states of mind, and is indestructible in that it constantly arises. It is the power which drives emotion and thought in the confused state, and wisdom and compassion in the enlightened state" (quotation from *Kriyayoga Tantra*).

7 Father HUGUENY, O.P. has extended his study of these questions in two articles in *Supplément à la Vie Spirituelle: Le fond de l'âme, le mens et l'image de la Sainte Trinité*, January 1932, pp. 1–25, and *Le vouloir foncier*, mars 1932, pp. 129–157. He is clearly to be situated within the Thomistic framework, which might at times divert him from the outlook of the Rhineland mystics.

8 *Le récit du pèlerin. Autobiographie de S. Ignace de Loyola*. Translated and annotated by Eugène Thibaut, S.J., 2nd edition, Bruges, Beyaert, 1924, pp. 70–71; 3rd edition, revised by André Thiry, S.J., Desclée de Brouwer, 1956, pp. 74–75. In the Museum Lessianum collection, ascetical and mystical section, No. 15.

9 SAINT GREGORY the GREAT: *Dialogues,* Book 2, chapter 35, PL 66, cols. 198 & 200. The following English translation and commentary is recommended: GREGORY the GREAT: *The Life of Saint Benedict*. Commentary by Adalbert de Vogüe, O.S.B., translated by Hilary Costello and Eoin de Baldraithe (Saint Bede's Publications, Petersham, Mass., 1993).

10 Cf. I. VALLERY-RADOT, Bernard de Fontaines, volume I, Tournai, Desclée, 1963, p. 254.

11 *Bellum civile*, II, 27, 2. He had already said in his Gallic War (B.G., III, 18, 6): *fere libenter homines id quod volunt credunt,* "the general tendency among men to believe what they wish should be true".

12 F. TAYMANS d'EYPERNON, S.J., Museum Lessianum, 1942. Other paradoxes, the resolution of which appears to be impossible, are pointed out by J. MASSON, S.J. *Le Bouddhisme, chemin de libération*, Desclée de Brouwer, 1975, pp. 36–37, note 50: "How is one to reconcile *karma,* the responsibility for subsequent effects, with the absence of a *bearer* of this responsibility, and this *karma,* with its mechanical and compulsive nature, with the exercise of a genuine *liberty*?" ("Comment concilier un *karma,* responsabilité à effets subséquents, avec l'absence d'un *porteur* de cette responsabilité? Et ce *karma* au caractère mécanique et contraignant, avec l'exercice d'une vraie *liberté*?")

13 See above, note 6.

14 TRUNGPA, op cit., pp. 190–191

15 See above, note 12; see pp. 53–56 of the author referred to.

16 "That's why the Hīnayānists, too, describe the universe in terms of atoms in

The Subject of Religious Experience 23

space and of moments in time. In this respect, they are atomistic pluralists" (CHÖGYAM TRUNGPA, op. cit., p. 188).

[17] W. RĀHULA, *L'enseignement du Bouddha d'après les textes les plus anciens.* Éd. du Seuil, Points. Sagesses, 1978. He returns insistently to this non-existence of a self: pp. 45–46, 48–49, 77–78, 81–83, 86–89, 95. This title is available in English as *What the Buddha Taught*, Gordon Frazer, 1978.

[18] *Visuddhi-Magga*, XVI, in WARREN, *Buddhism in Translations*. Quoted by MASSON, op. cit., p. 57.

[19] See also MASSON, op. cit., p. 112: "In the spiritual quest of the *Hīnayāna*, the first axiom is, in the truest sense, the non-existence of the person. The latter is a mere aggregate of particles artificially joined, of elements without extension or duration. The history of self is a succession of pearls on a string – except that there is no string." ("Dans la recherche spirituelle du *Hīnayāna*, l'axiome préliminaire, c'est, au plus vrai, la non-existence de la personne. Celle-ci est un pur agrégat de parties artificiellement conjointes, d'éléments sans étendue ni durée. L'histoire du moi, c'est la suite des perles sur un fil, sauf qu'il n'y a pas de fil.")

[20] SUBHĀDRA BHIKKU, *A Buddhist Catechism*, 1970, pp. 130–132.

[21] A psychological presentation is to be found of the origin of the empirical self or "ego", according to the classical doctrine of the five *skandha* or aggregates, in the book by CHÖGYAM TRUNGPA already quoted. Worthy of notice, from the outset, is a *complete rejection of the metaphysical self* which should not surprise us in the least; this is the first of the Four Noble Truths taught by the Buddha at Benares (see MASSON, op. cit., pp. 59–60). The same concept holds good in the mind of the *Mādhyamikas*, and so is shared byTrungpa (pp. 190–191).

[22] MASSON, op. cit., p. 64.

[23] R. DE SMET and J. NEUNER: *La quête de l' éternel. Approches chrétiennes de l'hindouisme.* Desclée de Brouwer, 1967, Museum Lessianum.

[24] We are following here R.C. ZAEHNER, *Inde, Israël, Islam. Religions mystiques et révélations prophétiques*, Desclée de Brouwer, 1965. This is the translation of his *At Sundry Times*, London, Faber and Faber, 1958.

[25] On the *Brahman-Ātman* identification, see R.C. ZAEHNER, *Hinduism*, Oxford University Press, 1966, pp. 52–56; M. ÉLIADE, *Histoire des croyances et des idées religieuses*, vol. I, Payot, 1976, pp. 254–257. On the *Vedānta* see, for example, R. GROUSSET, *Les philosophies indiennes*, vol. II, Desclée de Brouwer, 1931, pp. 160–403.

[26] P. JOHANNS, *La pensée religieuse de l'Inde*, Paris, Vrin; Louvain, Nauwelaerts, 1952, p. III.

[27] *Les moines chrétiens face aux religions d'Asie.* Bangalore, 1973. Vanves, A.I.M. Secrétariat, pp. 52–54.

[28] Cf. R.C. ZAEHNER, *Inde, Israël, Islam*, p. 121.

[29] *Les moines chrétiens*, pp. 42–45.

[30] Rāmānuja's doctrine, full of delicate shading and obliged to fight simultaneously on two fronts, is not without complexity. See P. JOHANNS, S.J., *Vers le Christ par le Vedānta*, vol. I: *Çankara et Rāmānuja*, Louvain, 1933, Museum Lessianum. For a summary, but fair, explanation, see the short work by A.M.

ESNOUL, *Rāmānuja et la mystique vishnouite*, Coll. Maîtres spirituels, Éd. du Seuil, 1964, pp. 113–122

[31] P. JOHANNS, *La penseé religieuse de l'Inde*, pp. 9–11. R. DE SMET and J. NEUNER, *La quête de l'éternel*, pp. 79–83.

[32] *Les moines chrétiens*, pp. 105–106.

[33] One finds, however, in this path an ultra-lucid, remorseless manner of tracking down to the very roots the most secret wiles of self-love.

Chapter II
Tibetan Monasticism

The life led by monks in Tibet. At first sight, it could seem that to discuss a subject like this in our times shows a complete loss of any sense of reality. It is well known that, in 1950, the Chinese invaded the country and, making full use of their overwhelming military superiority, they drove the monks from their monasteries, reduced most of these to ruins, as was shown in a photographic exhibition at Dharamsala in February 1980. As for those thousands of cenobites, reduced to slavery, it was now practically impossible for them to maintain the observances handed down for so many centuries. The final blow fell on 10 March 1959, when the popular uprising of the Tibetan nation was savagely suppressed by the Chinese Communists. However, as a result of the exodus of more than 80,000 Tibetans to India, or even to the West, this was also the beginning of a new era in which the great, traditional monastic Orders took root in a strange land, while a significant number of Westerners saw in the Buddhist Dharma the answer to their aspirations, an alternative to the oppressive structures of our own society.

The monasteries

It is not our intention to retrace the evolution which has taken place in recent times. If we remain within the classical framework of the life as actually lived by monks in Tibet, it is because this framework is still the indispensable reference point of the monks in exile, just as it is for those Tibetans who remain attached to the religion of their ancestors. It is the ancient monasteries which remain the template. It is the way of life which, however greatly adapted to new circumstances, remains in their view the ideal to be pursued in the foundations to be re-established. There is a good deal more to this than archaeology.

In the pages which follow, I am indebted to a well-considered chapter on *Le mysticisme tibétain* by T.-Y. Dokan.[1] The whole existence of a Tibetan unfolded in the midst of reminders intended to show him the path to follow. Living under the constant protection of the Liberated Ones, above all, the great Bodhisattva Chenrezig, who reincarnated in order to help human beings, Tibet offered the image of an entire people en route towards a glorious apotheosis, with acceptance pervaded by joy which is, for Westerners, one of the most surprising aspects of Buddhism. In such a framework and, no less, in such a wild and naturally awe-inspiring environment, where the human being experiences his smallness, his frailty and his impermanence, where he cannot feel anything but ephemeral, the very numerous monasteries stood out as havens of peace in which to dedicate oneself to what was essential, or — in a manner of speaking — as powerful magnets. In addition, in pre-revolutionary Tibet, one person in six entered religious life and, among the laypeople, many were either stewards to monasteries, whose material welfare they guaranteed, or else made themselves responsible for an isolated monk, a *naldjor-pa,* that is an experienced ascetic of the "direct path", living in seclusion.

As for the monasteries, in Tibet there was every kind, from great cities such as were, for example, Drepung, near Lhasa, with some ten thousand monks, Sera, Ganden or Kumbum which counted several thousand, down to minute religious houses, consisting of no more than a little temple, an assembly hall and a few other buildings, perched on wind-buffeted peaks or sheltered in the hollow of some remote valley. However, in the one case as in the other, between Tibetan *gonpas* and Christian monasteries practically no similarity existed. Drepung or Kumbum were more like towns, with numberless ill-assorted buildings which formed unities more or less independent of each other and separated by streets which, for many hours of the day, teemed with noisy, ill-smelling and ragged crowds. Within the *gonpa* itself, the monk's life differed even more from that lived, for example, by Catholic monks. There was no church, nor even a chapel, simply a dark temple, the *lhakhang,* the house of the gods, the worship offered to them being limited to the lighting of a butter-lamp, the burning of incense and the making of a triple reverence to the statue representing the lord of the house. It was in the assembly-hall, vast enough to accommodate the entire monastic population, decorated by frescos thronged with benign or terrifying figures, bristling with banners hanging from the ceiling and bearing images of Buddhas and deities, at the back of which gleamed gilded statues of great deceased lamas and the reliquaries containing their mortal remains, that the *trapa* (monastic students) gathered, cross-legged and motionless, kept under control by dignitaries on thrones whose height indicated their rank. Here, for hours at a time, the rounds of the *sūtras* unfolded in a slow rhythm, punctuated by the sounding of bells, trumpets and tambourines and chanted in a very deep voice, coming from the pit of the abdomen. To all intents and purposes, it was to this morning assembly, along with certain other ceremonies, that community life was limited,[2] while, in parallel with it ran the long cycle of studies, as each of the great monasteries was a university – and novices from those religious houses not possessing a school would come there to study – consisting of several sections: philosophy and metaphysics; sacred Scriptures and monastic rule, the tantric school, where ritual, magic and astrology were taught, and the school of medicine.[3]

The rule for religious

The rule for religious is not uniform.[4] The basic thing is to distinguish between the ordained monks and the married religious. The *ordained monks* are the successors to the Indian *sangha*; they follow the disciplinary rules (*vinaya*), which include the vow of celibacy. Nevertheless, not all the obligations and prohibitions of the *vinaya*, such as the eating of meat, are scrupulously upheld. As in Indian Buddhism, several stages serve as landmarks in a monk's life: renunciation of the world, novitiate, full ordination. Monastic vows are, in principle, lifelong. In reality, however, various grounds are accepted for a monk's giving up his vows and being reduced to the lay state. Monks lived in the monasteries. The future monk would enter very young, perhaps around eight years, on his parents' decision, rarely on his own account. He was entrusted to a master, a relative or acquaintance, with whom he would live and who would take responsibility for his initial instructions: reading, writing, elementary grammar, and the memorisation of texts. In return, the disciple was obliged to serve his master and to participate in the corporate menial work of the monastery, such as the gathering of firewood. Later, depending on his wishes and capabilities, he could decide his own future course: study, the carrying out of rituals, temple maintenance, the service of the lamas and administration of their property or that of the monastery. Some, who were unwilling to accept monastic life, joined a very special group: often called warrior-monks, they served as bodyguards and spent the rest of their time in competitive sports and in fighting.

In principle, parents had their child enrolled in the monastery nearest their home. He could remain there for the whole of his life, or he could transfer at his own wish. In order to pursue higher studies, he would eventually join one of the university-monasteries of his tradition. These great monasteries often consisted of several thousand monks, divided into colleges (*tra - ts'ang*). In the case of the *Gelugpa*, for whom the mastery of the intellect is an essential preliminary to the practice of *tantra*, studies in philosophy, metaphysics and so forth lasted seventeen years, ratified each year by an examination in the form of a disputation, ritual in its unfolding. These are public discussions between students, highly picturesque and full of liveliness and good humour. This reminds us, but without such brilliance, of the scholastic training of our mediaeval Schools and the famous *disputationes* still known to religious of my generation. In the case of the *Nyingmapa* and the *Kagyupa*, the young monk could choose between following intellectual studies or the immediate practice of *tantra*, in which case he would enter the college of *tantric* achievement, and be attached to a lama who would confer on him the initiations and the successive teachings of mystical experience. Each monastery had a fixed annual programme, for study and ritual alike, varying from one monastery to another, recorded in a charter either granted or approved by the government.

The *married religious (tantrists)* could also live in the monasteries, although, if they chose to do so, their families remained outside. In the majority of cases they lived in the village, leading a life similar to that of laypeople apart from their religious services. Others, again, led a wandering existence. Recruitment was usually through the family: they handed on the teaching from father to son or from uncle to nephew and they formed an endogamous class. They belonged, for the most part, to the ancient Orders, the *Nyingmapa* and the *Bönpo*. Their long hair, braided with wool and rolled up into a "bun", made them easy to recognise. As their title implies, they devoted themselves to tantric rites and to meditation.

They did not make monastic vows, but simply that of attaining Awakening by the *Bodhisattva* path and the *tantra* vows.

Eremitical life

The desert is, according to Dokan,[5] the place to look for genuine practitioners of the "direct way" of *Vajrayāna*. They lived in hermitages, *ts'am khang*, often built in uninhabited regions near high, snow-covered peaks. A retreat of this kind, moreover, could be more or less strict, and more or less extended. *Ts'am*, in fact, means simply to isolate oneself. This could be done by shutting oneself up in one's own room and leaving it only to perform some act of devotion. Some devout laypeople would isolate themselves in this way within their own homes. One could do *ts'am* in monasteries which owned separate cottages set aside for such use and provided with an internal courtyard; this made it possible to stand in the open air without being seen. There are monks who shut themselves away, there, for several years – often for three years, three months and three days[6] – or even remain there until their death. Isolation of the utmost strictness can also be practised in the dark, and some hermits would wall themselves up for life in something resembling tombs.[7] More often, however, seclusion was observed in the *riteu*, scattered hermitages on mountainsides, sometimes grouped together. The *riteupa* were generally *naldjorpa*, practitioners of the "direct way" and living in total solitude.

The first contact, rather disconcerting in its nature

One of the best Tibetologists of our times was undoubtedly Professor Giuseppe Tucci (+1984). In the book entitled *Tibet: Land of Snows*,[8] he shares with us his mixed feelings on approaching a strange civilisation, one which, to him, was ever so slightly ambiguous. He warns us, however, that there are two dangers to be avoided: of seeing only magic, on the one hand, and of seeing only pure, ancient wisdom, in a good state of preservation, on the other. This is how he sums up his impressions:

> Of course the first contact with the world of Tibet was not edifying, any more than was that of India.. Then there was, in Tibet, the disproportionate number of monks in relation to the population, worship

reduced to an elaborate ritualism, the daily recourse to exorcists to avert some calamity or to cure some illness, the intrusion of financial interests in religious communities and their wealth, as well, could not fail to give rise to an unfavourable impression of the Tibetan religion. Such an impression might well be confirmed and reinforced by visits to the temples, with their innumerable statues and images of bizarre and monstrous appearance, represented as often as not in a manner quite different from that in which we would conceive a divine form.

An unmistakable tone

Nevertheless, monastic life was a hard apprenticeship and imposed years of sacrifice: the best years of life domesticated by an iron discipline, regulated in a rhythm divided equally between liturgical ceremonies and study; the obligation of committing to memory books thousands of pages long; and, for the best, meditation or further study in dogmatics.

All this was achieved in a school under the surveillance of masters, in shrewdly judged proportions of trials and examinations, which unfolded with such wisdom and in such skilfully ordered magnificence of rites that the neophyte approached, with something very like anguish, the decisive moment which, by the assigning of a grade in the ecclesiastical hierarchy, ratified a transformation of mind and soul.

I often had occasion, when speaking to such people, to see how vivid were the memory and emotion associated with the waiting for this decisive moment in their lives, and how perturbed they were in reviewing the stages of their spiritual lives. This emotion was the mark of a sincerity before which all must bow, for it was clear that these persons had succeeded in the most difficult of achievements: that of eradicating the Man from man, completely, without turning back or repentance.

Even after our efforts to sketch, as above, the structure of Tibetan monasteries, the different classes of monks and the stages of their formation, we would remain unsatisfied. All this, after all, is no more than the framework, I might almost say the decoration, of any monastic life. It is nothing without reference to the *interior life*, the means employed for progress towards liberation. The substance, however, I have brought together elsewhere under the title: "*Voies et moyens de salut dans le bouddhisme tibétain*".[9]

Monks at prayer?

On the face of it, Tibetan monks pray a great deal. The order of their day differs little from that followed in our monasteries. Even the material layout of their *lhakhang* reminds us of the double choir familiar to us monks, and we retain a tender memory of the "canonical hours" in the *gonpas* in various countries. Fascinating, too, in its simplicity and "Franciscan" poverty is the daily liturgy in the temple that hugs the road at the foot of *Sonada* hill (Darjeeling district). But sentiment is not enough and, when the texts used are examined more closely, little is to be found but praises of the *Dharma*, exhortations to a higher ethical standard and, here and there, the invocation of a "deity", terrible or beneficent; in short, little in the way of prayer, in the strict sense and, despite the exuberance of the symbols and the beauty of the *thankas*, we are worlds away from the prayer of the Psalms.

This impression has been renforced, for me, by the careful reading of a de luxe presentation brochure entitled *Tushita*[10]. This contains closely argued explanations emanating from well-known masters, spokesmen for various Tibetan traditions within the framework of *Mahāyāna* Buddhism. The interest of this publication is obvious, but one is struck, in the course of reading it, by the insistence upon No-self and emptiness, the constant exhortations to personal effort without recourse to prayer, and the absence of God. Man is alone in his arduous quest. Even what seems to be a prayer is rather an exhortation addressed to oneself: in this connection, the opening invocation to Manjushri and the response of the Dalai Lama on the subject merits re-reading.

Prayer and personal relationship

In December 1986, Lama Denys Teundroup, the spiritual director of the Karma-Ling Institute, Savoy, gave a teaching entitled, *Aperçu sur la prière et les mantras dans le Mahāyāna -Vajrayāna*. His explanation subsequently appeared in *Les Cahiers du bouddhisme* (N° 31). He listed there a series of types of prayers in a Tibetan context, highly instructive and similar, here and there, to the forms with which the Judaeo-Christian tradition has familiarised us. What, however, is fundamentally different, if I am not mistaken, is the ideological basis, the doctrinal background. This is not a criticism of anyone, but an endorsement of the sincerity shown. This is what Lama Denys says:

> Although the *Vajrayāna* stresses the interpersonal relationship and insists upon the importance of prayer, this is not in any sense a relationship in which the mind of the practitioner focuses on the other, reifying him in an anthropomorphic sense, since such a focusing has the effect, on a fundamental level, of consolidating the I-other duality and of stressing its polarising in terms of "you" and "I". Even the relative humility of devotion should be properly understood; it does not consist of diminishing oneself by placing God at an infinite distance from ourselves; to establish oneself in this way, albeit tiny in the face of the divine immensity, is thereby, subtly, to be maintained in duality. The proper attitude is in forgetfulness and abandonment of self, an abandonment which makes access possible to a state of transparency; this is to say that in self-forgetfulness the "I" becomes transparent, and in this transparency, which begins the dissolution of duality, the other also becomes more translucent. It is then that a mutual participation of the "I" and the Other is set up, an essential unifying of these two terms which constitute duality; this way Divinity is to an ever-increasing degree in us and we are to an ever-increasing degree in It. From this perspective, it is clear that profound prayer is not a conversation with the Other but, rather, it is founded in the abandonment of self and a direct participation in the Divine nature. It is clear, too, that even when one speaks of prayer as communication with the Divinity, the question does not arise of a conversation with God. Such a conversation is always part and parcel of our discursive thought processes and would be, in its innermost reality, a conversation with ourselves, with our *alter ego*. In Buddhism, Divinity yoga ultimately makes possible ... the non-dual union of *Mahāmudrā*, in which there is no longer either God or practitioner.[11]

This quotation by Lama Denys shows, to say the least, how much separates a Buddhist spirituality, however profound, from the intimate union of the soul with its God which characterises Christian mysticism. However, I take the view that this passage, to cut a long story short, is somewhat rigid. Anyone who wished better to grasp the worth and the fine shadings of the final goal of *Vajrayāna* should be encouraged to read one of the more recent issues of the magazine *Dharma* on this very theme: *Mahāmudrā, l'ultime pratique de l'esprit*.[12] In it can be read some excellent explanations by masters representing this tradition: Kalu Rinpoche, Bokar Rinpoche and Lama Denys Teundroup.

A graduated path: Lam Rim

Perhaps, however, we are discussing mysticism too easily. This was not the tradition of our novitiates, and it is not that of the Tibetan lamas, either.

It must be recognised that their religion encompasses the Three Vehicles, and must begin with the first of them; that is to say, a long ethical training is presupposed. The Christian who endeavours to practise all the virtues, and is acquainted with the manuals of ascetic theology, is aware of the conflicts involved. To sum up, it is comforting to rediscover, in the clothing of a different terminology, a collection of moral categories similar to those of one's own religion. Although the context is clearly Tibetan, with all the Buddhist philosophy that this entails, I think that a Christian reader would be able to read with profit and understand without difficulty the fine little book by Geshe Rabten, director of the Tibetan centres in Switzerland: *Enseignement oral du bouddhisme tibétain*.[13] This should also be the case with the consecutive volumes of *La grande voie graduée vers l'éveil, de l'incomparable Tsong-kha-pa* (founder of the *Gelugpa* tradition), which have been published with a commentary by Mr Yonten Gyatso, and whose very titles indicate their progression: *L'individu de motivation inférieure ... intermédiaire ... supérieure*.[14]

At the level of Mahāyāna

The twin mainstays are emptiness and compassion. Emptiness is as good a translation as any for *shūnyatā*. Professor Guenther, opposing this to the form of an object, say a potter's vessel, sees attention being drawn, here, to a space, a field (and not to a void).[15] "To use a simple image, the nature of the mind could be compared to the sky, open and shining; but as, when the sky is darkened by clouds and fog, it is veiled from us, in the same way, the veils of our mind conceal its true nature from us," says Kalu Rinpoche. What are these veils? They are, first and foremost, the illusion which ascribes a real existence to phenomenal appearances when, in fact, they are projections of the mind, or the illusion ascribing a real existence to the mind, whereas it is empty of essential being.[16] Here, the philosophy of Nāgārjuna and of the *Madhyamaka* school can be identified.

As for compassion *(karuṇā)*, it would be an aid to understanding to read and meditate on *Les trente-sept pratiques des Bodhisattvas,* compiled by Tho-me Zang-po (1245–1369), which we were able to translate, at Plaige *(Kagyu-Ling),* from the Tibetan and of which the present Dalai Lama likes to give oral explanations.[17] One of the greatest *Kagyupa* masters of the previous century, Djamgœun Kongtrul, is the author of an admirable little treatise, the translation of which has been published under the title *L'alchimie de la souffrance.*[18] He reports the Tibetan system of spiritual apprenticeship, centred entirely upon compassion. The parallels with Christian texts struck me immediately and, for this reason, I gave a lecture on this subject[19] at Plaige. Speaking more broadly, it will be readily granted that it is on this terrain that the two religions come closest. As the comparison calls for serious study, we shall refer to it later.[20]

The practice of Guruyoga

The importance of the choice of a guru is stressed, and his line of conduct towards his disciple is described, for example, in the *Encyclopédie des mystiques orientales,* in the course of the chapter entitled *Le mysticisme tibétain.*[21] Blofeld, too, has dealt with this subject.[22] If a closer examination is desired, the first chapter of *L'Aube du Tantra*[23] should be studied. In this, Professor Guenther simultaneously presents a synthesis of this "spiritual friendship" and the characteristics of the four stages of the evolution described, continuing, moreover:

1. *Kriyatantra:* action viewed symbolically and treated as ritual, as ablutions, for instance; the relationship of a child with its parents, transposed into a religious context, submission to a transcendent being.
2. *Caryātantra:* the pursuit of the meaning of these rules of behaviour; progress from the master-servant relationship to that existing between friends, on an equal footing.
3. *Yogatantra:* the harnessing of everything in us to gaining the maximum degree of insight into this friendship.
4. *Mahā-yogatantra:* no further distinction is made; the question of knowing whether or not the other is my friend no longer arises, since we simply are one.[24]

Further on, Professor Guenther observes: "This profound experience is brought about by the guru and he exercises, by means of such highly intense experiences, a powerful influence on the pattern of our spiritual growth. This is because, ultimately, the guru is none other than the Buddha – not the historical Buddha, but Buddhahood itself. All the empowerments are to be seen as progress in *guruyoga*. In *guruyoga*, we endeavour to approach our true and fundamental nature in drawing closer to the guru. We are also connected with his lineage; that is, with all those who preceded him in the direct transmission of the teaching and who remain connected with him".[25]

All this unerringly evokes the degrees of mystical union, as they are described by Saint Teresa of Avila or, for that matter, as studied by the theoreticians of Christian mysticism, such as Father Augustin-François Poulain in his classic, *The Graces of Interior Prayer*.[26] But who would have the competence, and even the beginning of the experience required, to carry through a comparison between the latter and the stages of realisation in *Vajrayāna*? It is better by far to try, in respectful silence, to attempt to grasp something of the matter from outside. The difficulties which Father Le Saux had in reconciling his Christian faith and his experience of Hindu *advaita* are common knowledge.

The manner of conceiving (let alone realising) the ultimate union depends upon the total mental and psychological structure of the believer, and this point is of the utmost importance. A union of love with God in a personal and theistic perspective, on the one hand, and the realisation of total liberation in the impersonal context of Buddhist *anattā* on the other, cannot be conceived of other than in totally different frameworks. The centrality of this divergence cannot lightly be set aside, so we shall examine it more closely, as far as our limited abilities allow, in the penultimate chapter of this book.

General survey of the means

A brochure entitled *Ladakh*,[27] well-illustrated and showing careful research on this Tibetan enclave within India, provides an outstanding chapter on *Le bouddhisme tibétain ou bouddhisme tantrique,* and we quote the following passage from it:

Vajrayāna offers a wealth of symbols, rites, formulas and psychic exercises which give the disciple the necessary aids for attaining Illumination and for transcending the dualism which handicaps the non-awakened mind. To the same end, *Vajrayāna* presents a considerable number of deities both of terrible or peaceable aspects which serve as auxiliaries or mediums for knowledge, each of them tied to particular rites and functions. *Vajrayāna* has constructed, in this way, an enormous pantheon founded upon a complex system of references and cross-references: each deity, conferred upon the disciple who is initiated into him or her as a tutelary deity or *yidam*, refers him in this way to a colour, a cardinal point, a season, a diagram (*mandala*), an incantation (*mantra*), a letter (*bija*), a posture (*mudrā*) and to a visualisation or mental image (*yantra*).

Explanations on each of these means are beginning to be available. We could, by way of a preliminary study, refer to our article in *Studia Missionalia: Voies et moyens de salut dans le bouddhisme tibétain*.[28] But it is time to close with an important point.

The symbolism of sexual union

Tantrism is most often seen as offering ample liberty for sexual propensities. The iconography appears to offer ample testimony to this conception. Whether statues or *thankas* are in question, female forms abound, as do scenes of copulation. This much is undeniable, and with reference, above all, to the usual *yab-yum* (father-mother) imagery of deities entwined in ecstatic embrace. We shall not claim that none of this is related to the spiritual path we are considering. The subject really calls for a study which will take all the fine shades into consideration. We shall, however, allow ourselves three observations.

1. *Tantric Buddhism* and *Hindu Shaktiism* should not be confused with each other. John Blofeld[29] and H. V. Guenther[30] emphasise that neither the term nor the concept of *shakti* occur in Buddhist texts. This eliminates a disagreeable way of conceiving the union between man and woman from the start.

2. Even if, at least in the past as Daniel Snellgrove believes must be admitted,[31] such a method could call for a physical union, the fullest weight should be given to Professor Guenther's all-round

view. He shows, in fact, in *The Tantric View of Life*,[32] how there is as much difference between their perspectives of love and of sex as there is between moral laxity and ascetic obsession. He establishes, between the former pair, a *gradation*, founded upon the texts. He might not wish us to speak, in this context, of sublimation of the sexual instinct, nor of escape into another world, but sex and love are certainly well-fitted to give access to the most real, not to say metaphysical, perception of existence. There is a danger, here, of words betraying us, as the author takes a firm stand against the Western manner of representing this union.

3. What is certain is that it has a fundamentally *symbolic value*. Like the *bell* that is rung by the left hand in the course of rituals, the feminine deity symbolises *Wisdom*, whereas the *vajra-sceptre* (diamond-thunderbolt) held in the right hand, and the masculine god, represent the skilful means (*upāya*), amongst which compassion plays a prominent role. All the serious authors[33] agree in saying that a pinnacle is attained here, the union of deities showing that in this *intimate conjunction of Compassion and Wisdom*, all dichotomies have been overcome and one has attained Buddhahood.

This area of iconography and its profound symbolism have, without our intending it, drawn our attention to the feminine pole of the spiritual adventure. Is it not under the aegis of these deities that we shall penetrate more deeply into the study of *Tibetan nuns?* Regardless of a widespread ignorance in their regard, they have existed since the dawn of *Vajrayāna* on the roof of the world.

Notes

[1] In the *Encyclopédie des mystiques orientales,* under the editorship of M.-M. Davy, Robert Laffont, 1975. Our quotations, pp. 158–160.

[2] Here we are quoting Dokan, but anyone who has stayed in Tibetan centres such as *Kagyu-Ling, Tharpa Choeling* or the *Manjushri Institute* will have been present each day at other liturgical offices occurring in the evening and which might continue for some hours. It would be surprising if these practices had been established in exile.

[3] This description applies, above all, to the *Gelugpa* monasteries, where stress is laid upon a long intellectual formation. The *Kagyupa*, for example, are known

to initiate their disciples much more quickly into contemplative life.
4 Here we are following the explanation found in the *Encyclopaedia Universalis*, vol. 4, 1989, art. *Bouddhisme tibétain* by A.-M. BLONDEAU, pp. 412–413.
5 See above, note 1.
6 It is known that certain Tibetan Orders, with a stroke of audacity, and seeing the spiritual thirst and generous disposition of Western practitioners, have allowed ordinary laypeople to attempt this experience, which was traditionally reserved for fully-fledged monks. Several *Kagyupa* and *Nyingmapa* centres in India, France, Scotland and Canada have acted in this way.
7 There is ample evidence for this. The practice was highly regarded in the old, indigenous *Bönpo* religion, which transmitted this very austere usage to the *Nyingmapa* hermits. See G. TUCCI and W. HEISSIG: *Les religions du Tibet et de la Mongolie*, Payot, 1973, pp. 202–204.
8 Giuseppe TUCCI: *Tibet, Land of Snows* (Centres of Art and Civilisations) Elek, 1967. Translated from *Tibet paese delle nevi*, Novara, Istituto Geografico De Agostini, 1967, page 64 in the Italian text.
9 In the Gregorian University magazine, *Studia Missionalia*, vol. 30, 1981, pp. 207–232.
10 This brochure was produced by Éditions Dharma, Les Jacourets, F – 06530 Peymeinade (now out of print)
11 Pages 28–29 of the article quoted.
12 *Dharma* magazine. Institut Karma-Ling, Hameau de Saint-Hugon, F – 73110 Arvillard. See no. 7 of this magazine, winter 1989–1990.
13 Compiled by M.T. PAULAUSKI. Paris, Maisonneuve, 1976.
14 Centre d'Études Tibétaines, 6, Boulevard d'Indochine, F – 75019 Paris (3 typescript volumes).
15 CHÖGYAM TRUNGPA & H.V. GUENTHER: *The Dawn of Tantra*, Shambhala Publications (London, Boston, Mass. and Boulder, Colorado, 2001). An earlier edition was translated into French and published as *L'Aube du Tantra* in Coll. Mystiques et Religions, Paris, Dervy-Livres, 1980; pages 39–40 are referred to here.
16 *Dharma* magazine (see above, note 12), no. 7, pp. 5 and 29–30, and no. 21 of this magazine: *Illusion et réalité*.
17 Published under the title *L'Enseignement du Dalaï-Lama*. Coll. Spiritualités Vivantes, Albin Michel, 1976.
18 *L'alchimie de la souffrance. La voie droite vers l'éveil*. Translated from the Tibetan, with notes and glossary by Ken McLeod. Éd. Yiga Tcheu Dzinn, Château de Plaige, F – 71320, Toulon-sur-Arroux, 1982.
19 *L'alchimie de la souffrance et les textes chrétiens primitifs* (May 1986).
20 See Chapter X: *Mahāyāna Compassion and Christian Charity*.
21 See above, note 1 of this chapter. On the guru, see pp. 162–163.
22 *The Tantric Buddhism of Tibet*, Arkana, 1992.
23 See above, note 15, pp. 12–15.
24 It goes without saying that *The Dawn of Tantra* provides a fuller description of the varying states, particularly at the higher levels, of the initiate on this path. See also, in *Dharma* magazine, no. 2, p. 43 and no. 9, pp. 59–60, some important notions of vocabulary referring to this topic. A very detailed

explanation is to be found in the article on *Vajrayāna* by Lama DENYS TEUN-DROUP in the *Dictionnaire des religions* published under the editorship of Paul Poupard by the Presses Universitaires de France, 3rd ed., pp. 2080–2096.

[25] *The Dawn of Tantra* (p. 77 in the French edition).

[26] A. POULAIN, S.J.: *The Graces of Interior Prayer*, London, 1910.

[27] By G. DOUX-LACOMBE. Coll. Les grands voyages. Éd. Centre Delta, Librairie Armand Colin, 1978. The text quoted, p. 84.

[28] See above, note 9, pp. 226–230. On the *mandala*, see, in this article in *Studia Missionalia*, page 228 and the relevant notes. In Poupard's *Dictionnaire des religions*, volume II, the article by M. DELAHOUTRE, p. 1221.

[29] See above, note 22; see his page 89, note 1.

[30] *The Dawn of Tantra*, (pp. 11–12 and 86 in the French edition).

[31] *À la rencontre du bouddhisme*. Published by the Secretariat for non-Christians, Rome, Ancora, 1st volume, 1970, pp. 146–149.

[32] Shambhala Publications, Boulder (Colorado) and London, 1976. See especially the chapter *The Way and the Apparent Eroticism of Tantrism*, pp. 55–57.

[33] We quote seven of them as supporting references, at the end of our article *Voies et moyens de salut* (see above note 9), p. 231, no. 86. This point, nevertheless, is hardly in dispute.

Chapter III
Tibetan Nuns

A NEGLECTED GROUP: BUDDHIST NUNS

In our day and age, when some subjects are worked to death, others, one knows not why, are generally neglected. Even without being a feminist, one has good reason to be astonished that so little is said about Buddhist nuns and that the general public is completely unaware of the existence of nuns in the Tibetan tradition. Our essay is intended to fill a gap. I have been interested for a long time in this matter, and have done everything in my power to acquire information, particularly during my travels in India, believing as I did at the time that Tibet was inaccessible.

A congress in Spain provided me with the opportunity to give, at Valladolid, a report entitled: *El monacato femenino en el budismo tibetano*. This was in the context of the 20th *Semana de Estudios Monásticos* (1984).[1] This lecture subsequently appeared in French in the journal *Collectanea Cisterciensia*, 1987, pp. 260–277. Revised and updated, it later appeared in *Studia Missionalia*, published by the Gregorian University (Vol. 40, 1991, pp. 287–313): *Des nonnes bouddhistes sur le toit du monde*. It will be noticed that the content of this chapter, as to essentials, was already published when our friend Môhan Wijayaratna brought out his book, *Les nonnes bouddhistes. Naissance et développement du monachisme féminin*.[2] We wrote a congratulatory review of it. However, it covers only part of our topic, for it is concerned, above all, with the origins of the institute of nuns and with the various rules to which they were subject during the primitive period, in the context of the *Theravāda*. A book has been published, more recently, by a Norwegian, a disciple of Professor Per Kvaerne, at the University of Oslo: Hanna Havnevik – *Combats des nonnes tibétaines. Religieuses bouddhistes du Pays des neiges*.[3]

Subsequent to our encounter with Tibetan monasticism in India in the month of November 1992, and then in the course of our pilgrimage to Tibet in July 1994, new experiences came our way. We will refer to these again in the chapter reserved for them in the second part.

On feminine monasticism in Buddhism, very little has been written. The best account that I know is by Father Jesús López-Gay, S.J., Dean of the Faculty of Missiology at the Gregorian University: *Origen del monacato femenino budista*.[4] We may be permitted to summarise it here, my personal contribution being to consider what is peculiar to Tibetan monasticism, which circumstances have led me to know best.

Tracing the historical roots

In *pre-Aryan India,* woman enjoyed a position fully comparable to that of man; it was with the invasion of the Aryans that she passed into a condition of inferiority. *Vedic* literature shows us a double type of woman: the one who centred her life on the home, and the one who followed an ascetic life, dedicated to the quest of her own spiritual realisation. The women who consecrated themselves to this kind of life did not at that time form communities; they were characterised by a contempt for worldly things and by their outstanding wisdom.

Jainism is one of the reformed sects contemporary with Buddhism. Its founder, Mahāvīra or Jina, halfway through the sixth century before Christ, organized it into a movement in which liberation is simply the fruit of knowledge and of a life of sometimes exaggerated asceticism. Texts referring to the period, and even to earlier periods, mention in this tradition thousands of nuns and one may deduce from their rules that, from this period, they lived in communities, old and young together, under a superior whose pardon must be sought in case of community disputes. We know their innumerable and detailed rules, their four vows: "not to kill (even an insect), nor to lie, nor to steal nor to possess anything whatsoever". When Mahāvīra introduced a fifth vow, that of chastity *(brahma-carya),* certain of his disciples broke away from him and formed a new sect. However, whether the Jains or the *ājīvikas* are in question, history has preserved the memory of famous vocations and their recital reveals the, often austere, life led by the nuns who are contemporary with the beginnings of Buddhism. So it would be a mistake to suppose that the Buddha was the first to institute a feminine form of monasticism, even more so to ascribe it to a much later date. It should also be observed that Jainism is far from having disappeared. Thousands of its nuns leave their trails on the dusty roads of India. We possess at this moment a work of great learning concerning them.[5] The visits, too, that we have been able to pay to their centres, focal points for meditation, intellectual life and beneficial work for society, have genuinely impressed us.[6]

What woman proposes – or founder in spite of himself

Many women, whether married or celibate, and while maintaining their secular state, accepted the Buddha's teaching from the earliest moment and promoted it with their material gifts and social support. It seems that the first laywomen to follow the Buddha were the mother and wife of Yasa, who had left his home in order to become a Buddhist monk. The Buddha himself, one day, praised the "nine unrivalled ones" among the women who followed him. In his teaching, constant references to women are encountered, generally full of appreciation and gratitude, at times with a certain irony. It is not until we come to the literature of later Buddhism that we see numerous texts imbued with a thoroughgoing anti-feminism, perhaps as a result of cultural influences (a return to the Vedic tradition?), perhaps through an evolution in Buddhist doctrine itself.

Certainly the Pāli literary sources are unanimous in praising *Pajāpatī*, aunt and nurse of the Buddha, who, in her desire to imitate the example of the monks, actually inaugurated monastic life for women. Her history is a moving one. Nevertheless, the Buddha was initially hesitant in the face of her request to abandon the world and be accepted into the Order. It required the intervention of Ānanda, a steadfast and forceful champion on behalf of these women. *Pajāpatī* was finally admitted to *ordination*, which, at this very early stage, consisted of no other ceremony than the fact of accepting the eight fundamental rules. Only later would it be carried out by repeating the triple formula: "I take refuge in the Buddha, in the Dharma, in the Sangha". Almost all the texts (with the exception of the book of *"Nuns' Songs"*, *Therīgathā)* include here the additions from a later age in which an anti-feminist trend is manifested. They stress that this acceptance of women into the

Order would be a source of harm for it, and the cause of the Order's lasting no more than 500 years. History has certainly given the lie to this prophecy.

Why leave the world? To what were they committing themselves?

From the texts it is possible to ascertain the location of the first monastery for nuns, their growing numbers, the virtues and higher "charisms" of certain among them, the list of their observances, the framework of their instructions, received entirely from monks. As for the *motive* for which so many women, married or virgins, entered upon this life of total renunciation and perfect chastity, it cannot, within Buddhism, be love for or fidelity to a person, Buddha, whom one has known and from whom one can no longer be separated. It is, rather, the desire to embrace an ascetic life, a life of renunciation of the world. Many factors are at work here, often of a domestic nature, the loss of a loved one, or else deriving from feminine psychology. Often vocations came from the aristocratic classes and from well-to-do families.

Chastity is an essential element of monastic life. Its rationale is not to be sought in the love of another person or in a mysticism of personal encounter. It should always be regarded in the light of a spirituality of liberation from the passions and from physical and psychological bondage. It is an attempt to return to a paradisiacal condition, to the original state where differences in sex were non-existent and where everyone lived like angels, spiritual and luminous beings. Also involved is a battle against the temptations of the demon Māra, who makes every effort to inhibit these vocations. As for the *earliest basic rules for nuns,* they revolved round these few themes: the respect which the nuns must show towards the monks, the faithfulness with which they should seek their spiritual instructions and resort, also, to public confession at a chapter of faults. The memory is preserved of two nuns endowed with spiritual gifts who, being as the "voice of the Buddha", had the privilege of instructing the sisters, the laypeople and even the monks. There were *two years of noviciate*. The nun in charge of instructing the novice came to be the one who conferred *ordination* on her, although, strictly speaking, it was the Order who ordained "through a nun". From earliest times, the Order of monks could delegate a nun for the juridical act of ordination.

The greatness and decline of feminine monasticism

1. According to the canonical texts there was, in the bosom of the Order, a well-organised and properly regulated community of nuns.[7] The community of monks and that of the nuns, taken together, were called *ubhato sangha* (the monastic Order under its two faces). The organisation of the community of nuns was entirely similar to that of the monks. They too had their full disciplinary code, the same corporate legal acts and two ordinations as well. It is true that the monks had the right to advise the nuns, but not to supervise them.

2. According to a brief historical overview by Father López-Gay, which he placed in the appendix to a chapter of his book *La Mística del Budismo*,[8] it is possible to see a very clear evolution. Feminine monasticism flourished greatly during the lifetime of the Buddha and that of his disciple Ānanda. However, when the latter was accused at the first Buddhist council of having opened the monastery door to nuns, there was a crisis. Their vitality could be maintained for a certain time, but a progressive decline was subsequently to be observed in all the Theravāda countries: mutually supportive testimonies are given for Sri Lanka, Burma, Laos, etc.

3. It has come to the point where an authority on the matter, Mr. Môhan Wijayaratna,[9] can make the following declaration: "It should be noted that, since the twelfth century, no Buddhist nuns have existed *in Theravāda countries*. Their disappearance seems to be due to political, social and climatic problems. At the present time, it is possible to see women dressed in ochre garments and observing the ten precepts but without having received ordination, since this has become juridically impossible."

4. On the other hand, *the Mahāyāna countries* experienced an evolution in the opposite direction. A remarkable growth in feminine monasticism was to be seen. In *China*, the nuns enjoyed the favour of an empress, with the result that they acquired, in the fourth and fifth centuries, almost too much power, including the political kind. Via *Korea*, the movement extended to *Japan*.

5. However, little by little, in these countries the splendour of femi-

nine monasticism has steadily dimmed. At the present time there are only two monasteries of Zen nuns in *Japan*, one of them, moreover, having at its head an abbess of great stature. At the same time, Zen monastic centres are known to be flourishing in the United States. Inspiration comes above all from a convent of Zen nuns in California. They publish a monastic periodical: *The Journal of Shasta Abbey*.

6. As for the vitality of monasteries for nuns in *Tibet*, I wonder if this is not due to the prominence of feminine deities and to the importance of everything feminine in the atmosphere of Tantra?[10]

In the land of the Rising Sun

A Belgian Benedictine nun who spent a month in Japan had the opportunity to stay in a monastery of nuns in the *Sōtō-Zen* tradition. This monastery, *Nisido,* at *Nagoya*, consists at the present time of 22 nuns, of whom several have come from the United States, because of the reputation of the abbess, *Aoyama Sensei,* a person of great wisdom. She is responsible both for the government of the monastery and for the spiritual formation of her disciples. Each of these, in addition, is in communication with a *roshi* of her own choice, on whom she will depend for her spiritual direction throughout her life, beyond her years of formation in the monastery, a monastery, in Japan, being essentially a house of formation for *temporary* monks and nuns.

Zazen, the sitting meditation carried out in a very precise posture, in normal circumstances takes up about three hours a day. In special session (*sesshin*), for seven weeks of the year, meditation lasts for almost the entire day, which is gruelling. Roughly a further three hours a day are spent in liturgical prayer (the recitation of *sūtras*).

This monastery is a relatively recent foundation. Since the Second World War, Japanese women became free, bit by bit, from the guardianship of men and, for the last twenty years, it has been possible for a nun to rise through all the grades of the monastic hierarchy, including that of responsibility for a monastery and of officiating at services. The nuns remain in the *Nisido* monastery for from two to five years. The rules of life are very strict: attentiveness to everyday actions, bodily postures, manual work, but there is also a properly Buddhist insistence on good will, sisterly spirit and hospitality.

In the context of *spiritual exchanges* between monks and nuns of our two traditions, abbess Aoyama Sensei, with two of her community, stayed for three weeks in 1987 with the Benedictine nuns at *Pradines*, taking part in all the Offices and the manual work of the community. This was a source of mutual edification, as the monthly magazine *Prier*[11] testifies. The abbess narrates her life and experiences, as much psychological as spiritual, in an attractive little book: *Zen Seeds*.[12]

In the tradition of Tibetan nuns

The first half of the twentieth century, before the Chinese invasion, that is, saw an exceptional nun who died in 1953. She was born in Milarepa's district of origin, the north-east of Tibet. As a very beautiful young girl, she had refused several offers of marriage. She came to Central Tibet and settled in a juniper plantation, her purpose being to establish a retreat centre. Before long, her disciples were numerous and the place became a *nunnery* with five hundred nuns. The monastery was named *Chouk-seb* and the foundress was distinguished with the title of Manjushri *(Dje-tsun)*. She was addressed as *Chouk-se-tsun-ma*, the Venerable Mistress of *Chouk-seb*.

From time to time, monks of the four Orders came by the hundreds to listen to her and to attend to her teachings. She visited Himāchal Pradesh. Having great compassion, she experienced acute suffering when she heard talk about murders and wars.[13] In *Eastern Tibet,* another monastery had 600 to 700 nuns.

The fact that Tibetan nuns could no longer attain to full ordination and become *gelong-ma* is due to the persecution of the last king, Langdarma (ninth century), who massacred thousands of nuns and forced others to marry.[14]

Prior to the Chinese invasion suffered by Tibet in 1950, the most famous monastery with a nun at its head was that of *Samding*, close to the famous lake Yamdrok, in Central Tibet. Contrary to popular belief, its members were all monks, only the superior or *head* being a nun. This was *Samding Dorje Phagmo*, the only feminine reincarnation in Tibet. The present Samding Dorje Phagmo escaped from the Chinese invasion of Tibet in 1950, but because of the extreme heat of India, she returned to Chinese-occupied Tibet, where she is still resident at the present time.[15]

The only women's monastery *(nunnery)* which could have been founded by a nun was *Zangri Karma*, in Central Tibet. It would have been founded by Shungsib Jetsun, a nun with a reputation for great sanctity.[16] Apart from this case, there are no other instances of nuns founding monasteries for women, although the wives of the Tibetan king Songsten Gampo had temples built, such as Ramoche and Tsuglhakhang, two of the holiest places of pilgrimage for all Tibetans. Here are some of the most memorable women's monasteries: in the vicinity of Lhasa, Drigung Terdrom, Tsang-gun and Gyari Gompo. At Lhasa itself, Michung Ri.

A famous *nunnery* in Eastern Tibet was that at Nangchen, called Garchag Thekchen Jangchub Ling, belonging to the Nyingma school of Tibetan Buddhism.[17]

The state of monasticism in Tibet before the Chinese invasion of 1950

Monks and their monasteries[18]

School	Number of Monasteries	Number of Monks
Gelug	2,827	323,392
Nyingma	1,597	124,040
Sakya	388	53,396
Kagyu	480	39,007
TOTAL	5,292	539,835

Nuns and their monasteries[19]

School	Number of monasteries	Number of nuns
Gelug	220	11,589
Nyingma	320	9,638
Sakya	41	1,239
Kagyu	137	4,714
TOTAL	718	27,180

EXILE AND RENAISSANCE: TIBETAN NUNS IN INDIA

In the shadow of Tai Situ: Sherab Ling

In the context of the relations to be established between the monks of our two religions, I have, for many years, had contact with Tibetan Buddhist monasteries. I was able, once again, in 1983, to stay in various Tibetan centres in India and Nepal. In particular, I lived for five months close to their *Library* at Dharamsala, North India, in the mountainous State of *Himāchal Pradesh*.[20] I went there in the first place to learn the language, but this also gave me the opportunity to visit a certain number of their monasteries. This is how I went to spend a week at *Sherab Ling*. It is a centre destined for great things, the undertaking of a very senior lama in the Karma Kagyu Order, who launched the enterprise when he was not yet thirty and whom I had had the good fortune of meeting at a centre in the Dordogne. *Tai Situ Rinpoche* is at one and the same time a model of Buddhist realisation and very open to the values of Christianity. He has read the whole of the New Testament three times in Tibetan. Amongst those engaged in interreligious dialogue, he is certainly amongst the most competent and the most agreeable. He has established his monastery on a wonderful site, on the heights beyond Baijnāth. He has built it in the middle of a pine forest, with a splendid view over a chain of snowy mountains. When the sun shines overhead, it is quite superb. In 1983, the monastery contained fifty or so monks, the majority being of school age (both primary and secondary).

A little distance away (seven or eight minutes' walk and on the far side of a stream in full spate), threading our way between bushes along a muddy path, slippery under the rain, an energetic little nun led us to a building which was already partly completed. These Tibetan nuns, belonging to the same Karma Kagyu[21] tradition, have actually undertaken to build a small retreat house[22] in the middle of a wood under very difficult conditions. No road has been built up this steep hill; bricks have to be carried on one's back and large stones on mules. They lack money, too, but not motivation. This modest house, of which the sanctuary and a few rooms have already been built, is not destined in the first place for laypeople, but for Sisters, particularly those at Tilokpur, of whom we shall speak presently. They are longing to find themselves a place for prayer and meditation in silence.

The little nun leading the way speaks adequate English. Courteous and very practical, she is directing the construction work on the future *nunnery* single-handedly. Her name is Anila Pema Zangmo. She gives me a photograph of the Karmapa and an article written by herself on *The Last Days of Sister Palmo*. She had been the most devoted disciple of this Englishwoman, whom she calls *Holy Mother:* Mrs Freda Bedi, who took the name Gelongma Karma Khechog Palmo. To judge from her photograph, she was a very strong, virile person. She lived in Sikkim, with the Karmapa as her guide. In 1968, coming from Dalhousie with some companions, she arrived at Tilokpur, bought the land and began building in 1969. This monastery for women was completed in 1973. She came to Sherab Ling in 1975, and Tai Situ Rinpoche encouraged her to settle there; he helped her with building plans.

Sister Palmo, who had divided her life between contemplative meditation and organizational activity, died peacefully at Delhi in 1977. Her faithful disciple entertained us in a wretched wooden cabin covered with black slates where, two minutes away from the *nunnery* under construction, she lived alone in an atmosphere reminiscent of the Desert Fathers.

This stay at Sherab Ling was also distinguished by conversations with several twenty-year-old monks and also with some Buddhist nuns, who urged us to go and see their monastery.

Tilokpur, on the summit of the holy hill

Some days later, we were at Tilokpur, on the road for Pathānkot (west of Dharamsala). This site is famous in the history of Tibetan Buddhism, and venerated by the *Kagyupa* above all, for this is where their ancestor *Tilopa* lived for very many years as a hermit. Visits are still made to the various caves, in the side of the rock, where he is believed to have lived. The countryside is made spectacular by the presence of the river Brahal (tributary of the Bias) at the bottom of a gorge. On the top of the hill the nuns, at the present time sixty in number,[23] have their little temple and their row of cells. Everything is simple and clearly marked by devotion. Their offices are sometimes very long, lasting for hours and, on certain feasts, the entire day. In the latter case, it is enough that some should be there to represent the community, other Sisters going about their different duties for, it goes without saying. they do everything themselves. Account is taken of the climate regarding prostrations. In Tibet, these are made in summer and the other "preliminary practices" (recitation of *mantras,* offering of the *mandala,* practice of *guruyoga*) in winter. In India, the reverse is done.

The majority of the nuns are young, but it seemed to us that their poverty prevents them from obtaining teaching adequate for their vocation. It is not enough that a passing lama should give them a short series of conferences. Every effort will be made to remedy this for the future. The abbess herself is an intellectual; she has just received her doctorate in Sanskrit from Sārnāth. Two of the nuns know English, having been educated in Christian schools, but the education of the others is deficient. Every sensible person will concede that, in this day and age, nuns cannot make do with an exclusively spiritual and liturgical formation, without any contact with the secular world. Even their spirituality would stagnate as a result. At Tilokpur, they struggle to exist and an interview with the Mother Abbess showed us how concerned they are over their want of income; it is not the ideal that is lacking but financial means. However, they are something like Poor Clares. What is most striking is that their poverty does not prevent them from being joyful, laughing even in the temple over the little mistakes to which a fairly complicated ritual gives rise.

In the atmosphere of the Gelugpa: McLeod Ganj

On Easter Monday, under the guidance of a German *anila* (nun), we ascended to the *nunnery* at *McLeod Ganj,* which we had already visited in 1980. A little topography would not be out of place here. *Dharamsala* is a town of about 11,000 inhabitants, but it is spread out on a steep hill. Right at the bottom, there is the post office, a hospital and a thriving and important market; the population is largely Indian. This is *Lower Dharamsala* or *Kotwali.* If one climbs for twenty minutes using a shortcut, one arrives on the terrace of the *Library,* a well-organized Tibetan one, surrounded by "ministries" of the Tibetan Government in Exile. A further half-hour's climb brings one up to *McLeod Ganj.* On one side is a rather picturesque market where Tibetans are numerous (there are about 5,000 on the hill), as are also Westerners, including hippies and drug-addicts. On another slope is located the monks' *School of Dialectics, Namgyal Monastery* and, finally, the Dalai Lama's residence. The nuns are settled just in front of the entrance to this village, close both to the popular market and to the centres of their religion. When I say "settled", this is something of an exaggeration, since they are sheltered in sorry-looking huts on the side of the road.

Strictly speaking, a *nunnery* does not have an abbess. Her true title is *U-mdze Ani,* from "head" (an honorific) and "to do" *(ze-pa).* Thus "Superior", maybe also a man; it is the Sister who is in charge of the daily affairs. In practice it is: she who has the responsibility for beginning the recitation of the prayers. For convenience I shall say "the abbess", but the word must not mislead us. Several Sisters act as a group for the administration of the monastery. In Tibet, the *Nechung ri nunnery* had more than a hundred nuns. The abbess, now in retirement and in poor health, entered the convent at the age of ten and left Tibet when she was 33. To begin with, she had only one companion, but thirteen more were to rejoin them. Two monks and two laymen helped them to build their present monastery. Ling Rinpoche then lived at *Tushita,* a little higher on the mountain, and came to their assistance. They are attached to the *Gelugpa* Order, the most powerful in Tibet and that to which the Dalai Lama belongs. It was in 1964 that the abbess left for Europe and lived, for the most part, in Scandinavia (Sweden and Denmark), where she was well received by Christian Sisters.

The offices in the monastery are renewed every two years; a Sister may be re-elected to the same office. In 1983, the Community numbered 40 Sisters on site, with another score working elsewhere, as nurses for example. Girls may enter the *nunnery* as young as seven, the youngest at that time being eleven. Those who are of school age attend the school in the *Tibetan Children's Village,* which occupies the summit of the hill. That apart, there are no classes at the monastery. They study the *Dharma* in community. Most decisions are made jointly, for which a monthly or three-monthly meeting is held, but day-to-day matters are settled each morning. The monastery has an abbot, a monk from Ganden, who sometimes goes to *Tushita,* where he spends some time in retreat. He carries out a great many rituals in his room and, from time to time, he gives *teachings,* whether on request, or for an initiation, or in order to comment on some special texts. These teachings might last for about ten days.

As regards vocations, the little girls come of their own accord, but with the approval of their parents. They learn by heart the texts used for *pūjās* (devotional rites) and are supervised by the *U-mdze.* The female novices *(ge-tsul-ma)* have the same vows as the males. Every fourth month of each year, there is a period of partial fasting *(nyung-ne)* which lasts for sixteen days and allows a single meal a day. There is, however, no deprivation of sleep, as in the Thai monasteries. Here, one goes to bed at ten, but the hour of rising is early.

The abbess draws attention to the poverty of the monastery. Only one part of the building is in solid material; a whole row of narrow rooms is of mere planks, which allow the winter cold, the monsoon damp and the summer heat to penetrate. The Sisters genuinely have no income, and they hope that help will be forthcoming for the maintenance of their community.[24]

Their life is marked, even more than that of their sisters at Tilokpur, by great poverty (buildings, food and everything else). This has the same regrettable consequences: a lack of both general formation and a broader spiritual training, because of the lack of means for obtaining teachers.[25] In the temple, their bearing is dignified and recollected. As far as outward appearance is concerned, you will be aware that, exactly like the monks, they have their heads completely shaved. They wear a light yellow shirt and an ample, wine-coloured robe over it.

During my stays at Dharamsala, I often had the privilege of saying Mass in the valley for the Sisters of Charity of Jesus and Mary, at their school in *Sidhpur*. In March 1980, shortly before I left, the Superior offered me a beautiful picture representing the Sacred Heart, for the Tibetan nuns. The abbess accepted it with deep emotion and, three years later, spoke to me of it, as soon as we met. However, since I could see that it was not in her room, she admitted that she had given it to a poor Tibetan family, about to set out for their homeland.

The visit we have just described took place on 4 April 1983. During our journey in India in November 1992, a Belgian Benedictine nun, Sister Marie-André Houdart, had the privilege of spending four days in the heart of the community. She gave a lively account of this experience, which we shall take up again in the appropriate place.[26]

A recent evolution

Can it be said that an evolution is becoming apparent in the life of this community? It would seem so, if one credits an article signed by a nun, *Karma Lekshe Tsomo,* and published in the *Bulletin* of N.A.B.E.W.D.[27] We here sum up the salient points.

1. Among the nuns, a real interest in the intellectual life is making itself felt. Close to the convent, a School of Dialectics has been established. The monks there attach great importance to scholastic debating contests. This has particularly attracted the nuns. But such endeavours presuppose a basic knowledge of logic; the nuns are therefore seeking instruction in this area.

2. The youngest recruits, who have an aptitude for bookkeeping and languages, are bringing a breath of new life. There are classes in Tibetan, at several levels.

3. Although, generally speaking, the study-courses are usually followed through, they are all too often interrupted by *pūjās* of long duration. These rituals and ceremonies are requested by various members of the lay community. In an atmosphere of faith, they are highly regarded as means for deepening the spiritual life, a source of great merit for the person who performs them and an effective means of removing the obstacles encountered by the *sponsor*. The gifts offered by the latter on such occasions form the greater part of the community's income, but these long rituals, which last for days or even weeks, inevitably disrupt the course of studies, which does not facilitate progress. Of course, *primum vivere* ...

4. The situation is complicated by the fact that this monastery-school is the victim of its own success. *Vocations abound.* Most of the nuns at *Geden Chöling* are Tibetans, but a good number are from mountainous districts which, while ethnically Tibetan, are located within the Indian frontier: Lahaul, Spiti, which we are

about to discuss, Kinnaur, Sanskar and Ladakh. Language and customs being related, these young postulants integrate well into Tibetan communities. However, in receiving them, resources are severely strained and the premises are becoming more and more inadequate. The community (in 1987) numbered about 80 nuns, of whom only 60 could be accommodated on site.

The nuns of Spiti: new horizons

If we may introduce a monastery which exists so far only as a project, let us say a few words about *Spiti,* a mountainous region with a scattered population. This district in the north-east of Himāchal Pradesh is close to Tibet and the means of access are difficult and dangerous. The countryside is fearsome and awe-inspiring, and it is here that the nuns long to settle. In terms of birth and nationality, they are Indian, but all their customs and religious practices are Tibetan. There are seven of them at the moment, all young, intelligent and fervent. The monk who will direct the group and be its "spiritual father" is a twenty-four-year-old lama, Lobchen Rinpoche, who was still studying at the School of Dialectics when I stayed there. The foundation was consecrated with a special ceremony: a Kalachakra initiation carried out by the Dalai Lama in July 1983, in the presence of 10,000 people. As a beginning, the nuns wish to open a school in which they will be teachers, for the region has a great need of it. While waiting, however, these young *Spiti nuns* must themselves be educated. They are temporarily members of the McLeod Ganj community.

Provisional survey

According to the magazine *Dreloma*[28] published by Loseling College of the University of Drepung in Karnataka State (South India), in 1981 there were in INDIA: 6,278 Tibetan monks, 653 tantric lamas and 340 nuns, there having always been significantly fewer nuns than monks. These figures have now been exceeded. The statistics provided by the Dharamsala *Information Office* state that there were, in India in 1984, in Tibetan monasticism, 12,615 monks and 993 nuns.

As to the division by countries and by religious Orders: in INDIA, it was *Geden Chöling* at McLeod Ganj which had the most nuns. There were 60 at *Tilokpur* (Kagyu) in 1984. At *Tsopema* (Rewālsar), Himāchal Pradesh, the monastery of Drigung Kagyu, beside the lake, had fourteen anilas, which is a good proportion of a community of fifty. Besides, a dozen nuns live as hermits on the hill, as associates of Lama Wangdor. At *Darjeeling*: Nyingma. In SIKKIM: Rumtek (Kagyu). In BHUTAN: Kagyu. In NEPAL: Nyingma, Abbot Trulshik Rinpoche, *Thubten Chöling,* at *Jumbesi*; this monastery held (in 1994) 250 nuns and 150 monks. There is a Kagyu-Nyingma monastery on higher ground than Kopan, and at a distance of two or three hours' walking: *Nagui-Gompa,* which is particularly for nuns who are meditating for ten years or more. Their director, now in old age, is particularly suited to nuns; his name is *Urgyen Tulku*. He has two sons who are tulkus: one of them is *Chö-Kyi Nyima*, at Bodnath. A *nunnery* with the name of *Bigu Gompa* is located at four days' walking distance from Kathmandu, and reached via the pass of Tisangla. It is Sherpa in origin.

Between Kathmandu and Lawudo (Mount Everest) is to be found a monk, *Thukse Rinpoche,* who belongs to the Kagyu-Nyingma and Rime (ecumenical) traditions. He specialises in contacts with nuns who are carrying out fifteen years of meditation.[29]

Since the beginning of the nineties, a monastery of Tibetan and Sherpa nuns, under the guidance of Lama Zopa Rinpoche, is being developed on the verdant plain at the foot of the hill of Kopan. It is known as *Khachö Ghakyil Nunnery*. These nuns already numbered about thirty in 1991. On returning to the great stūpa of Bodnath, in July 1994, they could be seen from a distance, washing their clothes in the pool.[30]

IN TIBET, prior to the expulsions of the Chinese communists, nuns were numbered by the thousands. Who would be equal to reporting on their current situation? Although reduced in number, they are known to exist, since from time to time, news bulletins in the media lift a corner of the veil concealing the atrocities, frequently marked by sadism, which they have to endure from the hands of the occupying power.[31]

There have been stirring events. Nuns who left *Lithang* (in the far east of Tibet) made the whole pilgrimage to Lhasa in prostrations along the road, crossing Nepal and arriving (there were 90 of them) at Dharamsala at the end of December 1990.[32] The same year, 35 nuns from *Chouk-seb* in the Nyingmapa tradition, arrived at

Dharamsala. They had put up a stiff resistance to the Chinese, and several had experienced torture.[33]

VOWS AND OBSERVANCES

In the early stages of dialogue, one thing never fails to cause amazement: "You Christian monks have only three vows, and we have 250 of them". It is perfectly clear that underlying the same word there are two distinct meanings. To simplify the matter a little, I would say that when they say "vows", this means *rules* that they have promised to keep. This interpretation is confirmed by the reading of a little book, published in 1982 by Tenzin Gyatso, the fourteenth Dalai Lama. It is entitled *"Advice from Buddha Shakyamuni. An abridged exposition of the precepts of the Bikkshu"* (i.e. a wandering mendicant).[34] The book makes no claims to originality: it is the same *Vinaya* that enacts the precepts of a Buddhist monk, no matter to what Vehicle he belongs. In this area, the Tibetan monks endeavour to be faithful to the primitive tradition. As to the content, it is a long and detailed list of the faults that the monk must avoid, from the gravest (that we would call "mortal sins") down to prescriptions regarding good manners and etiquette. In looking for *our vows*, we will find *chastity* in a prominent position and, above all, very many regulations which, as far as we can see, aim at preserving *poverty*, something which a Buddhist would list rather under the term *non-attachment*. The tradition followed by the Tibetans numbers 253 precepts, a certain number of which govern relations between monks and nuns.

What, however, are the *obligations of the nuns*? In the Tibetan context, there is no "full ordination" for them and they are bound by only a small number of vows, on an equal footing with the novices.[35] In the schools where the unbroken lineage is preserved, as in China, the nuns have even more vows than the monks. We shall return to this subject later.

To the extent that our observations can be relied on, their life of prayer is comparable to that of our contemplatives. They are daily in the temple for hours of liturgical services. Because of their present circumstances in exile, they are obliged to do much manual work, which makes them similar to the Trappistines, poorer than our Poor Clares, much less intellectual than our Benedictines. Their enclosure is certainly much less strict than that which holds good in our monasteries, so it should be no surprise to see them travelling, on their way to receive such and such a teaching from a lama of repute. As for the purity of their lives, their simplicity and their active kindness, they are very like Christian Religious. It is very much to be hoped that contacts between nuns of our two religions will be established and become frequent.

As regards their poverty, a Dutchwoman pointed out to me one day that the nuns of *Geden Chöling* are not in a position to act as do the monks of the *Tantric College*, who go to private houses to recite prayers and perform *pūjās* for the intentions of the families, and so earn money. This is quite true, but the faithful come to them with offerings, to ask them to recite prayers for them in their own *gonpa*.

Tuesday 15 February 1983:[36] Since about 5.30 p.m. on Sunday, it has rained continuously, with an extraordinary heaviness, particularly at night; in fact, the downpour has sometimes been quite violent. Last night, there was a storm that lasted for most of the night. The gutters were swamped with muddy waves and it is to be feared that a good deal of soil was lost that way. By turns, two "nuns" came to knock at my door. They were genuine beggars, deplorable in appearance: running noses, broken teeth, untidily dressed, though their clothes were those that nuns usually wear. No doubt these were some kind of hermits.

What is their motivation?

As regards the regularity of their lives and their monastic training, the parallels between our two religions are many, but this is not the place to develop such a theme. Much can be learnt on the subject from the dialogue amongst monks.[37] A more fundamental question arises: what is the *motivation* that actuates them? This cannot be the love of God or the desire for intimate union with him, since the belief in a personal and loving God is absent from their Buddhist doctrine. The desire to understand them involves putting oneself in their position. The deep convictions of the Buddha colour the whole of his spiritual path: the universality of suffering, the impermanence of the world, the inexorable law of karma, the necessity for total detachment, the renunciation of every form of selfishness; the sense of community, as well. All this is summed up in the formula of the Three Jewels: *Buddha, Dharma, Sangha*, which draws their entire lives into a spiritual ascent, galvanised by an aspiration towards purity, wisdom and infinite peace. Add to this the sacrifice of self to which the *Mahāyāna* invites for the liberation of all sentient beings, and the fact that the Vacuity (*Shūnyatā*) of Nāgārjuna could well correspond to our God, according to the approach of apophatic theology. This, however, is a delicate issue, and should not be conceded without the most searching inquiry by the experts.[38] By any reckoning, the ideal enshrined in Buddhism is sufficient to lead its monks and nuns to a high degree of spiritual realisation. Should they chance upon St Teresa of Avila or St John of the Cross, this is a real delight for them, as the best of them recognise themselves in their writings.

On the quest for full ordination, or the lure of the Chinese tradition

Three days after our visit to Tilokpur, we had some dialogue with a rather different kind of nun. There were two of them, come from Australia and New Zealand, clearly well educated and highly intelligent. Although they had received direction from some of the lamas of McLeod Ganj, they had gone to *Taiwan*, in order to receive the full ordination which Tibetans are unable to confer upon women. Naturally, this brings with it the obligation to keep a large number of vows, more even than the monks,[39] but they were not in the least daunted by this consideration, as it corresponded to their inner calling. They were obliged to adapt to Chinese culture and, on arrival in Taiwan, they felt thoroughly out of their element as even the signposts were unreadable. However, their stay was made easier by the readiness to help shown by the local people and by the respect shown by these for the nuns, of whom there were thousands. The majority of these, in fact almost all, entered the monastery only after completing their secondary studies; some, indeed, had been to university. The intellectual level was quite high, in contrast with that of the Tibetan nuns in India who have neither secular nor religious doctrinal education. In Taiwan, the laity contribute in significant measure to the financial upkeep of the monastery and all its material needs. As a result, the monks can dedicate themselves completely to liturgy, meditation and Dharma-study. The nuns we met could not speak too highly of the perfect bearing of the monks and nuns, the strictness of their observances and the beauty of a life directed towards unfailing order. None of this is achieved without hardship. They showed us photographs of a ceremony which involved having their shaved heads marked with indelible burns (in their case six). The long ceremonies, lasting more than three months, caused them acute physical discomfort, notably in the joints, through their remaining for long periods on their knees, or through the impossibility of relaxing a faultless deportment ... but this brought them great spiritual profit, relief and peace.

We looked at photographs of the largest Buddhist monastery in Taiwan,[40] where they lived for four months and were fully ordained. This monastery holds 170 nuns and 50 monks. The architecture is imposing, in the classical Chinese style, and with raised ceilings; certain statues, for example that of Kuan-yin, are very tall. The chants, which they recorded, are impressive in their volume, like a Beethoven symphony, but with simpler, repetitive melodies, like the ocean waves. Monks and nuns sing in turn; while one part of the choir is giving voice, the part facing it bows and bends low. The assembly following their ordination ceremony was admirable in its dignity: 300 newly-ordained people, both monks and nuns; a slow walk, regular lines, remaining standing for a long period, prostrations and the presence of ten abbots.

Since that time, they have been wearing an ample black robe which, in its cut, is reminiscent of the habit of Zen bonzes. In the summer, they wear a lighter robe, pale blue in colour. The dream is one day to lead some Tibetan nuns, perhaps a whole community, to follow their example and commit themselves to the road to full ordination. This, however, involves sacrifices and, given the present mentality of the McLeod Ganj community, they must expect a conservative reaction. These two nuns have in consequence to persevere in spite of their isolation. They do, nevertheless, have the approval of the Dalai Lama.

The case of which we speak is not unique. A certain number of Western nuns belonging to the Tibetan tradition are going, with the approval of the Dalai Lama, to receive full ordination in Hong Kong, Taiwan or Singapore.[41]

A young Tibetan nun from *Tilokpur* arranged a lecture for us at the *Asirvanam* meeting[42] on 27 November 1992. Two days later, she entrusted me with a secret. She had been part of a group of three Tibetan nuns who received complete ordination at a monastery for Chinese women in *Hong Kong*. Another group of three went there in 1987. Total: 6.

I shall add a comment which was made to me by a young Westerner who has committed herself as a novice in the Vietnamese path. This latter having preserved the unbroken lineage within the Mahāyāna, there is no need to run to south-east Asia to receive full ordination; the monks of Vietnam confer it on Tibetan nuns at their centres in Joinville[43] or Meyrac,[44] without leaving the Hexagon.

WESTERN NUNS ON THE TIBETAN WAY

As is well known, there has been for the last two decades a strong current in favour of Tibetan Buddhism in most Western countries. The proof lies in the number of centres opened, the success of retreats directed by great lamas and, deeper and more problematic, the fact that numerous young Westerners, men and women, are undaunted by the prospect of the austerity of a strictly enclosed retreat lasting three years and three months. Amongst the young people, there are already a good number who have put on the Buddhist monks' robe. The same phenomenon is at work amongst women and girls. God alone knows the depths of the heart; it is not for us to judge the sincerity of these "conversions". There are many factors to be considered: rejection of a technological and materialistic civilisation, dissatisfaction with the traditional Churches, the personal trauma of misunderstood young people, divorcees. What can I say? It is simply impossible to deal with the subject as though this phenomenon did not exist. There are hundreds of Western women of most nationalities who, in America, Europe, India or Nepal, have shaved their heads and put on the wine-coloured robe. What is their rule of life? Do they have convents, or organized communities? Although circumstances have brought me the acquaintance of a good number of these often most praiseworthy people, I believe I can safely say that regular communities are very rare. Without actually forming a true community, certain nuns at Lavaur, in the Tarn, gravitate around the *Vajra Yoginī* centre and *Nālandā Monastery* for men, where they go to receive teachings. The magazine *Mandala,* published at Soquel, California, contains an article entitled *Nuns around the World* in its issue for October 1990, on page 6. It provides information on an international meeting attended by a score of nuns at Dharamsala and on two communities coming into being, in Australia and in Italy. This same magazine describes the beginnings of the Australian *nunnery* in its October 1992 issue, page 11.

Advantages and drawbacks

The lack of regular communities brings with it disastrous consequences, born of a certain *individualism*. If the person concerned is generous, and if she has the privilege of a very spiritual lama with sound judgement for her director, this Western nun will be able to do good and to persevere in her quest for the interior life. The best outcome would seem to me to be the nun putting herself at the service of a Tibetan community and dedicating herself to the assistance of its members. That American nun comes to mind who was for many months in charge of the dispensary at Kopan (Nepal), where the little boy-monks quickly develop health problems, or of this German *anila* who quietly rendered many a service to the community at McLeod Ganj or, again, of another such, attentive in hospitality at the *Manjushri Institute* in Ulverston (England). Anila Rinchen is well known as the valued assistant to the lamas of Kagyu-Ling (Château de Plaige) and Anila Zangmo, while loving the solitude of her hermitage, helps the faithful of Karma-Ling, in the Savoy, with her teachings.

However, it is impossible to generalise; perhaps good examples are the exception. I have heard *many complaints* from feminine informants who, for instance, put all their confidence in such and such a lama to whom, as he is always on the move, access is difficult. Rare, too, are those lamas who are sufficiently open to the Western mentality or sufficiently prudent to grasp the implications of our psychological problems and give suitable advice to the directee, who is in any case often too docile. Situations have been witnessed which led to disaster.

Quite apart from what has just been said, from the viewpoint of *monastic formation*, is it reasonable for a young Western woman to go and lead the life of a "freelance" nun, without proper direction or any supervision, in today's world? Addressing monks and nuns with a certain amount of experience behind them, I leave it to them to answer. Under such conditions, who can be surprised if many of the women and girls who embark with such enthusiasm on this way of life should encounter great obstacles to their perseverance or quite simply *disrobe*?

Far be it from me to end on such a pessimistic note. After all, as regards those who are *Tibetans* by birth, their convents, despite certain remediable defects, have left me with the impression of great single-mindedness, real courage and a benevolent peace. One defect which women observers from the West have pointed out to me is that Tibetan women are still all too often maintained in a condition of dependency in relation to the monks. Can this not be remedied?

Prospects for the future

The beginnings of an organization with international scope are taking shape. From the 11–17 February 1987, there took place at Bodhgaya in India, an *International Conference for Buddhist nuns*. There were 120 of them, from 24 countries. The organizers belonged to various traditions: Sri Lankan, Thai, Tibetan. In front of a thousand people, the Dalai Lama upheld the idea that women should have the opportunity of attaining to complete ordination and drew attention to the positive role that they would be able to play in the *Sangha*. An organization, *Sakyadhita*, was established and sixteen resolutions outlined its aims.[45]

Some women will be interested in a genuinely new and sensible project. At the time of writing, several Western nuns practising in the Tibetan tradition are organizing a three-week programme which is to take place at *Bodhgaya* in February 1996. The programme will include teachings on the *Vinaya*, and reflections on adaptation to modern Western culture. Although it is intended in the first place for nuns in the Tibetan tradition, it will gladly accept nuns from the other traditions. There will even be contributions from Chinese *bhikshuṇīs*. There will be discussions on the way nuns' communities are organized, and also on a programme of education similar to the strict apprenticeship for ordination in the Chinese tradition.[46]

However, whatever their country of origin, one can have but one wish for them: that they remain faithful to their vows. There is a *sūtra* in which the Buddha said: "Wherever there is a monk observing the *Vinaya*, that place is luminous, it is radiant. I see that place as not empty: I myself abide there peacefully."[47] And, in order to emphasise that to observe the eternal law is to see himself, he says in another place: "Whoever sees the Dharma sees me. Whoever does not see the Dharma cannot see me, even if he takes hold of my robe."[48]

Many Westerners had the advantage, or possibly the drawback, of a more or less Christian childhood. Many of them have unhappy memories of it, whether in the Catholic Church or in Protestantism. Might they not, thanks to encounters with monks and nuns who strive to be faithful to the Gospel, discover something of the true face of Jesus and – why not? – of his Church?

Notes

[1] Its proceedings have been published under the title *Mujeres del Absoluto. El monacato femenino. Historia, instituciones, actualidad* in *Studia Silensia* of Silos Abbey (Burgos), vol. XII, 1986. Our lecture, pp. 159–179.
[2] Paris, Éditions du Cerf, 1991.
[3] Éditions Dharma, St. Michel en l'Herm, 1995.
[4] In *Studia Missionalia*, vol. 28, 1979, pp. 231–263. See also his book *La Mística del Budismo. Los monjes no cristianos del Oriente.* Madrid, Biblioteca de Autores Cristianos, 1974, chapter 5, on the rules of Buddhist monasticism.
[5] N. SHĀNTĀ, *La voie jaina. Histoire, spiritualité, vie des ascètes pèlerines de l'Inde.* Introduction by R. PANIKKAR. Coll. Les deux rives. Paris, O.E.I.L., 1985.
[6] Especially at *Rājgir* and *Viraithan* (Bihār State) in 1983. See below in chapter VII, page 199, to say nothing of our enjoyable conversations in Paris with the Jain monk *Kirtichandra Vijayaji* (24 June 1992 and 18 June 1994).
[7] M. WIJAYARATNA, *Les débuts du monachisme bouddhique comparés à ceux du monachisme chrétien*, in *Collectanea Cisterciensia*, t. 45, 1983, pp. 69–76; see the end of this article, p. 75.
[8] See above, note 4; the appendix to chapter 3 is entitled *Las monjas budistas*, pp. 110–115.
[9] Article quoted above, note 7; page 76, note 21.
[10] See R. SAILLEY: *Le bouddhisme "tantrique" indo-tibétain ou "Véhicle du Diamant".* Coll. Le Soleil dans le coeur. Éditions Présences, Saint-Vincent-sur-Jabron, F-04200 Sisteron, 1980. Especially p. 42 and the following: *Les divinités féminines.*
[11] No. 98, janvier-fevrier, 1988, pp. 8–9.
[12] SHUNDO AOYAMA: *Zen Seeds: Reflections of a female priest,* Tokyo, 1990. See the review by Kathleen England in *Bulletin du Conseil Pontifical pour le Dialogue*, 1991, XXVI-1, No. 76, pp. 146–149.

13 We had the privilege of visiting this monastery during our pilgrimage to Tibet in 1994. This was a real adventure, to which we shall refer again in chapter VIII.
14 Information supplied by Tenpa Negi, then a teacher at *Kagyu-Ling*. Other sources say that they had never received full ordination.
15 This monastery, belonging to one of the Kagyupa sects, is located to the east of Gyantse. The feminine incarnation is reputed to be that of the tantric goddess *Dorje Phagmo, Vajra Vārāhī* (wild sow of thunder, or of diamond). In the past she was awarded a high degree from the Emperor of China and maintained a court and a monastery occupied exclusively by monks. See the *Tibetan Bulletin* of Dharamsala (vol. XVII, No. 5, December 1986–January 1987, p. 8) The article *The Gonpas of Tibet*, by DEKI C. GYAMTSHO, pp. 6–8 & 12, contains a good description of the organization of monasteries in Tibet. On *Samding*, see S. BATCHELOR, *The Tibet Guide*, Wisdom Publications, London, 1987.
16 Doubtless another, less correct, manner of referring to the Jetsun-ma of *Choukseb* whom we have just mentioned.
17 Information received from the *Information Office, Central Tibetan Secretariat, Gangchen Kyishong*, Dharamsala, H.P., India. The same Office gave us the following statistics.
18 These figures refer only to Buddhism, and do not consider the ancient religion of Tibet, *Bön*, with which we have had favourable contacts. See chapter VII.
19 It will be noticed that the latter are, and always have been, much less numerous than the monks.
20 See the more detailed account in chapter VII.
21 The *Karmapa*, whose principal monastery today is at Rumtek (Sikkim), are by far the most prosperous branch of the *Kagyupa* Order. They have several important centres in France.
22 It is not simply a question of an eight-day, or even of a month-long retreat. The Tibetan *Nyingma* and *Kagyu* Orders preserve the very austere usage of a retreat lasting three years, three months and three days, with strict enclosure; during this period they devote themselves to the "preliminary practices" and (at least in the case of the Kagyu), to the exercise of the six yogas of Naropa. Since the exile which began in 1959, they have been admitting to such retreats those Westerners who are judged to have the capacity for it.
23 In June 1984.
24 *Geden Chöling Monastery*, McLeod Ganj – 176.219, Dharamsala, Distt. Kāngra, H.P., India.
25 A German anila (Buddhist nun) obtains alms for them to ensure that they have a hot meal every day. She observed to me: "It is not true to say that the lack of income prevents them from receiving suitable instruction. They have had lessons from the principal Gelugpa masters, who give them free of charge. But everything depends on the nuns' intellectual capacity. Some of them are limited in what they can assimilate, but those whose responsibility it is are unwilling to refuse all but the most gifted candidates; all who offer themselves must have their opportunity. One thing is obvious: the present buildings are inadequate. The superior plans to have an extension built, in order to increase the number of cells." Although the case is not peculiar to McLeod Ganj, there should be

taken into account a kind of occasional teaching which must have been frequent in Tibet. When a highly reputable lama gives a series of lectures or some sought-after initiation, disciples are seen to flow in from all directions and, amongst them, nuns eager for these instructions. They cover enormous distances in order to benefit from them. Outside of the sessions, their families feed and shelter them.

[26] In chapter VIII, pp. 154–156.
[27] In North America, the equivalent of our European Commission for Monastic Interreligious Dialogue is the *North American Board for East-West Dialogue*. Their *Bulletin* was published by Osage Monastery, 18701 W. Monastery Road, Sand Springs, Oklahoma 74063, U.S.A. See *Bulletin* No. 32, May 1988, pp. 10–12: *A Brief Glimpse at Tibetan Refugee Nunneries*.
[28] Volume VI, 1981, p. 8
[29] This information was given to me by a Swiss monk, Gelong Sangye Samdrup, the first Westerner to obtain the rank of *Geshe Lharampa;* it was complemented by the French monk, Matthieu Ricard, interpreter to the Dalai Lama.
[30] See *Mandala* magazine from Soquel, California, No. 9, October 1991, p. 6: *Women in Tibetan Buddhism: Tibetan Nuns*.
[31] See, for example, the *Tibetan Bulletin* published by the *Information Office* of Dharamsala: Gangchen Kyishong, Dharamsala 176 215, Distt. Kāngra, H.P., India: vol. XIX, No. 1, p. 28; XX, No. 3, p. 4; XX, No. 4, p. 3; also the magazine published in French at the same address: *Actualités tibétaines:* Vol. I, No. 1, 1989, pp. 4 and 6–7; No. 2, p. 2; No. 3, 1990, p. 1.
[32] Article by M. FINK: *Un exemple de courage: les nonnes tibétaines*, in *Actualités tibétaine*s, vol. II, No. 3, juillet 1991, pp. 14–16.
[33] *Actualités tibétaines*, vol. III, no. 4, Hiver 1992–1993, pp. 13–14. I have before me the account by *Ani Kalsang Pelmo*.
[34] *Advice from Buddha Shakyamuni. An abridged exposition of the Bikkshu's precepts*. Dharamsala, Library of Tibetan Works and Archives, 1982.
[35] Both men (*ge-tsul*) and women (*ge-tsul-ma*) novices must observe the same vows, to which are added *many rules*, according to the interpreter at Tilokpur. All this must be preceded by the *taking refuge* in the Three Jewels: Buddha, Dharma, Sangha. At the beginning, the male novices were required to observe ten precepts, the women novices six. Cf. the article by P. López-Gay, quoted at note 4: *Origen del monacato femenino budista* in *Studia Missionalia*, 1979, pp. 260–261.
[36] This paragraph is an extract from my journal.
[37] We shall refer to this again, particularly with regard to the two interreligious meetings at the Abbey of Praglia, in chapter VI, pp. 94–97.
[38] We intend to return to this in chapter XI.
[39] For full ordination, whereas the monks have 253 vows (see above, note 34: *Advice from Buddha,* page 12); the nuns have 348. The additional ones aim at protecting them from men.
[40] Hai Ming Temple, Taipei, R.O.C., Taiwan.
[41] See a detailed description of the ceremony in the Dutch *Maitreya Magazine*, 1985, No. 4, pp. 4–6 (Stichting Maitreya Institute, Heemhoeveweg 2, 8166 HA Emst, Nederland).

42 We shall give an account of this encounter in chapter VIII.
43 Ven. Thich Huyen Vi, Monastère Linh Son, 9 avenue Jean Jaurès, F-94340, Joinville le-Pont.
44 Venerable Thich Nhat Hahn, Village des Pruniers, Meyrac, F-47120 Loubes-Bernac.
45 See *Tibetan Bulletin*, for February-March 1987, vol. XVII No. 6, p.18 and, especially, the most detailed account in *Maitreya Magazine,* 1987, No. 3, pp. 16–18.
46 For fuller details, see the magazine *Dharma,* No. 22, January-May 1995, p. 41: *La vie comme nonne bouddhiste.*
47 See the compendium quoted at note 34: *Advice from Buddha*, p. 2.
48 *Itivittuka Khuddaka-Nikaya,* quoted by Buddhadāsa Indapañño, Thailand, in *Christianity and Buddhism,* Bangkok, 1967, 2nd edition, p. 106.

Chapter IV
Cistercian Spirituality

What is the purpose of this chapter?

Let there be no misunderstanding over the aim of this chapter. It is not due in the least to a desire to trace the history of Christian monasticism. Nor, to narrow the field somewhat, is it for the sake of tracing the origins of Cîteaux. Let us recall our outline. Since a meeting between monks of two religions is under discussion, the book began with an explanation that would answer the question, "What is Tibetan monasticism? Does it concern monks or nuns?" Now the second panel of our diptych is revealed. Since Trappists are going out to meet them, what is this Cistercian tradition which they call to witness? On this topic there is no lack of competent authors: Father Louis Lekai, Dom Jean Leclercq and, slightly earlier, Dom Anselme Le Bail. We can do no better than to refer to their writings. A style both learned and clear in explaining their history is found in the writing of Father Edmond Mikkers, in the article *Robert de Molesme* in the *Dictionnaire de Spiritualité* (vol. 13, col. 734–814). To summarise, we shall refer to a History of the Church which effectively locates our movement in the context of the period.[1] Subsequently we shall consider the spirituality, properly so called, of this tradition.

The founding of Cîteaux

> Lord, make me know your ways,
> Lord, teach me your paths.
> (*Psalm 24.4*)
> I shall bring her into the wilderness
> and I shall speak tenderly to her.
> (*Hosea 2.16*)

By way of introduction, a few words should be said about the immediate context. In the eleventh century, a movement of reform which had been launched by monastic elites was seized upon and developed by various popes, most notably Hildebrand, a former Benedictine of Cluny, who took the name Gregory VII: hence the name Gregorian reform. But the very success of Cluny was its greatest danger; it became too rich, too proud of the vastness of its buildings, the learning of its writers and the grandeur of its offices. What a falling away from the strict monastic ideal as St Benedict taught it to his sons! It was thus in reaction to this state of affairs, these ingrained habits, these superfluous observances and a certain collusion with the temporal, that a small group of heroic pioneers had left Molesme, daughterhouse of Cluny: Saint Robert, its founder, and many of his monks were not in the least satisfied with the ideal, austere though it already was, as practised in this house.[2] It was against this background that *Robert de Molesme* left the monastery which he founded and where the quantity of benefactions was conducive to laxity in the monks' lives. He withdrew, with a score of companions, to a lonely district, Cîteaux, in 1098. On a marshy site (cistels = reeds) he founded the new monastery (*novum monasterium*) whose essential novelty was to be the return to a literal observance of the rule of St Benedict. Recalled by his monks, Robert was obliged to return to Molesme, but he left at Cîteaux the prior *Alberic*, who succeeded him as abbot (1099–1109) and committed the community to the path of asceticism. The third abbot of Cîteaux, *Stephen Harding* (1109–1133), played an important part in Cistercian organization, made essential by the spectacular development of the foundation.

In 1132, as a matter of fact, at a time when Cîteaux was passing through a critical stage, following many deaths, a young nobleman, *Bernard,* arrived at the monastery from Fontaines-lès-Dijon. He was accompanied by about thirty companions whom he had won over for the monastic ideal. In his wake, a multitude of men representing every social class were to knock on the monastery door throughout the twelfth century. It became necessary to make new foundations: La Ferté, Pontigny, Clairvaux and Morimond.

In the face of such rapid expansion, Stephen Harding undertook the task of drawing up a statute which would make possible the maintaining of unity of observance between Cîteaux and its foundations. This was the Charter of Charity *(Carta Caritatis)*. It anticipated a certain dependence of the abbeys which were answerable to the summit, not of a single house (as at Cluny), but to

Cîteaux and its first four foundations. These five abbeys are the origins of the filiations, in which each of the founding abbeys has the duty of visiting annually and the responsibility for supervising elections. But in every monastery the abbot is elected by the monks of his own abbey, together with the abbots of the houses which it had founded.

In addition, all the abbots met annually at Cîteaux, for a general chapter, responsible for defining observances, correcting irregularities and considering any opportunities for making new foundations. In this way, Cîteaux was prevented from giving rise to an abbot with excessive power. The Order avoided the kind of centralisation represented by Cluny, while providing against the danger of monasteries becoming isolated: the unity of Cîteaux was defined before all else as unity of observance.

Cistercian observance

> Then are they truly monks
> when they live by the work of their hands
> as did our fathers and the apostles.
> (*Rule of St Benedict, ch. XLVIII*)

Cîteaux had no wish to draw up a new monastic constitution. Its intention, on the contrary, was to return to the Rule of St Benedict, followed to the letter, by way of a thoroughgoing renunciation and a life lived completely in common. Consequently, Cîteaux cut back everything that Cluny had added to the choral duties, supplementary psalms and litanies. The Cistercians themselves were obliged to give up, as regards clothing, food and drink, everything whose use had not been provided for in the Rule. Their clothing was to retain its natural colour, grey, to eliminate the expense of dyeing. So they were known as "white monks" to distinguish them from Cluniac monks, whose habits were black. The monk was to cut out fat and daintily varied dishes from his diet. The Cistercians would sleep fully clothed, on straw mattresses, in a common dormitory.

Following the example of Cîteaux, the monasteries were to be established in uninhabited places, far from other people, in a complete break with the world. The Order of Cîteaux desired to return to poverty and refused to live from the labour of others. In consequence, it would accept no lands given as benefices, from which they need only anticipate the income, nor tithes, nor serfs. The monks were to cultivate their own lands. They were to settle in waste places in order to bring them under cultivation. They also renounced the possession of mills and communal bakeries, not to mention revenues, which would put them on the same footing as landed gentry.

The desire to work their lands themselves was not compatible with a liturgical life, even in a simplified form, nor with all the monastic exercises. The Cistercians would create a new institution, unforeseen by St Benedict: *lay-brothers*. Bearded and often illiterate, they would be responsible for agricultural work on the abbey's more distant property. During the summer months, they would live in a "grange", a kind of farm building located at their place of work, about a day's walk from their monastery, to which they would return on Sunday. These lay-brothers were dispensed from the full practice of the Rule of St Benedict and from residence within the enclosure, and they had no voice in chapter. As for the choir-monks, they cultivated the land nearest to the enclosure.

The expansion of Cîteaux

The expansion of the Order of Cîteaux in the twelfth century proved sensational, and extended into the greater part of the thirteenth century. It was possible, thanks to the flexibility of the Charter of Charity, which allowed the affiliation to the Order of such monasteries as were anxious to preserve their independence. It was due, too, to the tireless industry of St Bernard, whose fiery sermons gave rise to vocations and who multiplied monastic foundations. At his death (1153), the Cistercian Order already numbered 343 abbeys. He had personally founded 70 communities, and the prestige of Clairvaux with its 700 religious overshadowed the mother abbey, which had a mere 250.

All this having been said, it is only right to acknowledge the *shadow side* of a reality which did not always tally with the ideal. Even in the lifetime of St Bernard, Cistercian foundations were not always established in uninhabited regions but sometimes also on lands already under cultivation.

In the course of centuries there was also cause for regret, in the Order of Cîteaux as in the majority of the monastic Orders, in an encroachment of the temporal, an extravagant wealth and a relaxation of regular discipline. On coming to the seventeenth century one can truthfully speak, concerning many of their houses, of a *decline*. They manifested, in fact, a lack of impetus, diminishing vocations and a kind of dreary pessimism concerning the monastic institution.[3]

The lamentable institution of *commendam* entrusted to a secular the temporary administration of an ecclesiastical benefice. The commendatory, not being even a religious, had no concern for enforcing observances; in fact he had no other cares than that of collecting the revenues of an abbey. This deprived the community of a true abbot, solicitous for the spiritual welfare of the monks and brought the spirit of the world into the cloisters. The abbeys produced revenues increasingly disproportionate to the small number of monks.

Attempts at reform

In the seventeenth century, a certain number of Cistercians wished to return to the primitive customs, restoring to honour the prohibition on eating meat, for example. The chapters were unsuccessful in preserving unity, even within monasteries, between the *Strict Observance* (the advocates of reform) and the *Common Observance* (the opponents of reform). The interference of Richelieu succeeded only in aggravating the conflict. The reform effected by Pope Alexander VII, in 1666, did not satisfy the supporters of the Strict Observance, among them the Abbot de Rancé, who made up his mind to carry out his reform in his own monastery.

Rancé and the La Trappe reform

Armand-Jean Le Bouthillier de Rancé was born in 1626, the son of a Councillor of State and godson of Richelieu. A worldly abbot, suddenly converted in 1657, he made a noviciate at the Cistercian abbey of Perseigne and withdrew to the abbey of La Trappe, which he held *in commendam*, and where a few monks lived an aimless life devoid of godliness and rule. He then undertook the reform of La Trappe, giving his monks the example of the most austere of lives. After becoming abbot regular in 1664, he set himself to go further than the reformers of the Strict Observance. He restored to honour perpetual silence, manual work, prayer, solitude, fasting, sleeping on the bare ground, voluntary humiliations and public reprimands. In 1683, he published *La sainteté et les devoirs de la vie monastique,* in which he criticised the life lived in other monasteries, going so far as to regard study as contrary to the life of a monk, which brought upon him a long-drawn-out controversy with Dom Mabillon and the Benedictines of the Congregation of Saint-Maur. In his zeal he sometimes exceeded the dictates of moderation, but till the end of his life (1700) he gave an example of asceticism. He remains a master of the spiritual life. Clement XI approved the reform in 1705 and a number of monasteries imitated La Trappe in the course of the eighteenth century. This reform was to bring new life to the Cistercian Order after the Revolution.[4]

The epic of Augustin de Lestrange

Dom Augustin de Lestrange (1754–1827) entered La Trappe in 1780. As master of novices (1785), when the Constituant Assembly suppressed the vows of religious, he conceived the project of settling with his brothers abroad.[5] In May 1791, he set out with a score of La Trappe monks to settle at *La Valsainte* (Switzerland). Having been elected superior, he drew up *Regulations* even more austere than those of La Trappe, with the object of making reparation for the excesses of the Revolution. Vocations were very numerous, and Lestrange made foundations in Belgium, England, Piedmont, Westphalia, Spain and at Valais (Switzerland). On his election as abbot in 1794, he received full power over all the monasteries of his reform. He brought together at Sembrancher (Valais) nuns of various Orders (1796) and made the first *Trappistines*[6] of them. Successive advances on the part of the French armies obliged Lestrange to withdraw all his subjects (about 250 persons) across Bavaria, Austria and Poland, till they reached Russia, but the tsar expelled all French emigrés (1800). Lestrange set out again towards Danzig, Lubeck and Hamburg. He was able to send a small group of monks to the New World and soon settled anew at La Valsainte (1802), where the foundation prospered until 1811, when the conflict between the pope and the emperor reached breaking-point. Lestrange escaped secretly to the United States, from whence he travelled back to England (1815). From there he took possession of La Trappe abbey, but a conflict with the bishop of Séez over jurisdiction obliged him to withdraw to the abbey of Bellefontaine.

Accused of abuse of power and of excessive severity, Lestrange was summoned to Rome in 1825. He was about to be deposed when he died, on the return journey, on 16 July 1827. The saviour of La Trappe left sixteen communities, comprising 934 religious. Among his written works we will quote *Règlements (Regulations) ... de la Valsainte*. This is the principal text of his reform, which was an attempt to return to the fullness of the Rule of St Benedict and the observances of the primitive Cîteaux. Its defect, as a code for monastic life, was the multiplication of minutiae, the excessive rigour in observances and the practices of supererogation. The sound balance necessary in a rule is lost. These regulations have exercised a great influence, albeit accompanied by difficulties which increased with time; they were abandoned in 1834.

Growth in fidelity

> Like a tree that is planted
> beside the flowing waters ...
> *(Psalm 1.3)*

When at the end of the Empire the Trappists were able to return to France, several groups of monks resumed possession of former Cistercian monasteries.[7] Often, too, buildings which had belonged to other Orders were occupied. Certain abbeys were foundations on new sites; this was the case with several monasteries in Belgium. The geographical expansion of the Order should be noted: Ireland, the United States, Canada and Spain. The population of the majority of monasteries was high (from 60 to 175 members), with many lay-brothers. This makes it easy to understand the numerous foundations. Material conditions were often hard, and the poverty real; simply making a livelihood was a problem. The Trappistines courageously followed the monks; they made foundations under what were frequently very difficult conditions.

The return to the sources

> Like the deer that yearns for running streams,
> so my soul is yearning for you, my God.
> *(Psalm 41.1)*

So Lestrange was the origin of the remarkable recovery of the Cistercian Order. Many of the communities which revived in the course of the nineteenth century abandoned his regulations and took again those of Rancé. This is the origin of the diversity of usages which led to the splitting up of the Trappists into three congregations: those of Sept-fons and those of Westmalle who followed Rancé, and those of La Trappe who retained, in a mitigated form, the regulations of Lestrange. The three congregations reunited at the end of the century, in 1892. It was at the instance of Leo XIII that the three congregations came together to form the Order of Cistercians of Our Lady of La Trappe. This reunion marks a definite distancing from Rancé and, at the same time, a return to the primitive Cîteaux, in its government and structures, as in the spiritual life of the monks. Austerity was to be restored to its proper place, as a means in the service of charity.[8] The new *Spiritual Directory* of 1910 bore witness to this development, as did other works by Cistercians which appeared at around that time. This movement cleared the ground for the rediscovery of the Cistercian writers of the twelfth century, in whom the most recent centuries had seen no more than pious authors. Henceforward, on the contrary, and above all from 1920 onwards, it would be recognised that, in renewing monastic observance, the first Cistercians had actually founded it upon a profound and original spiritual doctrine, which retains its full force today.

From 1955 onwards, there was a greater concern for achieving a more balanced life. Customs, the details of which were judged too burdensome, were pruned; the liturgy was relieved of a certain number of vocal prayers; free periods were built into the timetable – all to the benefit of *Lectio divina* (meditative spiritual reading), on which emphasis was placed. In addition, the formation of both novices and monks became the object of renewed attention. This internal renewal went hand-in-hand with a major expansion of the Order, particularly outside Europe. It was especially rapid in the United States: from three houses in 1940 to sixteen in 1975.

Cistercian monasteries were founded in Asia, Africa, Latin America and Oceania. Japan alone now has six. A list of these monasteries can be found in the article by Father Edmond Mikkers already quoted.[9] It makes impressive reading but, as he tactfully points out, this worldwide expansion in diverse situations can bring its own problems.

SPIRITUALITY IN THE COURSE OF THEIR HISTORY

> There is one thing I ask of the Lord
> for this I long,
> to live in the house of the Lord
> all the days of my life.
> (*Psalm* 26.4)

Of its very nature, the history we have just traced with broad strokes reveals a spirituality, in the sense of the prime mover in such initiatives, such revivals in the course of the centuries. Their written works cannot do other than reveal the deep feelings of the monks who were their authors, caught up as they were in the slipstream of their time. To go into detail would be irksome and beyond the scope of this book. Perhaps I may be allowed to summarise the historical perspective of Father Edmond Mikkers,[10] and then say a word about the psychological standpoint of Thomas Merton on this subject, before closing with some personal remarks. Without denying the interest of the intervening centuries, we are limiting our summary to the most important periods from the viewpoint of our Order.

The period of origins

The century and a half from 1098 to 1250 was the golden age of Cistercian spirituality. From the primitive texts there emerge three principal elements: a firm attachment to the Rule of St Benedict, the quest for solitude and the imitation of Christ as poor man. The great authors of the twelfth century are St Bernard, William of Saint-Thierry, Aelred of Rievaulx and Guerric of Igny; then come their disciples in various European countries. The fairly homogeneous teaching of this Cistercian school can be arranged under four headings:

1. *The human aspect.* The first element is an instruction on man, on the human soul and its abilities. It is actual and concrete man with his faculties and all his varied states of mind, with his faults and shortcomings. It is man who, created and intended by God to be in his own likeness, is called to live in union with him, but it is also man broken by sin, rendered weak and subject to suffering, wandering in the night of ignorance and weakness, with his inquisitiveness, his covetousness and his taste for what is earthly. However, this same man possesses, at the very heart of his disordered being, fundamental, inborn capabilities for knowledge and love, as also a fundamental orientation towards the good. This conception of man as image and likeness of God is invariably to be found among Cistercians. By his nature, man is and always remains image, from his origin and by grace he receives a beginning of likeness which is called to open out according to the true Image and perfect likeness of God, the eternal Word, the Incarnate Son.

2. *Asceticism.* The ascetic element, second panel of Cistercian spirituality, is not to be understood in a narrow or one-sided manner. Man's true liberation from his malady and the restoration of his original likeness to God is the result of a spiritual practice involving his whole being and of a continuous asceticism and conversion. The acquisition of the virtues is, in the language of the first Cistercians, a *vita activa* which, of its nature, includes the service of one's neighbour.

A double aspect needs to be examined: first, the negative aspect with renunciation, distancing, the living apart from and withdrawal in relation both to visible appearances and to the interior, invisible world. Man experiences this "world" as the cause of the disorder in his inclinations and longings. This is why he must put it behind him *(fuga mundi)* in order to meet Christ and, through Christ, God; the latter can be found only beyond all the sensations and superficial impressions of the soul. Man has to learn to live within himself *(habitare secum)* and to observe himself as though from a distance, because it is only in this way that he will find in himself the basis and capacity for the knowledge and love of God.

The positive aspect is the acquisition of the virtues proper to the transformed spiritual life: the Christian virtues (faith, hope and charity) and the more specifically monastic virtues: obedience, humility, silence and fraternal charity in the framework of the monastic community. Here, the full reach of the observance of the Rule, its customs, its varied activities, work, fasting, vigils, solitude and poverty finds its proper place. The goal of the ascetic process is the rule of charity, the reign of love *(ordo caritatis)*. It is there that is found the profound and complete rest of the human faculties, stability of soul and mind, peace in the presence of God.

3. *The sense of the sacred.* The return of man to God invariably takes place within the context of salvation history: man showing the marks of sin and its consequence is existentially delivered by Christ and enters, in him, into communion with God. Amongst the Cistercians, the mystery of the incarnation occupies the centre of the stage. This centring on Jesus, the man-God, had never yet been so strongly emphasised in the history of Christian spirituality. They insist upon the imitation of Christ, not only in the sense whereby Christ has become a model for man, but in that whereby, through his nature as divine Image of the Father, he has the power to restore in man the original image and likeness to God.

4. *The experience of God* is the final goal of the whole spiritual process: it is the complete unfolding of love, the resemblance to Christ, the restoration of the image of God or, simply, life with God as union with him. This, however, is always brought about in the human context of life on earth and, consequently, in the darkness of faith. It is completely bound up with charity, following the demands of the fraternal community.

The spirituality of La Trappe

Although Rancé was already, since before 1665, allied to the strict observance, he lost no time in putting ever more severe observances into effect and in following his own conceptions of reform. He too wished to return to the practice of the Benedictine rule according to the primitive usages of Cîteaux but, under the influence of the Desert Fathers who had been instrumental in his conversion, he actually established a more austere and radical form of life, made up of abnegation, penance, silence and prayer. He attracted numerous vocations and was soon imitated by several other monasteries.

Rancé's reform differed from the others in that it was inspired and upheld by a spirituality. This latter, by way of a radical break with current opinion, set his sights just as radically on the origins of monasticism, that is, on the Fathers of the Desert. In this, just as in the practices which flowed from it, he went further than the primitive Cîteaux. But Rancé, in a way, rediscovered and handed on to his disciples and contemporaries the true meaning of monastic life, the quest for God alone, the imitation of Christ and the total abandonment of all the world could offer. This attention to fundamentals has certainly been one of the characteristics of his reform and the source of his success and fruitfulness right down to the twentieth century. In the history of Cistercian spirituality, Rancé is the link which connects the Trappist Cistercians of the nineteenth and twentieth centuries with the sources and the beginnings of the Order.

Towards a new equilibrium[11]

The Trappists having been reunited in 1892 into a single Order, particular attention was paid to the setting up of a structure inspired by the Charter of Charity and to rediscovering Cistercian life as the Fathers of Cîteaux had prescribed, with its liturgy, observances, etc. Certain spiritual publications support this return to the sources, the principal being *La Règle de saint Benoît méditée* (Nevers, 1909) by Dom Symphorien Bernigaud.

Around the same time, three spiritual authors exercised a deep and lasting influence: Dom J.-B. Chautard, *L' âme de tout apostololat*; Dom Vital Lehodey, *Les voies de l'oraison mentale* (1908), *Directoire spirituel* (1910), *Le saint abandon* (1919), and Dom Anselme Le Bail, to whom the *Dictionnaire de Spiritualité* owes its article on Saint Bernard.

The influence of these three abbots within the Order coincided with the movement then under way to rediscover the riches of prayer and mysticism. The Order did not remain out on a limb; it found support for rediscovering its own tradition of prayer and a life of withdrawal from the world.

Moving on from false images

> Lord, who shall be admitted to your tent
> and dwell on your holy mountain?
> *(Psalm 14.1)*

At this point we draw inspiration from one of the spiritual giants of our century, the American Trappist Thomas Merton (1915–1968), of Gethsemani Abbey, Kentucky. This choice is not in the least fortuitous; in fact, it is highly appropriate that he should appear in such a book, for he was one of the pioneers of monastic interreligious dialogue. His relations with Suzuki, the propagator of Zen in the West, are well-known. He was fortunate enough to attend the Congress at Bangkok organized by A.I.M.[12] and, just a month before his death, he had, with the Dalai Lama[13] at Dharamsala, Himāchal Pradesh, some most enjoyable conversations, which made a deep impression on the latter; indeed, he refers to them with deep feeling in a recent book[14] and, when he visited the State of Kentucky in April 1994, he made a point of going to the Gethsemani La Trappe, he, the Dalai Lama, wishing to pray at the tomb of his "good spiritual friend".[15]

We may therefore be permitted to quote a couple of pages in which Thomas Merton, in his own style, dismisses the false ideas in circulation on the subject of our life. They are reproduced in French in a brochure on the *Vie Cistercienne* published by the Abbey of Timadeuc.[16]

> It is a custom of contemplative monasteries to issue booklets which will inform visitors and postulants about the life led by the monks. The present pamphlet is something more than a plain "postulant's guide", and more than an apologetic justification of monastic life. Such books are now plentiful and, in any case, the *apologia* for monastic life tends to be overworked. It is true that explanations are owed, and must be given. The monastery is so radically different from the "world"! Monasticism seems so much a thing of the past and so alien to technological society. The life of the monks seems on many counts to be pointless. And these objections themselves dictate replies. It is natural to argue that the monk is not so different after all and to assert that he has a very definite role to play in the modern world, that he is part of it, and that he is not useless at all. Frankly, these arguments are often misleading and unsatisfactory. To say that the

monks are justified because they "practise scientific agriculture" and that the monastery is a kind of "powerhouse of prayer" is often to compromise the true meaning of monastic life. Actually what matters about the monastery is precisely that it *is* radically different from the world. The apparent "pointlessness" of the monastery in the eyes of the world is exactly what gives it a real reason for existing. In a world of noise, confusion and conflict it is necessary that there be places of silence, inner discipline and peace: not a peace of relaxation, but a peace of inner clarity and love, based on ascetic renunciation. In a world of tension and breakdown, it is necessary for there to be men who seek to integrate their inner lives not by avoiding anguish and running away from problems, but by facing them in all their naked reality and in their ordinariness! Let no one justify the monastery as a place from which anguish is utterly absent or where men "have no problems". This is a myth. It is not by extraordinary spiritual adventures or by dramatic and heroic exploits that a man comes to terms with life. The monastery teaches men to take their own measure and to accept their ordinariness; in a word, it teaches them that truth about themselves that is called humility.

A powerhouse of prayer?

It is true that monks pray for the world. But this expression unfortunately suggests a kind of interior busyness and bustle that is quite foreign to the monastic spirit. The monk does not offer large quantities of prayers to God, then look out upon the world and count the converts that must result. Monastic life is not quantitative. What counts is not the number of prayers and good works, nor the multitude and variety of ascetic practices, nor the ascent of the various "degrees of sanctity" and "degrees of prayer". What counts is not to count, and not to be counted.

"Love", says St. Bernard, "seeks no justification outside itself. Love is sufficient to itself, is pleasing in itself, and for its own sake. Love is its own merit and its own reward. Love seeks no cause outside itself and no results other than itself. The fruit of love is love." And he adds that the reason for this all-sufficient character of love is that it comes from God as its source and returns to God as its end, because God Himself is love.

The seemingly fruitless existence of the monk is therefore centred upon the ultimate meaning and the highest value: he loves the truth for its own sake, and he gives away everything in order to hear the Word of God and do it. The monk is valuable to the world precisely in so far as he is not part of it; and hence it is futile to try to make him acceptable by giving him a place of honour in it.

While our monasteries are careful to help the poor in their vicinity, La Trappe cannot be regarded above all as a work of charity, nor as a centre for regional development.

Nearer to you, my God

Father Raymond Flanagan[17] one day pronounced this terse and thought-provoking formula: "Trappist life is not something, but rather Someone." It would be a mistake, therefore, to overlook the end for the sake of the means, and see these monks as ascetics practising excessive mortifications. In the course of the century which has just closed, mitigations to their observances were brought in, while safeguarding a moderately penitential life. The monks of my generation knew a time when the Office of Vigils began at 2 a.m., and that on weekdays; on Sundays and on the greater feasts, the Office being longer, it began at 1 a.m. Little by little, these observances were alleviated. In a good number of present-day Trappist monasteries, the monks rise in time to be in choir at 3.30 a.m., which, even so, hardly amounts to sloth.

Objectivity is gained, too, in seeing in them something other than cultivators of vast farms or brewers of good beer, right and proper though it is to gain one's livelihood by one's work.

Another image could profitably be dispelled: that of the monk who is doubtless faithful to his strict observances but hardly open to things of the mind, a backward anti-intellectual. To speak only of the abbey God has given me the blessing of living in, Scourmont has counted several monks with university degrees (Rome, Louvain, Paris). Father Joseph Canivez (+1952) published the *Statuta Capitulorum Generalium Ordinis Cisterciensis* in eight volumes (1933–1941). It was our abbey which founded and for many years ran the monastic journal *Collectanea Cisterciensia*. The works of Father Anselme Dimier (+1975) on Cistercian architecture and the studies of Father Charles Dumont on Aelred of Rievaulx and Saint Bernard are well known.

Without wishing to lay claim on any monopoly, may we say a word on devotion to Mary. Where is the Order, whether monastic or apostolic, which does not claim a special devotion to the Mother of God? It would, nevertheless, be unjust to forget the place which she holds in our Cistercian life, from the ardent devotion of Saint Bernard, Our Lady's cantor, to the *Salve Regina*, full of earnest sweetness, which closes the often arduous and testing day in our community of Trappists.

One is a bad judge in one's own cause, but I believe I am correct in saying that, even in our own days, La Trappe does exercise a certain attraction, and one of the most genuine kind. I have in mind these active religious, those diocesan priests and committed laypeople, yes, even unbelievers who, by chance, come to spend some days of retreat in a haven of peace, in the shadow of one of our abbeys. Many of them will tell you that they experienced here a mixture of work and prayer, of austerity and joy, of silence and sacred chant, which enabled them, in the bareness of our church, to discern something of the Divine Presence which they have not found elsewhere, and they return to the busyness of the world with this calming and invigorating memory of a stay at La Trappe.

Notes

[1] P. CHRISTOPHE, *L'Église dans l'histoire des hommes. Des origines au XVe siècle*. Droguet-Ardant, 1982, pp. 333–336.

[2] DANIEL-ROPS, *Saint Bernard et ses fils*. Mame, 1962, pp. 19–21.

[3] We draw inspiration here from the second volume of the work mentioned at note 1: *Du quinzième siècle à nos jours*. Droguet-Ardant, 1983, pp. 264–266.

[4] See the article *Rancé* by Fr. A. DIMIER in the Encyclopædia *Catholicisme*, vol. 12, col. 478–479, and the article *Rancé* by A.J. KRAILSHEIMER in the *Dictionnaire de Spiritualité*, vol. 13, col. 81–90.

[5] See the article *Robert de Molesme* by Fr. E. MIKKERS in the *Dictionnaire de Spiritualité*, vol.13, col. 805–806.

[6] Concerning these adventures, see the well-documented work, as readable as a novel: *Des moniales face à la Révolution française. Aux origines des Cisterciennes-Trappistines,* by Mère Marie de la Trinité KERVINGANT, O.C.S.O. (1903–1990). Bibliothèque Beauchesne 14, 1989, 408. A more amplified work was published by the Commission pour l'Histoire de l'Ordre de Cîteaux under the direction of Jean de la Croix BOUTON, Abbaye d'Aiguebelle, F – 26230 Grignan: *Les Moniales Cisterciennes, Histoire externe et interne*, 4 volumes, 1986–1989 (so not Trappistines only).

[7] Article quoted at note 5, col. 806–807.

[8] We are following here an illustrated brochure: *Vie Cistercienne* published in 1977 by Timadeuc Abbey, F – 56580 Rohan, pp. 39–40.

[9] Article quoted at note 5, col. 811–814. The directory of our Order, *Elenchus Monasteriorum O.C.S.O.* for 1995 lists 93 monasteries of monks in various countries and 65 of nuns. Statistics for the end of 1993 numbered 2,656 Trappists and 1,866 Trappistines. These figures have fallen slightly, but the number of foundations, particularly in the Third World, continues to grow.

[10] According to the article referred to in note 5, col. 741, 743–747, 768–772, 798.
[11] The same article, col. 809–810.
[12] See *A New Charter for Monasticism. Proceedings of the Meeting of the Monastic Superiors in the Far East. Bangkok, December 9–15, 1968.* Ed. John Moffitt, Univ. of Notre Dame Press, 1970.
[13] *The Asian Journal of Thomas Merton.* A New Directions Book, New York, 1973, pp. 100–102, 112–113, 124–125, 321–323. Harold Talbott accompanied Merton during his journey in North India. He was present at the three conversations with the Dalai Lama and gave an account of them in the American magazine *Tricycle. The Buddhist Review,* Summer 1992, pp. 14–24.
[14] *Au loin la liberté. Mémoires.* Fayard, 1990, pp. 268–269.
[15] *Dalai Lama visits Thomas Merton grave* in the *Bulletin of Monastic Interreligious Dialogue,* Abbey of Gethsemani, Kentucky, no. 50, May 1994, pp. 2–3, with photographs.
[16] See above, note 8, pp. 45–48. The original text is to be found in the brochure *Cistercian Life.* Cistercian Book Service, Spencer, Massachusetts, 1974.
[17] A former Jesuit, Father Raymond (died 1990) entered Gethsemani Abbey. He wrote several books on the origins of Cîteaux and biographies of Trappists, in a brisk and personal style.

Lhasa, the Potala

At Lhasa, on a little bridge over the river Kyichu, with Potala in the background

Temple of the Thousand Buddhas at Kagyu-Ling, Saône-et-Loire

With Kalu Rinpoche at Kagyu-Ling, 14 November 1984, planting a tree together

With Bokar Rinpoche at Kagyu-Ling in November 1988

Karma-Ling: The former Charterhouse of St Hugh and the Chorten

Karma-Ling: The entire complex

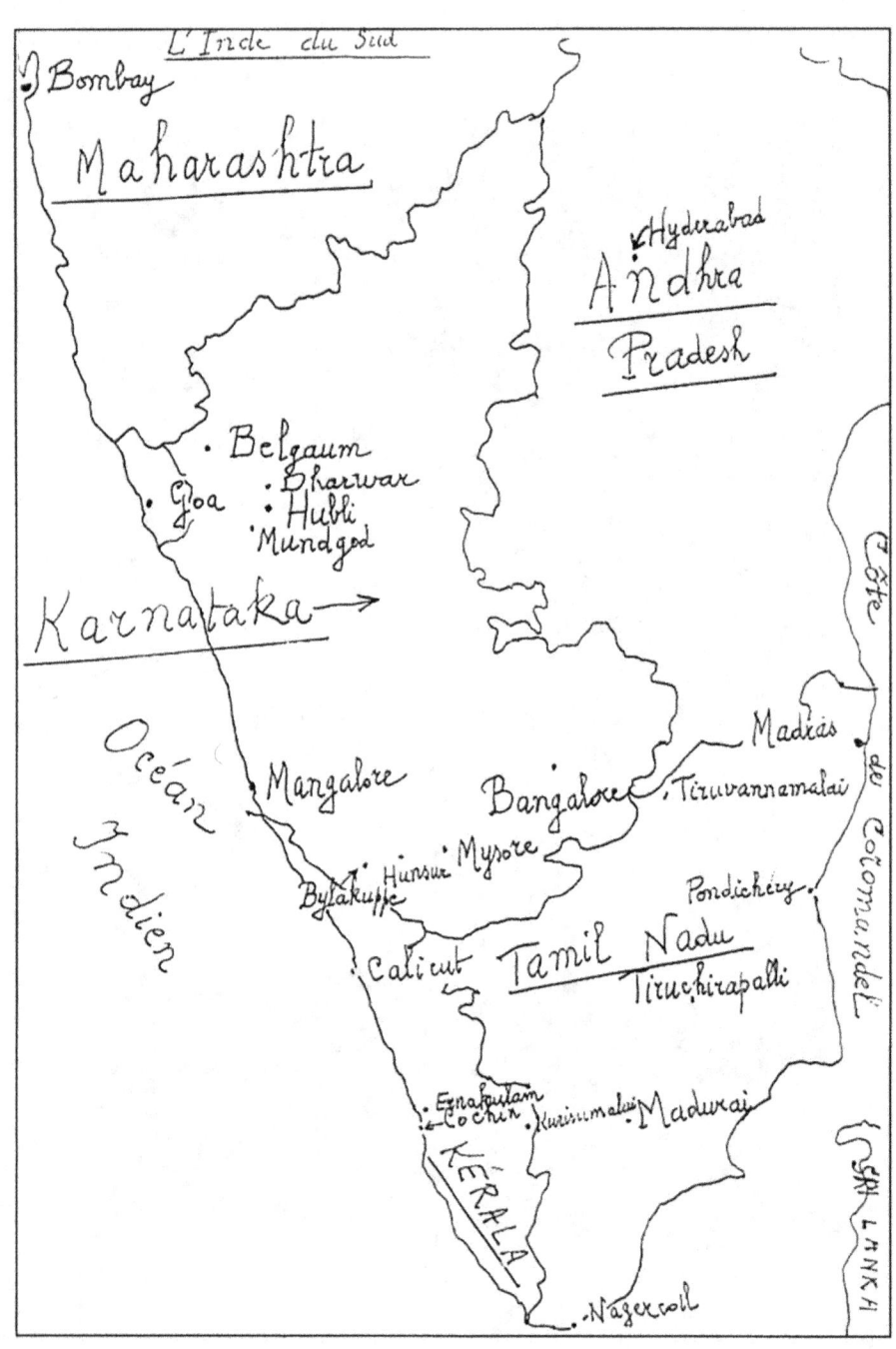

Southern India

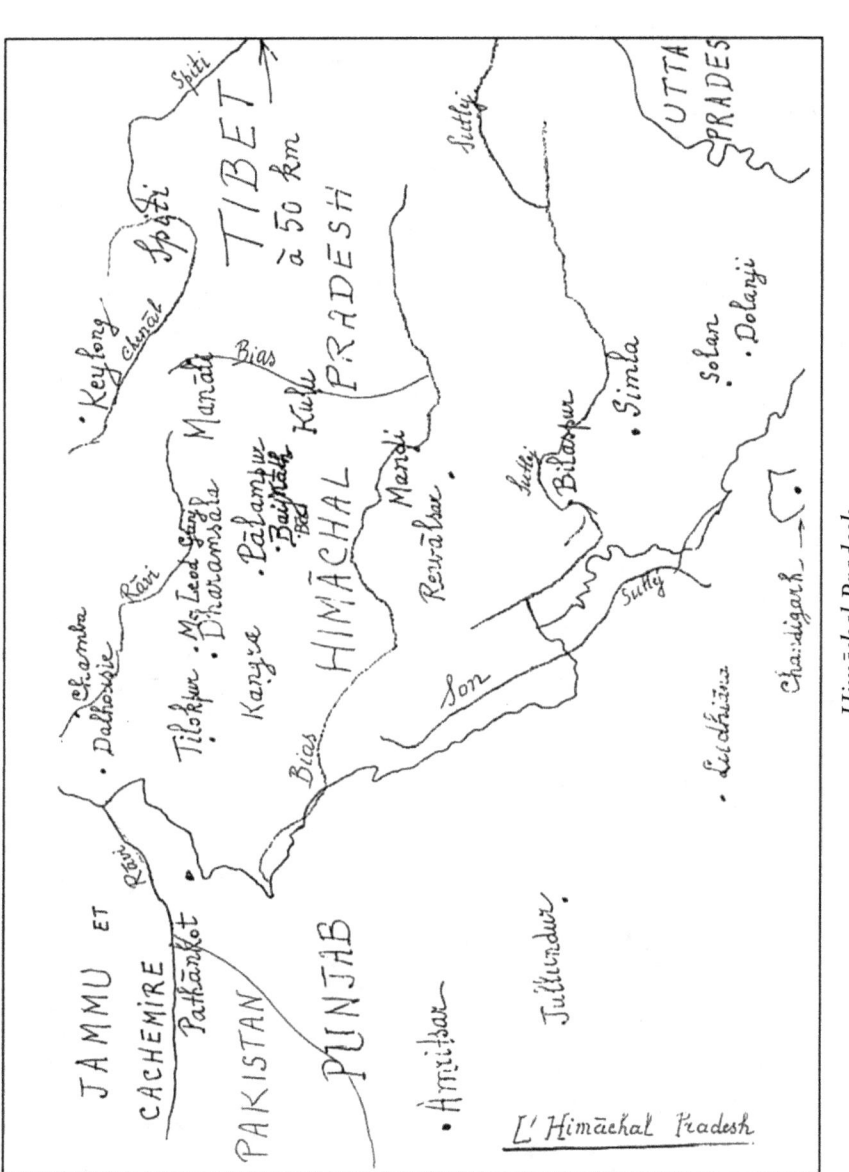

Himāchal Pradesh

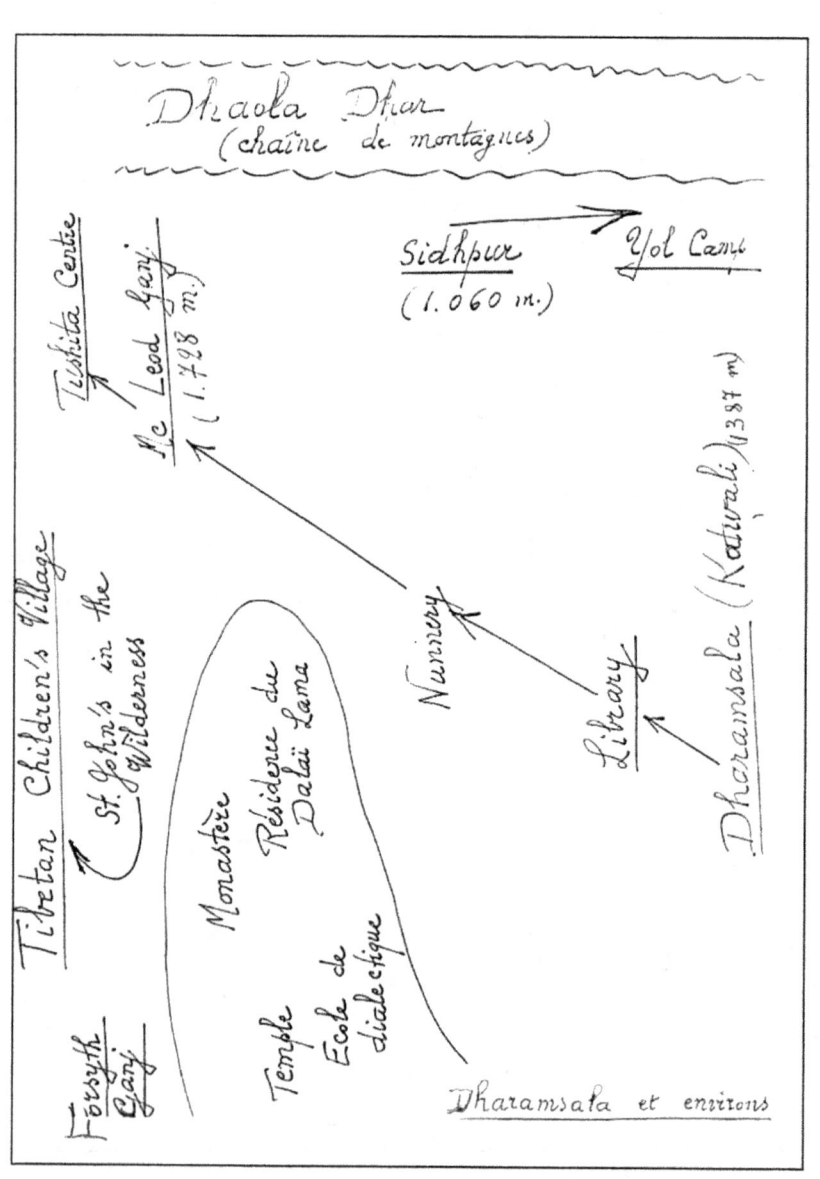

Dharamsala and environs

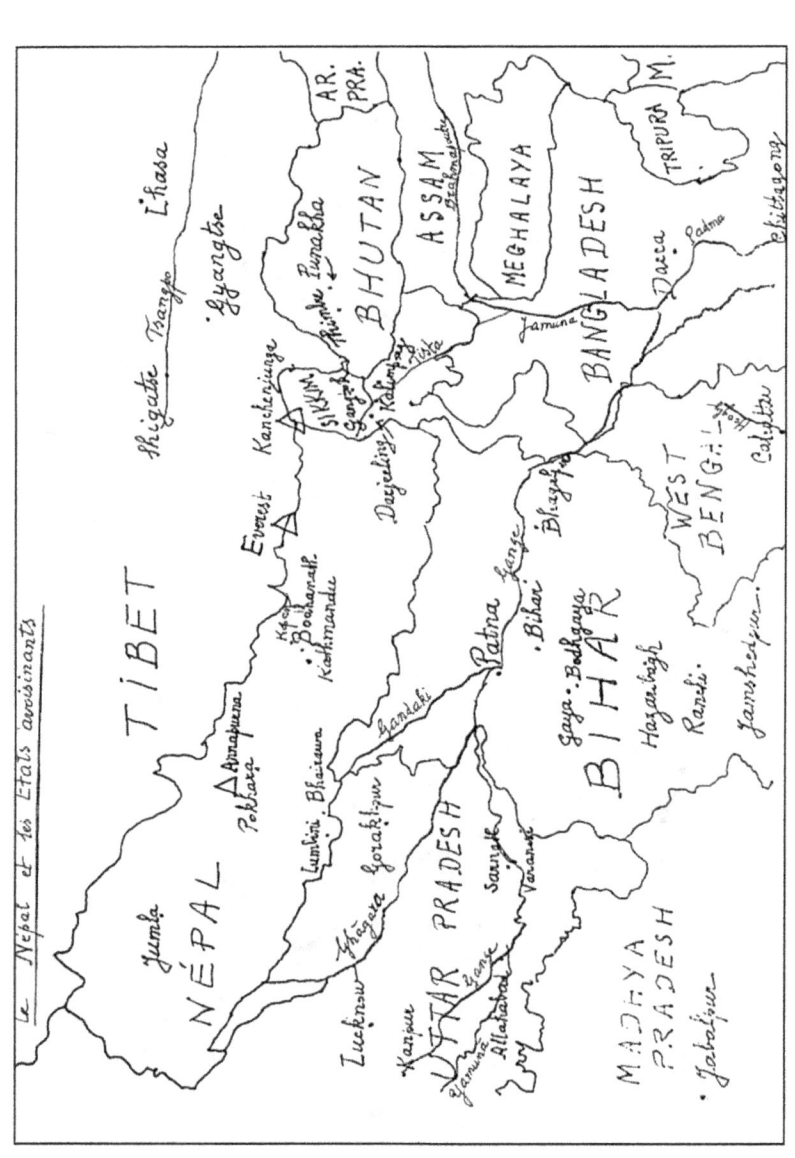

Nepal and Neighbouring States

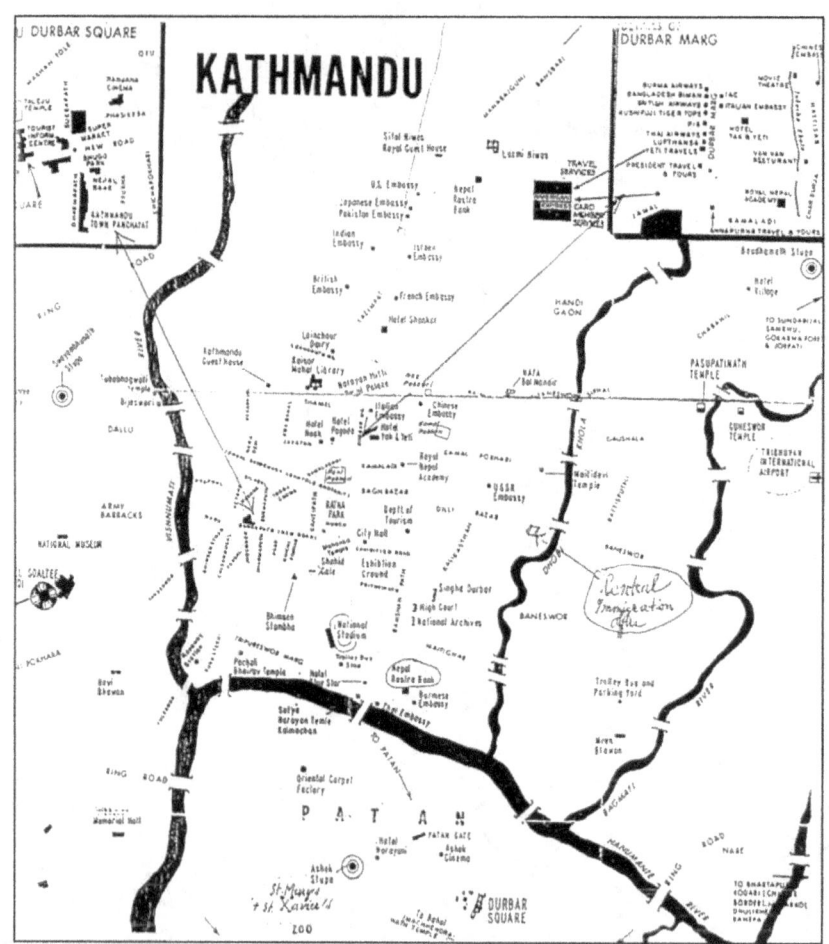

Kathmandu

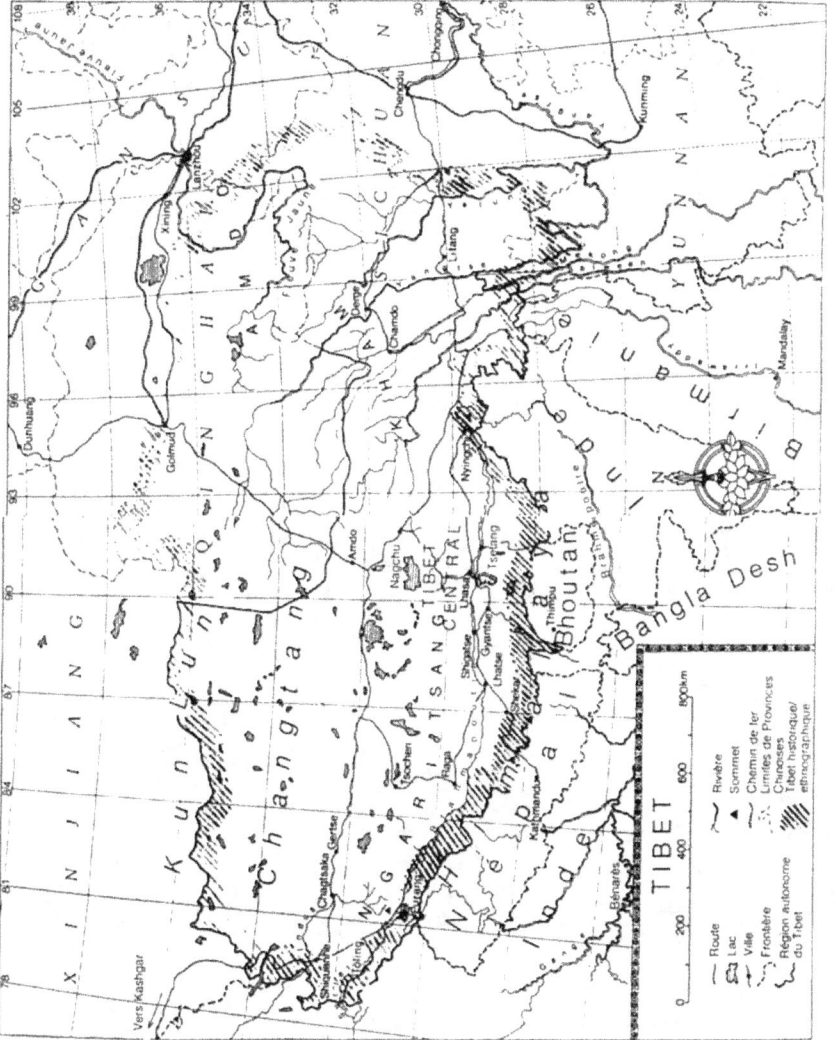

Tibet

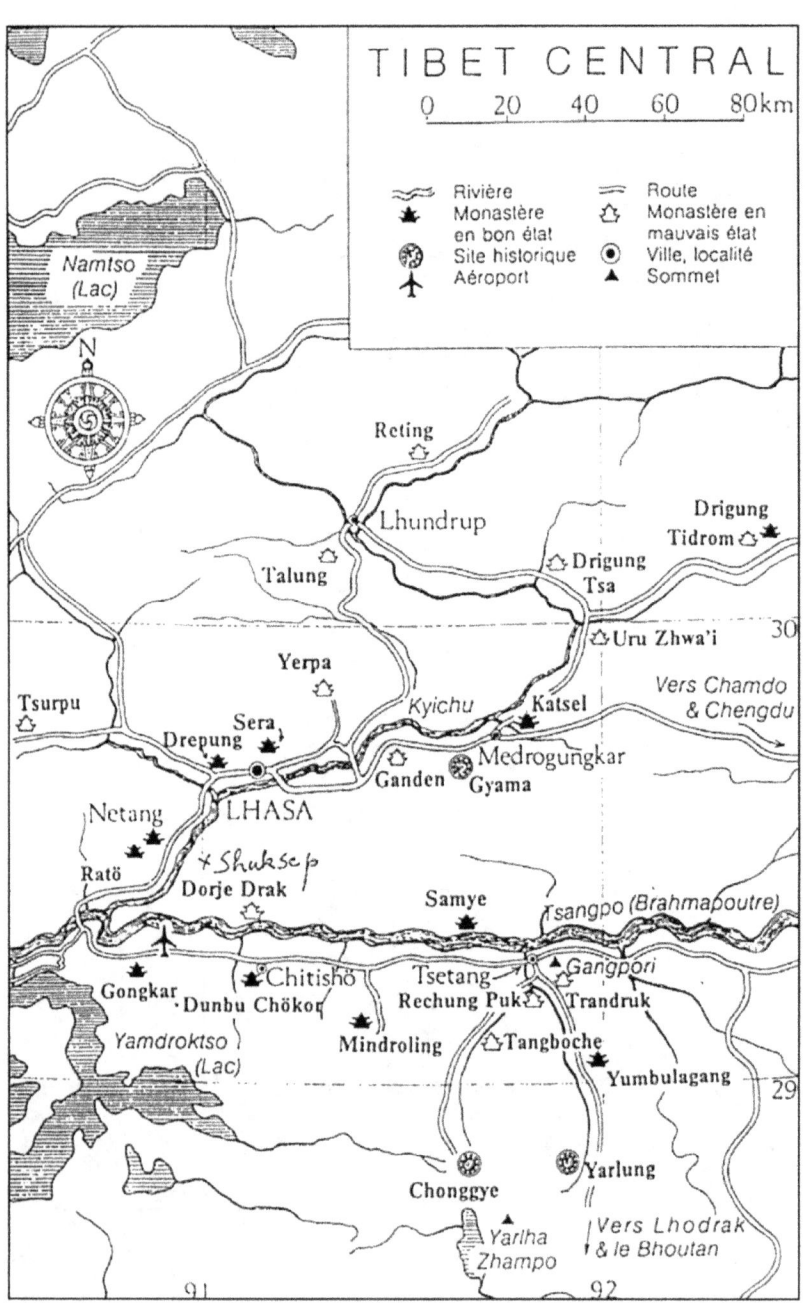

Central Tibet

Lhasa

Part Two
The Meeting

Chapter V

First Encounters (India)

MEETING OTHER RELIGIONS

Is the current infatuation of a great many Westerners, both young and not so young, with Oriental religions a passing fashion, or a more lasting phenomenon whose consequences cannot yet be seen? One way or the other, we are confronted with an undeniable fact. Rather than making an abstract and doubtless artificial survey, we intend in these pages to emphasise a far from negligible aspect of this movement: *the interreligious meeting of monasticisms.*

The Vatican II declaration *Nostra Aetate* on non-Christian religions, evidence of openness and sympathy, may be considered a seal of official approval. It was not an absolute beginning: to see this, one has only to recall the names of such pioneers of adaptation as De Nobili in India or Ricci in China. In our own century, to take only Catholic thinkers, the same spirit, well before the Council, motivated the Jesuits Dandoy and Johanns in Bengal and, in the South, Father Jules Monchanin and Dom Henri Le Saux, whose writings are still in process of being published. A whole group of theologians in India are examining the problem, and Raimundo Panikkar and Fathers Yves Raguin and William Johnston are names to be reckoned with for their depth of reflection.

Falling within this great movement of openness and doubtless corresponding with its deepest intuition, a *properly monastic* interest in the "monks of the other side" is developing. Is it not truly astonishing that so many centuries of feigned mutual ignorance could have elapsed, as in the case of the religious in Sri Lanka who, in the 1950s, meeting a group of saffron-robed monks on the road close to a famous Buddhist temple, looked to the right, pretending not to have seen them, whereas the *bhikkhus* looked to the left? I cannot suppress the thought that neither Jesus nor Shakyamuni would have approved of such behaviour.

That is a thing of the past. The importance of monasticism in dialogue with non-Christian religions was highlighted by a letter from Cardinal Serge Pignedoli to Dom Rembert Weakland, the Abbot Primate, on 12 June 1974: "Historically, the monk is the outstanding type of *homo religiosus* for all time, and as such, he attracts and serves as reference point for both Christians and non-Christians. The existence of monasticism at the heart of the Catholic Church is, in itself, a bridge connecting all religions. If we were to approach Hinduism and Buddhism, not to mention others, without monastic experience, we should hardly be considered religious men."[1]

This was already clear to Father Monchanin, as can be seen from his description of the complementary qualities which would bring mutual enrichment to the two partners: "India must give the West a keener sense of the Eternal and the primacy of being over becoming, and receive in turn from the West a more concrete sense of the temporal, becoming, the person and love."

Jacques-Albert Cuttat, too, in his book *The Encounter of Religions,* offered a golden rule: "The more deeply one enters into one's own religion, the better able he is to understand other religions from within, and the more deeply one enters into other faiths, the better he penetrates the depths of his own."[2]

This also means that we have no need to set aside our faith in Christ in order to engage in this meeting. As was very well put in the booklet published at Vārāṇasī in 1977 by the Indian Episcopal Commission for Dialogue: "Dialogue is the response of Christian faith to the saving presence of God in other religious traditions and the expression of a firm hope of their fulfilment in Christ."

The pioneers of this wider ecumenism, whose names are found in this account, clearly laboured in the spirit just described. To mention only one engaging personality, whose memory is still vivid for many, Thomas Merton was a model of such a combination of full monastic life with warm openness to the spiritual values of other religions. His sympathy with Zen was especially noteworthy. McInerny was able to say of him: "Merton was not a systematic thinker, but he had powers of penetration which few scholars possess. He had a genius for getting to the heart of complicated thought-processes and returning from the venture with what was essential to those processes. Merton deserves to be ranked as one of the major modern explicators of Oriental lore for Western audiences. He went East as a monk, knowing well his own tradition, which is the condition of a true dialogue."[3]

PRELIMINARY STAGES OF DIALOGUE

Bangkok – Bangalore

The activities of A.I.M. – an acronym originally representing *Aide à l'Implantation Monastique,* but now *Aide Inter-Monastères* – are well known. To mention Asia alone, it has to its credit two major congresses of monastic superiors: that held at Bangkok in 1968, marked by the tragic death of Thomas Merton,[4] and that in Bangalore in 1973, the Proceedings of which were published under the title: *Les moines chrétiens face aux religions d' Asie.*[5] At the end of this highly fruitful meeting, Dom Rembert Weakland, Abbot Primate of the Benedictine Order, threw out a suggestion which was to make its mark. Without denying the contribution of lay or religious specialists to meetings of different religions, was there not a particular vocation for monks to dedicate themselves to contacts with their "equivalents" in the major non-Christian religions?

Béthanie (Loppem) – Petersham

The call was heard and, soon, parallel initiatives were to be witnessed in this field. First of all, in August 1977, A.I.M. brought together at *Béthanie,* a monastery of Benedictine nuns at Loppem, near Bruges, a score of monks and nuns interested in this project and representing various Orders and congregations. They had the benefit of the information shared by theologians or missionaries well acquainted with the questions which arise in the course of interreligious dialogue. The participants, from a dozen countries, were thirty-six in number, with many areas of expertise. The majority had not only a theoretical knowledge of religions of the East, but could draw on a more or less extensive experience acquired in this or that Asian country: India, China, Japan, Thailand, Laos, Cambodia or Sri Lanka. The day would begin with a period of communal meditation. We were introduced each day to a particular method of Eastern meditation: an explanation would be given by an expert who would then help us to practise it. In this way we had the opportunity of becoming acquainted, in turn, with different forms of yoga, Zen and *Theravāda* Buddhist meditation. Particular care was taken over the Eucharistic liturgy and the establishing of an oriental atmosphere with the chants and symbols used. Other times of prayer during the day provided the opportunity for meditation on beautiful texts from the *Upanishads,* the *Bhagavad-gītā* or mystical poems from Hinduism or Amidism.

Over the course of the week, the lectures had for their subject a comparative study of the methods of interior life in the major religions. There was no suggestion of syncretism, care being taken to bring out the character proper to each religion. This, however, did not prevent us from finding points of similarity. A number of more concrete exchanges introduced us to the way of life of several centres or monasteries already centred on the meeting of the spiritual paths of the East.

As for the tangible results of the Encounter, I see them as falling under three headings: first of all a very clear awareness of the present situation, in which the religions come into contact but in a way that is sometimes confused and disorganised; secondly, a theoretical task for which theologians should equip themselves; finally, a collection of practical suggestions concerning hospitality and information. There was no evidence of idealism; on the contrary, the impression was that the road would be long and any results a distant prospect.[6]

Whereas the monks and nuns who came to Béthanie represented the countries of Western Europe, a meeting of the same kind, also held under the auspices of A.I.M., had taken place in the United States, at *Petersham*, from 4–13 July 1977. Participants came from North America (the United States and Canada). Apart from the monks and nuns, there were present a group of young people and some non-Christian meditation masters. However, the outcome was very similar.[7]

A TOUR OF MONASTIC INDIA

On the initiative of the Abbey of Praglia, near Padua, and thanks to the organisational skills of P.I.M.E. (Milan Foreign Missions), a group of Western monks, nearly all Italian, could be seen taking flight for India on 16 January 1979. This was not a piece of tourism: our intention in setting out was to meet other monks who, at least in principle, constitute the spiritual and contemplative elite of the major non-Christian religions in this vast country. We were all overwhelmed by the sheer quantity of information received and by truly fruitful contacts, for the hospitality shown us everywhere was excellent, the prayers in common exemplary, the intellectual exchanges most profitable. The journey lasted almost forty days, taking us at a spanking pace through the most varied regions and a great diversity of monastic communities. Rather than resorting to a list of place-names and communities, perhaps I may be allowed to bring these encounters together in a more thematic manner, even if this prevents me from preserving the chronological order of this "pilgrimage to the sources". Let us say at the outset that we were helped over the choice of ashrams and throughout the journey by a vigilant Brahmin, Sri Trivadi Ramachandra, a disciple of Gandhi.

To speak only of Christian monasteries, the group spent some days at *Shāntivanam*, not far from Kulittalai, 30 kilometres from Tiruchirapalli. On the banks of the Kāverī this peaceful Indian-style dwelling is situated, sanctified by its associations with its founders, Fathers Monchanin and Le Saux, the "hermits of *Saccidānanda*". Dom *Bede Griffiths* has taken up the torch, and the great tradition continues. Some of us made our way through the South as far as the hills of Kerala where, in an active seclusion, *Kurisumala*, an ashram of the Syro-malankaran rite under the direction of Father Francis Acharya, stood open to view.

Our objective, however, was to visit *Hindu ashrams*. It would be irksome to give a list of them, but such a list would show that the majority of the States were crossed, from East to West, from the extreme South to the Himalayas. To describe the way of life encountered in them would be very time-consuming and, in any case, it should be borne in mind that we were confronted by enormous diversity. What was most striking everywhere was the poverty, detachment and a quest for the Absolute to which everything else was sacrificed. The ashram which most greatly edified us, and which enjoys great renown amongst Hindus also, was the *Divine Life Society* at Rishikesh. Its founder, venerated as a saint, was Shivānanda, and his present successor, *Swāmi Chidānanda,* is rightly considered a spiritual master of the highest order, combining with a thorough knowledge of the Scriptures an intense contemplative experience. He is, moreover, very open to the values of Christian mysticism, which makes him an outstanding partner in interreligious dialogue.

Similar remarks can be made regarding *Sandeepany Ashram,* under the direction of *Swāmi Chinmāyānanda,* at Powai Hill Park, Bombay. A very searching formation is given there to future promoters of Hinduism in its most orthodox *advaitic* form. As at Rishikesh, where thousands of monks live as hermits in a kind of Thebaid of the mountains, urban ashrams, too, attract seekers of the Absolute who come from Western countries.

As a group highly qualified for dialogue, the *Ramakrishna Mission* merits particular attention. From its very beginnings, at the instance of Vivekānanda, it has had simultaneously a monastic and a missionary orientation. Imitating the methods much used by Christian Churches, it founded social and educational institutes. The calibre of its members, their intellectual formation, to say nothing of a considerable knowledge of Christianity makes them shrewd participants in dialogue. This is the impression we have brought away from our exchanges with their communities, at Calcutta, Mylapore and Belur Math, still thrilling with the memory of Ramakrishna.

Another group notable for its sympathy and openness is that of the *Tibetans.* Driven from their country in 1959, there were, as of 1979, more than 80,000 of them in India. Their highest priority, in exile, has been the refounding of their great monasteries. At *Bylakuppe,* accordingly, there are already 500 monks, many of them young, to revive the ancient monastery of *Sera.* At *Sārnāth,* a genuine Tibetan district shelters a college where 150 monks are studying, to say nothing of *Dharamsala* (Himāchal Pradesh State), residence of the Dalai Lama, who granted our group of monks a long audience.

Finally, it should be noted – a surprising discovery, this, for many of us – that foundations of *nuns* exist also in the non-Christian religions of India. We will mention only three, which we visited: the community of *Hindu nuns* of *Paunar,* at *Wardha,* founded by Vinoba Bhave not far from Sevagram, Gandhi's ashram; the *Jain nuns,* whose highly austere life rivals that of the *sannyāsis* and, finally the *Tibetan Buddhist nuns,* rivalling their brothers at Dharamsala for zeal.[8]

Notes

[1] The full text of this letter was published in *Bulletin of A.I.M.*, Vanves, No 17, pp. 61–63. For the original context, see Jean LECLERCQ, O.S.B., *Nouvelle page d'histoire monastique. Histoire de l'A.I.M. (1960–1985)*, A.I.M. Secretariat, 1985, pp. 133–136.

[2] *The Encounter of Religions,* New York, Desclée, 1969, p. 118.

[3] Dennis McINERNY, *Thomas Merton and Oriental Thought* in *Cistercian Studies,* 1979 – 1, pp. 59–72.

[4] See chapter IV, note 12.

[5] Bangalore, 1973, A.I.M. Secretariat, 7, rue d'Issy, F-92170, Vanves.

[6] See our article, *La rencontre monastique interreligieuse de Béthanie, Loppem, 20–29 août 1977,* in *Collectanea Cisterciensia,* 1977 – 4, pp. 310–321.

[7] *Été 1977 – deux rencontres: Petersham (U.S.A.) et Loppem (Belgique)* in *Bulletin de l'A.I.M.,* (Vanves), 1977, No 23, pp. 71–81.

[8] A more detailed account of this journey may be read in: *Un tour de l'Inde monastique* in *Collectanea Cistersiensia,* 1979 – 2, pp. 182–199. For Tibetan nuns, see chapter III, above. For the Jain tradition, see pp. 41–42, and notes 5 and 6 on p. 63.

Chapter VI
Meetings in Europe

THE INTERRELIGIOUS MEETING AT PRAGLIA

"Christian monks face to face with the religions of Asia" was the title of the Congress at *Bangalore* in 1973. In actual fact, although representatives of Hinduism and Buddhism were present and it was possible to begin a dialogue with them, the speakers were Christian and it was they who explained the spiritual values of those other religions. At *Petersham* the same conditions prevailed, although notice was taken of the attraction of the non-Christian East for young people and adults of the West. Emphasis was laid on a "global" culture in which all the major religions would be in communication for the greater well-being of the world. At *Béthanie,* stress was laid, as also at *Petersham,* on the necessary conditions for the preparation of our communities for receiving our brothers, monks of the East or Westerners seeking sound information on methods for meditation, whether Asian or traditional.

The meeting at the Benedictine Abbey of *Praglia*, not far from Padua, from 2–8 October 1977, had no longer merely a distant goal, the chances of success of which had still to be assessed; a resolute commitment to the path had been made. It was a matter of living together for a whole week, Christian monks and those of the Asian religions being alike resolved to share their monastic life in a concrete and reciprocal manner. Those fortunate enough to take part, first in the encounter at Béthanie and then in the experience at Praglia, experienced something very like stupefaction before that grace of God which made possible the realisation, after so few weeks, of an ideal which had seemed attainable only with great difficulty. No doubt Providence wished to show us the path, rediscovered after so many centuries, on which the Spirit, at work in all religions, wished to lead us.

The initiative for this meeting, endorsed by A.I.M., came from two brothers, Fr Cesare Bonivento and Mgr Agostino Bonivento.

The former belongs to the Milan Foreign Missions (P.I.M.E.), the members of which (Fr Muratori, Fr Manca and the others) gave evidence, during the session, of their organisational skills and their dedication. Under the guidance of their Abbot, Dom Giorgio Giurisato, the Benedictine monks showed their gift for hospitality and the grandeur of their liturgy. Their sense of humour, their charity and their eagerness to listen to these Eastern monks made a deep impression on these latter.

The participants

Christians: a good number of Benedictines, almost all Italian, Mgr Luigi Sartori, from the seminary at Padua, several Italian and Sardinian Abbots, Abbot Tholens from Amsterdam, one of the founders of A.I.M., five priests from the Milan Foreign Missions, three young Camaldolese monks and a Trappist from Scourmont. Mgr Rossano, from the Secretariat for Non-Christians, took part in the week.
Hindus: Swāmi Bhavyānanda, from the Ramakrishna Mission, Mr Trivadi Ramachandra, disciple of Gandhi, Swāmi Sadānanda from Rishikesh (Himalaya).
Buddhists: the Venerable Saddhatissa, originally from Sri Lanka, at the head of the Mahābodhi Society of London. From Tibet, Geshe Rabten and his young disciple, Gonsar. From Burma, the Venerable Rewata Dhamma, a learned master of the school of meditation.

The order of the day

Since it was understood that a shared experience of monastic life was to be made, the Hindus and Buddhists took part in community life from morning to evening, attending Mass, of which the clearest possible explanation was given, and part of the *opus Dei*.

For our part, we were able to participate in their liturgy. Each morning, in fact, was kept free for them to this end. In the meeting hall, where everything was prepared and where the Easterners sat in the lotus position as did several of our Fathers, we took part in turn in Tibetan, Theravāda Buddhist and Hindu ceremonies, this last presided over by the Swāmi from the Ramakrishna Mission. Both before each ceremony and while it was taking place, explanations were provided which enabled us to appreciate the import of the symbols and the meaning of the prayers and chants. The same procedure was followed over the meditation. The afternoon was given up to more doctrinal exchanges. A representative of each religion spoke from the standpoint of the latter on the theme of the day. The following day, this was discussed in small groups.

The themes put forward

These were as follows:
- monastic life at the personal level
- monastic life from the standpoint of the community
- monastic life and society

The text of the addresses was subsequently published in Italian.[1] The participants came away with the desire to become better acquainted with Christian monasticism in all its forms. The Christian monks were struck by several points of convergence. It might be said that these Eastern monks were far from us in their doctrines but close in their quest of the Absolute. Their life showed us a greater concern for detachment and for austerities, and they seemed to us more committed to meditation, more contemplative in the strict sense, though the quest for a union of love with God seems strange to their standpoint (and even this point requires slight distinctions to be taken into account). They, at any rate, were delighted by this experience of life in common,[2] and a decision was made to repeat it.[3]

It was while listening to the addresses given by these Eastern monks that I inwardly made the resolution of devoting what free time I might have to the study of Tibetan Buddhism and to making contact with its monasteries. The meeting with Geshe Rabten played a part in this decision which, it seems to me, was well-advised, if not downright providential.

The second meeting at Praglia

This took place, with the same results, from 23–29 September 1979. The majority of the participants had also attended the first meeting. There was the additional benefit of the presence of Bede Griffiths and Swāmi Shraddhānanda, a member of a Shankarian ashram at Hardwar. This time, the overall theme was *the monastic rule*. Whereas, in 1977, we experienced with regret a certain bittiness owing to the severe restriction in the time allotted to each speaker, care was given on this occasion to provide sufficient time for them to give proper lectures. Each day had a greater unity, focusing interest on one of the great traditions.[4]

The dialogue commission

A.I.M., for its own part, did not remain idle but persevered in creating a structure for its work. Its preliminary action was to establish a commission entitled D.I.M. *(Dialogue interreligieux monastique)* in which different Orders and the principal countries of Western Europe were all represented. A similar effort was put into concrete form in North America by the setting up of a parallel commission, the N.A.B.E.W.D. *(North American Board for East-West Dialogue)* for the United States and Canada.[5]

TWO TIBETAN MONASTERIES IN SWITZERLAND

Rikon

The tragic predicament of Tibet, its invasion in 1950 by the Chinese Communists, the revolt in 1959 soon followed by the voluntary exile of the Dalai Lama and more than 80,000 refugees need no introduction. Many of them found a refuge in India and Nepal. In the West, by far the most welcoming country was Switzerland and at the time of writing more than 1,300 Tibetans live there. Over and above housing and employment, the means have been provided for the preservation of their culture and religion. Their benefactors were sufficiently enlightened to establish, at *Rikon*, about ten kilometers' distance from Winterthur, a little monastery where seven monks live in community and care for the spiritual well-being of the neighbouring colony, where 200 Tibetans, accommodated in white cottages, work at the factory close at hand.

At 800 metres above sea-level, amongst trees hung with prayer-flags in vivid colours, there stands on the hillside, in an atmosphere of beauty and calm, the little monastery which is also a study centre. A healthy balance may be seen here between religious life in the strict sense (the large chapel decorated with *thankas* where bodhisattvas are enthroned, with bowls of bright metal, their ritual lamps) and, on the other hand, a library well equipped with everything concerning Tibet, its geography, art, explorers' reports and, needless to say, its religion. I can safely say that, in the field of works in Western languages on Tibet and Tibetan Buddhism, you would have to visit the Guimet Museum in Paris or the Library of Congress in Washington to find its match. Moreover, this centre is beginning to be well known and is attracting seekers or sympathisers with the Buddhism of the Lamas who come to stay, and ten cells have been built to accommodate them. Although the language of the monks is Tibetan, most of them are able to converse in English or German. Care had been taken in their selection and, in fact, some are actively engaged in translating Tibetan works into European languages. Their smiling and straightforward manner with visitors, imbued as it is with Buddhist benevolence, makes contact with them very pleasant. Attendance at their early morning liturgy can only edify guests, no matter what their religion. Great reverence and inwardness is to be observed; the deep voices of the monks is accompanied, here and there, by the tinkle of their bells or the sounding of drums and cymbals.

On the upper storey are to be found the departments of the *Tibetan Office*, which has the heavy responsibility of watching over the material well-being of all their refugees across the West. Despite its modest size, Rikon is simultaneously a centre for monastic life, culture and mutual aid in the social sphere. On this point it is comparable to some of our Christian monasteries. But there is to be found, throughout the enterprise, an intense inner life. For some years, actually, Abbot *Geshe Rabten* has been giving his teachings here, and hours spent in his little chamber, a genuine oratory, can be extremely worthwhile. He answers with great wisdom, not unmixed with humour, all the questions touching doctrine and monastic life that Western monks,[6] put to him. His interpreter is an intelligent and sympathetic young lama, *Gonsar Tulku*, whose tact at Praglia had been appreciated by all.

At Mont-Pèlerin: Tharpa Chœling

At their urging, we set out to visit their foundation at Mont-Pèlerin, Vevey, at the other end of Switzerland on Lake Geneva.

Meetings in Europe

From the windows of this monastery there is a magnificent view of the lake and the snow-covered mountains on the far side. It is at one and the same time a home for monks in wine-coloured robes and a study centre, with the added novelty that the monastic community that they are establishing here is intended for Western monks. It has been open for hardly a year and already vocations are flowing in. A dozen monks, from a variety of countries, have already found their mode of life here. As at Rikon, the visitor is edified by the seriousness of their monastic commitment, the recollected dignity of their liturgical office, the zeal they show for their studies (they are all required to learn Tibetan and some of them speak it already) and the warmth of their welcome. Even if one arrives with prejudices – objections, for instance, to the passing over to Buddhism of young people with a Christian upbringing – it very soon has to be admitted that they are, simply, totally committed souls who, at the end of frequently tragic adventures (conflict, even drugs in some cases) have ended up in India to find in this way of life, both regular and remote from the world, the path that leads to inner peace and to a deep-seated ambition for the heights of the Spirit. Their sincerity is moving and, since they make no effort to conceal it, let us add that their interest in the great Christian monastic Orders arouses in them an unquenchable curiosity and a lively fellow-feeling.

In the case of both Rikon, the beautiful white bird poised on the lonely hill, and Mont-Pèlerin, the lively young foundation overlooking the lake and the further shore, we have experienced the joy of a meeting or, even better, of a recognition. Contacts like this cry out to be renewed and deepened. One experiences there that monasticism is *in fact* a bridge between two religions, so different in other respects. They need to know each other better, understand each other more fully and, please God, provide mutual support.

Vevey and Rikon revisited

These first meetings took place between 28 March and 1 April 1978. I was able to revisit these two centres of Tibetan life in Switzerland from 30 May to 3 June 1985. My original impressions were, if anything, reinforced. At *Vevey,* these young monks took me into their confidence as though I were their spiritual father. I was allowed a long conversation on comparative religion with

Madame Ansermet, widow of the famous conductor, and found her very committed to the *Dharma*, while at the same time open to other traditions. Geshe Rabten, his health already undermined by the illness which was soon to end his life, spoke hardly at all, but listened benevolently.

At *Rikon,* I noticed the greater extent to which German was becoming the lingua franca, even among the Tibetan monks. I happened to be present for some exceptional days from the liturgical standpoint. The Dalai Lama's former envoy in Switzerland had recently died and Tibetans came to Rikon for this occasion, not only from neighbouring cantons but from Austria as well, in order to take part in lengthy funeral rites. This was the first occasion on which, here in the West, I had felt myself immersed in the culture and devotion of Tibet.

A BUDDHIST MONASTERY IN BURGUNDY

Kagyu-Ling

At about thirty kilometers to the south of Autun, the nearest small town being Toulon-sur-Arroux, the château of *Plaige* is to be found at the turning of a narrow path, its slender turrets pointing to the sky. This dilapidated edifice was acquired by an association the object of which is to assist the establishment of monks of a great tradition while at the same time maintaining friendly contacts with Christianity. The founder of the monastery is the Venerable *Kalu Rinpoche. Ling* means a centre; *Kagyu* the oral tradition. This is not the most official Order of Lamaism, the *Gelugpa*, to which the Dalai Lama belongs and which is sometimes referred to as the "yellow church". The *Kagyupa* go back to Marpa and Milarepa; their main branch has, as "Abbot General", the Karmapa XVI. Whereas the *Gelugpa* have a scholastic and intellectual propensity, forming "Doctors of Theology" who bear the title *Geshe,* the ideal of the *Kagyu* monks is more definitely spiritual and mystical. At Rikon and Vevey, the *Gelugpa* edified us with the level of their studies and the simplicity of their welcome.

It is good to make the acquaintance, through face-to-face meetings, with the other stream, in which, as it seems to us, the majesty of their liturgy and their concern for austerity are to the forefront. We took part in an intensive study of the Tibetan language which lasted a fortnight. Excellent handbooks were provided for our use. The courses were arranged on three levels, each with its own teacher, two Frenchwomen and one Frenchman, this arrangement being best suited to the difficulties experienced by beginners. Tibetan has nothing in common, so to speak, with our Western languages. The sole point of contact with the Indo-European languages being an alphabet used by the Indians who took Buddhism to Tibet; it shows similarities with the alphabets of North India.

The day at Kagyu-Ling is divided between the liturgical office, which consists of two long services, each lasting between one-and-a-half to two hours, periods of study and those allotted to solitary meditation. The food is frugal but wholesome, the atmosphere favourable to recollection, and to fraternal contacts between the resident monks and the temporary guests. We are witnessing a *recent foundation*, and who is unaware of the difficulties which are part and parcel of every beginning? Not the least are arranging an old château and managing both the formation of monastic recruits and the broader hospitality to visitors; they are still, I believe, experiencing financial difficulties. They would like to put up a building in the park for monks only, including the temple and their cells, and the château would become the guest house. These, at least, were their plans at the time of my first visit to Plaige, in August 1978.

The Liturgy, of a very oriental style, has among its attractions the extensive employment of symbolism, and the use of what will impinge on the senses. From this standpoint, it differs sharply from the bare and cerebral character of our modern Western liturgy. The Tibetans readily make use of long, booming trumpets, the deep tones of which seem to call forth echoes from deep valleys; they shake tambourines and mingle the clear tone of cymbals, the melodies of conches and the rhythm of bells with the sounding of enormous drums.[7] Flowers, fruit and the light from little lamps envelop the altar, which enthrones the solemn Bodhisattvas in their variety of vivid colours. The entire office is in Tibetan but, to help the numerous laypeople taking part, either Buddhist already or close to becoming so, assistants distribute oblong texts, resting on stands, which give the Tibetan prayers with a French translation interlined.

The completely essential feature of the monastery, however, is the existence of *two separate buildings reserved for the retreatants*.

This word has lost in our languages its primary meaning and a reference to the Desert Fathers is called for in order to recover the strong sense of complete separation from the world. It is here, however, that the final goal of the *Kagyu* tradition comes into its own. In Tibet, this total retreat was permitted only to seasoned monks who had long since passed the preliminary stages and whose spiritual progress, after years of meditation, empowered their access. For three years, three months and three days, the retreatants live shut up in an enclosure from which they never come out and where no one enters except an attendant bringing food for their kitchen; he himself is a trustworthy monk. They divide their time between the study of texts, receiving teachings, prolonged meditation and the practice of a form of yoga. Their austerity is unquestionable. They sleep for little more than four hours and that without a bed, or even the possibility of stretching out on the ground; they maintain the lotus position and sleep in a kind of box which supports their arms. For a long time there was no form of heating, not even in winter.

At Kagyu-Ling, the retreatants themselves constructed two buildings, white windowless "carmels" completely turned toward the interior. Seven boys between the ages of twenty and thirty are enclosed in one of them; at the further end of the robinia wood, seven young girls. They are all from different Western countries, several from California, and English is the language of the majority. Almost all, on the men's side, will remain monks (or so it is hoped). They are counted upon to be the leaven in the lump for the future. As for the girls, the nun's vocation is stricter and, traditionally, less promoted in Buddhism.[8] Nevertheless, there are already at Kagyu-Ling besides the retreatants, two fervent nuns who help with hospitality for guests of their own sex.

The hidden presence of the two buildings under the trees is like a constant reminder of the ideal to be followed. Fully occupied with housework, answering visitors' queries and language studies, the eight French *residents*, under the direction of three lamas from Bhutan, are clearly less contemplative, but they aspire to become so and, for this, they count upon our help. Having not the slightest feeling of antagonism towards genuine Christianity and the Gospel, they would like to be better acquainted with our monastic traditions, for which they express a high regard.

As for guests and sympathisers, they may lodge and meditate in thin-walled wooden *cabins*, small and quiet, which, situated in the thicket at the bottom of the park, provide a foretaste of the eremitical life. You may imagine that this arrangement is congenial to me; I have been back each summer for ten years, in very much the same conditions.

Over the course of the years

Life inevitably brings with it growth and change. The small cabins have multiplied, and I have moved from one to another. My fellow-disciples have changed: this one and that of the men and women have gone into retreat, or even departed to help maintain centres in the South of France or abroad. In the course of time, our language studies have led us to tackle, in the form of an anthology, fundamental texts in the Mahāyāna and Tibetan tradition. The premises are being improved and modernised. A *chorten* of enlightenment stands on the edge of the meadow. Soon there will be buildings in the Bhutanese style of the great *Temple of the Thousand Buddhas*, the first instance in the West of this architecture, very spacious and covered with frescos, suitable for sumptuous festivities. Then the functional storeys of the *Marpa Institute* are being erected and fabulous figures brought to life to decorate the *Dzambala* fountain. I shared in the joy of these developments.

It goes without saying that the architecture of the new temple, with its gilded dragons, gigantic statues and vivid frescos, an out-and-out oriental palace dropped into Saône-et-Loire, is drawing the curious in large numbers at weekends and on summer days. In the course of the years, the number of residents and the variety of nationalities represented at Plaige has grown visibly. However, the young men who might, at the termination of their retreat, have been expected to remain as monks are fewer than expected, and this to the extent of weakening the hope of a genuinely stable community. Even the staff of directing *lamas* has changed, though without losing its family atmosphere; Bhutanese is spoken on the first floor of the old château.

Despite being a foreigner to the institution, I am more familiar than most with the history of its origins. Where, in 1995, are the men and women who witnessed the clearing-out of the old house? The important thing is that the spirit, or as they say, the *motivation* of the beginnings should not have been lowered.

Is interreligious dialogue taking place?

From time to time, though less frequently than at St. Hugh's Charterhouse, the opportunity arises of holding *Conversations on comparative religion* at Kagyu-Ling. Certain dates may be highlighted:

1. A *first meeting* between Christians and Buddhists took place 11–13 November 1984, with the Venerable *Kalu Rinpoche*. Among the participants, leaving aside two diocesan priests, most noteworthy were some monks from La Pierre-qui-Vire. The encounter was an informal one, with spontaneous questions and answers. The whole event was recorded and the contents – both simple and invigorating – may be read in an attractive booklet.[9]

2. A *second meeting,* 8–11 May 1986, with *François Chenique* taking part, provided the opportunity for me to present, in turn:
   – Three methods of Christian meditation
   – The Imitation of Jesus Christ
   – Mahāyāna compassion and Christian charity[10]
   – The alchemy of suffering and early Christian texts.

3. The *inauguration of the temple,* 22–24 August 1987, was attended by a round of festivities. As might be imagined, one was able to hear, both in public and private talks, people coming from a great variety of spiritual horizons; hence, comparisons, most often beneficent and educative, arose continually.

4. An *interreligious Conversation dedicated to peace* took place with *Bokar Rinpoche* in the chair, 10–14 November 1988. We had the benefit of hearing Arnaud Desjardins, a Lebanese Sufi and a learned Jew on "Bible and Kabbala". At this encounter, I gave an account of the history of Monastic Interreligious Dialogue.[11]

5. Finally, a teaching from *Tai Situ Rinpoche* on 27 November 1994 was followed by a lecture on *the Catholic teaching on peace*. The same evening saw the inauguration of the *Marpa Institute* and the dedication of the *Dzambala* fountain, fully illuminated in the night.

It will be clear that so many encounters, whether on the school benches, in the course of a ritual or at the speakers' table, have given rise to numerous friendships.

A BUDDHIST RETREAT AT SAINTE-BAUME

Wishing to be better acquainted with the spiritual techniques of Buddhism and to make contact with Tibetan Lamas, I was delighted to take part in a *Buddhist meditation session* which was held on the delightful site of Sainte-Baume, Provence. For ten days, 23 September to 3 October 1978, around 200 persons, all coming from different religious horizons, were initiated into the Graduated Path towards Awakening. The majority of the retreatants were French, but others came from Italy, Germany, Switzerland or America. The atmosphere was both recollected and relaxed. Every generation was represented, although the majority were young people. The day was divided between periods of directed meditation and those spent in listening to teachings given by lamas from India and Nepal. Discussion groups made possible more dialectic exchanges. Taken as a whole, many of the retreatants of both genders were Christian by upbringing and did not set out to repudiate Christianity, but the majority had had a deficient theological formation, and their ignorance in this field made it possible for them to admit several of the doctrines of Buddhism (transmigration, for example, generally accepted by them) which are clearly incompatible with our Christian faith. The exchanges were marked by cordiality and frankness. The lamas, whilst being the focus of great veneration, did not dominate, and the public, particularly after explanations generally found to be too hard, or too greatly pervaded by a mythology worthy of the Middle Ages, did not hesitate to express strong criticism. There are, after all, on the Buddhist path, certain emphases which are unacceptable (elaboration, for example, of the tortures of hell). *Lama Thubten Yeshe*, with his humour and irony in satirising Western society had more influence on the assembly than the possibly more standard, but also more chilly and distant teaching, of *Lama Song Rinpoche*, who presented more the figure of a mandarin.[12]

To sum up, a great deal was learnt and the spiritual atmosphere was favourable. Speaking as a priest, I was entrusted with a great many secrets. So many souls are troubled and seeking, often at a loss in the face of the present situation of the Church, and they experience a want of spiritual direction. Amongst the assembly, there were several attached to Buddhism and accustomed to making use of its techniques, up to a point. Many actually "took refuge" during the retreat.

The criticism could be made against this week of having overdeveloped the intellectual and doctrinal side. More time could have been made for meditation, even if undirected. As for the liturgy, leaving aside the closing *pūjā,* it was regrettably absent, whereas a stay at Kagyu-Ling made a favourable impression on both counts.

A Mahāyānist retreat at the Viviers seminary (Ardèche)

Following the meditation week of the previous year at Sainte-Baume, the retreat held from 21–31 July 1979 at *Viviers,* beside the Rhône, formed its extension and complement. The participants, fewer in number, came to about a hundred, including around twenty Spaniards, mostly from the centre on Ibiza (Balearic Isles). Consequently there was simultaneous translation into both their language and French. Two meditation courses unfolded in parallel; one setting out the Graduated Path to awakening, the other for more advanced disciples. Certain teachings were intended for all, which allowed both groups to be present. We had the advantage of doctrinal lessons from *Lama Thubten Yeshe,* whose spiritual influence was unquestionable, while *Lama Zopa* explained for us, with simplicity and conviction, the most important points of Mahāyāna philosophy. Care was taken to reserve the last four days for a retreat in the strict sense, the doctrinal side yielding to a deep and recollected practice of the teachings we had received.

This priest, who had the privilege of participating fully in both aspects (intellectual and contemplative) and was in a position to receive quite a number of secrets, came away with a very positive overall impression. This is not at all to say that the two religions are similar, as their fundamental doctrines can hardly be reconciled. With goodwill, however, and a modicum of intuition, it is possible to discover parallels and resonances between them. At all events, it is important to respect the avowals of many who say that their journey on the Mahāyānist way has made possible a loving rediscovery of Jesus and of the value of his message.

I had a lengthy conversation, one evening, with two young Scandinavian women, a Swede and a Finn who, though Lutheran by origin, showed a keen interest in matters to do with my monastic vocation.

Another day, wishing to talk with a family from beyond the Pyrenees, I asked a little Spanish boy, "What is your name?" To my surprise, he answered, "Siddhārtha!"

A great heart: Lama Thubten Yeshe

Ubi caritas et amor, Deus ibi est
Where charity and love are, God is there

This marvellous being who was all smiles and whose very breath was love, he has left us.[13] I believe I am conveying the feelings of those men and women who had known him by saying that it is difficult to hold back tears at the thought of never again seeing that beaming figure, himself enjoying life but fully aware of those ills that afflict the depths of the human heart. It is for others to record which of his ancestors he reincarnated, the early stages of his monastic life, his studies in Tibet and the responsibilities he shouldered in exile. A Christian monk may be permitted simply to recall a few memories of the man who was a teacher and friend to many.

We met him for the first time at *Sainte-Baume,* during the retreat we described above. He accompanied, and appeared in sharp contrast to, Song Rinpoche, who was more solemn and more aloof. After very few minutes, it could safely be said that Lama Yeshe had his audience in his pocket. With his sense of humour, he excelled in satirising our Western society. He was a matchless impresario, I would almost use the word clown, with his often highly comical mimicry. Nevertheless, for all his success in exposing oddities and absurdities, the illusions of the majority of people and their slavery to the passions, he never wounded, so palpable was his compassion and his sense of certainty that good would triumph. When he gave himself up to peals of laughter, everyone did the same, convinced that with him, they were on the road to freedom. I saw him again the following year, this time with Lama Zopa, at the time of the second retreat, at *Viviers* on the Rhône.

It was always a great joy and advantage to meet him on subsequent occasions, whether on the picturesque hill of *Kopan,* beyond

Bodnath in Nepal,[14] or in his much-loved refuge, *Tushita*, in the woods which crown McLeod Ganj, not far from his Holiness the Dalai Lama, but above the commotion of the Tibetan market. Such a location aptly sums him up: close enough to the crowd to be of benefit to it, but a lover of solitude where his favourite disciples could follow him in the most secret and most severe practices. He did not grant unconditional admittance to retreats of so searching a character.

That he should have had so great an influence of persons encountered almost by chance would seem to suffice. He was, however, behind the demeanour of a kindly father or a cute child, an organiser of the highest order. This may be deduced by the great number (over thirty) of centres founded by him *For the preservation of the Mahāyāna Tradition* in most countries of the West, from France to the United States, from the Netherlands or England to Spain, from Italy to Australia. Wherever he went, he knew just how to found, organise and sustain, and in all these countries he will be mourned.

The cost of Lama Yeshe's perseverance, during his last years, in his tireless apostolate across the world, is well known. In view of his heart condition alone, his doctors would have ordered complete rest and offered only the most slender hope of a cure, but in addition to this, he suffered greatly from a gastric ulcer. However, ardent *bodhisattva* that he was, he continued to spend himself for the salvation of all beings. Had he been a Christian, he would have merited canonisation.

May a Catholic monk be permitted to describe yet another essential aspect of his personality? He was a true *ecumenist,* capable of passing beyond the frontiers which all too often hold the major religions apart. Does his action at Kopan on behalf of his retreatants, come from such distances to learn Buddhist meditation techniques, need to be recalled? A week before Christmas, he gave them the most profound conferences imaginable on the coming of Jesus into this world, its true meaning and the best way to prepare for it.[15] During the Sainte-Baume retreat, also, not only was he amongst a group of lamas who climbed the hill to carry out their *pūjā* in the grotto of St. Mary Magdalene but, one fine morning, he slipped away to make a visit with us to the church of St. Maximinus, where he demonstrated a lively devotion to Mary, the Mother of Jesus. He is nevertheless well known as a faithful promoter of the *Dharma*, and with what fidelity he held to his own tradition. He would happily reminisce about the days at *Lawudo*, on the slopes of Mount Everest, where he trained his young monks with such thoroughness.

When, in 1982, the opportunity arose for him to make a pilgrimage to Tibet, he returned to his original monastery, *Sera*, where he had received his formation in the *Sera-jé* college. In its current ruinous condition, the cell he had formerly occupied no longer had a roof. Nevertheless, Lama Thubten Yeshe installed himself there in the lotus position, and remained for long hours in meditation, under the open sky.

VISITING NON-CHRISTIAN MONASTERIES IN GREAT BRITAIN

Having spent nearly three months on the little island of Caldey, off the coast of Tenby,[16] where the monastery required assistance, I took the opportunity on leaving[17] to visit four Buddhist monasteries and a *Vedānta* centre in England and Wales. It was an experience which, without being entirely ground-breaking, was, I believe, beneficial for all concerned. I rediscovered old friends and came to know their home ground.

In Wales: Penrhos

Heading North from Newport, Wales, one reaches first Raglan, and then the peaceful village of *Penrhos*. This, since July 1978, has been the home of a little Tibetan Buddhist centre named *Lam Rim* (The Gradual Way).[18] The house and grounds were purchased by some Western laymen who had sold their possessions and given up what were in many cases very successful careers in order to establish a centre for the *Dharma*. They were fortunate enough to attract and maintain in residence thereafter an excellent "Master of theology" in the Gelugpa tradition, the Venerable *Geshe Damcho Yonten*, who had been an abbot in Ladakh and, since 1966, has had Western disciples in India. The contacts which I had with him were on the meeting of our respective forms of monastic life, whereas I questioned the residents about their means of livelihood. To earn a living, many of them go out to work, giving yoga courses, running a welfare centre for the mentally handicapped, as well as other, more modest occupations. The maintenance of the house and gardens rests entirely on them. The little monastery is, in consequence, as much a place of work as it is one of meditation under the direction of a good spiritual master. Peace reigns in the neighbourhood, which is in the open countryside with its great fields. Courses for retreatants are regularly organised there.

In October 1981, I was to return for several days to this peaceful centre, and I found it a more beneficial stay. I enjoyed longer conversations with the Geshe, who threw light for me on essential points of their doctrine, even though he knew all too little about Christianity. Moreover, in private conversations, each of the men and women residents showed me absolute trust, explaining often bewildering situations for me. As individuals, their generosity is outstanding, but the future of the centre would be more assured if there were a stronger sense of a common life. I returned yet again in October 1982, and took part in a course in Tibetan given there. Certain of the residents had left, while new faces appeared among them; the ladies had remained, devout and faithful.

Manjushri Institute, Ulverston

Much better known is the *Manjushri Institute,* at Ulverston.[19] Reached only at the end of a long journey, it is in the South of the County of Cumbria, not far from the Lake District, on Morcombe Bay. The present buildings, the work of a rich landowner in the 1820s, have something showy, even pretentious, about them. But these edifices with worm-eaten beams, having been left in poor condition since 1976, required a complete restoration with which the present occupiers are still contending. The place still has something sacred about it, as what is still known as *Conishead Priory* was an Augustinian monastery for more than three centuries until its suppression by Henry VIII. The Buddhists who live there now and their sympathisers love this link with an ancient monastic tradition. It is a privilege to lead a contemplative life in a place sanctified by centuries of prayer, and they readily underline the fact.

This is undoubtedly the most flourishing Dharma centre in Great Britain – not only owing to the grandeur of the property, with a park showing magnificent autumn foliage close to the sea, but above all for the dynamism of the latest residents. It was established by four young English engineers on a spiritual quest, who came to know Tibetan Buddhism in India. They renounced their possessions, acquired this old manor-house and made it an important base for *Lama Thubten Yeshe's* great organisation, the *Foundation for the Preservation of the Mahāyāna Tradition*, which already has several centres worldwide. The heart of the undertaking is in Nepal, at *Kopan*, where we stayed at the beginning of this year.[20] We had earlier had the benefit of following two retreats, in the South of France, directed by that great spiritual master and having deep conversations with him. In recent times, the Institute has been organised in a fashion that might be described as academic. The novelty is this: the scheme has actually been devised of providing Westerners with access, by means of a course of studies lasting for many years, to the ambitious grade of *Geshe*. The most highly qualified masters in this field come from the famous Tibetan college of *Sera*: Geshe Kelsang Gyatso and Geshe Jampa Tegchok. We had with the latter a long and most cordial conversation touching, first, on the dialogue between monks, and then on a comparative study of our two religions and their fundamental doctrines.

It should not be supposed that all this boils down to a mere intellectual discipline. In this centre, the spiritual dominates: early morning *pūjā* and the recitation of prayers, meditation techniques and work in a monastic spirit. Leaving aside the passing guests and the numerous retreatants on certain ocasions, the long-term community counted (as of 1980) 80 members: ordained monks, nuns, laypeople and their children. The fact of spending a number of days in such an environment not only gives rise to appreciation of the attentive and obliging attitude of those in charge, but allows one to engage the residents in confidential conversations where an intense thirst for an inner life and a confrontation between Christian faith and the methods of the Dharma are mingled. The grace of God fashions souls of good will in unexpected ways. Naturally the Institute, well known abroad, attracts followers from a great many countries.

I was in the park, looking for a path to the bay and a lady pointed it out to me. This proved to be an opportunity for a discussion of the two religions. This journalist from London, Vicki Mackenzie, both faithful to Christianity and an admirer of the person and teaching of Lama Yeshe, was later to write an attractive little book, *The Boy Lama*, in which I see that she has not forgotten our conversation. It concerns a little Spaniard in whom the upholders of reincarnation see Lama Yeshe reborn.[21] While staying at his monastery, *Sera*, I was to encounter this likeable child, who has been named Ösel, that is to say, Bright Light. He enjoys, it must be said, what some would consider an excessive degree of publicity.[22]

A Vedānta Centre: Bourne End

The *Vedānta Centre* of the *Ramakrishna Mission* is located not far from a loop of the Thames at *Bourne End*, in the County of Buckinghamshire. All the streets are decked with magnificent autumnal foliage and, surrounding the little monastery is a wide variety of trees. We arrived just in time for "Vespers": chants in honour of Ramakrishna, whose impressive portrait occupies a central place in this most peaceful chapel where ewers and copper vases holding China asters, chrysanthemums and gladioli contribute to the worship. Even more impressive than the music, however, there was silence and a long, motionless meditation. Then the community welcomed me. I had met the Swāmi at Praglia, where he appreciated the Benedictine atmosphere.[23] *Swāmi Bhavyānanda* is simultaneously an organiser, a religious preacher and a man of prayer. He took the initiative of inviting to stay with him most of the monks who had, in 1979, made their "tour of monastic India",[24] as guests of a great many ashrams. From 16 to 22 June 1980 they found themselves here, sharing the community's life of prayer with the two *swāmis* and four novices or *brahmacaris* and having discussions with them which were appreciated by both parties. This very evening I was invited to recall my own experiences of contacts in this field: Praglia, India and the Tibetan monasteries. Despite the somewhat cramped quarters, one could only admire the way the life was organised, with its regular observance, enclosure and concern for the offices. Without bearing the name, it is in fact a noviciate. Hospitality also is offered to guests and day-visitors, who include Indians. Certain services, such as accounting and printing are guaranteed by lay followers who come to the centre every weekend.

Being the man of dialogue that he is, the Swāmi invited me to come on a visit to the Anglican Benedictine monastery, *Nashdom*,[25] a mere ten minutes away by car. I arrived shortly before the Sunday High Mass, which corresponded in every way to our renewed Roman Liturgy. One felt fully at home and the hospitality also was genuinely Benedictine.

Swāmi Bhavyānanda has a real sympathy for Christianity. Without any confusion over the distinctions between our faiths, his appreciation of the Christian religion is based upon personal conviction. The Refectory is dominated by an admirable painting of the Madonna of the Grand Duke by Raphael, whereas in the library the place of honour is occupied by an attractive picture of Christ.[26]

TWO THERAVĀDA BUDDHIST CENTRES

The Mahābodhi Society, London

I was taken, after this, to London, where I had an evening appointment with the *Venerable Saddhatissa*, also known to me from Praglia and full of the same zeal for interreligious dialogue. As soon as I left the car I noticed a great bustle in front of the premises of the *Mahābodhi Society*,[27] with Sri Lankan children playing on the pavement. The very narrow entrance hall and the stairwell were crowded with people, and the ground floor hall was also packed with people sitting on the floor, listening to an exhortation from the Venerable Sadhatissa. This festival is called the *Kaṭhina*, the feast which closes the rainy season and at which pious laypeople offer monks of the *Sangha* a brand new saffron robe which they are supposed to have cut out, made up and dyed on the same day. These details are no longer followed to the letter, but the feast is very real and has drawn Sri Lankan Buddhists, numerous in England, from all parts of the country. While awaiting the close of the ceremony, I was welcomed by a pleasant British secretary and, when at last the Venerable Sadhatissa was free, he gave me the warmest reception imaginable, full of kindliness. Despite his age, this zealous monk had recently returned from Germany, where he brought about the restoration of the *Mahābodhi Society,* which had been allowed to lapse there. The next day, he was due to set out for Sri Lanka in order to obtain funding for an extension of the London Vihāra. His amiability was almost excessive; he introduced me as his *"teacher"*, saying that I had taught him about Christianity!

I came to see him again, in the company of Father Vincent Cooper of Ealing Abbey, on 30 October 1981. Seven Sri Lankan monks were in residence and the premises were too cramped; they still had not received permission to build their extension. The Venerable Sadhatissa died in 1990.

The Wimbledon Vihāra

Whereas, in Sri Lankan company, everyone would beam on hearing me say that I had spent six happy years at Ampitiya, I could make no comparable claims on the sympathy of the *Thais*. It was, however, with courtesy that I was received at their *Wimbledon Vihāra*.[28] Calonne Road winds gently towards the park, the villas which line it concealed behind the magic of trees with their golden foliage. The Thai centre on which I called seems to be reserved for their expatriates; all the staff are Thais. The monastery is a small one and can accommodate only a few monks. Nevertheless, there is a chapel for the liturgy and an impressive Buddha is enthroned there, a beautiful black image dating from the thirteenth century which was presented by the king of Thailand. To the left is a meditation room for guests. In the garden rises a new building in their national style, a vast *Wat* which will offer the full range of facilities of a monastery. Westerners are more readily welcomed at another centre which has been opened for them at some distance from London, in Hampshire.[29] This is under the direction of the *Venerable Sumedho,* who is highly regarded by all.

The monk who welcomed me was the Abbot's secretary. Acquainted with several oriental languages, he also speaks fluent English and is in frequent demand for conferences. I have the impression, however, that his acquaintance with Christianity is more limited than that, generally speaking, of the Tibetan and Indian masters, and monastic interreligious dialogue appears to be a new experience for him.

A TIBETAN MONASTERY IN SCOTLAND: SAMYE LING

I had for a long time wished to make a brief stay at *Samye Ling,* in the south of Scotland. This centre has in fact become famous and was the first foundation of Tibetan Buddhism to have been made, not only in Europe but in the entire Western world. The very name "Scotland" suggests both landscapes imbued with poetry and an undeniable severity of climate. In Dumfriesshire, the autumns are long, permeated by moist winds blowing off the Irish sea, and the winters are famous for their cold, accompanied by ice and snow. However, it was during a rainy but mild week, when the boughs of the trees were golden and the foliage at the height of its splendour, just before it dropped, that I succeeded in making contact with a centre of spirituality with a reputation it fully deserves.

Thirty years ago, it was a hunting lodge and this is still the main residence, with its series of roofs steeply pitched to allow the rain to run off. A small but serviceable block has been added, however, with well-kept bedrooms. An electric heater and any number of blankets may be borrowed to ward off the cold. At the beginning, the spiritual aspect was already taking shape, but all would agree that in 1964 and the following years, the Johnstone House Community lacked consistency and stability. It was then that the providential meeting occurred between a lonely spot at some distance from any town, in a wooded solitude on a riverside, and two young but high-ranking Tibetan lamas who were looking for somewhere to establish a centre of their ancient tradition. One of these was the Venerable *Chögyam Trungpa Rinpoche*, with whom we had spent an academic year at Oxford in 1963–64, and who had just come to public notice by means of an enthralling little book: *Born in Tibet,*[30] in which he recounted his training as a young *trulku*, his responsibilities as an abbot and the stages of his flight from Tibet into exile in 1959.

His companion, *Akong Rinpoche,* both monk and doctor and trained, like him, in the most reputable traditions, came with him to Scotland and continues to preside over the destiny of the centre. It was called *Samye Ling*, the name in fact of the first of all the monasteries to be founded in Tibet, during the heroic period of Padmasambhava, in the eighth century of our era.[31] It is still this same *Guru Rinpoche*, seated on his lotus in the middle of a lake, who is depicted as a backdrop to their sanctuary wall. It seems that after a certain length of time, differences of opinion arose between the two founding monks. This was certainly not over the main doctrines but, if I am not mistaken, over the manner of approach and the degree of adaptation to a culture very different from that of Tibet. *Trungpa* had, it seems to me, a more liberal attitude towards the ancestral structures, was more free and easy over ceremonies and doubtless more radical with regard to interior resolution. He left in 1970 for the United States and there publicised Tibetan spirituality by his many writings, the greater part available in French translation,[32] and the influence of the centre he founded in Boulder, Colorado, amounts to a stage in the cultural evolution of that country.

Meanwhile, *Akong Rinpoche*, more faithful to traditional methods, to liturgical symbols, the recitation of *mantras* and the numerous subdivisions of the religious art of Tibet, has contributed with his strong personality to giving Samye Ling that atmosphere, both recollected and full of very varied activity for which it has been well known for twenty-five years. It is thanks to him that it has passed through being an over-fashionable place, visited without discrimination, to acquire a reputation for seriousness and commitment which corresponds more to what one expects of a meditation centre or a monastery.

The two visits from His Holiness the XVIth Karmapa were for a good deal a kind of reinforcement of the new direction. This latter, the Abbot Primate as it were of the Karmapa Order, with its more contemplative propensity, is known to have left this world in early December 1981, leaving a great void. Meanwhile, Samye Ling has continued to develop and is putting forth new shoots which will doubtless increase in vigour, at Brussels, Barcelona, Madrid, Berlin and Dublin.

On site, progress is being made on the construction of the future monastery. Detailed plans may be seen, and are truly beautiful: the style of Tibetan monasteries is retained. Part is already near completion: that consisting of the temple properly so called and a great meditation hall. There will be three floors. The other wings of the quadrangle will house series of bedrooms, the usual offices, kitchen, refectory, etc. At present all that is contained in temporary premises, ill-suited and manifestly not designed to house so many residents. At the time of my visit, the centre numbered between thirty and forty persons living there long-term, all of them on a voluntary basis; each works according to his skills and aptitudes and the needs of the community. But in the summer there are also numerous visitors, occasional retreatants and, above all, participants on the courses held when come high-ranking lamas or *rinpoches* who are sometimes brought over from India, or who are making a tour of Western countries.

From the terrace of the building under construction, the eye takes in the property as a whole, the trees in the park, the outlines of the river, the hills and the glen. But one must, above all, in order to be fully aware of their life, go and visit, beyond the puddles and the muddy paths, the numerous temporary huts where numerous arts and crafts are in a thriving state. For, in addition to the builders, the electricians and the plumbers who are erecting the new temple, you see the products of their printing press, which publishes the classical works of Tibet and the oblong prayer cards; the painting studio where the disciples of Mr Sherab, an artist faithful to the Kagyu tradition, are being trained in the composition of admirable *thankas*; an outstanding woodcarving studio; the workshop for pottery and ceramics; the dairy where cheeses are made; the dairy farm; the small kitchen garden. None of this differs greatly from what one would find at a Christian monastery, whether Benedictine or Trappist, and everything is based on voluntary service, on free offering, the sense of community and the primacy of the spiritual.

A Buddhist nun lives alone, withdrawn in almost constant prayer. The liturgy, with its rituals of Guru Rinpoche, Chenrezig, Tara and Mahākāla, unfolds according to the best traditions, with the fullness of pictorial representations, the richness of musical instruments, offerings of flowers, of fruits and of figurines known as *torma*.[33] The surrounding countryside is populated with male and female pheasants, while the immediate vicinity of the house is a breeding ground for peacocks. It goes without saying that the sanctuary is at the heart of everything and provides the inspiration for it all. A very wide-ranging library (Christian mystics are represented there) aids doctrinal nourishment, while courses in the Tibetan language are given with great competence and teaching ability by a young Canadian.

Since Akong Rinpoche was abroad at the time of my visit, I asked for an interview with *Lama Ganga*, his undoubted deputy in the community of monks, and I had the pleasure of talking for an hour with a relaxed and modest monk. He said at the outset that he knew nothing of Christianity, but his sympathetic curiosity was worth more than a great deal of knowledge. He added that he was nothing in his own religion, and was there by accident, if not by mistake. In fact he is known to have made the terrible retreat of three years and three months,[34] three times in Tibet, which means that he has spent a decade in solitude. It is he who carried out the visitation of most of the centres in California. Here, indeed, it is to him that has been entrusted the training of a dozen Westerners, coming from several countries (one group comes from Spain). And he claims to know nothing and be nowhere.[35]

The *inauguration of the temple* was the occasion of great festivities, from 15 July to 18 August 1988; they assumed an interreligious character since dignitaries from non-Buddhist traditions were invited. The same spirit of openness can be seen in a daring project: just off the Isle of Arran (Firth of Clyde) on the west coast of Scotland is a small island that they have bought. Sanctified already by the presence of a hermit in the sixth century, it is known as *Holy Island*. Samye Ling dreams of making this a place where different religions might, side by side, dedicate themselves to prayer and contemplation.

A MEETING BETWEEN CHRISTIAN AND BUDDHIST MONKS IN HOLLAND: MAITREYA INSTITUUT, EMST (25–27 AUGUST 1988)

It was under the inspiration of the Gelugpa monk Thubten Yeshe – to whom we have already referred[36] – that the *Foundation for the Preservation of the Mahāyāna Tradition* was organized. It consists, most notably, of a monastery on the hill of Kopan, not far from Kathmandu, several centres in India and a good many in Western countries (Australia, United States, England, Italy and France).

Their centre in Holland, called *Maitreya Instituut*, had obtained official recognition as "stichting" on 21 December 1979. Initially established at Groenhoven, *Bruchem*, it did not for long remain there, but relocated to *Maasbommel*, on a bend of the Meuse, where it remained for four years, from 1983 to 1987. On 1 September 1987, the Institute moved again, becoming established at *Emst*, its present home.[37] Emst is halfway between Apeldoorn and Zwolle, where Thomas à Kempis lived and where his body is buried.

They have not had either to build or convert, here; their centre is a former youth hostel. It is a quiet country residence, shaded by, without being in, a wood. Gelderland is very pretty.

The Institute publishes a Dutch-language three-monthly magazine, the quality of which can be seen in both content and presentation: it is called *Maitreya Magazine*.

It is here that, on the initiative of Dom Cornelius Tholens, O.S.B., a co-founder of A.I.M. and an ardent promoter of dialogue, days of encounter (25–27 August 1988) between Catholic and Buddhist monks were organized.

Participants on the Catholic side were: Dom Tholens, former abbot of Slangenburg, who directs a centre in Amsterdam; Father Bernard de Give, Trappist of Scourmont; Father Jaap Hendrix O.S.B., who directs a Benedictine centre at Nijmegen; Father Chris Smoorenburg, O.P. who, at the Nijmegen Albertinum, is on the staff of an Institute attached to the University, where he teaches the meditation techniques of Eastern religions. Neither of the two just mentioned derives his knowledge of Buddhism from books alone: they described for us their stay in the Zen monasteries of Japan, including their experience of begging for food.

On the Tibetan side, Geshe Konchok Lhundup, who heads the Community, raised questions about Christianity. The intelligent and faithful translation was provided by a Dutch monk, Gelong Thubten Tsepel. A number of apposite questions were raised by a young Tibetan monk, Tenzin Lama, who was open toward Christian doctrines. Three Dutch novices of the Community also took part. The Catholic monks questioned the Geshe.

It will be guessed that such questions, spread out over several hours of exchange, were of an enthralling nature; both sides learned a great deal. The atmosphere was not in the least polemic; on the contrary, we were trying, in fraternal dialogue, to discover the points of contact and to understand the other religion in depth.

The same atmosphere prevailed on the afternoon of the following day, with an important difference: people from outside who knew the centre were invited to take part. Besides, the house staff were freed from their duties for two hours, both to listen and to take part in the discussion. We were quite thirty in number, which at first sight could have weighed down this meeting round long tables, all the more so as the most recondite theological problems were unhesitatingly raised.

Some of the points raised

1. A preliminary series of questions touched on *their monastic life*. For the training of a Tibetan monk: he chooses a *tutor* for himself. The monastery is marked by a hierarchy of personal relations. Particular reference is made to the *university-monasteries*, where study has pride of place. There is no obligatory period set aside for meditation: this is done on an individual basis, when silence prevails, particularly at night. As regards discipline, to which we shall refer presently, that of the *tantric colleges* is much stricter and more severe. In them the sense of community life is much more developed: there is a common dormitory and their whole life is dedicated to rituals, liturgy and meditation. The particularly austere life of the *naldjorpas,* yogis of tantric Buddhism. The symbolism of colours, in visualisations, their habits (their violet colour comes from Kashmir: the robe of the *Mūlasarvāstivādin).* The very deep sounds of the monks' chant at the Tantric College. The relationship between contemplative life and ordinary life.

2. A second series of questions tended to penetrate further towards understanding the *spiritual doctrines of Buddhism*. Taking refuge in the Community: a sort of "communion of saints". The Buddha-nature in every living being, even the animals. Universal spirit and individual spirits, these latter subdividing into spheres of consciousness. At the deepest level, the subtle mental consciousness: it is to this that karmic residues are attached. A question as to the different terms used to designate the final stages of realisation: Nibbāna, Dzogchen, Mahāmudrā, Shūnyatā, the Bright Light (Ösel).

3. Certain questions embarked directly on a *comparison between Buddhism and Christianity* on those areas where they appear close. What does the word *blessings* mean in a Buddhist context, on the one hand, and in a Catholic context, on the other? What are grace, and initiation?

4. The Lama, in his turn, raised questions about *Jesus* (the man-

God), his prayer, his ethics, his meditation techniques. The meaning of the name "Christ". They entered on a better understanding of the *Christian life*. The threefold division of the human being, according to the doctrine of St. Paul writing to the Thessalonians: body, soul and spirit. The relationship between our spirit and the Holy Spirit. God in me and I in God. God as creator and "creation" by the mind in Buddhism. Religions of experience and religions of revelation. Human liberty and the nature of God in me.

So the kind of problems tackled can be seen. The best of it is doubtless the fact that no one felt wounded by any of it. Besides, rather than being left tired by discussions on such a high level, all went away declaring themselves delighted and expressing the desire to repeat the experience.

A GELUGPA PRESENCE IN THE TARN: A CENTRE AND A MONASTERY AT LAVAUR

Before travelling to Spain in order to take part in a congress at León, I took advantage of the journey to give a full week (late November to early December 1988) to visiting Tibetan centres in the Tarn and in Spain.

Vajra Yoginī

I was collected from the station by *Denis Huet*, director of the centre for the last six or seven years, and responsible for the *Vajra Yoginī* buildings (Château d'En Clausade, Marzens). We had met at a retreat conducted by Lama Thubten Yeshe, their founder,[38] and he had, like his companions, been particularly moved by my obituary for Lama Yeshe[39] and subsequently for Song Rinpoche.[40] As at Plaige,[41] in Saône-et-Loire, they had bought an old château and slowly restored it, in stages (roof, heating). Here, however, rather than turrets at the corner, there was a broad frontage. The interior boasted a white marble staircase without banisters. The external walls are in a lamentable condition; part of the building must have undergone a serious fire. The stables built by the counts were being converted for other uses, as well as could be managed.

The ladies whom I met in the secretary's office at reception had known Lama Yeshe and made visits to Kopan, not far from Kathmandu. The château is well situated, with a panoramic view of the surrounding countryside, at the centre of a wooded park of almost twenty acres which, during the summer, allows them to run courses with several hundred participants, taking advantage of the meadows and woodland paths. I had an interview with Geshe Tengye, spiritual director of the centre, thanks to his Tibetan interpreter Tenzin, who has a good understanding of doctrine. We spoke about the Holy Spirit.

I returned the following year, in June 1989, and saw signs of progress. A magnificent balustrade, made of wood from tropical islands, was to be seen on either side of the marble staircase. They had had a visit from a *high healing lama* who uses tantric formulae; he cures certain cases of AIDS and cancer. A good conversation with *Geshe Tengye* turned on the distressing predicament of Tibet under the Chinese regime.

After a great deal of conversion work and effective preparatory measures, *Vajra Yoginī* was able to offer accommodation to the numerous participants at the great doctrinal course of November 1993. His Holiness the Dalai Lama, over the course of a week, provided the commentary on a difficult chapter of *The Path Toward Awakening* by *Shāntideva*. A group of Christian monks were amongst the audience. One could only wonder that such an intricate topic could warrant the assembly of 2,500 persons.[42]

Nālandā Monastery

One has to travel right across Lavaur to reach Labastide Saint-Georges where there is, not a centre in this case, but a real monastery, *Nālandā Monastery*, within the same allegiance.[43] This is yet another of Lama Yeshe's foundations, thus belonging to the Gelugpa tradition, with a sympathetic openness to the Western world and everything it contains that is of value, Christianity in particular. But there is no question of syncretism; it is a genuinely Buddhist monastery. The building, low and on the small side, is set a little distance back from the road. The garden, where flowers are plentiful and which includes a kitchen section, backs onto a river and is surrounded by a copse. On the premises at the present time are a score of monks, young people and adults, from a variety of countries. English has been the medium of communication since the beginning in 1983. Leaving aside those who earn their living by working outside, I have come into contact with monks in wine-coloured robes from almost a dozen countries: Germany, England, Australia, Belgium, Spain, France, Italy, New Zealand, Holland, Reunion Island and Switzerland. The Australian Adrian Feldmann, who was for many years director of the monastery and watched over its growth, has returned to Australia to give teachings. The present director is an American by the name of Pende. The translator is a Sherpa, Thubten Sherab. The building was purchased in 1979. Community life began there in 1983 when *Geshe Jampa Tegchok*, coming from the *Manjushri Institute* at Ulverston (Cumbria),[44] where he had been teaching for three years, accepted an invitation from Lama Yeshe to become abbot of Nālandā. It is he, therefore, who is responsible for the daily instructions and for higher studies for obtaining the grade of *Geshe*. Like Lama Yeshe, he was originally from the monastery of *Sera-jé*, where I met him in 1983.

The atmosphere at Nālandā is excellent; any monk with a Cistercian training would recognise in it many aspects of his own life in community since, apart from the ceremonies and the periods of private meditation, the importance attached to manual work is quite clear, all participating in the kitchen and maintenance work.

A subsequent visit in June 1989 enabled me to meet acquaintances again and to converse with the American Pende, who is *manager* of Nālandā. They were creating small bedrooms in the shell of the former sheep-run, as well as giving it a new roof and putting roughcast on the walls. They were very pleasant toward me.

I met the same courtesy and even candour during my third stay, in October 1991. Several Frenchmen have joined their community, an occurrence which, until now, has been rather rare. Upstairs, I admired a beautiful statue of Lama Yeshe; great pains had been taken to convey his welcoming expression.

We had one further opportunity (13 and 14 October 2005) of visiting both the Nālandā monastery, in full work of constructions, and the Vajra Yoginī Centre, where we had a very good exchange with the current director and with the Venerable Lama Tenzin Dorje. We were coming as a group from a session of Interreligious Dialogue at the Benedictine Abbey of En-Calcat (Tarn).

UNDER SPANISH SKIES

Barcelona – Madrid

1. On 25 November 1988, I left that little monastery and the surrounding countryside. There exists a stark contrast between the landscapes worthy of Lamartine that I was leaving behind and the bustling cities of the Iberian peninsula. *Barcelona*, vast and regular. A few yards from a great crossroads, dominated by an important Jesuit college, stands *Samye Dzong*,[45] the centre founded by Akong Rinpoche, the "mother house" of which is at Samye Ling in Scotland.[46] They belong to the Karmapa Order. The director of the centre was in conference with the supreme head of the Nyingmapa, having in view a series of teachings, so I had a cordial conversation with one of the residents, a Portuguese Buddhist who spoke several languages. Here they hold courses in the Tibetan language, given by a Canadian who is an excellent teacher. On a blackboard facing us was written out a liturgical text in that language. I believe I would still understand it now.

I returned to this centre on a fine summer evening, the following year, and received a very warm welcome from the director, a doctor of Barcelona, who did me the honours of his house. A spacious hall upstairs served as temple for them. As they were about to welcome Akong Rinpoche for a week, a young monk had gone out to buy some magnificent bouquets with which to decorate their altar. At the top stood a tiny bronze statue: a Nepalese Buddha, surrounded by bright silk. I took part in their "Vespers", the ritual of Chenrezig, while the Rinpoche was being collected from the airport.

2. Barcelona is certainly very extensive, like Nineveh, which was several days' journey across on foot. I finally arrived at Calle Rosellón, 298, where I was expecting to give a lecture. As a matter of fact, things turned out differently, perhaps better: instead I had a satisfying conversation with the Tibetan Lama, *Geshe Lobsang Tsultrim,* from *Sera-jé* at the *Nāgārjuna Centre*.[47] This is a foundation of Lama Yeshe's, so we had a good many shared memories. Here, in addition, there are two Spanish Lamas.[48] The ritual of *Tara (Dreulma* in Tibetan) began forthwith. This deity is reminiscent, for Christians, of the Virgin Mary. The name *Tara* signifies

that she carries supplicants over all obstacles, hence the ardour shown by Tibetans towards her. She is the equivalent of Our Lady Help of Christians. Furthermore, in the eyes of the intellectuals, as the Mother of all Buddhas she is the source of Wisdom, to say nothing of twenty-one other titles under which she is invoked, reminiscent of the Litanies of Loreto. Taking part in this ritual, in the lotus position on little cushions, were about fifteen of the faithful, both men and women. The ceremony, which takes place several times a week on set days, lasts an hour and a half with a break for taking tea and biscuits in silence.

3. At Madrid, I stayed at *Kagyu Dechen Ling*,[49] where I had had friends for several years. I had been witness to the beginnings of their centre, in Calle Limón, in 1982; at its transfer to Sáinz de Baranda Street, and currently to the ups and downs of a foundation to which inculturation did not come easily. Let such monasteries as experience no difficulties cast the first stone at them! In any case, the artistic and practical way in which they have converted their apartment is most admirable. Everything has been repainted in vivid colours, in the Tibetan style. The temple is very large, and the best bedroom is reserved for the Lama, a Bhutanese who is adapting only with difficulty to his public. Two rituals are held each week. I was particularly struck, and deeply moved, by a rare occurrence: despite my being a foreigner (and that twice over: by both nationality and religion), they felt free to confide in me over their problems, just as though I were a member of their group. I should add that my affection for them is manifest, and has been so for six years.

When I returned to Madrid the following year, without any idea as to where I might stay, they showed me their capacity for welcoming even strangers. Many personal exchanges had alerted me to the difficulties that several of them had been experiencing on their journey. I stayed with them. They showed me a trust which I have to describe as excessive. As each of the men and women were obliged to go out to work that morning, these loveable people left me completely alone in the residence, with the key to the apartment. I could have gone off with everything. As it was, I merely raided the refrigerator at mealtimes and begged them to take me to another centre in Madrid, where I was expected for an evening lecture.

4. As for this other centre in Madrid, the *Nāgārjuna Institute*, of Lama Yeshe's tradition, it is of much more recent date, at least under its present form.[50] Situated in the heart of Madrid, it is led by an extremely pleasant young director. *Antonio Pascual* lived for twelve years in Nepal, in particular on the hill of Kopan, where he recalled our having met in 1983. But he has also associated with the other Tibetan Schools (Kagyu, Nyingma) and, furthermore, is adamant that he has remained a Christian. All those present, around ten, both men and women, were waiting for me; I was installed in an armchair in the middle of their "temple" and, from the time of my arrival until ten in the evening, they plied me with the most profound questions on the relationship between Buddhism and Christianity, and on those points of doctrine which were either comparable or incompatible. It was a simply marvellous evening of intelligent and understanding inquiry.

I returned there the following year, 1 July 1989, to find an audience three times as large. I gave a lecture on "The Ideal of Compassion in the Mahāyāna tradition compared with Christian Charity".[51] Due, no doubt, to the absence of the director, the atmosphere of this meeting was a good deal less relaxed, certain of the participants adopting a polemic tone to which I am quite unaccustomed; several apologised as they left.

Kalu Rinpoche and the Rimé movement

The name of Kalu Rinpoche (1904–1989) will recur on a number of occasions in these pages; an emaciated face, an extraordinary gaze, the unquestionable influence of a mystic. Anyone who had the opportunity to be near him would confirm this testimony. He had lived for many years in solitude before establishing his monastery at *Sonada*, a little way below Darjeeling in North India.[52] He then sent his disciples to Canada and Europe at the request of Westerners. Kagyu-Ling in Burgundy and Karma-Ling in Savoy were amongst his first foundations and Spain, in its turn, would benefit from this movement. Enjoying the privilege of being initiated into the main lineages of the Vajrayāna and venerated as a master in each of them, Kalu Rinpoche was, in our century, the most active representative of the *Rimé* movement.

Rimé (ris-med), in Tibetan, means "no-party", *impartial*, that is to say, rejecting any kind of sectarianism between the traditions.

The great promoter of this movement, comparable to ecumenism amongst the Christian Churches, was *Djamgoeun Kongtrul* (1813–1899). Educated in the Bön tradition, this young monk underwent a Buddhist apprenticeship in that of the Nyingmapa, before becoming master at the Kagyu monastery of Palpung. Having been initiated into various lineages, he was distressed above all by the sectarianism which reigned in Kham (Eastern Tibet). He therefore launched the Rimé or "impartial" movement, the forerunners of which go back to the fourteenth century. Its members did not abandon their own tradition or their centre of interest, but considered the Lamas and the teachings of all the schools as equally worthy of respect and in freedom of spirit pursued a varied programme of study and practice. The *Rimé* movement attracted many distinguished scholars, whose works brought together famous texts used by any number of modern Tibetan masters, particularly those of the Nyingma and Kagyu[53] traditions.

It is the latter tradition that is followed by the *Panillo* Tibetan centre, in Huesca province, of which we shall now speak.

Panillo (Huesca)

I was most anxious to visit, for however brief a stay (it lasted in fact a day and a night), the *Dag Shang Kagyu* centre,[54] founded by Kalu Rinpoche in 1984. I reached it on 26 June 1989, thus during the period of its infancy. It was in a solitary spot in the province of Huesca (Aragon). If you set out from the small market town of *Graus*, you reach the virtually abandoned village of *Panillo*, after climbing these picturesque hills for 7 kilometres. It is hot and dry in this landscape of rather arid mountains; the woods have a conservation order on them and hunting is prohibited. The village, which seems poor and dilapidated, has a good many olive trees. The temple may be seen from some distance. The interior conversion has not yet been carried out; there are a few bedrooms upstairs. Facing it, and under construction, is a small building intended for reception and a gift shop. At some distance, a kilometre away, in fact, are the kitchen, the refectory and, upstairs, a dormitory in an old house which from a distance looks almost as though in ruins. It bears the dates of several different periods; the oldest could be the eleventh or twelfth centuries: massive walls and round arches; it would be the ideal setting for a play by Claudel, several large barrels, some of them of enormous capacity, in a cave. In the course of a tour of the exterior, you come across a small and very ancient chapel. Despite the precariousness of the rest of the premises, Lama Sherab will not allow the cooking to be done there. The land which has been purchased amounts to almost 250 acres and is wooded and uncultivable. The local Council is sympathetic towards the centre but will not allow indiscriminate building work; the character of the site must be maintained.

In such a context, it is easy to have good communications with the small group of residents, highly motivated as they are in a period calling for heroism: there were encounters in the areas both of comparative religion and of personal confidences.

The opportunity has not arisen for a return to these solitary places, but the people who run the centre were kind enough to send me news of it, so it was with great surprise that I saw on the cover page of their most recent programme the measure of progress that has been made. In 1994, it was an admirable *chorten*, the base of the dome illuminated on all sides; it is not for nothing that this is named "the *stūpa* of many auspicious doors". In 1995, bearing the signatures of the three Bhutanese lamas, there was a photograph of the little temple completely finished, smart and dainty, its whiteness radiating out against a background of bluish hills. As for the regular life, it is now under way, including courses of teachings, to say nothing of visits from high lamas in the course of their travels. After a rather slow start, we see here a promising future, above all for souls eager for solitude and silence.

TWO TIBETAN CENTRES IN BELGIUM

Yeunten Ling, Tihange

In the Meuse valley, not far from Huy, the milky clouds from a nuclear power station may be seen rising into the sky. Once you have crossed the river by a wide bridge, you are surrounded by picturesque rural scenery and must climb towards the leafy summit of the hill of *Tihange*. A pleasing chestnut avenue leads you towards a wood of full-grown trees, tranquil and favourable to meditation. After skirting a pond, you see the structures of a classical château, in red brick with stone window recesses, calm in its balanced proportions.⁵⁵ This is *Yeunten Ling,* which loses nothing by its associations with an early mediaeval hermit, St. Jean l'Agneau (beginning of the seventh century). I have been there on several occasions, whether in the depth of winter to hear Tai Situ Rinpoche (13–15 November 1985) or in the summer, when everyone partook of lunch at small tables out-of-doors in the inner court. The Belgian Commission for Dialogue, as also the directors of *Voies de l'Orient,* met there again on 26 April 1990, when the Dalai Lama came to consecrate the *chorten* (or *stūpa*). His Holiness, in the middle of a very busy day, was kind enough to meet our group for almost an hour, recalling his meeting with Thomas Merton and praising Christian monasticism.⁵⁶

I am writing these lines on my return from yet another visit to *Yeunten Ling.* Most of us had taken part, in May 1988, with *Lama Ogyen,* now deceased, who had shown us the kindliest attention.

This Sunday, 28 May 1995, the genial welcome shown to us was given by *Lama Karta.* We had come at just the right time: he was to give the last lecture in a course on preparation for death.⁵⁷ Then we were present in the afternoon at a long ritual of Amitabha. This visit was an opportunity, above all, for informal discussions touching on the fundamentals of both our religions, taking care to pick out the points of convergence. The nuns, therefore, whose first visit it was were immersed in the atmosphere of kindliness and recollection which marks a *Dharma* centre. We were welcomed, too, by nature: the beauty of the great trees and the wind rippling a multitude of prayer flags hanging from their tops and, along the path to the *chorten,* the tall poles supporting streamers in vivid colours.

Founded in 1973 under the auspices of Kalu Rinpoche by the Tibetan centre of Antwerp (now at Schoten), Yeunten Ling has been, from the beginning, completely bilingual. It numbers at the present time, beside the three Tibetan lamas, around fifteen residents including a few Belgian monks. On the first floor of the château, the main room is decorated with frescos from the hand of Gega Lama. The same artist is responsible for the statue with gilded draperies to be admired at the heart of the *chorten*: The Buddha Shakyamuni, standing majestically and making the teaching gesture with his right hand.

Brussels, rue Capouillet

You will not expect to hear about rustic charm or wide horizons in the centre of *Brussels*, just a few minutes' walk from the *Place Louise*. There is, however, a great quietness in this little street where those who are enamoured of wisdom love to come and meditate, hear teachings or follow a ritual. I would not want to pass in silence over the good relationship I have for many years enjoyed with the directors of this centre, who always welcome me with genuine cordiality. These links go back to the time when I made the acquaintance of a Tibetan lama who is at one and the same time qualified in traditional medicine: *Akong Rinpoche,* founder of *Samye Ling* in Scotland. He was studying in Oxford at that time. I found myself at rue Capouillet when Tai Situ Rinpoche and the Dalai Lama came to Brussels (1981 and 1982 in the one case; 1990 in the other), to say nothing of various other stays.

CHRISTIAN-BUDDHIST ENCOUNTERS AT KARMA-LING (SAVOY)

On the borders of Savoy and the Dauphiné, the ancient *Charterhouse of St. Hugh,* situated in the mountain above Arvillard, close to La Rochette,[58] was in a dilapidated state and more or less abandoned when a Tibetan centre decided to revive the spiritual life there. Over the last few years, the ancient buildings of the Carthusians have been seen to take on a new life, and an almost monastic existence is taking shape there within the contemplative lineage of the Kagyupa, under the enlightened leadership of *Lama Denys Teundroup*. Faithful to their tradition, they have even constructed two separate buildings for the young men and women who have begun that austere retreat of three years and three months in the strictest enclosure, reserved in Tibet for monks already well advanced in contemplative practices.

It was in this Alpine setting, in a solitude conducive to meditation, that there took place, first a *René Guénon Encounter* in 1981, then meetings between Christians and Buddhists on themes common to both. The Encounter in 1985 was arranged for Pentecost and this was far from being a coincidence; despite their belonging to different traditions, the organizers were very much aware that the Holy Spirit plays a highly prominent role in spiritual movements, no matter what the religion invoked, and its universal, not to say cosmic, character cannot be put on hold – as indeed was keenly felt during the Mass of Pentecost, ardently celebrated with Gregorian chant.

We were present each year for three days surrounded by prayer and a whole series of lectures on the main theme. In 1983: *Meditation, Christian and Buddhist.* In 1984: *Word and Silence.*[59] In 1985: *Love and Knowledge.* The attentive audience was given the opportunity to respond with questions, above all at a round table at the end of a course. Coming as they did from different religious or philosophical horizons, the audience did not hesitate, any more than the lecturers, to bring up the most profound subjects. Numerous similarities between the two ways were shown up, but the temptation of blurring differences was avoided. Courtesy was maintained.

The speakers had a great deal of contact between sessions, taking their meals together, and real friendships sprang up amongst them, for all that so many different cultures were met with at every Encounter. The Venerable Thich Thien Chau represented Vietnam and was conversant with the practices of Zen. Tibetan lamas from different centres in France, Lama Denys, Superior at Karma-Ling, and competent laymen (Dr Jean-Pierre Schnetzler, François Chenique) helped us thoroughly to investigate the Tibetan tradition and to compare it with our own Christian spirituality. Fr Placide Deseille allowed us to hear the voice of Orthodoxy. While the Venerable Jean Éracle awoke an echo of the Pure Land, and was able, when occasion arose, to restate the fundamental principles of Buddhism, it can safely be said that a wide range of the currents of Western spirituality were well represented at every Encounter. To list all the speakers would be irksome, but Benedictines, Trappists, Carmelites and Jesuits in turn set out the different aspects of their respective practices, as did also a Canon Regular of Saint-Maurice (Valais).

When the Buddhist organizers sent the *Acts* of the second Encounter to the Secretariat for non-Christians, they received in reply a letter full of cordial congratulations. The participants in these meetings would have undoubtedly recognised in it their own sentiments.

During the discussions, it became clear on numerous occasions that the divergences between Christianity and Buddhism were located at a deeper level: the *problem of the person*. What exactly should we understand by this term? Does it suffice to point up the distinction between individual and person, or has not, rather, a properly theological examination of this point, and that of the mystery of the divine Persons in the Blessed Trinity, become essential?

The question thus raised at the end of May 1985 was not immediately made the object of communal reflection, but more than one of us continued to give it consideration. It came up again in public when Karma-Ling organized an inter-Buddhist Encounter on the theme of *anattā* (24–26 April 1992). I was present merely as an observer but experienced the meeting, nonetheless, as an opportunity to go into the subject a little more thoroughly. The outcome of these reflections are to be found in Chapter XI, below and, in Chapter IX, a more ambitious project: the examination, in a more exclusive group, of the possible relationship between the Mahāyāna doctrine of the Three Bodies, or *Trikāya*, of the Buddha, and the dogma of the Blessed *Trinity*. But let us not anticipate our doctrinal section. May we be permitted, rather, to give a rapid overview of Encounters IV and V between Christians and Buddhists.

Spirituality in daily life
Fourth Encounter (6–8 June 1987)

It was in the wonderful setting of the ancient Charterhouse of St. Hugh's, in Savoy, that the fourth encounter between representatives of Christian and of Buddhist monasticism took place. At the heart of the pine-forests surrounding this narrow valley right up to the snowy peaks, while the river rushed along below the mountain, we discussed the common theme: *Meditation and contemplation in action*. While it is relatively easy, after all, to construct a spirituality that is detached from the world, a certain skill is called for if its principles are to be incarnated within the reality of the routine and distracting activities of daily life. In the face of this difficulty, Christians and Buddhists alike must demonstrate a sense of realism and a use of certain skilful means in order that their beautiful theories do not remain divorced from reality and ineffective. As in previous years, we were able to observe both agreements and significant differences in the basic doctrines.

One of the most appreciated lectures was the first, going from the beginning to the heart of the matter. Madame Rose Degive, the Catholic mother of a family, committed to the reception of immigrants and director of the *Voies de l'Orient* centre at Brussels, enabled us, with a moving simplicity, to grasp how innumerable household duties can provide a summons to the most genuine spirituality. On the Christian side, we had the doctrinal explanations of Father Guy Boué, O.P., of the Facultés Catholiques de Lyon; a chapter on the history of spirituality from Father Bernard de Give on *The Brothers of the Common Life and the "Devotio Moderna"*; a remarkable testimony by Father Pierre de Béthune, a Belgian Benedictine from Clerlande: *Reinterpreting the Rule of Saint Benedict in a Zen monastery*, in which not only monastic texts but lifestyles were compared.

Dr Schnetzler, a psychoanalyst, reviewed several of the most familiar aspects of modern life: *(métro, boulot, dodo) hustling, toiling, sleeping*, showing how their tedious and degrading aspects actually derive from the loss of their traditional and sacred character. Given as it was by a Buddhist, this lecture was obviously valid for everyone. The *Dharma* was studied specifically in two explanations of the Tibetan tradition, one by the director and moving force of Karma-Ling, Lama Denys Teundroup, and the other by Lama Tcheuky, who directs the centres in Marseilles, while the voice of Japan was to be heard in the exhortations of the Reverend Yukai, a monk of *Shingon*, the Japanese Vajrayāna.

As had been the case in previous years, this Encounter took place at Pentecost, and thus unfolded under the auspices of the Holy Spirit, of whom we do not have the monopoly: *"Spiritus Domini replevit orbem terrarum, et hoc quod continet omnia scientiam habet vocis."*[60]

God and Emptiness
Fifth Encounter (2–4 September 1988)

From the time it was founded, the Karma-Ling Institute has dedicated a significant part of its activity to studying the relationship between Christianity and Buddhism. Its location in a former Carthusian monastery, and the fact that Kalu Rinpoche, spiritual master of Karma-Ling, belongs to the Tibetan ecumenical movement, *Rimé*, naturally leads to this.[61]

The first Encounters, which we have just described briefly, had as their aim the outlining of the bases for dialogue, areas of empirical agreement and the study of parallel advancement in the spiritual life in both religions. Assured of a solid fraternal basis and spiritual practices which show similarities, the organizers have seen fit to draw up a plan that is more theoretical, but which is of the utmost importance, that of endeavouring to compare the concept of God in Christianity and that of Emptiness, clearly central to Buddhism. Almost three full days were given up to these exchanges, in which about 80 persons, not counting the residents of Karma-Ling, participated. Here are the subjects that were ventured upon:

Father Bernard de Give, O.C.S.O. – *The search for God in a Carthusian monastery.*

Madame Mitchiko Ishigami, research worker at C.N.R.S. and graduate of the universities of Tokyo and Paris – *God and Emptiness according to Saint Paul and Dogen, Zen Master.*

Madame Odette Baumer-Despeigne – *Meaning and experience of emptiness in the writings of Hadewich of Antwerp*, a Flemish mystic of the thirteenth century.

Dr Jean-Pierre Schnetzler, psychiatrist, psychoanalyst and Buddhist – *The fear of the void.*

Reverend John Éracle, of Pure Land Japanese Buddhism and curator of the Ethnographic Museum at Geneva – *The true meaning of emptiness in Buddhist texts.*

Father Placide Deseille, of the Orthodox monastery of Saint Anthony the Great – *Theology, positive and negative, in the Orthodox tradition.*

François Chenique, Doctor of Religious Sciences and Professor at the École Française of Yoga – *The emptiness of God.*

On the last morning, a dialogue-lecture took place between Father Pierre de Béthune, Benedictine monk of Clerlande (Belgium) and Lama Denys Teundroup, spiritual director of Karma-Ling Institute entitled *Spiritual Methods for Realising God and Emptiness according to theistic and non-theistic approaches.* The meeting closed with a final round table.

Compared with the preceding Encounters, it will be admitted by all that the comparison attempted was more problematic. This was not due to any shortcoming in the audience, who were more attentive than ever and contributed more actively. Nor was it due to some doctrinaire *a priori*, lacking in openness regarding the opposite religion. It will be admitted, however, that a risk was taken in venturing upon a more profound subject, in which everyone felt personally involved, and by means of a more difficult route.

For it is not sufficient to give an account of our apophatic theology, and the experience of the Christian mystics to satisfy the requirements of a Buddhism with any desire for consistency. Radical non-duality cannot easily reach an accord with a philosophy of the person or theistic dogmas. There were even disputes from time to time. This however, does not mean in the least that such comparisons ought to be avoided, as they open our eyes to the true position of another religion. Provided that fraternal bonds are established, one is entitled to hope for progress in mutual understanding, as was the case in the ecumenical movement. Even though no further major Christian-Buddhist Encounters have been held at Saint Hugh's, this does not mean that they have been definitively given up. Preference is being temporarily given to discussions in smaller groups, as we are about to see.[62]

A shared linguistic research project

The scene of this activity was, once again, the Karma-Ling Institute in Savoy. Since 1988, a group styled *College of French-speaking translators* or *Lotsawa Board* has been organizing meetings for translators of Tibetan. The aim is to standardize the way in which Buddhist technical terms, but also those referring to psychology or the spiritual field, are translated. The specific task which they have in view is to compile a Tibetan-Sanskrit-French glossary comprising 500 entries. The tenth Encounter took place 17–18 April 1993. A dozen scholars took part in this work, which is not to say that all were present at each meeting. My knowledge of Tibetan being somewhat scanty, I attended primarily in order to learn by listening to these worthy philologists and linguists. To tell the truth, I caught the train after it had set off, and have participated only in the last five Encounters, that is, since 23 November 1990. None of us was idle during these days of compulsory work with dictionaries (including a large Chinese one) and of crucial debates; we value the memories of these seasoned combatants. The College, if it survives, will be integrated into the *Fédération du Bouddhisme Tibetain*, which already includes twenty-five French *Dharma* centres. It will fall to this latter to oversee the final editing of the *Glossary* and to ensure its distribution. It is intended in the first place for use by Buddhist centres, but its interest for interreligious dialogue may be imagined: that of knowing the exact meaning of the terms used in exchanges on comparative religion. Even if this lexicon never sees the light of day I shall retain, even more, perhaps, than the enrichment of my vocabulary, an ineffaceable impression in my memory: what psychological penetration Buddhism commands, and what subtlety of interpretation in the way it expresses everything connected with knowledge or intuition!

The Dalai Lama's visit to Karma-Ling, Saturday 30 October 1993

Preparations for the event had been made over a long period. A vast esplanade had been set up over several months. It was the foundation of a big top with tiers of blue tents with a capacity of 1,500 visitors. Everything was decorated and the brightly coloured banners in evidence along the paths to the *chorten* were as fresh as on the day they were put up. In the corridors of the Charterhouse a beautiful display of portraits of birds enhanced the welcome. A watchful security team was placed at intervals all the way from Pontcharra while a helicopter stood by a pavilion in case first aid was required. In spite of the cold in the morning and evening, the weather was splendid, the full moon a happy omen for the Tibetans. Arriving at the beginning of the afternoon, His Holiness was welcomed by the civil and religious authorities of the region. Some monks and nuns were present, mingling with the wine-coloured robes of the monks and nuns of the *Dharma*. Besides the blessing of the *chorten* and an address to those who were going into retreat, the main event of the day was an address by the Dalai Lama to the dignitaries present, followed by a short speech in which he emphasised the fraternal relationship which exists between Christianity and Buddhism. He made some very strong statements in well-weighed words, such as: "In the West, which is pervaded by a culture marked by Christianity, everyone who considers turning to the Buddhist Dharma must reflect deeply on what he is doing and be careful not to abandon the religion of his birth without mature consideration."[63]

We all have precious memories of this day, of the gentle smile of His Holiness, to say nothing of the reunions with sympathetic people whom one had met at various Dharma centres in the course of the years. On the previous evening, the Dalai Lama had visited the Grande Chartreuse and admired its simplicity. It is evident that he finds the life of our monks impressive. Some people criticised the reception for admitting too many journalists. While a press conference was given for them, the public went away, unable to wait any longer, and the cars went back down into the valley.

EAST-WEST SPIRITUAL EXCHANGES WITH JAPANESE ZEN MONKS

Since 1979, a most promising new venture has been taking shape, the fruits of which are already in evidence. This is an exchange of monks, brought about with two Oriental traditions marked by both particular interiority and particular openness. These are the Tibetan lamas and the Zen monks of Japan. Groups of Zen monks are coming to stay in Western monasteries, while monks and nuns from Europe go and observe Zen discipline for a month in Japan. These spiritual exchanges have been taking place alternately in Europe and Japan, *every four years*, since 1979. Such monastic visits make possible a reciprocal knowledge, both specific and in some depth. The address given by Pope John Paul II at the end of the first exchange may be read in the *Bulletin of the Pontifical Council for Interreligious Dialogue*.[64] The second was followed by the publication of a very lively book by Benoît Billot: *Voyage dans les monastères Zen*.[65] An account of exchanges II and III can be found in the same *Bulletin*.[66] For the fourth, see the article by Father (now Archbishop) Michael Fitzgerald in the *A.I.M. Bulletin*.[67] For the whole series, we are making use of the dossier compiled by Madam Mitchiko Ishigami-Iagolnitzer, research worker at C.N.R.S.: *Dialogue interreligieux monastique au Japon et en Europe*, which brings together a large number of reports and interviews published on the occasion of these *Échanges Spirituels de 1979 à 1987*.[68]

It should also be emphasised that we are not simply considering short-lived groups, leaving room to suppose that nothing happens in the intervals between their meeting. One Japanese Zen monk has been persevering enough to follow the theology courses at *Sankt Ottilien* abbey, Bavaria, for years. *Hozumi Roshi* is beginning to be a well-known and admired figure in the European communities for the lectures he gives and the courses he directs, while the radiant personality of the abbess *Aoyama Sensei*[69] gives rise to love, on her account, for the nuns of her Soto tradition.

EXCHANGES WITH TIBETAN MONKS
INTERMONASTIC HOSPITALITY PROGRAMME

In 1982, a thirty-year-old monk, student of the School of Dialectics at Dharamsala, spent four months in the United States, staying in turn in six Benedictine abbeys, sharing their life and exchanging information. Both sides were very pleased with this experiment, which was repeated the following year on a larger scale: three monks toured a dozen monasteries of Benedictines and Trappists in the United States and in Canada. In the other direction, a group of Catholic monks and nuns went off to India, during the autumn of 1986, in order to stay in a considerable number of Tibetan monasteries in the subcontinent.

These meetings as a whole come under the heading of the *Intermonastic Hospitality Programme*.[70] These exchanges, which began in 1982, were at the time of writing (1995) in their seventh phase. By 1993, around a hundred monasteries in Europe and America had welcomed Hindu or Buddhist monks and nuns, and more than seventy Christian monks and nuns had stayed in different monasteries in the East.[71] For phases VI and VII of the programme, involving monks and nuns travelling in both directions during 1994 and 1995, see the Bulletin of N.A.B.E.W.D. which, since 1993, has been entitled *Bulletin of Monastic Interreligious Dialogue*.

Independently of these exchanges, two English Benedictines, Dom Aldhelm Cameron-Brown, abbot of Prinknash, and Father Francis Baird, made a tour in 1988, under the auspices of D.I.M., of forty-eight Tibetan monasteries across the length and breadth of India.[72]

Before reporting our own adventures, it seems appropriate to record the growth of the Commission which encouraged these meetings.

THE DEVELOPMENT OF THE COMISSION FOR MONASTIC INTERRELIGIOUS DIALOGUE

The comission for *Monastic Interreligious Dialogue*, the acronym for which is D.I.M., watches over the establishment, or the reinforcement, of fraternal relations, in the majority of Western European countries, with monks of the Oriental religions. We have said a few words about its origins.[73] England is particularly active, as is also Dom Cornelius Tholens in Amsterdam, but so are our members in Germany, Belgium, France and Italy who include distinguished abbots in the Benedictine Order. N.A.B.E.W.D., in North America, publishes a bulletin, circulates cassettes, organizes meetings and collaborates with the *Naropa Institute* in Boulder, Colorado, which was founded by the Tibetan master Chögyam Trungpa Rinpoche (1939–1987).

Moved by the same spirit, the Benedictine abbey of La-Pierre-qui-Vire has had, for many years, the best possible relationship with the *Kagyu-Ling* centre, in Saône-et-Loire, while the Tamié La Trappe, in Savoy, maintains a neighbourly relationship with *Karma-Ling*, the former Charterhouse of St. Hugh.

The North American branch used to be called N.A.B.E.W.D. *(North American Board for East-West Dialogue)*. Recently, in order more clearly to demonstrate its monastic character, it has been renamed M.I.D. *(Monastic Interfaith Dialogue)*. This is the designation preferred also in Great Britain to D.I.M., which has an unfortunate sound in English. This is not the place in which to go into details of the activities of these groups, which are subdivided into *regional commissions:* France, Belgium, Germany, Great Britain, the Netherlands, French Switzerland, the Iberian Peninsula, and Italy. Since a meeting was held to which we shall refer later, there has even been an Indian commission.[74] We are justified in anticipating that, in the years to come, this tree may grow new branches: Poland, Australia, Eastern Asia.

A recent modification of the structures (1993) aims at giving a greater autonomy to D.I.M. (or M.I.D.), which will no longer be a subcommission of A.I.M., but the general secretariat of which will depend directly on the Abbot Primate of the Order of Saint Benedict and the Abbot General of the Trappists.

To anyone for whom our movement holds interest, one cannot do better than to recommend the book by Dom Jean Leclercq,

O.S.B.: *Nouvelle page d'histoire monastique. Histoire de l'A.I.M., 1960–1985.* Published by the Secretariat at Vanves in 1986, it is supported by ample documentation and written with ardour. In it one may see how the birth and development of D.I.M. are bound up with the initiatives of A.I.M. The general secretariat of the latter was entrusted to Father Abbot Robert de Floris, assisted from an early date by Sister Pia Valeri, from the monastery of Béthanie, Loppem. When Father de Floris retired, in July 1982, he was succeeded by Father Marie-Bernard de Soos, former Superior at Dzogbégan, in Togo. The new secretary has been, since 1984, Sister Teresa Rodriguez, from Stanbrook, England.[75] At the head of the commission for Dialogue is Father Pierre de Béthune, Prior of Clerlande, Belgium.

Each of the regional commissions reflects on the *doctrinal aspects of interreligious dialogue.* One of the best courses on this subject was held at La Pierre-qui-Vire from 19–24 April 1982.[76] However, there were others, later, in Belgium and France. For such comparisons, we are fortunate to be able to count on the collaboration of two religious who combine real modesty with great learning, clarity of expression and a most sound judgement: Father Pierre Massein, of Saint Wandrille's Abbey, who was for a long time responsible for teaching Buddhism at the Institut Catholique, and Father Jacques Scheuer, S.J., director of *Voies de l'Orient* at Brussels and Professor of Oriental Religions at the I.E.T. (Institut d'Études Théologiques) in that city.

Each regional commission takes pains to establish contacts and produce publications. In the case of France, and French-speaking Belgium and Switzerland, there is the *Bulletin du D.I.M. francophone.*[77] The English Benedictines made an excellent initiative, which could serve as a worthwhile model for other countries. Under the title: *Monastic Interfaith Directory,* they published in 1986 a very handy little Directory which gives a map of Great Britain and Ireland and mentions not only Catholic and Anglican monasteries, but also those of the different branches of Buddhism to be found in the countries concerned and even, with a good introduction, the Vedānta Centre of which we have already spoken.[78]

If one wishes to gain an idea of the different activities of each regional commission, the best way is to read one of their reports: for instance, in the *Bulletin of the Pontifical Council,* entitled, since 1994, *Pro Dialogo.* You will find in No. 88, for 1995, an account of the 23rd meeting of the Central Commission of the European

D.I.M. at Saint-Maurice (Valais, Switzerland) from 17–19 June 1994.[79] Each nation reports briefly on its activities, and a great diversity of approach will be noticed. While the spirit that moves us is clearly the same, the organizers adopt, according to the country, the methods best suited to the context of that nation and take into account the circumstances of the Eastern monks to be found there. Bavaria is not England, nor is French Switzerland the Iberian Peninsula. French-speaking Belgium not being as large as France, it is easier to bring together the "contact-persons". As for the young Dutch-speaking region, God has given it as director a native of Antwerp who has become a Trappist in Holland, and for whom it is easy to straddle the frontiers.

A DIALOGUE IN BOTH DIRECTIONS

Dialogue – as the word indicates – takes place in both directions. It would be an unrealistic project if we did not have responsible dialogue partners coming from the other side, eager to hold exchanges. Christian monks of our times have been fortunate to have, facing them, Japanese or Tibetan monks for whom encounter is highly valued. We have in mind certain great *Roshis* from Japan and, on the Tibetan side, him who, in his own person, symbolises the entire monasticism of the *Vajrayāna*. His Holiness the Dalai Lama was kind enough to address a message explicitly to Christian monks when, in 1991, the magazine *Monastic Studies* published a special issue: *Buddhist and Christian Monasticism*. The French translation of this message subsequently appeared in the *Bulletin de l'A.I.M.*[80] The Dalai Lama gave an interview to the Catholic monks and nuns who had come to hear his teachings at *Vajra Yoginī*, Lavaur, in November 1993.[81] At the same time, the Tibetan lamas from Tihange,[82] near Huy, in Belgium, were given a brotherly welcome at the abbey of Orval.

In the sphere of reflection, this same year of 1993 was distinguished by an important document. At the suggestion of the Pontifical Council for Interreligious Dialogue, the D.I.M. instituted an inquiry with the aim of thoroughly studying the nature of the dialogue of religious experience, particularly where prayer and contemplation are concerned. It was published under the title: *Contemplation and Interfaith Dialogue*.[83]

We share the conviction of *Father Le Saux* (Abishiktānanda): "If everyone lives at the depth of himself, as intimate as possible with the Spirit who is in him, under whatever name or form by which he makes himself known, a marvellous communication is set up between persons, beyond words, at the level of the Spirit. It is just such a communion of life and such a discovery of the Spirit, one in the other, that gives its momentum to the ecumenical movement, and to its pioneers their boldness in going forward and taking prophetic initiatives."[84]

Notes

[1] *Monachesimo Cristiano, Buddhista, Indù. Incontro interreligioso sulla vita monastica. Praglia 3–8 ottobre 1977.* Editrice Missionaria Italiana, 1978.

[2] A more detailed account of this course: *La rencontre interreligieuse de Praglia, 3–8 octobre 1977,* is to be found in *Collectanea Cisterciensia,* 1978-1, pp. 72–78.

[3] A slight disturbance of the chronological order will be noticed. The *tour of monastic India* described in the previous chapter actually took place *after* the first meeting at Praglia. This reversal has been made intentionally, in order to group together the different meetings in Europe. In any case, that held at Praglia had the same directors and, to some extent, the same participants on the Christian side.

[4] *Deuxième rencontre interreligieuse à l'Abbaye de Praglia, 23–29 September 1979,* in *Collectanea Cisterciensia,* 1979-4, pp. 356–359, or in the *A.I.M. Bulletin,* 1980, No. 28, pp. 54–57.

[5] *Two Commissions for East-West Dialogue* in the *A.I.M. Bulletin,* 1978, No. 24, pp. 50–57.

[6] There were three of us, from three Orders and three different countries: a Dutch Benedictine, an Italian Camaldolese and a Belgian Trappist.

[7] A detailed description of the various musical instruments used in the liturgy is to be found on pages 160–161 of G. TUCCI's and W. HEISSIG's work, *Les religions du Tibet et de la Mongolie,* Paris, Payot, 1973.

[8] See our chapter III.

[9] *Rencontre chrétiens-bouddhistes. Foi et amour, à Kagyu-Ling* with the Venerable Kalu Rinpoche. November 1984. Kagyu Yiga Tcheu Dzinn Éditions. Château de Plaige, F-71320 Toulon-sur-Arroux.

[10] See chapter X below.

[11] Published under the title *Une entreprise féconde: le dialogue interreligieux monastique* in the Gregorian University journal *Studia Missionalia,* vol. 43, 1994, pp. 95–113.

[12] The latter, less accustomed to an audience of Westerners, may have been nervous. The impression of coldness he gave at Sainte-Baume was rectified when I saw him again in January 1983, during a brief stay in his monastery,

Ganden, in Karnataka State. In private, he showed himself simple and kindly, fully prepared to answer questions.

[13] This Gelugpa monk, who died on 3 March 1984 at Los Angeles, California, was born in Tibet in 1935.

[14] See below, pages 111 and 122.

[15] The text of these lectures is to be found in his book: *Silent mind, holy mind*, edited by Jonathan Landaw. Wisdom Culture, Ulverston, Cumbria, England, 1978. Dutch translation: *Stille geest, heilige geest*. Maitreya Instituut, Heemhoeveweg, 2, NL-8166 HA Emst, Nederland. The same Institute publishes a fine Dutch-language journal, the *Maitreya Magazine*, which published, especially in 1984, various issues on Lama Yeshe and his successor, Lama Zopa Rinpoche.

[16] It is common knowledge that the Anglican Benedictines on Caldey Island were received into the Catholic Church in 1913. The Scourmont Trappists took their place on the island from the end of 1928.

[17] From 18–20 October 1980.

[18] Lam Rim Buddhist Centre, Pentwyn Manor, Penrhos, Raglan Gwent NP5 2LE.

[19] Manjushri Institute, Conishead Priory, Ulverston, Cumbria LA12 9QQ.

[20] See below in chapter VII. I spent ten days or so there in January 1980.

[21] Vicki MACKENZIE: *Reincarnation: The Boy Lama*. Bloomsbury, London. Translated into French as *L'Enfant Lama. Histoire d'une réincarnation,* by C. Vlérick, Collection *"Les énigmes de l'univers"*, Paris, Robert Laffont, 1991. The sequel to this work is: *Reborn in the West: The Reincarnation Masters.* Also Bloomsbury, London, 1995. The journals *Mandala* (Soquel, California) and *Maitreya Magazine* give regular news of him.

[22] Some years later, the *Manjushri Institute* was obliged to withdraw from the *Foundation for the Preservation of the Mahāyāna Tradition*, and since that time it has no longer been included in the list of their centres, published regularly by the journal *Mandala* (see note 21). Flourishing in Italy (Pomaia), the Foundation also has a good number of centres in Australia and in the United States.

[23] See above, pages 94–97.

[24] See above, pages 90–93.

[25] Nashdom Abbey, Burnham, Slough SL1 8NL. The Anglican Benedictines came here from Pershore, Worcestershire, in 1926 and moved again, in 1987, to Elmore Abbey, Church Lane, Speen, Newbury, Berkshire, RG14 1SA.

[26] I returned to the *Vedānta Centre* at the end of October 1981 and, this time, enjoyed a greater number of conversations with the novices. I was able to attend the Swāmi's classes, models of teaching skill and religious conviction. These all came very much within the framework of Hinduism, while fully acceptable to a Christian and possessing a vigour that we have perhaps lost. Address: Vedānta Centre, Unity House, Blind Lane, Bourne End, Bucks S18 5LG.

[27] British Mahābodhi Society, London Buddhist Vihāra, 5, Heathfield Gardens, London W4 4JU.

[28] Buddhapadipa Temple, 14 Calonne Road, Wimbledon Parkside, London SW19 5JH.

[29] The Venerable Ajahn Sumedho, Chithurst Forest Sanctuary, Chithurst House, Petersfield, Hants.
[30] *Born in Tibet,* as told to René Cramer Roberts. First edition, published in England, 1966, by Allen and Unwin, London; 3rd edition, the Clear Light Series, Shambala Publications, Boulder, Colorado, 1977. Translated into French as *Né au Tibet,* and published by Buchet-Chastel, 1968.
[31] See the article *Sam-yé* in the *Dictionnaire des religions,* under the editorship of Paul Poupard, Presses Universitaires de France, 3rd, revised and enlarged, edition, 1993, pp. 1816–1817. During our pilgrimage to Tibet in July 1994, our group visited this ancient monastery. See below in chapter VIII, pages 246–248.
[32] See B. de GIVE, *Bibliographie d'initiation aux religions orientales.* Published by A.I.M., 7, rue d' Issy, F-92170 Vanves. For works by Trungpa, see pages 29–30.
[33] See J. BLOFELD, *The Tantric Buddhism of Tibet,* London, Arkana, 1992. More detailed explanations are given in TUCCI, G. & HEISSIG, W. in *Les religions du Tibet et de la Mongolie,* Payot, 1973, in the references for the word *gtorma* in the index, p. 511.
[34] See above, pages 101–102.
[35] Samye Ling is situated on a railway branch-line between Lockerbie (Edinburgh line) and Langholm, to the north of Carlisle. Address: Kagyu Samye Ling, Tibetan Centre, Eskdalemuir, Nr. Langholm, Dumfriesshire DG 13 0QL, Scotland.
[36] See above, pages 78–79 and note 20. By 1995, the Foundation already had 74 centres in 18 countries.
[37] Maitreya Instituut, Heemhoeveweg, 2, NL-8166 HA, Emst, Nederland.
[38] See above, pages 107–109.
[39] See above, pages 107–109, also *Cahiers du bouddhisme,* n° 22, octobre 1984, pp. 40–43.
[40] *Les cahiers du bouddhisme,* n° 24, April 1985, pp. 42–43.
[41] See above, pages 100–105.
[42] See the account in the journal *Dharma,* no 19, January-May 1994, pp. 50–55.
[43] Monastère Nālandā, Château de Rouzegas, Labastide Saint-Georges, 81500 Lavaur.
[44] See above, pages 110–112.
[45] Centro Samye Dzong, Karma Lodrö Gyamtso Ling. Calle Pau Claris, 74, 2°, Barcelona 08010.
[46] See above, pages 115–118.
[47] Nāgārjuna Institute, C.E.T. Barcelona, Rosellón 298, Pral 2a, 08037 Barcelona.
[48] I did not see them again during a second visit in 1989.
[49] Kagyu Dechen Ling, Calle Sáinz de Baranda, n° 57, 8° D, Madrid 28009.
[50] Nāgārjuna Institute, Calle Costanilla de los Angeles, n° 2, 3 dcha, 20013 Madrid. Since then, they have changed address.
[51] See below, chapter X.
[52] On Sonada and my encounters with Kalu Rinpoche, see in chapter VII, pages 148–150 and page 200, note 4.
[53] See DJAMGOEUN KONTRUL, *Le flambeau de la certitude.* Translated from

the Tibetan by J. HANSON. Éditions Yiga Tcheu Dzinn, Château de Plaige, 71320 Toulon-sur-Arroux, 1980, pp. 19–20.
54 Dag Shang Kagyu. Centro de Estudios y de Meditación Budista. Aptdo. N° 17, E-22430 Graus (Huesca).
55 The château was rebuilt in 1576 but in their present state, the buildings date from the eighteenth century.
56 Subsequently, on the initiative of the Belgian D.I.M., the three lamas and the people who run the centre were welcomed at the abbey of Orval on the 11th November 1993 – a brotherly encounter of which a very pleasant memory has been preserved by both sides.
57 This morning, on the *bardo*, the intermediate period after death, crucial for the choice of a future life.
58 Institut Karma-Ling. Hameau de Saint-Hugon, 73110 Arvillard (Savoie), France.
59 The *Acts* of these two colloquia were subsequently duplicated and published by Éditions Prajna, du Centre Karma-Ling. The first contains 193 pages; the second, 247 pages.
60 Introit for Pentecost (Wisdom 1.27). The subsequent colloquium could not be held at Pentecost as most of the priests and Christian monks were summoned on that feast by the obligations of their ministry.
61 See above, pages 92–93.
62 In chapter IX, on the subject *Trinity and Trikāya*.
63 See the journal *Dharma*, n° 19, p. 46.
64 In 1980, n° 43, p. 15.
65 Paris, Desclée de Brouwer, 1987.
66 In 1984, n° 55, pp. 93–96. In 1988, n° 67, pp. 30–36.
67 Vanves, 1991, n° 50, pp. 120–124.
68 Sciences et Lettres, 38, rue de l'abbé Carton, 75014 Paris.
69 See above, page 45.
70 Further details of these meetings may be obtained by reading the accounts published regularly in the *Bulletin* of N.A.B.E.W.D. *(North American Board for East-West Dialogue,* formerly at Osage Monastery, 18701, W. Monastery Road, Sand Springs, OK 74063, U.S.A., but since January 1991 at Abbey of Gethsemani, 3642 Monks Road, Trappist KY 40051. See also *Pro Dialogo,* the Bulletin of the Pontifical Council for Interreligious Dialogue, 1981-1, n° 67, pp. 36–41, under the title *Intermonastic Hospitality Programme* (especially on Stage III). This text appeared in French under the title *Moines et moniales chrétiens en Inde* in the *Bulletin de l'A.I.M.*, 1987, n° 42, pp. 122–125. On Stage V, see the *Bulletin of N.A.B.E.W.D.*, n° 46, January 1993, pp. 1–3.
71 Extract from *Contemplation and Dialogue* in *Pro Dialogo,* 1993-3, n° 84, p. 264. This figure clearly refers to both the programmes we have just described and not simply the *Hospitality Programme* with the Tibetans.
72 See their report under the title *Tour of the Tibetan monasteries in India* in the *Bulletin of A.I.M.,* 1989, n° 46, pp. 83–92. The sheer number of monasteries visited is astonishing. Were these good monks trying to break a record? The value of such a course might be queried; would it not be better to visit fewer monasteries and stay longer at each?

73 See above, pages 89–90 and 97.
74 In chapter VIII, on *Asirvanam*, page 204.
75 She returned to her monastery at the end of 1994. The information from 1990 needs to be updated. The President of A.I.M. is Fr. Martin Neyt, from the monastery of Saint-André, Clerlande, and his Assistant is Sister Gisela Happ, from St. Hildegard Abbey, Eibingen.
76 Under the title: *Influence des religions orientales en Europe. Information et discernement*. A brief account of this is to be found in *Collectanea Cisterciensia*, 1983, pp. 77–79.
77 France and Switzerland: D.I.M., Monastère Ste-Bathilde, 7, rue d'Issy, F-92170 Vanves, France.
Belgium and Luxemburg: D.I.M., Rue Haute, 58, B-1348 Louvain-la-Neuve, Belgique.
78 Under the title: *A Working Guide to the Monasteries of the Christian, Buddhist and Hindu Traditions in Britain and Ireland*. Prepared by the *Monastic Inter-Faith Dialogue*, Douai Abbey, Upper Woolhampton, Reading RG7 5TQ, 1986. On the Vedānta Centre, see above, pp. 112–13.
79 *Pro Dialogo*, n° 88, 1995/1, pp. 92–97.
80 *Monastic Studies,* The Benedictine Priory of Montreal, n° 19, 1991. *A.I.M. Bulletin,* n° 54, pp. 117–118.
81 See above, pages 121–122.
82 See above, pages 128–129.
83 In the *Bulletin of the Pontifical Council for Interreligious Dialogue*, 1993-3, n° 84, pp. 250–270. This document has been published in several languages, and is reproduced (except for the *Fondamental Bibliography* with which it closes) in *Documentation Catholique,* n° 2090, of 20 mars 1994, pp. 291–297.
84 Quoted by J. DUPUIS, S.J., in *Jésus-Christ à la rencontre des religions*, Paris, Desclée, 1989, pp. 307–308.

Chapter VII

At Home with the Lamas

> Jesus said to Nathaniel:
> "When you were under the fig-tree
> I saw you" (*John 1.48*)

In the context of the establishment of relationships between Christianity and the Eastern religions, it is only very recently that there has been any awareness of the obvious: monasticism, which exists on both sides, is a bridge which should have been in use for a very long time in order to promote contacts. When Dom Rembert Weakland, at that time the Benedictine Abbot Primate, appealed to this effect to the Congress of Bangalore, he met with approval and A.I.M., where Asia was concerned, saw to the setting up of a structure which would meet the need. It was titled D.I.M., Dialogue Interreligieux Monastique. Its members meet regularly at Vanves,[1] each having chosen one of the Eastern paths: Hinduism, Zen Buddhism, or the Tibetan tradition. At the end of a tour which had led them through the most varied regions of India (17 January to 22 February 1979) about ten Italian monks had made the acquaintance of a good many ashrams amongst those most highly regarded in Hinduism.[2] This author was able to accompany them and derived great profit from doing so. His superiors permitting him to extend the experience, he had the happiness of becoming acquainted with the most important centres for Tibetans in exile. Short of a real exchange of monks between the two religions, it was educative for a European Trappist to live for three months with Tibetan Lamas. We make no great claims for these pages. It would take long studies, and practice too, to go deeply into this very special Buddhist path, often badly presented to the West by publications the main purpose of which is to cause a sensation. Besides, a choice had to be made. Even when living within easy reach of courses on doctrine given by well-known masters, living cheek by jowl with the initiated practising their meditation techniques, we preferred to abide by the study of the language, the prerequisite as it seems to us of a philosophical and spiritual investigation. It must also be pointed out that such visits are quite unlike attendance at a university seminar. Travelling is time-consuming, as are the necessities of life under conditions that are often primitive, to say nothing of the many conversations. But all this is real life, *living together*, whose value, probably unknown to intellectuals living in well-heated rooms, needs to be appreciated.

A MOUNTAIN MONASTERY ON THE DARJEELING ROAD: SONADA

I took flight from Brussels on 1 January 1980 at 12.15 p.m. Our actual flying time was ten hours, with a stop at Abu-Dhabi (United Arab Emirates). Almost the whole of Europe as we crossed it was covered with snow or hoar-frost: the landscapes were of white fields. The difference in time is four-and-a-half hours. We arrived in *Bombay* at 22.15 by our time, at 2.45 local time. I did not leave the very lively and noisy airport at all on 2 January. The departure from Bombay was at 6.30 p.m. and we arrived in *Calcutta* at 8.40. I spent that night at the airport, which was much quieter, remaining there until the plane took off at 13.10. We reached *Bagdogra*, near *Siliguri*, in North Bengal, at 14.00. At Bombay, the daytime temperature was 23°; at Calcutta, particularly at night, it was much cooler.

Bagdogra is almost fifty miles from Darjeeling, but I alighted from the bus just after Kurseong, where the Jesuits had their theology faculty till very recently. *Sonada* is a little further and higher. We were in the mountains here, the foothills of the Himalayas, and the road skirts a number of precipices; it actually follows the same route as a narrow-gauge steam railway line. In the course of the journey, I had several good conversations. India was in the throes of elections, set for the 3rd and 6th January. There were a good many placards in the Darjeeling area.

On my arrival at Sonada, I realized that they had not received my letter, although I knew for certain that it had been correctly addressed. Nonetheless, I was warmly welcomed. I had brought a copy of the letter of recommendation from the Lama at Plaige.[3] Everyone told me that it would take two months to obtain a visa for Sikkim, where the Karmapa, supreme head of the Kagyupa, has his residence, so I gave up that visit. The climate here is pretty severe: the nights are very cold and one wraps oneself up in blankets. The group of Western sympathisers, from the United States, Canada and France is particularly pleasant and obliging.

At Sonada, where I arrived on the evening of 3 January, the accommodation is frankly primitive. There is simply nothing in the way of Western comfort. An entire hill is occupied by a little hamlet of Tibetan refugees and by the monastery. Along the road, below, rise well-decorated *stūpas* or *chortens*. Then comes the housing for the monks and their temple, where I attended the morning and evening *pūjās*. There are a score of them, including a dozen boy-monks, some of them extremely young. A vast temple is under construction, also on this hill. Higher up is the residence of the Abbot, the *Venerable Kalu Rinpoche*. He is a man of deep spirituality, a kind of Buddhist saint, practising the greatest austerity. He is elderly now, his features are emaciated, but he radiates wisdom and goodness. Very open to the meeting of religions, he was received in audience by Pope Paul VI, who made a great impression on him. Doubtless this was mutual. I have had the opportunity for two interviews with him, but this was only the beginning of our dealings with each other.[4]

Here, and with several other lamas, I have been able to see the depth of the impression made by encounters with the American Trappist *Thomas Merton*, who stayed for a month at Darjeeling and its neighbourhood, only a short while before his death at Bangkok in 1968. He, for his part, had a high esteem for Tibetan lamas.[5]

At Sonada, life was marked by real poverty, especially when compared with our Western lifestyle. I had so much more esteem for the *Westerners* – Americans, Canadians and French – who came to live and meditate here, some of them for a year or more. Their religion of origin is often Christian (all denominations). There were, for example, two Ukrainian Orthodox, who celebrated Christmas on the date on which their church observed it. As the Westerners inevitably live among them, it is with their group that I had the most frequent contacts. The fact that almost all the monks spoke Tibetan only did not help communication, but we smiled at each other, making friendly gestures and performing little services for one another.

I had supposed that the isolation of such a place ruled out the possibility of a Catholic presence. However, I soon made contact with the *Salesians,* who maintain a philosophy faculty here for two provinces, with 120 scholastics. Almost all were on holiday, the colleges and schools being closed for the three winter months, which are intensely cold. For this reason also, there are practically no tourists in this season. The Salesians gave me the best possible welcome, as did the *Holy Cross* Sisters, a Swiss congregation of which the members here are all Indian. In my free time, I studied a little Tibetan.

On Thursday 10 January, I made my way to *Darjeeling,* the most important town of the district: 65,000 inhabitants, a lively market and many schools and colleges. I visited several of these, notably *North Point,* one of the best establishments in India, where the Jesuits have educated a real elite. The majority of the pupils are non-Christians, but they show themselves grateful for the education they received there. The same applies to the *Loreto Convent.*

From there I travelled the following day to *Kalimpong.* I arrived at the closing of a retreat for the diocesan clergy, amongst whom I met several of my former seminarians from Kandy. I was edified by the excellent outlook of the priests of the diocese and of their bishop, Mgr Eric Benjamin. I caught sight of some Canadian Jesuits and of some canons regular of Saint Maurice, in Valais. Several of them would like to see the foundation of a Trappist monastery in this frontier district, close to Tibet and strongly influenced by the traditions of Buddhism. I saw and admired at Kalimpong two beautiful Catholic churches which are constructed entirely in the style of Tibetan gonpas.

From Darjeeling one is able to watch a sunrise on Everest (Chomolungma). The peaks of the eternal snows of Kanchenjunga could be clearly seen, all the way to the outskirts of Kalimpong.

I had not wanted to leave the hill without "paying a visit" to the *Kurseong scholasticate* – or rather to its location, for the theology faculty, on reasonable grounds, had been transferred, in 1971, to Delhi, where it is now known as *Vidyajyoti* (the light of knowledge). Here had lived, as professors or students of theology, a good many Belgian Jesuits who were my brothers and friends. The names on several tombstones were familiar to me. These scenes, formerly enlivened by a crowd of young religious now conveyed solitude and melancholy.

Having descended once more into the valley, I attended a beautiful Religious Profession ceremony at the (Liège) Daughters of the Cross, at *Matigara*, near Siliguri. The Mother General was present and gave me the best possible welcome.[6]

FIRST STAY IN NEPAL

It was on 15 January that my plane landed in *Kathmandu* at about 11 a.m. The town is admirably located in a broad valley surrounded by hills. It holds a great deal of life and numerous sanctuaries. The neighbourhood has many famous pilgrimage sites for Buddhism: for instance *Svayambhu*, the *stūpa* of which is often reproduced in books on Nepal, and *Bodnath*, where I was able to visit two Orders known to me only by their names: the Nyingmapa (the Red Hats) and the Sakyapa. In particular, I spent ten days in a Tibetan monastery with a considerable influence (in the United States, Canada, France, England, Australia, Germany and Spain). Every year, they welcome on this hill more than 200 retreatants, come from every country in the West to make a long retreat. The Abbot is the *Lama Thubten Yeshe*, whom I know well, having been on two of his retreats in the south of France.[7] He is very open towards Christianity and has written some moving pages on Jesus. As I was on very good terms with his retreatants, they invited me to give two addresses, in the "meditation-tent", followed by questions on the relationship between Buddhism and Christianity. I admire the courage of these Westerners who commit themselves to such long periods of spiritual training. The accommodation is certainly primitive, and it is a luxury to have a narrow little room in one of the series of accommodation blocks. The majority have to be content with a simple mattress and living cheek by jowl under a vast tent. By way of compensation the view, for anyone who makes a circuit of the summit of the hill, is superb in every direction as far as the horizon, though you feel the wintry cold as long as you remain in the shade.[8]

At *Kopan* – this is the name of the monastery – there are also in permanent residence a score of Tibetan monks and, most noticeably, 70 little boy-monks in red robes and with shaven heads, receiving an austere and vigorous training in an atmosphere of joy. This alone is an eloquent testimony.

Kathmandu (5 miles from Kopan) also has an important college belonging to the Jesuits, who were invited there by the government in about 1953. I was warmly welcomed (spending a day and a night there), but I held to my intention of sharing the life of the Tibetan monasteries at all times.

RETURN TO INDIA

Travelling via Vārāṇasī, I reached the important town of *Gaya* on 25 January. I was given accommodation by the Sisters, whose parish priest was an American Jesuit, and spent the 26th and 27th on pilgrimage to *Bodhgaya*, the holiest place in Buddhism. The reason for this is that, under the Bodhi tree (a shoot of which has been preserved), Shakyamuni received the mystical grace of his Enlightenment, the starting point of Buddhism across the world. Here there are monasteries or guest houses belonging to almost every Buddhist country. I had, most notably, a long conversation with the Abbot and one of the monks of the Thai monastery, the temple of which is an architectural gem, but Japan, China, Burma and Sri Lanka are also represented. As for the pilgrims, it is unquestionably the Tibetans who are the most numerous and the most fervent. The Dalai Lama was there for a week, and hundreds of red-robed monks were seated, meditating and praying, in front of the great temple throughout the afternoon. As for the Indians, they too are numerous but come rather as tourists.

The plane being obliged to pass by *Delhi*, I took the opportunity of visiting the Jesuit theology faculty, transferred there in 1971 from Kurseong. I had the joy of a reunion with several Belgian Fathers who had been my fellow-students and friends. I also saw a beautiful Tibetan temple and Lama Yeshe's reception centre, which is close to the airport.

At *Amritsar*, I set my heart on seeing once more the Golden Temple, in the middle of a lake, marvellous in the late afternoon sun (it was 5 p.m.). This is the heart of the Sikh religion,[9] and also the base for several missionaries. They were all highly interested in my expedition, and understood its importance for the meeting of religions.

DHARAMSALA OR TIBETAN CULTURE IN EXILE (1980)

On Wednesday 30 January 1980, the bus from Amritsar brought me to *Pathāncot*, on the border with Pakistan, at the hour of the midday meal. I went to take it in a school run by Franciscan Sisters, almost all of them originally from Kerala. They gave me a tour of the *nursery*, where I was greeted by the singing of very young children. At about 5.30 p.m., I arrived at *Dharamsala*, where I expected to stay until 26 March. This was not my first visit here since, in the company of some Italian monks, our *Tour of Monastic India* [10] made it possible to pass this way, on 17–18 February 1979, two very full days in the course of which, most notably, we had the privilege of a long audience with the Dalai Lama.

As this is mountainous country, it would take a three-dimensional model to show the different levels of the neighbourhood. I have already mentioned the special circumstances of this small market town, which is on several tiers. It would be worth referring to the explanations given above with a view to locating the *gonpa* of the Tibetan nuns at McLeod Ganj.[11]

The *Dharamsala* market is fully halfway up the hill. It boasts a bus station and a densely populated village.[12] A shortcut brings one, rather out of breath, to the level which I have described. This is an important spot, where the *Library* can be admired. This is a specialised library, perhaps the best in the world for original works in Tibetan and English books on the history, geography, art and religions of Tibet. Each year, especially during the summer months, the very well equipped lecture room is full of Westerners come to carry out research. The Centre publishes a magazine, *The Tibet Journal,* and collections of classical works on Tibetan Buddhism. I have made the acquaintance of two Canadian translators: Glenn Mullin and Olivier de Féral.

This spot is, moreover, of equal interest from the *political* point of view. This is the seat of the Tibetan government-in-exile. A fine white building beside the library includes, on the first floor, the Council Chamber where the Dalai Lama calls his ministers together. There is a reception room on the ground floor. All round the esplanade are buildings housing the different *offices*: "ministries" such as Home Office, education, finance, foreign affairs. The modest canteen where I would take my meals is the place where one meets all the officials from these offices. Since they are all Tibetans, they speak their own language amongst themselves. Foreigners who so wish may, for a modest sum, take their meals at the *Staff Mess.*

I was very warmly received by the director of the Library, Mr. Gyatso Tshering, who at once took care to obtain a good room for me. I had for neighbours Amchok Rinpoche, an intellectual lama who had been *assistant librarian* the previous year and was writing a thesis for the University of Vienna and, most notably, a very pleasant young Tibetan by the name of Gokey, a former pupil of the Jesuits at Darjeeling,[13] and retaining still-vivid memories of them. He did me very many services.

The surroundings were highly picturesque, with a simply wonderful view over the hills and the plain. In the distance, a broad river, almost a lake, created by a dam, was visible . Above all, and very close, there was a chain of snow-covered mountains, the Dhaola Dhar, well over 13,000 feet high, which reflects the most wonderful colours when the sun is setting. If one continues up the precipitous slope of this hill, twenty-five minutes' climb brings one level with the convent of the Tibetan nuns we had visited the previous year and, a little further, the small village of *McLeod Ganj,* with a market and the hotel where we spent two nights. This village, due to the altitude and exposure, is much colder than our level. Another hill, of the same height, is occupied by the *School of Dialectics,* the temple and the residence of His Holiness the Dalai Lama. The latter was kind enough to grant me a private audience lasting half an hour. This gave me the opportunity to see, once again, how much he has at heart the meeting between Christianity and his own monks. For this occasion I put on my religious habit, as I did when I went, each Sunday, to say Mass at the military camp at Yol, in the valley.

Life at Dharamsala

I studied the language with a succession of *tutors.* For my first *tutor,* I had a competent layman, by the name of Tashi. Next came a monk, Yelo Rinpoche, less well acquainted with English. For my third I was promised someone really well informed, the best, they said: Lobsang Thönden, whose Tibetan manual for English speakers was about to be published.

Here are some of the minor occurrences of my life in these mountains. On 5 February, I saw the arrival, for the purpose of writing an article for the missionary magazine *Pro Apostolis*, the title of which has since been changed, of two Flemish Jesuits, one being the director of the magazine, the other attached to the mission at Ranchi. They had obtained an audience with the Dalai Lama and an interview with a member of the delegation which had returned from Tibet. They took photographs and drew me into conversation on the prospects of the encounter with Buddhism.

On Sundays, I would go to say Mass at Yol, in the Indian army's vast camp. A score of Catholic soldiers took part, along with their wives and children. The Chaplain, *a Carmelite* from Kerala, on learning my reason for coming, at once grasped the importance of the step I was taking. He would be only too glad to set himself, or one of his brethren, to the study of Tibetan and follow courses on doctrine at the Library. Up to now, leaving aside Mgr Lamotte and Professor Snellgrove, on the Catholic side I know only Father Sherburne, an American Jesuit, to have acquired any competence in this field, and that Father does not live in India. Later, I had the pleasure of coming to know Father Francis Tiso and actually to see him take part in our pilgrimage to Tibet in 1994. Father Ambrose, O.C.D., too, insisted that there should one day be a Trappist foundation in this region. At a short distance from here, there is an utterly beautiful spot, where nature is still completely unspoilt and there are broad hills entirely covered by forest. This is only a few minutes from the McLeod Ganj market and the only building is an almost completely abandoned Anglican chapel, *Saint John's in the Wilderness*. This place of utter solitude and silence would be the ideal site for a monastery.

While awaiting my interview with the Dalai Lama, I had been present at a picturesque and almost daily session of debating: with many a dramatic gesture, the young monks, philosophy students, engage in what our scholastics used to call *disputatio,* the very lively challengers remaining standing, delivering their objections with a sceptical and gleeful expression, the defenders of the thesis staying calmly seated, considering their replies. This *School of Dialectics* has around 70 students, all red-robed monks. On a higher level, one comes to the *Tibetan Children's Village*, under the patronage of the Dalai Lama's sister. It is both an ordinary and a vocational school where young Tibetans learn crafts at which they will excel. There are altogether a thousand children. Plans are under way for a branch at Mysore, in the Bylakuppe Settlement, the monastery of which I had visited the previous year.[14]

From 17–19 February, there took place the boisterous and largely secular celebrations for the Tibetan New Year, *Losar*. This actually lasts for six days, three of preparation and three of festivities. It is a real hullabaloo, with the accompaniment of firecrackers and rockets. While the normal fare is almost meagre, people give themselves up to feasting during these days: prolonged and superabundant meals, entertaining shows, even a night worthy of comparison with our best Christmas and New Year celebrations, with a great dinner at midnight preceded by hours of Western-style dancing. One wondered where religion entered into all this, as it resembled Christmas without a religious celebration. There were, however, daily *pūjās* for the monks and some duties in the temple. On further consideration, our Carnival and New Year's Eve are as little marked by Christianity.

From 20th February, the study courses, in both language and doctrine, resumed. There are about twenty-five Westerners following them; some stay here for months, or even years. Time being limited, I have opted for language-study, leaving to some future date the effort of grappling with Buddhist philosophy and of practising Tibetan meditation techniques. I do not have the space to describe here the *life of the people* amongst whom we live: the women carrying their well-swathed babies on their backs, the lively games of the children, the many dogs that bark during the night; in particular, on a higher level, the intense *devotion of the pilgrims*, prayerfully making circuits of the Library or prostrating at the entrance, for its portico is built of pillars decorated in vivid colours like those of a temple. This building houses, moreover, important collections of Tibetan manuscripts, including precious copies of the *Kangyur* and its ancient commentaries: this is their Holy Scripture, and the first floor includes a museum where there are hundreds of statuettes of the Buddha, of their most famous lamas and their deities. They carried away these treasures when they fled their homeland into pitiless years of exile.

On 21st February, Spring suddenly showed itself: birds grew excited, buds opened wide, the temperature rose. I was struck by the bright and tender foliage of certain trees; a wild cherry tree was in flower. There were great quantities of mauve and violet flowers, while the snowy mountain, close at hand, shone splendidly when the sun set.

A meeting with a young Indian

Towards the end of the month, I was drawn into an adventure which I had not in the least anticipated. I had bought a piece of cake from a young Indian of some sixteen years. Brown-faced and fine-featured, he was a Christian, which is exceptional in those regions. He openly wore a silver-plated cross and brandished a New Testament, which had been offered to him by a Christian from America. He invited me to go and see where he lived. It should be understood that the surroundings of the Library are still occupied by huts belonging to Indians, the original inhabitants of these hills. The child led me into a dark hole with no light but that which came through the entrance. In this cave-like space, there was nothing, no table, no chair, no lamp, no bed, not even a proper covering, and he shook with the cold every night. He had only the small portable stove on which he cooked his banana- or apple-tarts, so much appreciated by his customers. I did my best to come to his assistance, and wrote to eventual benefactors. He later insisted on my spending twenty-four hours with his family, who occupied one of the nearest hovels in a village in the valley. I agreed, though not without repugnance and, the following weekend, I stayed with that numerous family, who dragged out their existence in a state of poverty bordering on destitution. I must say that they gave me the best welcome possible, but it wrung my heart to reflect that such was the condition of millions of poor people all over India. Before these the Tibetans, exiled and starting from zero but diligent and skilful, passed almost as rich. It goes without saying that the little Indian invited me every day to help him make his cakes. These were evening hours apparently wasted, but in the course of which I learned something which books could not have taught me about the way of life of people stripped of everything but with a sensitive heart, overflowing with gratitude. Since my visits to him involved creeping along, threading my way between poor dwellings, the Indians came to recognize me and would smile as I passed them.

The influence of the hill:
political, educational, social and religious

> A city built on a hill-top
> cannot be hidden.
> (*Matthew 5.14*)

It is common knowledge that the Tibetan people, who had been invaded by the Chinese Communists in 1950, rose against their oppressors on 10 March 1959. This insurrectionary movement was brutally crushed but, every year since then, the Tibetans in free countries have kept this day as their national festival. Here, decorations are put up, and the sports-field just below the Library is encompassed with flags, placards and strips of calico bearing inscriptions. Tents were pitched for the Dalai Lama and his officials. Speeches were delivered and there was traditional dancing to watch. The orderly procession, which had been shouting slogans as it came down from the summit of the hill, did so with renewed enthusiasm as it progressed through the streets of Dharamsala. In the afternoon, a considerable crowd gathered to see an exhibition of photographs and documents brought back from Tibet by a delegation that had been able to spend three months there at the end of the previous year. The population there is forced to carry out heavy labour; the majority of the magnificent monasteries are in ruins.

After a few days of storm and hail, just before the middle of March, the fruit trees (apple and cherry) came into blossom, while the mountain of eternal snows was splendid in the setting sun.

On a fine afternoon, 19 March, I made a tour of the mountain. First of all I visited, in the *Tibetan Children's Village*, above McLeod Ganj, the vocational school where young Tibetans, both boys and girls, are taught to make those beautiful carpets, so sought after by Westerners. They are there at the looms, very industrious and skilful, and one can see the progress of their work. Similarly, at the school of art, *thankas* and *mandalas* are prepared in silence.

On the summit of the hill there stood, as modest proof of a far-reaching movement, the *Tushita Centre* of Lama Thubten Yeshe. A Dutchman and an American had taken great pains to level the very stony and uneven ground; the concrete of the foundations for the future house of lamas had not even set.

On the other hand, it is more than eight years since the establishment at McLeod Ganj of *the Tibetan nuns* whose convent I was about to visit for the second time.[15] There were about fifty nuns there, living a "Franciscan" life of poverty, in devotion and joy. Their Superior would be delighted if contacts were to be established between her community and Christian nuns. If a monastery of Trappistines or a Carmel could one day be founded in that region, this would make her deeply happy. This much is certain: an opening onto the monastic life of another religion would be the occasion of great consolation, a stimulus to fervour and mutual edification.

At the moment of my departure, I received once more great marks of esteem on the part of the director of the Library, from the Rinpoche who had been my tutor and the person in the room next to my own. A talk accompanied by slides on the most picturesque aspects of life in the Tibetan settlements of *Karnataka*, notably that of Mundgod, was well received by the public, who discovered anew its colourful folklore and the fascinating character of its liturgical celebrations. In other respects, concerned as I was over the poorest among the Indians, it wrung my heart that I had to leave them.

THE STAGES OF MY RETURN JOURNEY

At Kalimpong, I was fortunate enough to arrive at the very end of a retreat which had brought together all the priests of the diocese of Darjeeling;[16] in consequence I had numerous and easy contacts with these missionaries, visits to whom on their home ground would have been very time-consuming. The same good fortune led to my finding at *Jullundur*, in the Punjab, not only the bishop, a Capuchin, but a group of Carmelites who work in his diocese.[17] They were having a meeting with their superior. I discovered at first-hand the great interest they felt in the meeting of religions. They were evidently highly sensitive to the prominent part which the writings of Saint Teresa of Avila and Saint John of the Cross are required to play in this contact with the mystics of the Eastern religions.

On the following day, 27 March, one plane took me from Amritsar to Delhi, another from Delhi to Bombay but I narrowly missed the third, which was bound for Brussels. What was, at first sight, an unfortunate hitch proved to be in reality the gracious gift of Providence in allowing me five more days in India. The next departure for Belgium being set for 1 April, I was able to spend those five days in Bombay, where I was welcomed in the most cordial manner by the Jesuits of *Saint Xavier's College*. They saw in me the former Jesuit and missionary to India but, perhaps above all, the Trappist, so I was constantly bombarded with questions on our way of life. The keenness of their interest in a genuinely contemplative life was very obvious amongst the majority of Fathers and Brothers alike. As regards *Tibet*, some of them recalled that the first mission, over twenty years from 1624 onwards, was that of the Portuguese Jesuits under the leadership of *Father De Andrade*. A work newly published in Italian by Giuseppe Toscano gives a large part of their report.[18]

Being as close as I was, I could not fail to visit the cave-sculptures at *Elephanta*. These are reached by crossing a body of water on which the port of Bombay stands. A small island, actually a hill, is an hour's journey away. At the summit of the hill is a vast cave, the sculptures in which go back to anything between the second century B.C. to the tenth of our era. This is a temple to Shiva and there are, amongst other representations, three great statues of this god. Above all, and occupying a central position, there is a magnificent and famous three-headed statue known by the name of *Trimurti*. No mere reproductions can convey its impressiveness. An excellent guide explained these works of art to us, setting them in the perspective of the religious context of Hinduism.

Saint Xavier's College, Bombay has a museum and an important library specializing in the history and archaeology of India; the name of Father Heras (+1955) is linked with it. Here are assembled very many objects of art, fragments turned up during excavations and nearly 25,000 books. It is one of the best centres of information for researchers in these fields, especially on the prehistory and history of religion.[19]

By way of a conclusion

It should not be imagined that a stay in Tibetan monasteries could bear any resemblance to that in a Trappist monastery or a Benedictine Abbey. These *gonpas* are simultaneously more open and more closed. More open, since one frequently sees lamas mingling unhesitatingly with the population surrounding them. However, one does not enter at will into the regular life of the monks. For various reasons, I have not truly taken part in their liturgical activities nor stayed in one of their cells. To be accurate, it would have been quite impossible at Sonada, the building programme of which is still incomplete.[20] At Kopan, though one constantly meets both adult and boy-monks, it is not customary for visitors to attend their offices. This holds good also at Dharamsala, where the Westerners meditate alone in their little rooms,[21] whereas at McLeod Ganj, anyone wishing to take part fully in their life would have to master the Tibetan language in order to follow the teachings and participate in the contests in the School of Dialectics.[22]

This is not in any way to imply that we were kept at arm's length. Whenever the opportunity offered, our conversations with the highest lamas took place on a properly spiritual and monastic level. As for the others whom we met in the course of the day, our contacts were invariably of a friendly nature; a smile and an obliging gesture compensated for the lack of linguistic tools. I was aware that their timetable and rules included a good measure of austerity, but certainly their modesty and benevolence predominated.

If I did not achieve all that I had hoped for during this visit – I think, for example, of my slow progress in the study of a language completely unfamiliar to me – I had, as gifts from the Lord, many a profitable encounter by way of compensation. Then there was the edification I received from those Westerners who, for often similar, personal reasons, committed themselves to the path of Buddhism, the strength and simplicity of the Tibetan people in the midst of whom we lived, the testimony of their festivals, their folklore and of their daily life. There was also the open-mindedness and generosity of so many missionaries, priests and Sisters, who, living as close as they did to these Dharma centres, and knowing the region thoroughly, were happy to have frequent contact with the Tibetans, indeed, at least in some cases, to study their language and doctrine. I am particularly grateful to them for having this outlook and for their welcome, which was a comfort to me. This applies to all who worked in the diocese of Darjeeling, the Jesuits of Kathmandu and the missionaries of the diocese of Jullundur in which Dharamsala is located. If Christian monks are called to play a specific role in the meeting with the traditions of the East, they cannot claim to be alone in this, but in collaboration with the local Church, which is more closely in touch with the real circumstances of these regions.

In this connection, it is interesting to note that these priests, dedicated as they are to the active apostolate, have been the first to suggest, some of them most urgently, the foundation of a Trappist monastery on their territory. There, they are on the frontier of Tibet and, at least in the case of Dharamsala, only a short distance from important centres of the great religions. It would provide evidence of our monastic life for Buddhists, Hindus and Sikhs. It would also serve as a reminder to the Church of the primacy of a life completely consecrated to God.

THE TIBETAN MONASTERIES OF KARNATAKA (SOUTH INDIA) (1983)

> Yahweh said to Abraham
> "Leave your country, your family and your father's house and go to the land I will show you."
> (*Genesis* 12.1)

I had by now been committed for five years to monastic interreligious dialogue, an undertaking which, without being directly of an apostolic character, might prove very fruitful in the long term; witness the warm welcome that we have always encountered with the lamas of Europe and Asia. To make contact easier, it would be a good idea to speak their language, for the greater number of the great masters of Tibet have not had the opportunity to learn English, and one cannot count upon the services of an interpreter. Ideally, too, one should be able to read their doctrinal and liturgical texts, so permission was given me to return for five months to the excellent Dharamsala *Library*, close to the Dalai Lama's residence, with a view to making a more extended study of their language.

In Nepal

The journey was arranged in such a way as to devote about ten days to the monasteries we shall refer to (from 12–21 January

1983). Then, as we were unable to obtain a visa for Sikkim, where we had dreamed of visiting the principal monastery of the Karmapas, we opted for a stay in Nepal (24 January–2 February). This made possible the pleasure of revisiting on the summit of the hill of Kopan, the monastery founded by Lama Zopa Rinpoche and Lama Thubten Yeshe, with its boy-monks of school age (there are 83 on site) and the simple and courageous devotion of its retreatants.[23] There, it is a far cry from Western comfort, and the weather was cold at that time of year. Moreover, without really seeking it, it seemed possible for the project of a monastic foundation to take shape in that country. The priests and Sisters eagerly desire a community of contemplatives in these Himalayan regions, marked as they are by Buddhism. Finding our own desire anticipated in this way, let us hope the Lord will provide the means to make this project a reality. Moreover, the administrators of the Tibetan centre gave me the opportunity of giving two addresses at Kathmandu, on our two religions, their spiritual techniques and their forms of monastic life. Questions from the audience enlivened the encounter.

In Karnataka

Many educated people, even in India, are unaware of the existence of Tibetan settlements in Karnataka (South India). One tends to think of all the Tibetan refugees crowded into the Himalayan foothills, where one wonders how they can make a livelihood. There are, however, thirteen Tibetan settlements in the State of Himāchal Pradesh alone.[24] In point of fact, here are some figures for which we have been able to check the truth if not the exactitude. In chronological order of foundation:

1. Bylakuppe has two settlements (5 camps, 20 villages) each having 6,000 Tibetans (thus 12,000);
2. Mundgod: 6,000;
3. Hunsur: 3,500;
4. Kolligal (branch of the *Tantric College*, closer to Mysore): 6,000.

There may be more than 12,000 at Bylakuppe. In addition to the above figures, we have about 30,000 for the whole of Karnataka State.

There are other *settlements* in Orissa, perhaps 6 or 7,000 Tibetans, and in other States in Central India. At McLeod Ganj and its neighbourhood (in Himāchal Pradesh) there are several thousand. For the whole of India: 80,000.

In Switzerland: 1,300.

Outside Tibet (Nepal, Bhutan, Sikkim, India, the West), total: over 100,000.

In Tibet itself, the official figure is 6 million.

According to the *Council for Tibetan Education,* there are in India, distributed among the different regions, 50 schools, 4 private boarding schools and 2 homes. According to the magazine *Dreloma,* published by the monastic university of Drepung, there are at present about 150 Tibetan *Dharma* centres, that is, monasteries of their various Orders (including the Bön religion) in India, Nepal, Bhutan, Sikkim and Ladakh. This amounts to approximately 6,278 monks, 653 lamas and 340 nuns.[25] The latter, all too often neglected in studies on Buddhism, deserve to be made the subject of a special study. The reader would be well advised to refer to the chapter which we have dedicated to them.[26]

Tibetan monasteries in India

Perhaps it would be as well to take time to recall some of the stages of the history of the Tibetan monasteries in India.

It is common knowledge that Tibet was invaded in 1950 by the Chinese. The latter took ever-tighter control of this vast country. The compromises attempted by the Dalai Lama proved to be fruitless, and popular rage against the occupier broke in that uprising of 10 March 1959 which became, as it were, the national celebration of the Tibetans. The Dalai Lama succeeded in escaping, as did a number of notable persons and religious leaders, but also a good many families from among the ordinary people. This voluntary exile saved the Tibetan culture and religion from a very probable annihilation. The Chinese perpetrated such massacres, deportations, and destruction of monasteries that a report made by the United Nations described these actions as genocide. What has become of the exiled monks?

1. From 1959 to 1969. All the monasteries, of all the Orders, were grouped at *Buxaduar*, in *Assam*. There were then about 1,300 monks, Khensur Pema Gyaltsen (now at Drepung) being abbot over the whole.
2. The *Settlement at Bylakuppe* was the first to be established, in around 1960, with Sera, but also some of the Kagyupa.
3. The *Settlement at Mundgod* began in 1964. It was in December 1969 that this monastery of *Ganden* began here. There are also some Nyingmapa at Ganden. At *Drepung* there are also 180 Sakya and about 65 Nyingmapa.

I set out from Bombay, and headed southward to Belgaum. From there, a bus brought me to Dharwar, then to Hubli, and another to *Mundgod*. Finally, after a long wait, a third came to the Tibetan Settlement, where I asked to be put down at the monastery of *Ganden*. All this is simple only on paper ... This is the North of Karnataka.

There are, on *Mundgod* territory, two of the ancient monasteries of Tibet: Ganden and Drepung, about three or four kilometres apart. Each of these two monasteries is divided into two colleges: Ganden: Shartse (where I spent the first three days) and Jangtse (which I visited); Drepung: Loseling (where I spent the following three days) and Gomang (which I visited). Each college has an independent life, its temple or prayer-hall, its houses (for living in or for meetings), its abbot *(khenpo)*. One can see their twin temples, a short distance apart, on the hill. The division into separate colleges does not mean that there is any difference in spirituality or outlook. The separation into two communities was imposed, for practical reasons, by the sheer number of the monks in Tibet; relations between them are good.

Ganden

Ganden had more than 4,000 monks in Tibet. At the present moment, each of its two colleges numbers about 500, of all ages. More than two-thirds seem to be young people in training. There are many children of primary school age, slightly fewer of secondary. The religious aged between 20 and 35 are active, busy about varied services of the monastery, and also on building projects, of which there are many. There are numerous, but still insufficient, housing blocks (one per "house", that is subdivision of the college). There is a single kitchen for the whole college. Bricks, and the firing of these, were to be seen everywhere, and so were blacksmiths and joiners. One stable housed cows and buffaloes. The atmosphere was gay and hardworking.

This is not to say that prayer was absent, far from it! I was actually present during two days taken up with long periods of religious chants and prayers in the temple. It was particularly vigorous and extended, in honour of the tutelary divinities of the monastery, almost throughout the day and far into the night. There were chants of varied pitch, like the waves of the sea, drums arranged in rows, powerful and booming trumpets which made all the walls and the vaults vibrate; all this in both temples at once.

The order of the day: All rise at 5.00 a.m. For the eldest there is an "advanced Buddhist philosophical training". For the youngest, the memorising of texts. From 8 to 9 a.m.: special prayers. From 9 to 11 a.m.: the morning debating. This being Southern India and the hot season, the monsoon, the students sleep from noon till 2 p.m. in their classrooms. There are classes in the afternoon. The students go to the "teacher's" room. The upper classes have about ten students each. From 6.30 to 8 p.m.: once again, special prayers (in the open air, in the courtyard). From 8 to 11.30 p.m. or midnight: debating. I was glad to be present, on several occasions, at these debates, as also at the college of Jangtse and later at Loseling. This is as picturesque as could possibly be imagined. In short, it closely resembled the *disputatio scholastica* of our mediaeval tradition, having in addition the shimmer of colours, the theatrical gestures, the mimicry of the challenger and the unbelievable liveliness of an Eastern court where a hundred or more students gave themselves up to an unrelenting contest in groups of two or three. Just as our own ancients quoted Scripture, the authority here was invariably the word of the Buddha, the *sūtras*, correctly interpreted of course. And as a fine variety of philosophical schools have flourished in the heart of Buddhism, one saw the amazing feats of memory performed by these young scholastics, who know thousands of pages of their sacred texts and their commentaries by heart. This contest lasted for hours. I was surprised to see boy-monks there, as young as twelve or thirteen; I was assured that they are in no way inferior to their elders, but demonstrate a great liveliness of mind.[27]

Since discipline has to be maintained in such highly-populated monasteries, in Tibet there were two *masters of discipline*, the Shengo and the Geko. The latter maintained good order within a college, the Shengo in the main prayer-hall (Tsogchen). In India, the two prerogatives are exercised by a single Geko, and his assistant (chabril). They superintend from the side and from behind during assemblies. An election is held in order to choose them. The names are sent to the Dalai Lama, who appoints the one he considers the most suitable. This takes place every two years.[28] I was reminded of my years in college when I saw these prefects in action. In point of fact, they intervened rarely in the course of long prayer-sessions, where the very young children were restless and inattentive. On the other hand, I was present one evening at Shartse to hear a short but vigorous discourse in the course of which the master, in a clear, steady voice, reminded his audience of rules which were evidently not being properly observed. The elders, in particular, listened gravely.

A sorer point is the *work carried out by monks*. How are they to gain a livelihood, since there is no question of a salary being paid to them? The services they provide, at the printing press and in the library, are voluntary ones, free of charge, so they are obliged to take on outdoor work. From this standpoint, their circumstances in India are completely different from those in Tibet, where the monks were not obliged to engage in manual work and could devote themselves peacefully to their studies. Besides, at least in principle, field work is forbidden to monks, since a great many small animals and insects are inevitably killed but, in India, people have to earn their living in whatever way they can, and the majority must, without in any way seeking it, live a life burdened with both intellectual and manual work. One might see them as worker-priests or, perhaps, Trappist monks.

I shall keep two memories, above all others, of Ganden. The first is of the interview granted me by one of the greatest living lamas, a true master of all the spiritual paths of Tibet and, in our eyes at least, something of a mystic. I had already followed one of his retreats, at Sainte-Baume. The Venerable *Song Rinpoche* showed himself happy to see me again and our conversation, bearing as it did on the motivation of Buddhist monks, was illuminating for me.[29] I shall refer to this again. The second memory is of a sentimental nature. Despite the barrier created by my ignorance of the

Tibetan language and the fact that very few monks could speak English, I was shown such great kindness and willingness to be helpful that I was quite overwhelmed by it, to the extent that it was with a great pang that I left them to visit the monastery of Drepung.

Drepung

I must admit to having taken the road to this monastery with a feeling of apprehension, due entirely to my own fault. Shortly before my departure from Belgium on 27 December 1982, I had received a letter from the abbot of Drepung warning me that I would require a permit from Delhi in order to enter their *Settlement*. It being too late to alter my plans, I set out on the day appointed and, out of prudence, went first to the neighbouring monastery of Ganden. While I was taking an almost furtive look at the buildings of Drepung, a scholar monk who happened to catch sight of me on the road, urged me, in spite of the refusal, to come and stay with them. So I spent three days there and found myself the object of just as much kindness as I had already experienced.

A short history lesson would not be out of place here. Tibet, prior to the exile, had eight monastic Orders, four of which can be found today in India. The most well known is the *Gelugpa*, to which the Dalai Lama belongs. It took its origin from a great religious reformer, comparable to Saint Bernard: *Tsong-kha-pa* (1357–1419). In 1409, he himself founded *Ganden*, the premier monastery of his Gelugpa reform; it numbered more than 4,000 monks in Tibet. His two disciples founded *Drepung* and *Sera*, also in the fifteenth century. The buildings of Ganden, a vast white city covering an entire hill, were reduced by the Chinese to a heap of ruins (photograph displayed at Dharamsala).

Drepung was founded in 1416. Filled beyond its capacity from the outset, it grew continuously until it reached the number of 7,700 monks. This represented only the resident monks, but for great ceremonies, there might have been about 10,000. This makes it without doubt the largest monastery in the world.[30]

Like Ganden, it has two colleges. *Loseling* (the one in which I was invited to stay), whose population in India rose to 6,000 monks, then had 534,265 of them under the age of 18 (it is easy to imagine their financial difficulties). *Gomang* has about 300 monks; it seems also to have less vitality.

It was the first Dalai Lama, another disciple of Tsong-kha-pa, who founded the monastery of *Tashi Lhunpo* (the seat of the Panchen Lama), which has also been revived in Karnataka, at Bylakuppe. In Tibet Drepung, unusually, was saved by an old monk who, through sheer audacity, prevented the Chinese from destroying it. However, most of the monks were forced into labour gangs or died of starvation.

Anyone who is interested in the Tibetan lifestyle in a Gelugpa monastery of high intellectual repute can read the account given of it by their former abbot, Khensur Pema Gyaltsen, in the Loseling college magazine, *Dreloma* (N° VIII, June 1982). The same magazine (N° VII, 1981, pp. 33–34) provides the most specific information on their current programme of studies and their liturgical feasts. We cannot go into these details, which have the advantage of describing the current situation. In 1981 (N° VI), Loseling had 15 classes, 230 studying, and the number is given of those who passed examinations in the higher grades in this "monastic university".

As in the case of Ganden, each college of Drepung has its own temple or prayer-hall, as well as a central temple where both colleges often meet at once. In these assemblies, a rigorous order of precedence holds good. At the top are the abbots, the former abbots, the *trulkus* (reincarnations), the *Geshes* (masters in "theology"), then the students according to age. Every Tibetan temple is a work of art as regards the architecture, the vivid colours in which it is decorated, the statues of the Buddha and the divinities, the cultic offerings. One can easily understand how so many Westerners fall under its spell. Besides, it awakens deep emotions to see 500 or 600 red-robed monks with shaven heads, sitting in the lotus positions in orderly rows, chanting invocations and sacred texts, to the sound of the most varied musical instruments, often magnificently resonant! The Tibetan liturgy is amongst the most fascinating that exist.

Compared with Ganden, Drepung, at least in its *Loseling* college, appeared more outstanding for its intellectual level. The monks there readily refer to it by the term of university. Even without being able to draw a parallel between their teaching and the breadth of choice in the faculties of a Western university, they at least deserve that of a monastic university, all the courses being directed to the fullest possible knowledge of Buddhist philosophy and Tibetan culture. However, such subjects as mathematics, Hindi and English have evidently been added to the curriculum. Their printing press is well equipped, the content of their magazine, *Dreloma,* is interesting. There is real culture among the best of them. It was at Loseling that I was able to acquire, in a very few days, the maximum information on their monastic life and history, as also on their spirituality. As regards the latter, I had the privilege of a long conversation, by way of questions and answers, with one of their major superiors, *Khensur Pema Gyaltsen,* a monk of great age and of a delicate benevolence, the abbot of Loseling for several terms in Tibet (the abbots are elected for six years). In Assam, he was appointed to the assembly of all the exiled monks and remains at the head of their monastic universtiy.[31] Part of that conversation was published, a short time later, in the context of a more general account.[32]

The most beautiful aspect of my stay is undoubtedly the fact that having given me so much, the administrators of Loseling, who had welcomed me so warmly, apologised for not having been able to do better.

Sera

I travelled there via Bangalore, Mysore and Hunsur. Further to the West lies the *Settlement of Bylakuppe,* already visited, but all too rapidly, in 1979.[33]

Founded in 1419 by a disciple of Tsong-kha-pa, the monastery of Sera reached, in Tibet, the total of 7,000 monks. Like both Ganden and Drepung, it divided its members into two colleges, which exist side by side in total agreement: *Sera-jé* and *Sera-mé.* When they gather in the principal prayer-hall, as frequently happens, for shared ceremonies, they are not segregated by college, but the students are assembled by classes.

After exile in 1959, the *Settlement of Bylakuppe* was the first to be established in South India. In 1970, a group of 300 masters and students began to organize themselves with a view to the rebirth of their ancient monastic tradition. The Indian government gave them 200 acres of land, and, after seven years spent clearing the jungle and constructing buildings, the monastery was ready to resume its regular life with two colleges. *Sera-jé* alone, the college where I was expected, must exceed 400 monks by the present time.

All showed themselves very accommodating; although few spoke English, they showed their heart, their radiant kindness, their willingness to oblige. They gave me what may well have been the best room, even though they were full to capacity. In fact the monk occupying the highest grade of the Gelugpa Order, *Ling Rinpoche*, "Senior Tutor" to the Dalai Lama and instructor and guide of his youth, was actually giving in this place a series of formal teachings with which he intended to bring his career to a close. Venerable old man though he was, and of a marvellous goodness, he was gifted with a steadiness of voice which enables him to bring off this feat, consisting as it does of his reading, by himself, a very long commentary for hours at a time, over a period of five weeks. His reputation had drawn to him an impressive audience of 1,600 red-robed monks from all over India. They all came to sit, in regular rows, in the vast space of the college temple but, being so numerous, the students of Sera were squeezed into every nook and cranny, under the porch and on the stairs. Pious laypeople, including untaught but deeply devout women, completed the assembled company.

Tibetan kindness being what it is, time was made to give me a personal interview with Ling Rinpoche, the abbot of the monastery and two other important lamas whom I had previously met in the South of France and at Ulverston (England). Not only was my welcome a friendly one, but appreciation was shown for my special capacity as a Christian monk, beginner at dialogue though I was. I must stress this: it is not only we who desire such meetings. The Tibetan lamas have set their hearts on it as much as we ourselves and, when time for it can be found, the conversation is of a properly monastic character and touches a deep level in our two spiritual paths. At Bylakuppe, very good relations are enjoyed with the Sisters of the *Apostolic Carmel*, their neighbours, who run a school at Kushalnagar.

When one considers that, 25 years ago, Bylakuppe was no more than a modest village and that at the present moment it numbers more than 12,000 Tibetans, when one sees this region dominated by two monastic colleges where almost a thousand monks work and pray,[34] one cannot do other than admire the work that has been accomplished.

Tantric College

Time was lacking for me to visit, when I had wished to do so, another Gelugpa institution which, already in Tibet, was already the object of great veneration. It is there, I have often been told, that the most authentic religious life, as also (leaving aside the austerities of the hermits) the most demanding, was to be found. If one sets out southwards from Hunsur, one comes to this *Tantric College* in the neighbourhood of *Gurpura*. There are about 200 monks there at the present time. An austere life, surrounded by the strictest rules: sleeping position, a rising hour at 3.00 a.m., a prohibition against being out of the monastic habit, riding bicycles, etc. This *Lower Tantric College* has a foundation of about fifteen members at *McLeod Ganj*, close to the Dalai Lama, who holds them in great esteem. As to the *Higher Tantric College*, their monastery is at Bomdila (Aruṇāchal Pradesh) and numbers 300 monks. Here (at McLeod Ganj), after a very early rising, they hold a service in their temple which lasts until 6 a.m. During the day, they go out to perform *pūjās* in private homes. On their return, they do the same in the monastery. They spend hours in meditation alone: the total period spent daily in prayer is about ten hours. This makes me sceptical when certain Westerners claim that Buddhism is not a religion. As for those descriptions, "upper" and "lower", we should not be misled. These have nothing to do with superiority in terms of the value of their doctrine or observances; they are solely an indication of locality. In Tibet, the *Higher College (Gyu-tö, Ramoche)* was located directly to the North of Lhasa, the *Lower (Gyu-me)* further South.[35] Traditionally, the Tantric College admitted only those who had achieved the rank of *geshe* but, at the present time, it accepts also young *trulkus* in formation from the age of twelve upwards.

Finally, there is, close to the *Tantric College*, another (non-tantric) monastery which I have seen referred to as either *Dzhongkar Chöde Monastery* or *Zongchö Dratsang Monastery* (*dratsang* = college). There are enacted traditional religious dances such as those of the Karmapa at Rumtek (Sikkim). These are performed exclusively by monks, and are particularly extended on the 29th day of the last Tibetan month, two days before their New Year (*Losar*). This monastery, which has about 50 monks, is in the Camp itself, at Nº 3 of the Gurpura *Settlement*.

By way of a conclusion: The fact of having stayed, for a few days only but thoroughly well filled, in each of the three principal monasteries of Tibet, has, thanks to the welcome of the monks and the information which they supplied, considerably added to my knowledge of their life and their spirituality. Wherever I went, I encountered only kindness and openness to dialogue. It is high time that our respective religions came closer, for our mutual encouragement and the benefit of our shared humanity. To take the Tibetan standpoint, it is quite clear that it is the revival of their ancient monasteries in their country of exile that alone can save their culture and their ancestral traditions for the future. Such a people cannot be allowed to disappear.

RETURN TO NEPAL

I then returned to Nepal for ten days, staying, as in 1980, on the hill of *Kopan*, about 5 miles from Kathmandu. Of the series of Tibetan centres directed by Lama Zopa Rinpoche and Lama Thubten Yeshe, this is the principal one, and I was welcomed as an old friend. I have described this monastery in the course of my first journey,[36] and all that I said then was reinforced on this occasion. I noticed the discreet behaviour and the devotion of the Westerners, young men and girls, who were making their *Tara retreat*. This is a female divinity, symbol of compassion, who is invoked for aid in difficulties and whose cult and attributes recall for Christians many features of Our Lady, even as to her litanies. I was given the opportunity for conversation with two *geshes* who lived on site and had responsibility for the education of the young monks (about 83 at Kopan): learned monks, but also modest and open-minded.

In the town, *Kathmandu*, I was invited to give two addresses to an audience of about a dozen, mostly Westerners who were Buddhist sympathisers. This was a real doctrinal comparison, and almost all the questions raised touched on sore points, but I love and appreciate this kind of serious encounter. While making plain my sympathy for Buddhism, I took the opportunity to offer a reminder of the fundamental truths of our faith and the riches of our tradition: the history of Catholic religious Orders, references to our great mystics and spiritual authors.

It goes without saying that I paid a visit to the Jesuits at

Kathmandu. Strictly speaking, their principal high school is in the Jawalakhel district, in the neighbouring town of *Patan*. When it came out that I was a Trappist and interested in the Tibetans, a Father with a big beard and the build of St. Nicholas led me to the *Settlement* close at hand, where he taught English to the children of the refugees. He took me to see their carpet workshop, and there were smiles and greetings wherever he passed. My arrival brought back to the foreground the idea of a monastic foundation in Nepal. In fact, not only the Jesuits but the Sisters and the Church as such long ardently for the presence of a Christian monastery in these regions, which are so marked by the influence of Buddhism and where the inhabitants have never seen Christian monks. Everyone knew how difficult it was for foreigners to obtain visas for more than six months in the northern regions of India (northern Punjab, the neighbourhood of Dharamsala, the district of Darjeeling and Kalimpong), let alone Nepal, but the American Fathers had spared themselves no pains in providing me with all the information I would need. All missionaries in India, particularly the ones I met, have stressed the necessity of a monastic foundation in these parts. May this dream soon become a reality!

Patna – Rājgir – Amritsar – Bangalore

The Catholic Church in Nepal comes under the jurisdiction of the bishop of *Patna*, whom I had arranged to visit. He happened to be one of my former pupils, from the Juniorate at Ranchi. Even though a good many things had been arranged with Father Miller of Patan (Kathmandu), Mgr. Benedict Osta added his own full agreement. He proved to be the most obliging of men when it came to showing me the great town of Patna and its environs. I had worked for years on a thesis which should have borne the title: "*Chandragupta Maurya* and contacts between India and the West".[37] Now it is here, on the edge of the most recent town, that the ancient *Pātaliputra*, with its pillars, column-shafts and palings (partly eroded by the waters of the Ganges, but of which more than a few beams survive), is located; I took a walk above it. I would never have imagined, around 1968, that one day I would actually be inside this *Mauryan compound*. The archaeological museum of the town is very well stocked, particularly with statues of Hindu divinities. I was shown a bridge of over three miles which is considered the longest in the world over a river (the Ganges here). I visited a mission-post, near the sacred hill of *Rājgir*, where Shakyamuni meditated before and after his enlightenment. At its foot there is a Buddhist temple where a really charming Japanese monk of the Order of Nichiren showed himself highly desirous of contacts between religions.[38] In the neighbourhood of *Bihār-Shariff*, there are Hindus, Muslims, Jains, but very few Christians, due in part to a shortage of staff on the mission. The great majority of priests and Sisters in the northern dioceses come from Kerala. They are excellent, with a strong and generous Christian tradition.

This was brought home to me again at *Amritsar*, where I was edified once more by the sight of the admirable Golden Temple, which is the heart of the Sikh religion. Where the Fathers of *Saint Francis' School* are concerned, the Capuchins have given way to the diocesan clergy. Since about 1980, a *Minor Seminary*, for students of 17 years and upwards, has been established. There are 32 of them at the present time, from three dioceses. The outlook is simultaneously very spiritual and open. In the course of my journey, particularly at Patna, I encountered once more my former companions from Shembaganur and Ranchi. It was from *Bangalore* that I made my visit to the monastery of Sera. I took advantage of my stay in that great city to make the acquaintance of the *Bible Society of India*. This is an ecumenical enterprise with ambitious plans, since it is succeeding in publishing the Holy Scriptures in all the Indian languages, a good hundred in all. They were able at once to provide me with a *Bible* in Tibetan. This is the work of a pastor, the late Reverend *Phuntsog*, one of the second generation of Christians in his family. His work being less than completely satisfactory, a new translation is in hand.

The temperature in India is very pleasant at this time of year. In every one of the regions through which I travelled (Bombay, Bangalore, Madras, Calcutta, Patna, Amritsar), it fluctuated between 16 and 21 degrees at 10 a.m. It is quite different in *the foothills of the Himalayas*, whether in Nepal or at Dharamsala. Although the sun shines all day, it is cold, particularly at night, and there is no heating. Everyone manages as best he can by working, where possible, in the sun, and with blankets at night.

DHARAMSALA AND HIMĀCHAL PRADESH (1983)

> Master, where do you live?
> Come and see.
> *(John 1.38–39)*

Settling in and companions

It was on 7 February 1983 that I arrived at *Dharamsala*, in the Indian State of Himāchal Pradesh, a six-hour bus journey from Amritsar. The director of the Library was away, but I was given one of the best rooms. It is possible to take advantage of a side-room close at hand to cook for oneself, an arrangement of which I did not make use, preferring the inexpensive canteen. The first person I met was a Peruvian who, on the completion of his studies in Louvain, had visited Scourmont and asked me for information on Buddhism. I recommended Dharamsala, without expecting to see him there. He was a graduate in Economic Sciences but was interested above all in Eastern religions. We fell into the habit of talking in Spanish, which confirmed for me the usefulness of my visit to Spain. He was an agreeable companion; we visited together most of the places I shall mention. We were quite often accompanied by a Dutch lady who had been studying Tibetan for four months, with a good teacher who had himself published a manual. This lady had been to *Ladakh* the previous May and gave me information about this region, where ancient monasteries had maintained their traditional way of life. Their culture has remained Tibetan.

In the course of my first days there, I wrote an *Introduction to Buddhist monasticism*, as a follow-up to an address I had given the previous year at La Pierre-qui-Vire Abbey on *The life of monks in Tibet*.[39] Then, while the impressions of my visit to Ganden, Drepung and Sera were still fresh, I wrote a report on *The Tibetan monasteries in Karnataka*.[40] The surroundings of the Library had changed, in so far as the buildings had visibly grown up, some most conspicuously so: for example, their new temple, the interior decoration of which was now complete, and a vast edifice which is, in short, their Chamber of Deputies. This is in fact the seat of the Tibetan Government-in-exile. Their national festival took place on 10 March; on this date they celebrate the anniversary of the rising against the Chinese Communists at Lhasa in 1959. As in 1980, I was able to take part in a very dignified rally, the occasion of a long speech on the part of the Dalai Lama. He presided also over the religious ceremonies, such as the initiation of Avalokiteśvara, before a mixed crowd, at the McLeod Ganj temple opposite his residence. According to information given me, a significant number of his audience had come from Tibet. They were on pilgrimage to the sacred places of Buddhism in India. There were also to be seen quite a number of Bhutanese children who were to study at the *Tibetan Children's Village* at Bylakuppe.

The weather, which at first had been very cold, had gradually become milder. Spring arrived over the first days of March, with the beauty of the new green on the hills, the fields of mustard with its yellow flowers, the moist rice fields, the plantations of maize and the peach-trees with their pink blossom; later the cherry trees would be covered with masses of white blossoms.

Sherab Ling – Bīr Settlement

In order to know their monasteries better and increase the opportunities for dialogue, I went to *Sherab Ling*. I have already described this centre, for it was in these regions that I had my first contacts with *Tibetan nuns*. It would be as well to refer to what we wrote about it then.[41] A few days later, a bus brought us in an hour and a half to the holy hill of *Tilokpur*, to the West of Dharamsala, on the road to Pathāncot. We were to spend 24 hours there, in a monastery of nuns of the Karma Kagyu Order. Of this visit also, I have given an account already.[42] It was 8 March 1983.

At *Sherab Ling*, we were present to see a colourful spectacle: the solemn reception, one fine morning, of a famous Master from Bhutan. He was a Nyingmapa monk named *Dilgo Khyentse Rinpoche*. The monks on the roof, clad in their finest attire, were wearing the marvellous crested yellow headdresses, the shape of which is reminiscent of Mycenaean helmets, and they welcomed this notable guest with trumpets and flutes. An interview was arranged for me the following day with his grandson, a sixteen-year-old monk who seemed older: *Rabjam Rinpoche*, whom I would see again, in 1994, at the head of a great monastery at Bodnath (Nepal). We compared the respective religions and their forms of monastic life, and he gave me with information on the presence of the Nyingmapa in Bhutan and in the Dordogne.

From there, we went on to visit the *Settlement of Bīr*, which numbers 3,000 Tibetans and six monasteries of three different Orders (Nyingmapa, Kagyupa and Sakyapa). We were particularly moved to witness a long *pūjā* presided over by a little *trulku* aged four. Although I have seen not a few Tibetan liturgies in various countries, it was here that we had the feeling that we were living, for an hour, as they doubtless used to do in Tibet. All this took place in the school premises, as the permanent monastery buildings were still incomplete. At the request of the inhabitants, who had paid for this to take place, there were held over twenty days, continuous prayers and ceremonies, from the early morning until eleven in the evening, with only short intervals for meals. All the monks in the neighbourhood would take part, and this has been taking place since 1966. What is striking is that these proceedings are not at all the exclusive affair of the clergy, or *sangha*. In these classroom-blocks-turned-chapels, pious laypeople crowd round the monks and are packed on the veranda, sitting in prayer, men and women of all ages, from the aged down to the smallest children. The future Nyingmapa temple, all vivid colours and rich in symbols, will be one of the most fascinating in the region.

It is in these monastic surroundings, at Tilokpur, that we were able to enter into a most illuminating dialogue with one of the best masters of philosophy in Tibetan Buddhism. Belonging to the Kagyupa lineage, *Khenpo Tsultrim Gyamtso* possesses simultaneously a very keen intelligence and a deep spiritual awareness. His teachings have a lasting effect upon minds and hearts. He is a simple man, radiant with goodness. As Tai Situ Rinpoche, he draws all to himself. He is known in the West for an excellent short work on *Vacuity*,[43] and is in great demand for conferences in our countries (France, Belgium).

Catholic Presence

On my first Sunday I said Mass, as in 1980, in the camp chapel of the Indian army, at *Yol Camp*. The Chaplain was new to me but, like his predecessor, a Carmelite from Kerala. On the subsequent weekends, it was thought to be more convenient for me to come to the Sisters who have a flourishing school at *Sidhpur* (or *Sidhbari*). These are the Sisters of Charity of Jesus and Mary, better known at home as the *Sisters of Charity of Ghent*, and were invited here by the military families. At present they have 850 pupils, both girls and boys, who arrive in batches by special bus every morning. Their boarders are from well-to-do families, the majority from the Punjab, and always gave me a warm welcome. I became aware that most of them have travelled a good deal and are well acquainted with the the sacred cities of India; almost all are Hindus or Sikhs. There are about thirty Tibetan children, well integrated with the rest, at this *Sacred Heart High School*. I said Mass in the Sisters' Chapel on Saturday evenings and Sunday mornings. Their convent is in the valley, which is littered here and there with boulders.

At a Hindu ashram

On one occasion, they drew my attention to the presence, in their neighbourhood, of an important centre of Hindu monastic life, so I accompanied several of them to *Tapovan*, on the summit of a hill in Sidhbari. This is the residence of a famous master: *Swāmi Chinmāyānanda*, founder of the great ashram of *Powai*, on the outskirts of Bombay, which we visited with the group of Italian monks in 1979.[44] At *Tapovan*, the buildings are vast, bright and modern and can easily accommodate guests. A timetable is followed which allows for the study of the *Upanishads*, the *Gītā* and also for the carrying out of *pūjās* and meditations in the Shaivite tradition of the South. The *Swāmi* welcomed us cordially. He has an impetuous, violent, ultra-earnest temperament – Saint Paul must have been a man of the same stamp – not known to be given to tactfulness towards Christianity. However, he spoke with such sincerity about the deep unity of religions that I could find no fault with him. His reputation is considerable. In the morning of that same Sunday, 2,500 people from all over the world had come to be present at the "reception of the idols" for their future temple. The esplanade is already dominated by a colossal statue of the monkey-god Hanumān. As for the architecture, what was proposed was a faithfulness to the most ancient techniques used in Dravidian temples. We saw the architects and their plans: Rāma and Sītā were to be represented, for the Rāmāyaṇa is held in great honour here.

A dash of climatic information

By way of a reminder – the *Dharamsala* market, also known as *Kotwali*, is at 4,550 feet, and *McLeod Ganj*, about 5½ miles up by road, is at 5,800 feet; the *Library* is halfway between them. This makes for a marked difference in climate. At the summit, it is bitterly cold in winter; the spring, on the other hand, is very pleasant. In a few days more the tourists, including some ragged and outlandish-looking hippies, would start pouring in. Twenty-five years ago, there was hardly as much as a hamlet here; it consisted simply of some covered stalls. It had become a village with a good many Tibetan merchants. My companions said jokingly that Westerners dream of dressing in Tibetan robes, whereas the young Tibetan women follow the Western fashions.

I had for a long while been falling behind in my letter-writing, some of my correspondents having been waiting for several months for a reply. I therefore set aside the end of February and the beginning of March for writing a great many letters. On 19 March, there was a violent storm accompanied by hail; I had never seen hailstones come down with such force and in such quantities; the whole neighbourhood was covered with them, and the storm began again in the evening.

Tashi Jong and its ritual dances

On 21 March I travelled with my Peruvian companion and a Dutch lady to stay for five days at *Tashi Jong*, a bus journey of about an hour and a half from Dharamsala. We had been planning this for weeks. *Tashi Jong* is a Tibetan monastery of the *Drukpa Kagyu* Order. Its members are particularly numerous in Bhutan (in Tibetan, the word for Bhutanese is *drukpa*, which means "dragon"). Only a short while earlier, 4,000 people from every country had come to take part in the enthronement of the little *Kamtrul Rinpoche*, the ninth of this name; having been born on 6 December 1980, he was just over two years old. Being the head of this monastery, and occupying pride of place in the hierarchy of his Order, this child was, accordingly, the object of great veneration, as were all the "reincarnations" of the same age amongst the Sakyapa of Bīr, or the seven-year-old one at Tsopema. In every one of them, it was impossible not to see a wisdom and a seriousness well beyond their age. The young Kamtrul behaved admirably during the ceremonies. He laid his little hands with the utmost dignity on the heads of those who prostrated before him. He would of course have masters *(tutors)* to supervise his doctrinal education but, from the day he was recognized, he was considered to be the first Kamtrul returned to be amongst his people. The belief in reincarnation can seem unacceptable to us, but we here encountered one of its exceptional cases. Besides, the search for the *trulku*, later known as *Rinpoche*, is governed by the most detailed instructions: directions from his predecessor, a letter from the head of the relevant lineage, astrological data, on-site investigations, recognition by the child of objects which had belonged to the deceased. We made several visits to this captivating child, but as for dialogue, we had this of course *with other partners*. On each occasion we were welcomed with cordiality and kindness. Chogyal Rinpoche explained to us the symbolism of the traditional dances at which we were present over the following days. The essentials are described in a brochure titled: *Garcham – the Celebration of Padmasambhava's Birth*. Dorzong Rinpoche gave us information on the history of the monastery and of the *Settlement* associated with it. Chentse Rinpoche, eager for contacts with Christian monks, described the life in their community and his own vocation. They do not receive a real philosophical grounding, due to a temporary lack of teachers, but it is hoped that these will be acquired in the future. They have already put up, close to the esplanade in front of the temple, the first building of their *chedra*, or school of dialectics.

Our principal reason for coming here was to be present at the *ritual dances* which go back to the Nyingmapa and celebrate the birth of *Padmasambhava*. Their philosophical and religious content is very rich, reproducing in a scenic manner an arrangement of the fundamental themes of their beliefs, and therefore contemporaneous with the beginnings of Buddhism in Tibet (seventh century), or even earlier. These dances lasted for four days, that on the first being a general repetition *(rehearsal)* with neither costumes nor masks. Each of the following three days had its own character: the costumes and masks were suited to the sentiments to be expressed, to the mythical or "magical" episodes to be emphasised. Anyone who has seen Tibetan dances, if only in films, will already have some idea of the magnificence of this display. Unless I am mistaken, it is only at Rumtek, in Sikkim, or at

Zongchö Dratsang Monastery at Gurpura (near Hunsur), that one can find, once a year, something like these dances with a rhythm usually slow in character but occasionally enlivened by leaps and pirouettes of astonishing vigour. All the actors are monks, usually rather young. The ornaments, for example on the hats, and the rich variety of the colours of the robes make these costumes works of art, while the masks, whether peaceable or terrible, give a mystical dimension to the dancers who wear them. All this takes place in the open air, on the temple esplanade, the actors and the dignitaries of the monastery being sheltered by a tent which is re-erected each morning as a protection against sun or rain. There were hundreds of spectators: Tibetans from the *Settlement* (300 refugees), Western observers attracted by *vajrayāna* Buddhism or photographers on a quest for displays of any kind. It should be stressed that, for believers, it is simply not a matter of a theatrical show. The parallel comes to mind of the "Mysteries" performed during the Middle Ages in cathedral porches. These same monks who dance for so many hours, and their brothers in the community, are regularly woken at 4 a.m. and pass almost all the free time in the day in long *pūjās* with deep resonances. These days constitute both mediaeval theatre and monastic liturgy.

We had guessed all this simply on the basis of hearsay, but to see it for ourselves was a completely different matter, so we were grateful to a little Tibetan girl of fourteen, a boarder with the Sisters of Sidhpur. It was she who urged us to go, giving us precise information on the feasts. Her parents live at Tashi Jong, where their house overlooks the *Settlement* and where we were treated with the greatest hospitality.

On the hill in that area live Tibetan *yogis,* known by the name of *Njaldorpa.* Strictly speaking, they are not monks. They dress in white, with a shawl over their shoulders, with a plait of hair rolled up on their head and another knot of it higher up. The ones we met live in the neighbourhood of the monastery, with which they have many ties. Their bearing is dignified, austere and impressive. These practitioners of *Tantra* live an eremitical life, followers of the direct way. The opportunity did not arise for any conversation with them.

Rewālsar: its monasteries and hermits

From there we had a long journey. Travelling via Mandi, it takes many hours by bus to reach *Rewālsar*. The Tibetans call this holy place *Tsopema*. According to tradition, *Guru Rinpoche* was born miraculously from a lotus, hence his name *Padmasambhava*. He was to have been burnt alive by a Hindu Rajah, incensed by the relationship which the ascetic had with his daughter, but he emerged in the middle of the lake which lay before us, which subsequently became a place of pilgrimage, for the whole of the Tibetan Buddhist tradition considers Guru Rinpoche as its original founder, this being particularly evident in the oldest monastic schools: Nyingmapa and Kagyupa. Surrounding the lake, and on a modest scale, were various temples of these Orders and we visited these, but there were also Hindu sanctuaries to Shiva and Durga, and a Sikh temple *(Gurdwara)* with a white dome and a welcoming guest house, where we heard the evening music, with sacred chants like those employed at Amritsar.

The 26th and 27th were set aside for *Tsopema*. We twice climbed the very steep hill with its innumerable, irregularly-cut steps, finding ourselves out of breath well before reaching the summit, which is the home of a *Drukpa Kagyu* master, by the name of *Lama Wang-dor*; his disciples, both monks and nuns, and a few Western followers, are, like himself, hermits living in caves in the side of the mountain. Once a month, they meet for a day of prayer in common, and we had the opportunity of being present. This was a *pūjā* which lasted almost all day, in the Lama's primitive cave transformed into a rocky *gonpa*. Poorly, even shabbily, dressed, lacking frescos and *thankas*, they had nevertheless the bearing of genuine men and women of prayer, of authentically spiritual people. One of them, a Canadian with emaciated features, welcomed me to his cave while at the same time unfolding the depths of *Dzogchen*. What was totally unexpected, and caused us real surprise was to discover, at the back of a rocky cavity, reached only by stooping very low and seen by the light of a feeble lamp, an amazing statue of *Guru Rinpoche*, tall, broad and majestic, completely covered with gold leaf and backed against a rock with which it formed a perfect whole; the face of the great founder was illuminated by the light from a window cut into the rock opposite it. The ascent of the hill takes two hours, especially if one continues upwards, past the hermits' caves to the real summit, where there is a little temple to Durga and one looks out over a vast landscape of distant mountains, as far as the eye can see.

On reaching the lakeside once more, we admired an ancient statue of Guru Rinpoche and the frescos of the *Nyingmapa* temple. We then accepted the invitation of a monk who was supervising the construction of a monastic college for the *Drukpa Kagyu*. Finally, we went to see the *Drigung Kagyu*: their convent was a red block of recent construction, which in normal circumstances would house about fifty religious (monks and nuns) and we called on a little "abbot" of seven years. A young monk provided information on their "sect"; little known in the West, it nevertheless has monasteries in both India and Ladakh. Their principal centre is at Almora (Uttar Pradesh).

The return journey, despite the sunshine and the beautiful scenery was pretty uncomfortable. It was actually the day of the popular Hindu festival of *Holi* (Spring festival). In all the towns and localities there were bands of fanatics wandering round with pails of water and containers of green, violet, yellow and red paint, with which they sprinkled passers by full in the face and on their clothing. As a result, we were obliged to keep the windows of the bus completely shut for fear of being treated, in every hamlet, to a plentiful shower and to finding oneself covered in assorted colours like clowns.

An educational paradigm: the Tibetan Children's Village

On 29 March we climbed beyond McLeod Ganj to the *Tibetan Children's Village*, which I had visited in 1980.[45] My companions admired the workshops in which Tibetan children (both boys and girls) learn the art of carpet-work in the most varied designs, the painting of *thankas*, the tailor's trade, even the making of masks. Our plan, in the first place, was to pay a visit to the Dalai Lama's younger sister, *Mrs. Pema Gyalpo*, who is overall head of this organization. She is responsible for the Village for Tibetan children. The sides of the hill are covered by these buildings: children's houses, school buildings, playing fields. All these save from abandonment the "half-orphans" whose parents are incapable of looking after them, and guarantees them a good education. There were 1,338 at McLeod Ganj; an institution of the same kind in

Ladakh was intended to take 400, plus 1,300 for whom *sponsors* were to be found. At Bylakuppe, there were 250, plus 150 who had come from Bhutan, and whom we had seen lodging close to the *Library* around the New Year. Mrs. Pema Gyalpo is remarkable for her concern for these young people, but equally so for her intelligent views on the manner of their education and her concern to prepare a future for them that is both realistic and faithful to the cultural traditions of their people. I had been sent to her by Cardinal Picachy of Calcutta; they had known each other for a long while. That acquaintance goes back to the time when Father Picachy, Prefect of *Saint Xavier's*, used to preach retreats at Darjeeling; the sister of His Holiness the Dalai Lama was then a young boarding-pupil at *Loreto Convent*.

Holy Week

I presided over the ceremonies at Yol military camp, whilst lodging with the Sisters of Sidhpur. The faithful numbered more than a hundred, almost all being soldiers or officers with their families. The chants and the Stations of the Cross were sung and said in Hindi, but very many military families were originally from Kerala.

A provisional balance-sheet

It was by now almost three months since I left Brussels and, halfway through my stay in India, a simple balance-sheet seemed to be called for. I had had, up to that time, little time to spare for studying Tibetan but, on the other hand, I had taken care, more so than in 1980, to profit from opportunities for dialogue and to visit as many monasteries as possible, this being the objective of D.I.M. In Karnataka, these were the great monasteries of Tibet, belonging to the *Gelugpa* Order. I saw the *Sakyapa* at Bir, different "sects" of the *Kagyu* at Sherab Ling (*Karma Kagyu*), at Tashi Jong (*Drukpa*) and at Tsopema (*Drukpa* and *Drigung*), the *Nyingmapa* (their dances) at Tashi Jong, Bir and Tsopema. All this gave me an introduction to the less classical groups, hardly known in the West. We even planned to go, beyond Simla, to a monastery of the *Bön-po*, a "magic" religion or path, often regarded with suspicion, but whose regularity of observance and intensity of interior life was praised by a very serious Polish girl who had a scholarship at Oxford.

More than three years earlier, I had had the benefit of meetings with my brethren in Calcutta, and with the Jesuits of Kathmandu and Godavari. I had also had the joy of coming to know Patna, its archaeological sites, a little of its diocese and the pilgrimage to Rājgir. I was almost forgetting *the nuns*, about whom I would put something in writing a little later, particularly on their *Nunnery* at Tilokpur and on two days spent at McLeod Ganj.

Dharamsala, a centre for dialogue

I received news of the death of *Monsignor Lamotte*, to whom I owed a great deal. It was he who had given me my first lessons in Sanskrit, introduced me to Buddhism and took happiness in my dedicating myself to the Tibetans. He helped me in the drawing up of my thesis and I found him both teacher and father.

A letter reported that the weather in Belgium was very cold and wet. It was the same in North India. This would damage the harvest and be to the detriment of the poor. From a certain vantage point, this weather was beneficial for those studying or teaching for, under normal conditions, the heat was crushing during the months before the monsoon. In our hills, at somewhere around 4,900 feet, the climate is temperate, and we had some fine, sunny days in May.

While not travelling as much as in February and March, I did notably make, in April, the acquaintance of interesting persons and institutions in our immediate vicinity. First of all, I had the opportunity of having a conversation with a Tibetan who had, in childhood, been converted to Christianity as a result of an extraordinary grace. He persevered in his faith despite his isolation.

I had already visited in 1980[46] the *Nunnery* of *McLeod Ganj*, where the Buddhist nuns, about fifty of them, lived their lives of prayer in great poverty. They have the devotion and the smiles of our own contemplatives. Chance brought me into contact with two Western women, an Australian and a New Zealander who, despite having been trained by Tibetan lamas, had gone to *Taiwan* with a view to receiving full ordination, which brought with it the obligation of keeping a great number of vows.[47]

In 1981, the American commission of Monastic Interreligious Dialogue (N.A.B.E.W.D.) had sent an invitation to the Dalai Lama: that he should send one of his monks to stay in the Benedictine Abbeys of the United States.[48] A young monk aged thirty was chosen: *Kunchok Sithar*; over a period of four months he stayed in six abbeys, not counting the convents to which he paid afternoon visits. The outcome was entirely positive, and the accounts he gave of his stays gave great satisfaction, while he himself derived great edification from the experience. On his return to India, he published a good article in the *Tibetan Review*. As he was lodging a mere half-hour's distance from us, we spent two enjoyable hours of conversation on our monastic Orders. He is a well-balanced and kindly young monk, who deservedly meets with sympathy.

Having entered the monastery at the age of twenty, he completed ten years of studies at the *School of Dialectics* at McLeod Ganj, a few minutes from the Dalai Lama's residence. Two days later, he acted as our interpreter, for a conversation with the Principal of this School, which is, in short, an Institute of Buddhist philosophy. Another monk also gave us all the information we could desire on the *Higher Institute of Tibetan Studies* at *Sarnath*, affiliated to the University of Vārāṇasī.

On site, at the *Library*, another monk showed us *their sacred books and precious manuscripts* in the department set aside for them. These, together with the collection of statuettes on the first floor, were saved from destruction by the courage of the Tibetans who carried these heavy loads over the Himalayas as they went into exile, under the most distressing conditions.

Not far from where we were staying was the residence of the *Senior Tutor* to the Dalai Lama, *Ling Rinpoche*, whose teachings we had followed at *Sera* during a visit in January,[49] and who gave us an affectionate welcome. He died at Dharamsala on Christmas morning 1983. We had the pleasure of a reunion with *Lama Thubten Yeshe*, who had a retreat centre called *Tushita*, up the hill from McLeod Ganj. He died on 3 March 1984 at Los Angeles, California, where his cremation was a moving ceremony.[50]

I saw once more the tutor I had had in 1980: *Yelo Rinpoche*. He had returned from *Mongolia*, where the Gelugpa monks of Ganden have an important monastery; with another monk he was drawing up the catalogue for the library, which contains some ancient manuscripts. Close to the *Library* stood a new hospital built by the Tibetans: *Delek Hospital*. We visited it one afternoon, and the lady responsible for its administration talked to us about their problems. It is well known, for example, that many Tibetans have succumbed to tuberculosis.

Bön: an unappreciated tradition

The most important visit of all was undoubtedly the one I made to a monastery a good distance away, which belonged to the *Bön* religion. Most accounts of this religion have over a long period represented it in a rather inaccurate and disparaging fashion.[51] It was the religion of Tibet prior to the introduction of Buddhism in the seventh century of our era. It has usually been depicted as a conglomeration of magic rituals. A student from Poland who was preparing a thesis for Oxford University on this subject told me that in her opinion this *Bön* tradition merited an objective examination. She added that I would find a fervent monastery, and I found this to be the case. I set out for the region of Solan, to the south of Simla. At *Dolanji*, there is a Tibetan *Settlement* of 400 persons in the valley. The temple and monastery buildings are on the hill. At first sight, one would imagine oneself in Buddhist surroundings, the monks being clothed in the same red robes, although it might be the Buddhists who, in Tibet, imitated the *Bönpo*. In any case, there has been a reciprocal influence which persists to our own days. Their ceremonies are moving. There were 108 monks, more than half of whom were of school age; a group of 36 were pursuing studies at the School of Dialectics, to which I was honoured one day with an invitation; a first. Their separation from the world appeared to be greater than that observed in the Buddhist monasteries I had visited. The Father Abbot holds strictly to the regular observance. We both had a great surprise when I arrived: without our realizing it when we arranged this stay, given that I had changed both my Order and name, it turned out that we had known each other for a long time, for *Sangye Tendzin Jongdong* was my companion at Oxford in 1963–1964. It need hardly be said that I received a warm welcome. Being both intelligent and open, he is an invaluable partner in comparative religion.

The return journey (being in any case the shortest route) allowed me to travel via *Chandighar*, a town built by the French architect Le Corbusier. There I met the bishop, Mgr Rego.

Life at Dharamsala

Every year, the Tibetans in India send their representatives to a political *Assembly* of around 200 pesons, who meet in a building adjacent to the *Library*, and deal there with all their problems, including the cultural and religious kind. Monks are to be seen there, including four delegates from Dolanji for the *Bön* religion.

During the month of May I had a companion here in the person of an Italian Father who had just made his retreat as a professor of theology at a seminary and was going to publish a thesis on "Religious Experience and Ideology". We were received together by the Dalai Lama in private. This proved to be an hour of rather complex exchanges on the problems posed by the aforesaid subject and the comparison between Buddhism and Christianity. The Dalai Lama is impressive in his doctrinal steadfastness and in no way carried off into syncretism, while showing an obvious respect for the spiritual path of all the great religions.

During this and the following month, however, it was *the study of Tibetan* that occupied me every day.

One evening, in the open air on the Library lawn, we were shown a series of short films, documentaries of different aspects of Tibetan culture. I was particularly impressed by one of them, showing a liturgical office in the temple of the *Tantric College*, not far from Hunsur,[52] whose monks have an excellent reputation. Although they belong to the *Gelugpa* tradition, it strikes me that the tantric symbolism which they emphasise must contain some borrowing from the *Bön* religion. The hollow, and extremely deep voice of the officiants gives it an ultra-serious, almost sinister atmosphere, but the whole visual aspect is entrancing: the richness of the vivid colours, among which blue can be seen on the reverse side of their "humeral", the picturesque character of the headdress, a kind of black plait rising to a sharp-pointed pyramid above the head, which they wear for part of the ceremony, were all quite dazzling. But the extremely recollected expression on every face brings with it the conviction that here we were dealing with highly interior monks, savagely convinced as it were.

Several days later, a full-length film was shown in the newly-completed extension to the *Library*. It was a high-quality documentary, the work of the B.B.C., covering *the eventful history of Tibet since 1904* – this being the date of the British expedition to Lhasa – up to our own time: the journey made by the second official delegation to Tibet. It used authentic documents: photographs and films taken during missions by the British delegates or military operations, including documentaries made by the

Chinese during their attack, interviews with former foreign residents who had known Tibet when it was free and who praised it, films of great religious "festivals" of an unimagined pomp and splendour. Amongst the recent testimonies, that of Heinrich Harrer was the best. During the second delegation, the emotion and irrepressible enthusiasm of the crowd welcoming the Dalai Lama's envoys was much in evidence. The film was fine and objective, leaving a double impression of enchantment and sadness: such beauty gone with a vanished past.

Though my references to it are few, we were in fact in India, and our little Tibetan "island" is surrounded by little houses in which the people of the country live. My only contacts with them, apart from bus journeys and purchases in shops, is meeting little boys, shrewd and knowing, who live in the poorest conditions. I hardly know how it all began; I must, one morning, have given a biscuit to a little fellow who had hardly anything to eat. The next morning he came with his brother, then his friends came along so, little by little, I acquired several customers. They made a detour on their way back home from their school below to obtain a biscuit. The seven- or eight-year-olds were as proud as Punch to demonstrate that they could write, right there in front of me, all the letters of the Hindi alphabet and all the numbers up to 100 in Arabic numerals. They are both extremely cunning and tirelessly mischievous, real little devils, but behind these amusing meetings, the spectre of the frightening poverty of India is all too visible. The father being away, vanished in Assam, in fact, the sixteen-year-old eldest son described the predicament of the family for me, and it was no laughing matter.

June was warm, as is normal at that time of year, and one was heartily thankful to be living in the hills, away from the soaring temperatures of the Indian plain.

During my interview with the Dalai Lama in February 1980, I had noticed the interpreter, who had few occasions for intervening but did so with tact and competence. As I left, he had told me that His Holiness enjoyed this dialogue and that I would be granted a second audience. In fact, this did not prove possible at the time, but I was warmly welcomed again this year. In the presence of the Dalai Lama, the interpreter maintained an attitude of reserve and dignity towards all visitors. Two days later, I learnt that he was a Rinpoche, the reincarnation of a great personage, and the younger brother of the Dalai Lama. The first meeting was hilarious, for this man who was so polite, almost timid, during audiences, was in fact endowed with an almost violent nature, cracking so many jokes in general company that one wondered if he was capable of seriousness. In point of fact, *Tendzin Chögyal* had worn a monk's robe till the age of thirteen, accompanied his brother into exile during the uprising of 1959 and afterwards carried out all his secondary studies, then going on to his *College,* at *North Point,* Darjeeling. This meant that he had been for nine years a pupil of the Jesuits, and he retained a deep gratitude towards the Belgian and Canadian Fathers, with whom he enjoyed discussing religion. He was an engaging person of deep spirituality, with a high regard for the Catholic Church and was, which in no way detracts from what has already been said, the excellent father of a family. They invited me several times to their home, a quarter of an hour from the *Library,* at *Kashmir Cottage,* the former home of the Dalai Lama's mother. The latter, a very worthy lady, had died in 1981, having admirably brought up her six children; Tendzin Chögyal was the youngest.

My time at Dharamsala came to an end. The first months had been taken up principally with visits to several monasteries and meetings with people responsible for important projects. It was in the later months that I was able to proceed with *the study of Tibetan.* I had an excellent teacher, from a distinguished Lhasa family, Mr. Thonden. Together we looked through the whole of the manual from Plaige (Toulon-sur-Arroux, in Burgundy), of which an English translation exists.

From Delhi to Kathmandu

On 30 June 1983, I left Dharamsala for *Amritsar.* On the following day, I arrived by plane at *Delhi,* where I expected to spend just a few days. I had obtained a permit to return to Nepal for a month to examine the possibilities of a monastic foundation. I preferred to avoid flying, which was expensive, and the trains, which were highly uncomfortable in North India, when I travelled to Kathmandu. The tourist bus recommended to me postponed its departure several times, so I stayed at the Jesuits' theology faculty, *Vidyajyoti, from 1–18 July.* I took advantage of this free time by writing a lecture on *Feminine monasticism in Tibetan Buddhism* and making fresh copies of the notes I took during my course on the Tibetan language. One always learns something on site about the trends in Indian theology and the regionalisation of theological studies. The scholastics being on holiday, the house was quiet. When the time drew near for classes to begin again, the students arrived in large numbers from every corner of India, bringing news of the circumstances of the Church in this vast country.

The journey *from Delhi to Kathmandu* was due to take four days by tourist bus, which offered very little in the way of comfort. This German luxury bus was an old rattletrap with recurring mechanical problems. Having left Delhi behind schedule, we had to run through the following night and had no opportunity of seeing either Agra or Lucknow. We stayed overnight at *Gorakhpur*. On 20 July, at about 7 a.m., there was an accident which could have been more serious. In order to avoid an enormous vehicle which our driver saw too late approaching from ahead, he backed forcefully into the lorry behind us. The windows shattered. The driver escaped with a broken leg, but it took an hour to extricate him, wedged as he was between the steering wheel and his seat. We waited for hours on the road for a replacement bus, ours being fit for nothing but the scrap-heap.

THIRD STAY IN NEPAL (1983)

We stayed at *Bhairawa*, the first Nepalese locality we came to. I was to spend five days at *Kathmandu*, from 22–27 July. As soon as I arrived, I visited a *little Rinpoche*, aged nine, who was soon to return to his monastery, Sera (Bylakuppe), accompanied by his mother and a devoted aide. He struck me as an exceptional child: fine-featured, wise, with a smile that shone with intelligence. After this, I was obliged to busy myself with applications for visas. I had come with the principal aim of speaking to several Jesuits (Father Miller, episcopal vicar, and Father John Locke, a specialist in Nepalese Buddhism).

At the same time, my visit provided the opportunity of going to *Bodnath*, some miles away from Kathmandu. Around the colossal, much-photographed *stūpa* were clustered the monasteries of different Tibetan Orders. I had already visited, in January 1980, the *Gelugpa* monastery, whose monks were originally from one of the great Tibetan monasteries: *Kitong Samten Ling*, close to the

Nepalese border. At Bodnath, there were 68 monks. We were fortunate enough to be given a great deal of information by an accommodating monk, *Thubten Palden.*

What I wanted above all to see again this year was the most beautiful monastery at Bodnath, extensions to which were still under way. It belonged to the *Karma Kagyu* Order, but had friendly relations with the *Nyingmapa*, whose young abbot (aged twenty-three) appreciated their meditation techniques. *Chö-Kyi Nyima Rinpoche* proved to be one of the most likeable lamas I had met, raising questions of his own accord concerning the Pope, our Christian Orders and their rules. When he was travelling through Europe, he was impressed by the great Catholic ceremonies he witnessed at Cologne and Paris.

On a plateau, about a quarter of an hour away, there stood a new monastery intended to house 150 *Nyingmapa* monks, to say nothing of the buildings where passing monks, or those participating in sessions there, would be put up. I would have liked to have seen someone who would, if I was not mistaken, some day be their abbot: *Shechen Rabjam Tulku*, an eighteen-year-old monk with whom I had had a cordial conversation at *Sherab Ling*. He is the grandson of *Dilgo Khyentse Rinpoche*[53] and was at the time staying in *Bhutan* while the work on the monastery was being completed.

On another occasion I went to *Pharping*, a picturesque little market town, roughly eleven miles to the South of Kathmandu. There on a hill, two small *Nyingmapa* monasteries have been established, the higher of these being a place of pilgrimage for the Tibetans, who come to make offering there and have *pūjās* recited for their intentions: evidence of popular devotion and ritualism.[54]

Here the Buddha was born

On 28 July, I went on pilgrimage to *Lumbinī*, the birthplace of the Buddha and an hour's bus journey from Bhairawa. I was able to venerate the place and to visit two monasteries close at hand. One of these was maintained by the *Sakyapa*. Built in 1968, it had *Chö-Kyi Trichen Rinpoche* for abbot and about forty monks (several of whom were away).

The second was rather symbolic: a Nepalese monk trained in Sri Lanka guaranteed the presence of the Small Vehicle at the

Theravāda Temple. Robed in yellow, he was the guardian of a bare sanctuary. What was saddening about Lumbinī was its complete neglect: muddy paths, difficult road access, no construction of any merit except for a pillar of Ashoka, buried in the ground. There was a development project, sponsored by the United Nations, but so far it seemed to exist only on paper.

The Pokhara site

I then went for ten days (29 July to 7 August) to *Pokhara*, recommended to me by several people as a suitable site for establishing a monastery. I stayed at a modest little hotel, a half-hour's walk from a newly-established school run by Sisters. They belong to the *Institute of the Blessed Virgin Mary* founded by Mary Ward (1585–1645) at the beginning of the seventeenth century. Well established in India, they run a secondary school for girls at Kathmandu, the counterpart to *St. Xavier's*. I said Mass every day in their temporary building and learned much from them, as also from *Father Ooki*, a Japanese Jesuit and a zealous and likeable missionary, the parish priest of this young parish. We looked at every aspect of the question, on which I would have to write a report to be considered by a meeting of abbots of the Order. The impression made was a favourable one, on the whole; many positive aspects operated in favour of Pokhara.

Situated at roughly 125 miles to the west of Kathmandu, and connected to the capital by plane, the town had about 55,000 inhabitants, but did not correspond in any way to the image that such a figure suggests to us. It was a series of covered stalls, small shops and modest workrooms, strung out along an inconstant river. Building had been carried out in a haphazard fashion, and the most solid structures were a hospital, a few hotels, the *S.O.S. Tibetan Children* and a parallel establishment for Nepalese children. The population is rather poor but very likeable. The Nepalese are not overburdened with scruples about regulations; they give an easy welcome and are a smiling people.

The locality being very extended, there were plenty of possible sites. Although buildings were very numerous, it would be easy to find a peaceful site for founding a monastery. One would simply have to avoid the areas which attract tourists, since the very name of Pokhara calls up a famous landscape: *the lake,* which is between

At Home with the Lamas

two and two and a half miles long, and, above all, the great mountain. While the plain is no more than 2,625 feet high, on clear days one can see at close quarters, a large part of *the Himalayan chain*, with peaks rising to 23,000 feet (the *Machha-Puchare*) and 26,250 feet (the *Annapūrṇā*). The climate is warmer than that of Kathmandu, which is at 4,265 feet, but Pokhara receives double the rainfall. The monsoon lasts from June to mid-October and, during this period, rain falls every day, and clouds normally hide the mountains. I can safely say that I have only seen brief glimpses of them.

The monasteries at Pokhara

I took care, during my visit, to make contact with the Buddhist monasteries at Pokhara, and the welcome I was given was invariably a very warm one. The monks entered readily into conversation, very happy to talk to a Christian monk. Here is a list of them:

1. *Gurung Gompa*, close to *Ram Ghat*. The lama, who was married, kept watch over the development of this temple, which belongs to the *Nyingmapa* tradition. It is not a Tibetan, but a *Nepalese* foundation. This temple is situated on a hilltop overlooking a bend in the river *Seti*, which widens greatly at this point. They were neighbours to the Sisters in the premises of their temporary school. It is common knowledge that this *Gurung Temple* is eager to promote a renewal of Buddhism in this country, purifying it of many practices or superstitions borrowed from Hinduism. This may be the beginning of a purer religion amongst the Gurungs, who predominate in this province.
2. At the *Tibetan Handicraft Centre*, close to an important crossroads, *China Chok*, there is a *Gelugpa* monastery: *Shang Gaden Chökhor Ling*. It was in the centre of the compound of the *Handicraft Centre* that they had built their monastery, completed a few months earlier. This little red-brick edifice had nothing luxurious about it: it was high time for them to abandon a miserable bamboo shelter and occupy it but this, added to the fact that they had to feed thirteen elderly monks and fifteen young boy-monks, posed serious financial problems for them. This monastery had originated with the Karmapa; it was the fifth Dalai Lama who

incorporated them into the Gelugpa Order. In Tibet it had 500 monks and in fact it came to have more than a thousand. The abbot, whose name was *Chöding Trulkou Jampa Khedrup*, welcomed me in a friendly fashion on several occasions and showed himself highly desirous of contact with Christian monks. By the most extraordinary coincidence I met again here the sister of the monk who was sent to spend four months in the Benedictine abbeys of the United States, *Kunchok Sithar*.[55]

3. The best-situated monastery is undoubtedly the *Manange Gompa*, on a hill to the east of the town. Access to it is by 302 very regular steps, but there is also an alley with a gentle gradient running alongside their grounds. They are isolated there, far from any noise and with a view over the valley. We arrived there in a downpour, towards four in the afternoon. The community were engaged in celebrating a Mahākāla *pūjā*, with great numbers of musical instruments: long horns giving deep notes, trumpets, conches and large drums. Of the 25 persons present, only five monks were adults, but the others, both children and adolescents, showed no less seriousness or devotion in the way they played their instruments and chanted their prayers; the Sisters who accompanied me were really edified by them. The monastery is called *Manange Gompa* because the monks come from that region, *Manang*, to the north of Annapūrṇā. It belongs to the *Karma Kagyu* Order, as can be seen from the statues in their sanctuary and the heads of the Order who are represented. The abbot, whose name was *Sherab Gyaldje*, was at Darjeeling at that time. The name of the monastery was *Karma Dhubgyu Chhekhor Ling*. It was situated in the Matepani district and numbered 42 monks (of whom several were on holiday). As the community was at the office, we were unable to speak to any senior religious, but the few to whom we did speak gave rise to some surprise. The Sisters, knowing that they had been born in Nepal, addressed them in Nepalese but none of them understood this. They would have needed to speak to them *in Tibetan*, which demonstrated to me how faithful they were to their religion and culture, all the teachings and liturgy being carried out in that language of the tradition.

4. To the south-west of the town are the well-built and admirably laid-out houses of *S.O.S. Tibetan Children*, where 53 Tibetan children, the majority of them semi-orphans, were divided into "families". Nearby, we visited the workshops of a *vocational centre* where the oldest learn a trade. Close at hand is the *Tibetan Refugee*

Camp of *Tashi Ling* where about 200 refugees had found suitable housing. Almost all had previously lived in Southern Tibet, beyond the border with Mustang, which they crossed during the Chinese invasion; they came here in 1964 or 1965. It was in these rather poor surroundings that, having asked to see the monks, I was led into one of these residences amongst the refugees. A huge but dark building had raised benches the length of the walls. It was simultaneously their sanctuary where the liturgy is carried out, the instruction hall, the abbot's residence and, undoubtedly, the refectory. Their Rinpoche, who seemed delighted to welcome me, was called *Tharling Tulku Lobsang Jamyang*. In Tibet, this was the *Gelugpa* monastery of *Darghyeling*, which then numbered from 60 to 70 monks. There were no more than eight, and most seemed elderly. The whole atmosphere was very poor. They had plans, which they showed me, for the construction of a monastery to house 60 monks, including young ones in formation, but they lacked the financial means. This was the first exchange the abbot had had with a Christian monk, but he seemed happy to engage in it.

5. *Hyangja*, to the north-west of the town, in a *Settlement* numbering thousands of Tibetans, particularly those from Mustang, has a *Kagyu* monastery. The journey being long and rather difficult, I could not spare the time to go there. Besides, the abbot (who presided over about ten monks) was at that time in Malaysia, and several monks were meditating at Rumtek, in Sikkim. The place, which is called *Tashi Phalkhel*, is on the *Jomoson trail* ("trekking" path). There were also a score of boy-monks there. The abbot's name was *Shangpa Rinpoche*.

BIHĀR, A MONASTIC COUNTRY

> The place where you stand
> is holy ground.
> (*Exodus* 3.5)

1. The University of Nālandā

On the evening of 9 August, I took the night bus from Kathmandu to Birganj and then, at Raxaul, the Indian frontier, another bus to Patna.

On 10 August and the following days, I noticed on the roads a great number of *Hindu pilgrims*. These were laypeople who, for this pilgrimage, had put on robes or tunics of saffron, brand-new and shining in the sun. They travelled in groups, either walking or by bus, from the North of Bihār to a temple, known either as Deoghar or by the name of their god, Bhabadham, situated 125 miles to the east of Patna. Some would take water from the Ganges about 60 miles from there, at Sultanganj, in order to offer it in devotion, which demonstrates the vitality of popular Hinduism. Sometimes the vehicles carrying them, too, sported shining miniature banners of saffron.

Travelling from Bihār-Shariff, I reached *Nālandā*, where I counted on making a leisurely visit to the ancient university, so famous in the history of Buddhism. The museum contains numerous statues of the Buddha and some tantric divinities. Then, led by a good guide, we went over the ruins of *the ancient university*. This did not yet exist in 450; it was already flourishing greatly in 650, reached its zenith in the ninth and tenth centuries and was destroyed by the Muslims in 1200. I had not expected to see more than the outlines, with the remains of very low walls. In reality, from the height of a raised *chaitya*, a kind of funerary mausoleum with nine storeys superimposed, we admired simultaneously the extent of the buildings and, especially in the case of site Nº 1, the state of preservation of part of the monasteries. All the work has been carried out with bricks, and the plan is so clear that you can count the individual cells. Dark rooms are reserved for meditation, and there is a wide variety of chambers, classrooms, temples, a drainage system and bathrooms. It is said that Nālandā had as many as 10,000 monks. Eleven monasteries had been excavated; there had been many more. What is most noticeable is the different levels to a single site: when one complex had been destroyed through internal disputes, the following king had it rebuilt on a bigger scale.

Close to the *Institute of Pāli Studies* there is a *Wat Thai Nālandā* for Thai Buddhist nuns (only one being in residence at the time). A vast guest house for pilgrims was under construction. We entered the courtyard of the *Institute of Pāli Studies* and found a hostel, above all for monks from abroad. There were 10 from Thailand, 4 from Burma, 3 from Bangladesh and we had some good conversations. One teaching monk was from Sri Lanka. We had, in particular, a long conversation with a very likeable young Nepalese monk. He set great store by interreligious dialogue, having encountered the Church in Australia. He told us the story of his vocation and led us to one of his teachers, a learned Burmese monk, Dr. U. Jagarabhivamsa. This *Pāli Institute* had 200 students. Its director was a German, Professor Gustav Roth, who lived at Patna.

2. The magic of Rājgir

On Thursday 3 February, we had been able to visit only one hill of this holy place, that on which I admired a beautiful Japanese temple and an utterly beautiful *stūpa*.[56] However, if this *Shānti Stūpa* and temple are the chief attraction for tourists, the true interest of Rājgir lies elsewhere. To find it, you must go out at dawn and climb another hill, on the right. It was here that Shakyamuni did penance and meditated from the time of his Going Forth, and after his Enlightenment.[57] The solitude there is complete. From the height of that terrace, there is nothing to be seen throughout the valley but the green of the hills. It is an ideal place for silent meditation. All along the climbing road which leads there, one can see a kind of little square terrace made from bricks; to one side, there is a placard: "Here the king Bimbisāra stopped his chariot ... and dismissed his large retinue when he went to pay a visit to the Buddha." It is in this spot that many an archaeological find was made, now to be seen in museums.

3. Visiting the Jain nuns

The religion contemporary with Buddhism also has precious memories connected with this region. We travelled, on the plain, to *Viraithan*, where the Jain nuns have a very active centre: a temple, a printing press, a library (15,000 volumes), a school and a dispensary. Everything is inspired by religion and directed towards the social good. The director of the centre, Sister *Chandana-ji*, was a remarkable person, very anxious to promote "ecumenical" contacts between religions. We admired their series of representations of the life of the *Tīrthankaras* who preceded *Mahāvīra*, and then, above all, the episodes of the life of the latter. There are very artistic scenes, created from a kind of wax figurine, dolls sumptuously dressed, often in a lavish and regal setting. By way of contrast, the completely naked ascetic stands erect, totally dignified, a witness to the spiritual in the face of a transitory world: in short, a fundamental lesson related to that of Buddhism.[58] This is why we were eager to hear it at the end of our journey.

Notes

[1] Until December 1990. Since 1991, the central Commission has taken care to meet each year in a different country; hence the meetings at Ealing (London), Lérins, Göttweig (Austria), Saint Maurice (Canton of Valais), and Montserrat (Catalonia). The next has been arranged in Italy. There has been a meeting at Mariastein, near Basel, as early as 1985. The purpose is to raise the awareness of as many communities as possible.

[2] See above, pages 90–93: *A tour of monastic India*.

[3] See above, *Kagyu-Ling*, page 100ff.

[4] See, in fact, what has been said above, pp. 104, 126–127, 142, note 9. I saw him again and was able to speak to him on several occasions at Plaige Château, notably 22–24 August 1987, during *the inauguration of the temple*; we planted a tree together, hand in hand. At *Karma-Ling*, too, I was present on 23 January 1985, when the Rinpoche came to bless the chalets where a whole group of generous disciples were to enter to make their three-year retreat. It was in the depth of winter; the melting snow and the layer of ice made the path leading up to the hermitages extremely slippery; one risked falling at every step taken. There had been plenty of hectic and dramatic preparations; the Rinpoche spent himself in teachings and rituals, while many highly edifying and moving secrets were exchanged.

Much water has flowed under the bridges since our first meeting at Sonada in January 1980. The temple has been completed. Kalu Rinpoche left this world on 10 May 1989. The magazine *Dharma*, N° 6, reported in detail his last months. It reproduced, on pages 6–7, his *koudoung*, that is to say his mummified body, placed in a mausoleum in the temple. His rebirth has been acknowledged in the child known as *Yangsi Kalu Rinpoche*, born 17 September 1990. See the magazine *Dharma* N° 17, pp. 58–64. He was enthroned at Sonada 28 February 1993. I had made his acquaintance in the temple of the park at Vincennes. It was the afternoon of 3 September 1992 and, having played a good deal in the morning, the child was peacefully asleep, as beautiful as a little angel. This gave me the opportunity of talking to his mother, a likeable Bhutanese, the sister of Lama Gyourme. As for his father, he is none other than Kalu Rinpoche's own nephew and administrator of Sonada: Lama Gyaltsen. There is nothing to prevent one's being reborn in one's own family.

[5] See above, pages 79 and 83, notes 13–15.

[6] To tell the truth, I am one of their former pupils, in the city where I was born, as also my brother and my four sisters.

[7] See above, pages 105–109.

8   Graphic and realistic descriptions of Kopan at that period can be found in the book by Vicki MACKENZIE, indicated above in Chapter VI, note 21; see her pages 22–23.
9   Already visited the previous year in the course of the *Tour of Monastic India*, which we described above on pages 90–93.
10 See above, pages 90–93.
11 In Chapter III, pp. 50–51. Here are the (approximate) figures for the altitudes:
    Yol and Sidhpur   3,480 feet
    Library   4,760'
    McLeod Ganj   5,670'
    Children's Village   6,230'
    Dhaola Dhar   13,120'
12 This is what is known as *Lower Dharamsala*. If the hill in its entirety is considered, the population numbers about 10,000 Indians, 5,000 Tibetans and, in Spring and Summer, a thousand Westerners.
13 See above, page 150–151.
14 See above, page 92.
15 The first occasion was with the Italian monks on 18 February 1979. For the second, see pp. 51–52.
16 See above, pages 148–151.
17 The diocese of Jullundur includes not only the Northern *Punjab* (with Amritsar) but also the Northern districts of *Himāchal Pradesh*; it therefore contains the territories bordering on Tibet and includes the district of Kāngra, where Dharamsala is situated.
18 Giuseppe M. TOSCANO, *Alla scoperta del Tibet. Relazioni dei Missionari del sec. XVII*, Editrice Missionaria Italiana, Collana *Biblioteca Scientifica*, 4, 1977.
19 Some personal memories. A young Indian girl, Goanese by origin, went to stay with my family. A former student at *Saint Xavier's* – and this was not her only tie with the Society – she completed her university studies at Oxford, where she met my nephew. I took advantage of my being in the neighbourhood to present myself at the light-filled home of her parents, in *Bandra*. It was with them that I went, on 21 February 1979, to the feet of St. Mary of the Mount. Hindus would come to pray there, leaving their sandals at the entrance. It was in this way that my *Tour of monastic India* came to an end.
20 At that period, I found myself the only foreigner present at their offices in that hut which they used as their temple, beside the road.
21 Note, however, that they are welcome to the courses on Buddhist philosophy arranged especially for them.
22 There were instances, and very good ones, but out of the ordinary.
23 See above, pages 151–152.
24 According to the brochure of the *Delek Hospital* at Dharamsala: *Tuberculosis Problem among Tibetans*, 1982.
25 Drepung Loseling Magazine, N° VI, 1981, p. 8. The title *Dreloma* is made up of the first syllable of these three words. Address: D.L.L. Society, P.O. TIbetan Colony, Mundgod – 581 411. Dist. N.K. Karnataka, India. The above figures should be raised, since the number of monks and nuns has increased since 1981.

[26] See above, Chapter III.
[27] For a study of Tibetan debating, see *Introductory Debate in Tibetan Buddhism*, by Daniel PERDUE, Library of Tibetan Works and Archives, Dharamsala, H.P., 1980, 112 pp.: the object of the debate, syllogisms and consequences, theory; example of a debate, translation and commentary to it. See also the articles entitled *Tibetan Debate* in the magazine *Dreloma* (see above, note 25), numbers IV and VI.
[28] *Dreloma* magazine, N° VII, 1981, p. 1.
[29] On the retreat at Sainte-Baume and Song Rinpoche, see above, page 105 and note 12. When I learnt of his death at Ganden in 1985, I wrote a brief article in his memory: *Un grand sage nous a quittés*, in *Les cahiers du bouddhisme*, avril 1985, N° 24, pp. 42–43.
[30] Following the magazine *Dreloma*, N° IV, 1980, p. 8, here is a list of the principal *Gelugpa* monasteries with their date of foundation and the number of monks they had in Tibet (prior to 1959):

Ganden	1409	4,000
Drepung	1416	9,000
Sera	1419	7,000
Tashi Lhunpo	1447	3,800
Kumbum	1578	3,600
Tashi Kyil	1710	3,300

This magazine gives also the less-populated monasteries of the Kadampa, Sakya, Kagyud and Nyingma.
[31] Khensur Pema Gyaltsen died 30 June 1985.
[32] Session at the Abbey of La Pierre-qui-Vire (19–24 April 1982): *Influence des religions orientales en Europe. Information et discernement.* Fascicle III, which was published in 1985 and includes interviews with Song Rinpoche and Khensur Pema Gyaltsen, is obtainable from A.I.M. Secretariat, rue d'Issy, F-92170 Vanves. The proceedings are not available in English.
[33] See above, page 92.
[34] *Number of monks in the Tibetan monasteries in Karnataka*. At Dharamsala, I consulted *the Council for religious and cultural affairs*, but only the 1981 statistics were available, and these give 393 for Sera-jé and 290 for Sera-mé; the other monasteries were in keeping. I was assured that these numbers could safely be *doubled*. When one asks the monasteries how many monks took part in the *Meunlam* for the current month, one reaches a figure in the nine hundreds for Sera. The same thing could be said of Ganden and Drepung. Roughly speaking, there are as many as 1,000 monks for each of the three great monasteries. As for the colleges, Shartse outnumbers Jangtse, and Loseling Gomang, as does Sera-jé Sera-mé (17 February 1983).
[35] See *The Tibet Guide*, Wisdom Publications, 1987. We shall refer again to the *Tantric College* below, page 189.
[36] See above, pages 151–152.
[37] This thesis was recently published in Paris: Bernard de Give, *Les rapports de l'Inde et de l'Occident des origines au règne d'Aśoka*. Les Indes savantes, Paris, 2005.
[38] By now it was August. See below, page 199 and note 56.

39 See above, note 32.
40 In short, what has been read above, pages 162–173.
41 See above, pages 48–49.
42 See above, pages 49–50.
43 *Méditation progressive sur la Vacuité* according to the teachings of Khenpo Tsultrim Gyamtso. Translated and edited by Jérôme EDOU, Institute of Mahāyāna Buddhist Studies, Saint-Léon-sur-Vézère. F – 24290 Montignac, France, 1980.
44 See above, pages 91–92.
45 See above, page 158.
46 See above, p. 92 and corresponding note 8; pp. 50–54, and in particular pp. 208–211.
47 For further details, see pp. 58–59.
48 See above, page 138.
49 See above, page 171.
50 On Lama Thubten Yeshe, see pp. 105–109 and 151–152, and the magazine *Wisdom. Magazine of the FPMT*, N° 2, 1984, *Wisdom Publications*, 25 Stanley Road, Ilford, Essex IG1 1RW, England. This issue, copiously illustrated, contains testimonies concerning his personality and traces the last months of his life.
51 Thank God, there is now an excellent account, by Professor Per KVAERNE at the University of Oslo: the article *Bön* in the Poupard *Dictionnaire des religions*, 3rd edition, 1993, pp. 231–233.
52 See above, page 172.
53 See above, pages 177–178.
54 I revisited these places on our return from Tibet, 25 July 1994. See below, p. 193.
55 See above, pages 138 and 186–187.
56 See above, page 175.
57 For the geographical location and the events of the life of the Buddha which had *Rājagriha* for their setting, consult E. LAMOTTE, *Histoire du boudhisme indien des origines à l'ère Śaka*. University of Louvain, Institut Orientaliste, 1976, p. 10 and 17–19.
58 We have discussed the *Jain* monks and nuns above, pp. 41–42. A good account, under the title *Jaïnisme* by M. Delahoutre, is to be found in the Poupard *Dictionnaire des religions*, 3rd edition, 1993, pp. 999–1002.

Chapter VIII

More Recent Visits

A MAJOR SPIRITUAL EXCHANGE: CHRISTIAN AND BUDDHIST MONKS MEET IN INDIA
DHARAMSALA – ASIRVANAM: 15–29 NOVEMBER 1992

> For you has he commanded his angels
> to keep you in all your ways.
> (*Psalm 90.11*)

It can be safely said that the experience which we record below is a first in the history of intermonastic dialogue. It was no longer a matter of simple visits, but a dialogue officially organized between representatives of different branches of Tibetan monasticism, male and female, and Catholic monks and nuns from India and Europe. It was also the first time that the monasteries of India had taken part as a body in this dialogue, and the extremely generous welcome of our Brothers and Sisters in Tibetan monasticism made possible exchanges of an unusual quality. This encounter had been strongly encouraged by the Pontifical Council for Dialogue between Religions and by Mgr Patrick D'Souza, bishop of Vārāṇasī and president for interreligious dialogue of the Indian Episcopal Conference. The Union of Indian Benedictine Superiors took up, and entrusted to Fr. Cletus, a monk of Asirvanam, the practical organization of the encounter; it was borne, on the European side, by Fr. Mayeul de Dreuille, assistant to the Abbot President of the Subiaco Congregation.

Three years earlier, Tai Situ Rinpoche, one of the four regents of the Karma Kagyu Order, abbot of Palpung in Eastern Tibet, made a pilgrimage in Italy for justice and peace. At the head of about ten lamas, he spent several days at Camaldoli, visited Assisi and was welcomed in Rome by His Holiness John Paul II.[1] At the end of this encounter, he invited the Christian monks, in their turn, to visit him in India. This is the origin of our session in November 1992. There were five of us from Europe: Fr. Francis Baird, from Prinknash; Brother Maximilian, from La Pierre-qui-Vire, a Swedish doctor of medicine who had spent several months assisting Mother Teresa in Calcutta; Father Henry Eikhlein, from Burma, staying at the Abbey of Bellefontaine; Sister Marie-André Houdart, from St. Gertrude's monastery, Louvain-la-Neuve; and Fr Bernard de Give, from Scourmont Abbey. From Rome we were joined by Dom Mayeul de Dreuille and Canon Francis Tiso, an American by birth but exercising his ministry at Isernia in Italy; he is one of the real experts in Tibetan Buddhism, having defended a thesis on the biography of Milarepa at Columbia University. From India itself came seven monks and six nuns of the Benedictine Federation.

Eventful beginnings

The outward journey was highly eventful, in ways of which those who are experienced in travel in this country may already have some idea. They include the cancellation of the plane which was to have left Paris on 13 November, the loss of a suitcase found to be missing when the plane landed (it was recovered the following day), the absence of anyone to meet us at Delhi airport on account of our arriving a day late, the frequent near-accidents in the unrestrained traffic on India's roads and the skirting of mountain precipices by night. I draw a veil over the rest!

Yet each time our group encountered a serious complication, or might have been distressed by some major difficulty, an angel of the Lord came to deliver us! I will give one example; there were many others. We had taken the night bus to travel from Delhi to Dharamsala via Jullundur and Hoshiārpur. The bus arrived at the former at 5 a.m., putting us down, bags and baggage, on the road in an unknown district, without our knowing the way to the next station and in the pitch-dark. We were progressing with the greatest difficulty along a stony side-path when we distinguished on our left the white walls of some barracks. Before the main door stood a sentry with a machine-gun aimed ready to challenge any visitors. The sentry left his post, which he should not have done, and came towards us with a smile, noticing the cross on our overcoat and saying, "I am a Christian from Kerala". At once, he hurried to stop a rickshaw which had just passed us, settled the price, gave exact directions and returned to his guard-post. We arrived five minutes before the departure of the bus bound for the foothills of the Himalayas. For his part Fr Mayeul, along with the Brothers and Sisters of India, had experiences of the same kind. On more than one occasion in the course of the journey, our well-laid plans were overturned, the reality proving quite different and much better. We clearly saw the interventions of Providence.

The Lord's Day at Delhi

We must, however, return to the beginning of the adventure. Those unaware of this should understand that the Charles de Gaulle airport is divided into two tentacles which must not be confused: Terminal A and Terminal B. Of course the inevitable happened: while the two Belgians awaited their companions at Terminal B, the two "French" (a Burmese and a Swede) were waiting for them at Terminal A. The consequence of this "original sin" soon became clear. Our little Father Henry, after heart-rending farewells to his Burmese friends, was obliged to be swallowed up, alone, by a fine Lufthansa plane which left at once for Frankfurt, from whence an Air India plane bore him off, without mishap but not without anxiety, to Delhi airport. Once arrived, he had some difficulty in finding Fathers Mayeul de Dreuille and Francis Baird. They should really have held up a notice, for the benefit of the latest arrivals, stating "I am Father Mayeul". This trio was to arrive on time at Sherab Ling and, alone, participate in the opening session, on the day and at the hour announced, but without their tardy companions, *absente corpore.*

As for ourselves, it was an Air France plane which conveyed us by a non-stop flight from Paris to Delhi (4,100 miles) in the course of Saturday 14 November, at a more or less constant altitude of 37,000 feet and a speed of 635 m.p.h. Disembarking at Delhi around 22.30, there we waited in vain for Father Mayeul and went to spend the night in a fairly good little hotel with a glorious name: *Ashoka Palace.* Then we attempted, on the morning of Sunday 15 November, to make telephone contact with the others. We were used to the Indian climate, summer-like on the plain but not excessively hot at this time of year. New Delhi, with its wide tarmacked arterial roads and Western buildings, gives a false idea of the Indian heartland. We decided to leave Delhi for Jullundur in the evening of this same Sunday. Disinclined to spend hours in the immense, noisy and impersonal bus station, we located a nearby church: *St. James's Church,* of the *Church of North India*; this is a union, already achieved, of several Christian churches. The parish is one of the most ancient in the city, Anglican by tradition, ecumenical in its openness. It had had to undergo all the conflicts of the British community in the previous century, often bitter trials. The church was filled with silence, conducive to meditation. We had the opportunity to speak a little with two of the parishioners, cultivated gentlemen who introduced us to their vicar, a benevolent pastor in his white cassock. The courtyard of the school just beyond the church filled up with groups in their Sunday best, the music of a foreign festival could be heard and the winners of a tombola to support the good works of the parish were drawn.

The ascent to Sherab Ling

Three different buses conveyed us, across the Northern Punjab and Himāchal Pradesh, to the monastery of Sherab Ling, beyond Bajnāth. The journey which began in Delhi at 19.15 on the Sunday ended only on Monday 16th around 16.00. This meant that we spent almost 19 hours travelling by bus, but the roads were not too bad, nor the buses too uncomfortable. It was on the Monday morning, at around 5 o'clock that the episode recounted above took place. The reader who wished to follow the itinerary on a map would have the following reference-points: Jullundur, Hoshiārpur, Chintpurni, Dera, Kāngra, Pālampur and Baijnāth. Himāchal Pradesh is right at the North of India, only the State of Jammu-Kashmir being more northerly. Sherab Ling is located forty miles to the south-east of Dharamsala. From Baijnāth, famous for an ancient temple to Shiva, we were taken there by taxi. When we were almost at the summit of the hill, we were met by Father Cletus, who was on his way down in another taxi and at once took with him Sr. Marie-André, from Louvain-la-Neuve, who was to stay at Dharamsala. We were to be separated until Friday 20th, meeting with highly-edifying experiences, but each by him- or herself. This is the right point at which to let the Sister take up the story. I shall merely give the co-ordinates for that place and provide additional information in the notes.

The hospitality of the Tibetan nuns and the Nunnery of McLeod Ganj

Having left my companions close to Sherab Ling, I was taken nearly forty miles away, to the *Nunnery* at Dharamsala.[2] I was welcomed warmly and with (shared!) relief by the five Indian Benedictine nuns, who had been anxiously wondering what could have happened to us, since the cancellation of the Paris-New Delhi flight on Saturday 14th had brought in its train a whole series of adventures, with our finally reaching our destination twenty-four hours late.

Founded in Tibet at the beginning of the fifteenth century, the monastery, originally named *Nechung Ri*, was razed to the ground by the Chinese in 1959. Three nuns succeeded, after some unbelievable experiences, in fleeing to India. The two survivors (one of whom participated fully in the whole of our encounter) decided in 1973 to resume monastic life in some rented rooms close to *McLeod Ganj*. The news spread very quickly among the Tibetan refugees, and several former nuns came forward to join them. As they came from different monasteries in Tibet, they did not revive the name *Nechung Ri* (this at a time when the monasteries refounded in India regularly took up the ancient name to emphasise the continuity of monastic life), but adopted that of *Geden Chöling*, which means "House of virtuous women who consecrate their life to the Doctrine of the Buddha *(Buddha Dharma)*". They were soon obliged to think about building a larger monastery, for there were very many vocations. Sharing in the work by carrying heavy stones, and cooperating in every way with the workmen, the nuns, in 1975, had the joy of opening their new monastery. At an approximate altitude of 5,580 feet, series of cells were built onto the mountainside in such a way that any movement around them involved climbing or coming down very steep steps.

After 23 hours of travelling on an epic scale, I felt completely exhausted. It was 18.30, and the Benedictines led me to have supper in the cottage (normally used as a classroom) which had been put at our disposal. All the meals were on a generous scale and the nuns had the sensitivity and thoughtfulness to enhance the normal menu with soups, vegetable salads and piquant sauces which relieved the monotony of rice and bananas. An elderly nun had given up her room, which she normally shared with a younger one, to Sr Sarānanda (a nun from Pradines who had for some years been living as a hermit close to Fr Bede Griffiths' ashram) and myself. She waited each morning till we had dressed before coming to renew the flowers and cups of cold water arranged on her little personal altar, before which a lamp was always kept burning. The nights were rather cold at that altitude, and there was no question of heating, even in winter, so the morning ablutions called for some heroism.

Having risen at 5.30, we went to take our places in the *lhakhang* (prayer-hall), where the nuns quickly swathed us in blankets. They also set before us low tables laden with bowls, plates, butter, jam and hard-boiled eggs, which was hardly the usual custom of the Tibetan nuns. The celebration began with a thanksgiving for gifts received from benefactors, then came long repetitions of the same phrases; after a moment, all began to shake handbells, gongs and cymbals. A pause allowed everyone to swallow some mouthfuls of *tsampa*[3] and drink a little tea (a serving Sister went round continually between the rows to refill the bowls), after which the same procedure began with another phrase. The celebration lated until about 8.30. At a certain moment, a Sister came round with a huge bowl of rice, an incense stick burning in the centre. Everyone took a pinch, then, at a signal from the mistress of discipline, threw it into the air. I never learnt the meaning of this rite.[4]

The following day, the *Arya Tara* was celebrated. This is a special *pūjā* which is observed on the 10th and 25th days of each Tibetan month. It is preceded by the lengthy preparation of *torma*, slender cones about a foot high, painted in different colours and embellished with various decorations.[5] Monks take part in both preparation and celebration.

Ani Tenzin Tselha, our "guardian angel", took us around the monastery, the fittings of which were certainly very primitive. She also took us to meet her old Mama, whose welcoming smile compensated for the difficulties of communication. Her husband having been tortured and killed by the Chinese, she fled, carrying her two-year-old daughter (Tselha) and year-old son for more than ten days.

We were also welcomed by Lama Tashi Delek, whom the Dalai Lama had designated for three years as *khenpo* to the community: he is both abbot and spiritual director. With the face of a smiling ascetic, he brought up with us various questions on monastic life and had tea served to us by Tashi, the twelve-year-old boy-monk who is at his service and in his school.

For the Eucharistic celebration each day, we rejoined the six Indian Benedictine monks who were staying in two Tibetan monasteries in the village. A score of young nuns followed one of these celebrations very attentively. That evening, Ani Tenzin asked us, "Who is Jesus?", and answering this took us till well into the night. When we moved around on visits to temples and sacred places in the neighbourhood, to say nothing of the stalls in the village, we had occasion to put questions to Ani Tenzin and to answer hers. The language-barrier, however, did not permit us to go very far. We were delighted, therefore, to have a long encounter with two Buddhist nuns coming, one from California, the other from New Zealand. With these, it was possible for us to go further in mutual discovery. One of them concluded our meeting with these astonishing words: "If I had known that monastic life existed within Christianity, I would probably be a Catholic nun now."

We had also spent a highly interesting afternoon when, together with the Indian monks, we were invited to the *School of Dialectics*, a kind of philosophy faculty. The debates were, above all, on the subject of rebirth.

What was unexpected was a visit from two compatriots from Brussels, employed by the *Tibetan Society of Europe*, which maintained various aid-projects on behalf of Tibetan refugees. Their familiarity with Tibetan life enabled them to answer several of our questions. They were with us when Lama Tashi Delek came to offer each of us a *khata*, the silk scarf traditionally presented to visitors of note. When we left on Friday evening, the Lama, too, was set on accompanying us to the bus, taking part in the fervent farewells. Three Tibetan nuns were to come with us and participate with us in the second phase of the intermonastic encounter, and three nuns from the Tilokpur monastery, near Kāngra, joined the group.

It would be presumptuous of me to attempt to pass judgement on monastic life as led by Tibetan nuns after an experience lasting so few days. Nevertheless, I should like to pass on a few observations which made a strong impression on me:

– The Tibetan nuns show a strong attachment to their monastic life, and the difficulties which most of them have had to surmount to attain it bear eloquent witness to this.

- They are actuated by great zeal for their sacred texts and spend a considerable portion of each day in memorizing them and reciting them in the context of their celebrations.[6]
- They live in stark poverty but, the wherewithal for their daily lives once assured, they consecrate their resources to obtaining sacred books and the equipping of their temple, with a view to restoring something of the splendour of the past.
- Their peace and joy are most striking, especially when we consider how the slavery of their homeland weighs upon them. Hoping against hope, they share and sustain the expectation of their people. May Tibet once more be free, one day.

A Kagyupa monastery in full expansion: Sherab Ling

> Let the land and all it bears rejoice,
> all the trees of the wood shout for joy!
> *(Psalm 95.2)*

After this fine testimony from Sister Marie-André, let us take up our narrative at the point at which our companion was taken away, just before we reached the top of the hill, a little after 4 p.m. on Monday 16th November.

In order to broaden the experience of the group, the Christian monks were to be distributed amongst three Tibetan monasteries. The unforeseen contingencies of the journey meant that all the European monks, plus Fr Varkey Vithayathil, the superior of Asirvanam, were the guests of *Tai Situ* in his monastery of *Sherab Ling*, in Himāchal Pradesh, a beautiful mountainous region which has rather cold nights in November but is spring-like during the day. The Benedictine monks from different parts of India were, as we have just seen, lodged at Dharamsala itself, as were the nuns. Here we rediscovered our European companions, each of whom had arrived on a different aeroplane.

First of all Canon Francis Tiso. Then, when on visiting the temple where a *pūjā* was taking place, we saw once more, with mutual pleasure and relief, little Fr Henry Eikhlein, Fr Francis Baird and Dom Mayeul de Dreuille. We also made the acquaintance of Fr Varkey Vithayathil, the Redemptorist who is the current Superior of Asirvanam. We were accommodated, not in the monastery buildings, but at some distance. The *Kagyupa* are well known for their austere tradition of making retreats lasting three years and three months in strict enclosure, in order to give themselves up to *Tantrayāna* practices, and an isolated house is reserved for these exercises. Since, however, there was at that time a free period between two retreats, the house was unoccupied and put at our disposal. The little rooms there were simple and practical and the Indian-style food fully sufficient. *Tsultrim*, a young Kagyupa monk of British origin, attended efficiently to all our needs, and was to act as our guide both on site and on all our travels. He also had an open mind. Not content with answering our questions, he showed himself eager to make a closer acquaintance with the Christianity which he had rather neglected in his youth. I had stayed at Sherab Ling in 1983 and can refer the reader to the description given at that time,[7] but I have to say at once that there had been a great deal of change.

My first meeting with *Tai Situ Rinpoche* took place at Dhagpo Kagyu Ling (Saint-Léon-sur-Vézère) on 10 June 1981. I was able to talk with him for an hour and a half; he seemed well able to spare the time. I fell at once under his spell. He was twenty-seven years old, with a childlike face, and an indescribable blend of wisdom and charm, depth and freedom that one could not but wish for all spiritual men to have: as though he could freely draw upon some living source welling up within him. Now, at the end of some exchanges on points essential to religion, he produced from a drawer a bird's-eye view of a collection of buildings which, to date, existed only on paper. On it could be seen a great temple and its outbuildings, prayer-hall, lecture-rooms, monks' accommodation and even, at the foot of the hill, a shop and a dispensary. It should be realized that this spiritual master is also a poet, an architect and a contractor. I admired the plan while saying within myself, "This is all very well, but where will he find the means to realize it all?" That was my attitude in 1981, and now the utopia was on its way to fulfilment before our eyes. The hill was covered with huge concrete structures and, at nightfall, taking care to avoid the puddles, we ascended those flights of stairs and walked through those spacious halls, the high walls already telling us the purpose of the buildings: a monastic university, such as existed in his native Tibet before their savage destruction by the Chinese invaders. Tsultrim, the young British monk, must have taken pleasure, not unmixed with pride, in making us scale those daring constructions. It could not even be objected that they would offend the poor peasants who lived locally, working their meagre patch of land in the village of Bhattu, since the twelfth Tai Situ was enlightened enough to entrust the building of the future monastery to the local manpower.

There were under construction, on the right of the road which climbed to Sherab Ling, eight *chortens* (or stūpas). Were these intended for the protection of the place from all baleful influences? There had recently been a hunt of the leopards frequently to be seen in the neighbouring thickets. On the other hand, opposite the *Retreat Centre*, there stood a tree with pink blossoms similar to the cherry trees of Japan, the *jacarandas*, while the district was bright with bougainvilleas. Tea plantations and rice fields were also to be seen.

Even though we had arrived a day late, we had not lost the first day, as a recording had been made of *the opening session*: a welcoming speech from Tai Situ, a report by Fr Mayeul, calling to mind the ideal of Monastic Interreligious Dialogue and the commendations it has received in high places and an address by Fr. Varkey in the name of the Indian Benedictine Federation. All this for the benefit of the audience, composed of a score of younger Buddhist monks, of an age to be in higher education. The community were not all present, a certain number of monks having left to take part in funeral rites, since they had just lost two important lamas: *Dilgo Khyentse Rinpoche*, a Nyingmapa master of very high calibre,[8] and the young and charming *Djamgoeun Kongtrul,* killed in a car accident at Siliguri (Bengal), when he was on the point of travelling to Tibet as a member of an inquiry commission to discover the reincarnation of the sixteenth Karmapa. A videocassete recalled for us also the first return of Tai Situ Rinpoche to Eastern Tibet, in 1984, visiting once more the monasteries under his jurisdiction in the influence of Palpung.

Pilgrimage to Rewālsar

Tuesday 17th November. Despite the picturesque undergrowth, if you have a delicate frame avoid at all costs the immediate surroundings of Sherab Ling : the earth roads have shocks and jolts in store for you over a good quarter of an hour. Only arriving at the main road will bring you the relief of "normal" traffic. By hill and dale, right-hand bends, left-hand bends, the mountain road, made up of an endless succession of ascents and descents, is at many points really dangerous. On the positive side, the landscapes, plunging over green hills and valleys. The temperature, on all these days, is spring-like and very pleasant. Our itinerary takes us towards the south: Baijnāth, Jogindarnagar, Mandi, Rewālsar. Having set out from Sherab Ling in three cars at around 8 a.m., we arrive on the stroke of noon at the door of *Rewālsar*. This is the right point at which to situate this place of pilgrimage in its historical or mythological context. Rewālsar is the Hindu name, whereas the Tibetans call it *Tsok Pema*.

According to the tradition, *Guru Rinpoche*, the first founder of Tibetan Buddhism, was miraculously born from a lotus, hence his Sanskrit name *Padmasambhava*. He had as disciple a fervent Indian princess, *Mandarava*. The king, her father, was furious about this and decided to burn him; the ascetic, however, survived, safe and sound, and from the stake emerged the lake that is here. As an object of veneration for the most monastic traditions, the place is holy and attracts pilgrimages. On a rather modest scale around the lake, stand a number of temples belonging to these Orders, which I visited with two companions in 1983.[9] On that occasion, we stayed there for two days, gasping as we climbed the very steep hill with its countless, irregular steps. My Peruvian friend was so impressed by the hermits living at the summit that he was completely spellbound by the place and returned to spend a year there, living in a cave on the mountain in an atmosphere reminiscent of the Desert Fathers. I do not know if the ring road had been built nine years ago: the fact remains that, today, we came up in a very prosaic way by car.

On arrival we were welcomed by Franco, an Italian living in seclusion with his wife, close to the lake; he had an Italian-style reunion with our Father Tiso. For guide we had a Flemish woman from Courtrai, able to speak Tibetan and explain the iconography of the Nyingmapa temple. After an agreeable lunch, minus hot spices, at the *Tourist Inn*, we went to visit the caves at the summit, which were caverns of a sort in which the hermits lived. Within them, here and there, were statues and representations of Guru Rinpoche and various deities. Access to these caves was sometimes difficult, but Tibetan humour maintains its rights and esoterism permits smiles. Hence this notice in conspicuous letters resting against a rock: *"Welcome to the secret cave of Guru Rinpoche!"* Austerity, too, has another face: that of this little old lady, rising out of I know not what hole like something out of a fairy story, with a shaven head and a nun's robe, who loses no time in serving us with cups of tea, welcome at this altitude and looking out over such a landscape, the very incarnation of Buddhist benevolence.

Tashi Jong and its ritual dances

Wednesday 18th November. The day ahead of us being much less busy, *Tai Situ* took advantage of the fact to give us a lecture, in the presence of his monks. He set out the manner of life in Tibet before the Communist invasion and the more difficult situation in India. Here there is no support from either the surrounding population or the Indian administration. In Tibet, the laws of the country require proper discipline on the part of the monks. He told us that their Rule provides for the correction or dismissal of monks. Tai Situ has read the Gospels in Tibetan and expressed deep insights into the "Buddha-nature" (we would say: the image of God) in each of us. In Tibet, families offered the most gifted of their sons; here in India and the neighbouring countries, the reverse is happening: there is no shortage of aspirants, but they are not the best sort.

When we asked Tsultrim where Sherab Ling's recruits are drawn from, he answered, "Most often from Konnor" a region to the east of Himāchal Pradesh, South of Spiti.

On the programme was the visit to *Tashi Jong*, three-quarters of an hour north-west from Sherab Ling, between Baijnāth and Pālampur. This is a monastery of the *Drukpa Kagyu* Order. The temple is famous for the traditional dances performed there. I had witnessed these over four days in March 1983.[10] Today we would have to be content with an hour. I had, in addition to these dances, made the acquaintance of the little *Kamtrul Rinpoche*, the ninth of that name, who was then a little over two years old, but already behaved in a very worthy manner. Now, in his twelfth year, he was witnessing, at the level of a gallery, the dramatic performances of his masked monks. These latter, wearing animal heads, advanced at a slow pace; playing the role of Mahākāla and seven or eight "protectors".

While waiting, from 12.30 till 3 p.m. for a meal that was very long in coming, a conversation began over our teacups, amongst ourselves, Tsultrim and Khenpo Losel, on subjects of comparative religion: Shankara, *anattā*, God as Creator, *shūnyatā* and reincarnation, an effort being made to discover parallels. It was a time of deep searching, one of the best of the whole session.

The flourishing of gonpas in the Bīr Settlement

Thursday 19th November. There was a storm last night, hence there was less dust on the roads, a cloudless sky and the whole day was sunny. We arrived in half an hour at *Bīr Settlement*, which I visited in 1983;[11] it numbers 3,000 Tibetans grouped round the monastery of their particular Order. At the time, I had been deeply impressed by the long prayers and endless ceremonies, engaged in not only by the monks but also by the ordinary people. What struck me today was the considerable progress made in the monastic building programme. We shall give only essential information about the four monasteries we visited.

1. *Dzongskar Institute,* belonging to the *Sakyapa*. We viewed their prayer-hall. This is an Institute of philosophical studies. Those who persevere in them to the end have the title of *geshe*. The monk who showed us around is a former pupil of *St. Joseph's College*, Darjeeling. There are here seventy monks, students of philosophy, including about fifty from Tibet. We were shown their temple, with its Green Tara. The *Khenpo* of the Institute, Soskar Khyentse Rinpoche, a rather elderly monk, greeted us in a friendly manner but knows no English. This building was under construction in 1988.
2. *Nyingma Temple*, the oldest: *Chöling*, which I saw almost complete in 1983. Chöling is also the name of their founder, whose portrait is to be seen in the reception room; we also saw there the portrait of a great promotor of the *Rimé* movement. In the temple, there was a portrait of the Karmapa.
3. A smaller *Sakyapa* centre is a school: *Sakya Peru*. The central statue in their temple: the Buddha *"as a prince"*, highly decorated and has an amazing headdress.
4. Still under construction, a rather large temple having at its centre a really beautiful statue of the Buddha. This is *Biyul Chöling*: "higher school, college". On the façade, fine, large paintings of the guardians of the four directions.

In the course of the evening, a dinner by candlelight. *Tai Situ* further explained to us the contrast between the circumstances of the monasteries in Tibet prior to the invasion and those of today. He also talked to us about his Western disciples. He finds them intelligent but extreme, narrow in the literal way they take everything that the Rinpoche says to them. They do not have the good sense of the Tibetans, nor of Orientals in general.

Our visit ended with an exchange of gifts. It was with regret that we took our leave of so kind a host.

A momentous day at Dharamsala

Friday 20th November. Departure from Sherab Ling at 6.30 a.m. for Dharamsala, by way of Pālampur. It was with deep feeling that I saw familiar landscapes and places[12]: Yol camp, Sidhpur, the market, a route I had followed so many times. So many meetings and even the smallest events returned to my heart's memory. On arrival at about 9.45 a.m., our car put us down opposite the School of Dialectics. This day was intended to fulfil two objectives: to allow our "Europeans" to see the seat of the Tibetan government-in-exile and to allow us to make the acquaintance of the Benedictine monks and nuns of India who will from now on be our companions until the end of the session at Asirvanam. In fact the first object had to be carried out at high speed. We made a lightning tour of the Library, casting a hasty glance over the innumerable statuettes in the Museum on the first floor and visited the modest temple of the Oracle, *Nechung*[13] at a run. We had somewhat more leisure for that of the *Namgyal Monastery*, with its marvellous statues, which we visited with great respect since a *pūjā* was taking place. This is the Dalai Lama's monastery, but His Holiness was absent.

Reimmersed in my past as I was, I made inquiries. Where is Gokey, the librarian? Dead from tuberculosis before reaching forty. And my Tibetan teacher, Mr. Thonden? Transferred to New Delhi. What about the Indian boys, who must have grown up by now? Vanished into thin air. It is *saṃsāra* ... The places remain:

Inanimate objects, do you have a soul
which becomes attached to our soul and forces it to love? ...

I eluded our group in order to take a look, however briefly, at the little house where I lived on my own in 1983, raised on an incline two steps away from the Library. I had lived there in studious but occasionally eventful seclusion, surrounded by friendships both Indian and Tibetan. After nine years, the little house has not changed at all; the door was padlocked, the curtains drawn.

Here we met our Indian Sisters and Brothers. To tell the truth, the first of these was a Frenchwoman, Sister Sarānanda, a nun of Pradines who has for several years been living as a hermit in the shadow of *Shāntivanam*, Bede Griffiths' ashram and, after her, Sister Teresita D'Silva, Prioress of *Shānti Nilayam*, Bangalore and, for many years, President of the Indian Benedictine Federation. She knew the epic beginnings of foundations in India and was able to describe them candidly.[14] Father Paul, of Asirvanam, lived through the most stirring events on the masculine side. We made the acquaintance of the other nuns who stayed with Sister Marie-André at *Geden Chöling*. The Sylvestrines from Makkiyad in Kerala spoke readily to me of the Trappistines of Soleilmont (Belgium) who have a foundation not far from their monastery. They pointed out from above, the hillside *gonpa, Tse-chok Ling*, at McLeod Ganj, where they had just spent four days, admirably welcomed by the monks.

In the afternoon, an *academic session*. Besides our monastic group in full force, about thirty young nuns, with shaven heads and wine-coloured robes, all smiles and attention, came to sit in the lotus position on cushions. We noticed in the audience a group of Western men and women, Buddhist sympathisers. The speakers alternated between Tibetan lamas and Christian monks. Dom Mayeul asserted the importance of intermonastic dialogue, Father Varkey, going to the essential, stressed the similarities between our two religions. The Sylvestrine, Father Thomas, superior of their foundation in the neighbourhood of Jhansi and currently the president of the Indian Benedictine Federation, traced the growth of the Benedictines in India.[15] Everything had been organized by him, with the cooperation of the Secretary of the *Department of Religion and Culture*, who presided over the meeting. A lama provided statistics for the monasteries and Tibetan centres in India and the neighbouring countries. A professor from the School of Dialectics spoke appreciatively about the educational and charitable works of Christianity; as for Buddhism, it could bring to

Westerners the help of meditation techniques of which they experienced the need. The Rinpoche spoke of the differences between the two religions: "To make an issue of these is to obstruct dialogue. We need these differences, because beings have different propensities. These differences are fundamentally the same reality and have only one purpose: mutual help."

Then we were treated to a magnificent spectacle. *The Tibet Institute of Performing Arts* (TIPA) is a school of art, particularly in drama, music and dance. It performs dance scenes and rhythmic movements of remarkable harmony. The actors, both men and girls aged about twenty, wore Tibet's traditional costumes and robes: we saw a variety of colours, dignity of bearing and perfection of movements. Certain episodes, toward the end, were of a comic nature, yaks as a part of history. This was a spectacle of rare harmony and pure beauty, giving a very exalted idea of their culture.

At the evening meal, the red robes of lamas and the white of Christian monks alternated, while my neighbours pursued doctrinal exchanges on points of philosophy: the human soul, those of animals ...

Dharamsala – Delhi

We left Dharamsala at about 10 p.m., boarding the night bus which brought us to Delhi around 11 a.m. We passed, I believe, through Pālampur, Mandi, Sundarnagar, Bilāspur, Chandigarh and Ambāla. Rice fields in the plain; after that, it looked like Chota Nagpore and then there were eucalyptus trees. As we approached Delhi, we saw many industrial sites: factories, chemical products, brickworks. Our destination was the CBCI (*Catholic Bishops' Conference of India)* where we celebrated the Mass of Christ the King in the evening.

Delhi – Bangalore – Asirvanam

Sunday 22nd November. The plane on which we left Delhi at 11.30 a.m. arrived at *Bangalore* around 2 p.m. The temperature there was 27°. Father Cletus was waiting for us. *Asirvanam* is about twelve and a half miles from the city. We dropped Sister Marie-André at *Sneha-Jyoti (Love and Light)*. This was where our nuns were to be accommodated during the session. It was a fairly new Congregation: *Grace and Compassion*, which unites the contemplative life with works of charity: this is a home for the aged.

On our arrival, at around 4 p.m., at *Asirvanam*, we received a warm welcome from the two guest-masters, who took us to see the vast, light chapel, the well-proportioned cloister, the library and the crypt. We were also shown the farm, which, with all its goats and the 600 cows, on their way back to the cattle-shed, is very important. The retreat house is remote and its surroundings convey peace and recollection; it is there that the Tibetan monks were to be accommodated. This community was greatly tried by a number of departures, but now a renewal can be seen. At present there are 14 solemnly professed (the majority elderly), 2 juniors, 2 novices and 14 postulants. If only the latter persevere! They made a favourable impression.

Excursion to Mysore

Monday 23rd November. As the plane journey gave us twenty-four hours' advantage over our Indian and Tibetan brothers who travelled by train, we went off to visit *Mysore*, a great city with half a million inhabitants and the former capital of a minor kingdom. At the summer palace of *Sriranapatna*, we admired the frescos representing the battles of Sultan Tippu Sahib (1749–1799) against the British. At the temple of *Sri Ranganathaswāmy*, we saw the statues of Vishnu and the offerings of the devout which the brahmin presents to the god. The bus then left the city to climb the *Chamundi Hills* (altitude 3,500 feet) with their fine views over Mysore. Here stands the temple of the goddess *Chamundeswari* with its solemn *gopuram* and fine sculptures. Three times a week the park and the fountains are illuminated in the evening. I saw this during my visit to Bylakuppe in 1979; it is an absolute marvel. As for the church of Saint Philomena, the architecture is good in itself but, being pseudo-Gothic, it is out of place in India. A shop, the *Kāverī Emporium*, is well stocked with the most varied objects of art and novelty goods. Mysore is known above all else for its silks (there is a great variety of saris) and for its sandalwood, which is used for works of art as well as for small articles. The high point of the day was a visit to the Maharajah's palace, an imposing edifice in which Hindu and Muslim architecture go hand-in-hand.

Everything – the size of the rooms, the elegance of the archways, the fine work of the many sculptures in wood and stone – conveys magnificence. An immensely long fresco shows the inauguration of this palace, with a procession of every rank in the army. The palace is illuminated in the evening. In a normal day, it receives five thousand visitors of every social class; the poorer are not the least admiring.

A day of arrivals

Tuesday 24th November. The temperature was summer-like and it was rather hot in the afternoon. There were foxes in the neighbourhood, and jackals could sometimes be heard calling at night. India has the most delicious fruits. We went to see, a few miles from there, the *banyan tree*, the second in India, the first being at Calcutta. This one covers an area of 3 acres (=1.2 hectare) with its shoots, the mother-tree being dead, and now constitutes a real wood. It is the home of a colony of small monkeys, graceful and rather timid.

At around noon, Father Bede Griffiths arrived. By evening, all the other participants were assembled and took supper with us at the monastery, the Sisters and nuns being catered for in a guest house refectory. Father Tiso came from Vrindāvan, on the Yamunā, in the neighbourhood of Mathurā, outstanding for its associations with the young Krishna. Also there to take part in the meeting was a young Flemish woman, Ria Weyens who, as an Oblate of the monastery of Soleilmont, was cooperating with Sister Isabelle at the Trappistines' foundation in Kerala. We were happy to have among us Father Albert Nambiaparambil, Secretary for Interreligious Dialogue to the Episcopal Conference of India. He was my pupil at the Pontifical Seminary of Kandy. We made the acquaintance of the Tibetan monks who arrived then.

Beside the eight persons come from Europe by different airports (Fiumicino, Gatwick and Roissy), eleven monks and six nuns, all Catholics, and representing the Benedictine communities of India, took part in the session. Four Asirvanam monks took part in all our exchanges; for the liturgy, of course, the full community was present.

On the Tibetan side, there were nine monks and seven nuns from various traditions: Gelugpa, Sakyapa, Kagyupa, Nyingmapa and even Bönpo. Among them were some real scholars, but the majority had difficulty in expressing themselves in English. The same observation, with two shining exceptions, held good for the nuns.

THREE DAYS IN SESSION AT ASIRVANAM

First day: Wednesday 25th November

High Mass

The principal celebrant at the solemn High Mass was Mgr Alphonso Mathias, Archbishop of Bangalore and President of the Indian Episcopal Conference. He took care to give brief explanations, for the benefit of the Buddhist monks and nuns, of the meaning of each part of the Mass. He did this in simple and engaging words, a model of its kind. At the Offertory, the procession bearing offerings of flowers and fruits was a moving one, including as it did Tibetan monks and nuns with their gifts, symbolizing a future of perfect convergence: *Reges Tharsis et insulae munera offerent. Reges Arabum et Saba dona adducent. Omnes gentes servient ei!*[16] In return, over the tea which followed, the tall archbishop, seated among the maroon robes, answered many questions put to him with great interest concerning the Mass. He had to help them to understand the reason for their exclusion from Holy Communion. Monsignor had the tact not to draw attention to canonical prohibitions but to resort to comparisons drawn from social psychology: "Just as people show a courteous welcome to passing guests, but do not admit them to the heart of the home as they do intimate friends or family members ..."

None of this seemed to convince his hearers. It struck me that one might, without giving offence to anyone, refer them to their own usages. Does one, in the *Vajrayāna*, at once admit to some advanced initiation, just any amateur, without his first taking refuge, following preliminary practices and receiving an appropriate initiation *(ouang)*? Besides, one finds such requirements in all the great, traditional Ways.

Opening Session

Father Varkey, Superior of Asirvanam, thanked the Tibetans for their generous welcome at Dharamsala. Father Mayeul, who organized the session, announced the programme for it. The first speaker was Father Bede Griffiths. It is well known that, for the *Nyingmapa*, *Dzogchen* is the final goal, the ultimate experience. Guru Rinpoche is invoked for it. Far from making it the special prerogative of their school, the Nyingmapa themselves regard it as a profound experience which goes beyond the framework of particular sects. According to Lobsang Yeshi, Thomas Merton had already noticed "the correspondence between this *Dzogchen* and Christian contemplation." Father Bede took the same stand, seeing in it *"a direct transmission of Supreme Wisdom"*, and laid himself out to show its agreement with the mystical tradition of Christianity but, also, as is currently being brought to light, with the outlook of modern science which sees in the universe and in the human body, not a fragmentation of distinct material beings but a complex of energies.[17]

Lobsang Yeshi Rinpoche addressed us at 4.30 p.m. and assumed, thereafter, the role of facilitator of the discussions, doing this with both intelligence and tact. Having attended a Catholic priests' school at Calcutta, he showed a real openness to our doctrines.

The director of the *Sakya Centre* at Dehra Dūn is Jamyang Lekshe. He said that poverty, taken to extremes by Milarepa, is not found in the monasteries. Chastity, as an aspect of morality, is the "apple of the eye" to the Buddha. Obedience must be given to the rules, infraction of which incurs corporal punishment. Purgatory does not exist in Tibetan Buddhism; the *bardo* is a pause, in order to choose another path. Hell is simply *a mental experience*.

Second Day: Thursday 26th November

Lecture on Exegesis

Father John Kurichianil, former Superior of Asirvanam, is at the head of a flourishing Syro-Malabar foundation in Kerala: *St. Thomas' Benedictine Monastery*,[18] and he is also a good exegete. He gave us an exposition on the theme: "The compassion of God in the Old Testament. The revelation of the God of compassion in the ministry of Jesus". While we do not wish to call into question the competence of the speaker, who carefully gave chapters and verses, something made us feel uncomfortable. Supposing a Buddhist comes across certain pages of the Bible, he could well notice narratives that shock him. Such a person, with scruples over killing so much as a mosquito, comes to an episode in which, on Yahweh's orders, Israel gives itself up to massacring Canaanite peoples. Father Griffiths, also, was frank enough to observe that the God of the Old Testament is not only compassion but sometimes takes on a contrary aspect which poses a problem for us Christians, too. As for the second part, in which Jesus appears as a model of compassion, that would not create difficulties for any observer from outside. This lecture gave rise to no fewer questions: God the creator, the welfare of the animals, God creating suffering and evil ...

The Silk farm

After lunch, we were taken to see the monastery's silk farm, and each stage of the development (including that of the cocoon) of the silkworms.

Expositions by the Tibetan monks

Nyima Tapa, a monk of *Dolanji*,[19] described for us the principal features of the Bön tradition. Bhikshu Karma did likewise for the doctrines of the *Nyingmapa* school.

Third Day: Friday 27th November

On the Rule of Saint Benedict

In the morning, there was a lecture by Father Thomas T. T., Sylvestrine, on "Humility in the *Rule of Saint Benedict*", a subject which gave rise to many contributions in both directions, both Christian and Buddhist monks wishing to make a contribution on this subject.

Testimonies from the nuns

This day gave a large place to the nuns. First of all the Tibetans: an elderly nun, from *Geden Chöling*, recounted the epic history of her monastery.[20] A young nun from *Tilokpur*,[21] speaking good English, described the present circumstances of her convent and their monastic usages. Then, at the request of the Tibetan nuns, Sister Iona gave, in simple and moving terms, an account of the life of Mary, mother of Jesus, following the Gospels step by step.

Celebration of Light

Finally, in a clearing at nightfall, each monk and nun holding a lighted candle, a celebration of light, with readings from Oriental poets, chants and prayers. The ceremony was directed by Father Albert Nambiaparambil and Father Francis Tiso.

At the monasteries of Bylakuppe

Saturday 28th November. Excursion to the *Settlement* of *Bylakuppe*. The bus journey took over four hours. The *Settlement*, which I visited in 1979 and 1983,[22] now numbers fifteen thousand Tibetan refugees. In the course of a decade, they have certainly developed this place, which had been a desert. Fields of maize and new buildings were visible. Welcomed first at the Dalai Lama's office, we had the midday meal in the *lhakhang* of *Sera-jé*, which at the office time of writing numbered 1,400 monks, including 400 boys of school age. The other college, *Sera-mé*, has 600. This whole monastic population lives in a small town surrounding the two temples, each house accommodating some tens of monks. The abbot of *Sera-jé* is Lobsang Tsering; that of *Sera-mé*, a younger man, Gosok Rinpoche, had just visited France. We have spoken above of a great Tibetan lama, *Lama Thubten Yeshe*, who died in 1984.[23] He is considered to be reincarnated in a little Spanish boy, Ösel, spoken of in the media and even the subject of a book.[24] Having known Lama Yeshe at close quarters, I wished to see his reincarnation. I knew that he had been at Sera for some time. He was brought at my request, accompanied by his Spanish tutor, whom I had met at *Nālandā Monastery*, near Lavaur.[25] I was able to talk with this little boy of seven, with his shaven head and wine-coloured robe, who is destined for an important role. For the time being he is captivating, reserved, almost timid, with the freshness of childhood.

At some distance from *Sera (Gelugpa)*, the Nyingmapa have their monastery of *Nambu Ling* (600 monks) and the *Nyingmapa Institute*, a school of philosophy with 1,600 students.

The Benedictine monasteries of Bangalore

The meeting ended on the morning of *Sunday 29th* November with a *closing session* at which Christians and Buddhists alike expressed their desire to see their dialogue continued on an organized basis. However, since the obligatory point of departure for the majority is Bangalore, we remained together for a quick tour of the botanical garden of the great city and, above all, for a visit to two Benedictine monasteries in its suburbs. We were welcomed for lunch at *Vanashram*. This is no more than a pied-à-terre for the Sylvestrines following theology courses with the Salesians, but the monastic character is evident in the style of building and the atmosphere of the Chapel. They also have plantations, and a well-stocked poultry yard.

We had tea with the nuns of *Shānti Nilayam*, after an Indian-style reception by a merry community of nuns in saffron saris.

On *Monday 30th November*, at *Asirvanam*, our group of five "Europeans", plus Father Tiso, came together around Father Mayeul to arrange the distribution of photographs after the meeting and to make suggestions with an eye to the meeting of Indian Superiors who would have to draw up their findings regarding this time of dialogue. In the evening, we boarded the bus for *Madurai*, in Tamil Nadu. It was seen fit to set aside three days for a more explicit contact with Hinduism, for it would have been a pity for several of us to have come so far and seen nothing of the principal religion of India.

MADURAI

Minakshi Temple

Tuesday 1st December. Our destination was *Archbishop's House*, in *Madurai*, which doubled as a guest house where we boarded and took our meals, to say nothing of the Chapel, where we celebrated the Eucharist, taking advantage of our meetings with the Archbishop, Mgr Arokiaswamy, who gave us an overview of the circumstances of the Church in this country. We visited the magnificent temple of *Minakshi*, the wife of Shiva. This temple is the largest in India, and one of the most beautiful, with its archways, its statues, its carvings and the devotion of the faithful. At the four cardinal points, there rise its *gopurams*, multi-storied towers sculpted with scenes from Hindu mythology, teeming with male and female deities. Although the temple has a geometric structure, the interior takes you past shadowy corners holding private sanctuaries. The space is partly occupied by shops, workshops for cutting-out and for luxury carpets. At the entrance, we watched the antics of a band of very slender monkeys with delicate features, and an ungainly elephant who, on being presented with an offering, takes hold of it, passes it up to his mahout, then slowly brings the end of his trunk down on your head in a gesture of blessing. There is no lack of amusements for a tourist! However, let us go to the essential of this luxuriant work of art. However shrewd one might be, the scholar who knows it all and can look down on the exuberance of popular devotion, who could remain indifferent to the profound *bhakti* of that noble old man, or of this poor woman who, having caressed the feet of their god, the sumptuous Vishnu or this funny little Ganesh with the elephant's trunk, prostrates before him, her forehead in the dust?

Madurai Mission

A car was put at our disposal for two days. On *Wednesday 2nd December,* it took us to *Dindigul*. Although we had not given notice of our visit, we were received with great kindness by the Jesuit Fathers of *Beschi College*. This is their large house of formation for four Provinces, speaking four different languages. Here they have their novitiate, juniorate, third year and a retirement home for elderly religious. We recalled that this Madurai Mission wrote a glorious page in the history of the Church. This was the place of residence of Fathers De Nobili and Beschi, those courageous pioneers of inculturation. As a former Jesuit, I felt thoroughly at my ease, but it was clear that they were happy to welcome monks and set no stint upon time for showing us everything. In the cemetery, I saw with emotion the graves of Fathers who were my colleagues at Kandy and Shembaganur. We then went to the hospital close at hand, *St. Joseph's Hospital*, run by the Sisters of a Congregation founded in Belgium,[26] and found five Belgian Sisters remaining. It is a very well-run hospital, with a dozen doctors, a nursing school, almost every department, solid and practical buildings.

During the return journey, we were allowed to enter the courtyard of a *mosque*. On the left, the long building serving as the Islamic school, on the right, a "temple" surmounted by a fine dome (all in blue) which is used every evening for instructions; the mosque is below. Dindigul, with nearly 500,000 inhabitants, has a population equally divided between Hindus and Muslims; these are factory workers at a leather works. The enormous rock overlooking it bears the palace of the rajah, a Muslim ruler. It is well known that India was shaken, around those days, by an event capable of unleashing a civil war: the destruction of the *Ayodhya* mosque by Hindu extremists.[27] It actually occurred on 6th December, at the time of our flight from Bombay to Paris. Before that, the newspaper headlines had predicted the event.

Hindu temples in the neighbourhood of Madurai

Thursday 3rd December is the feast of *Saint Francis Xavier*. It was moving to say the Mass in his honour so close to the region which he evangelized, the fishing coast where he made so many converts. It rained heavily the previous night and the road was covered with great puddles. In the morning, we visited the temple of *Thirupparankuntram*, about six miles to the south of Madurai, one of six famous temples dedicated to the god Murugan. It is a very ancient *cave-temple*, the forty-eight pillars of which carry beautiful carvings. A modest bribe enabled us to enter an enclosure normally reserved for Hindus. This did not seem to surprise the big Brahmin, bare-chested and with the thread of his caste much in evidence, who was on duty, for he proclaimed majestically, for the benefit of the outsiders who might have difficulty in identifying the idol: "Shiva! ... Vishnu! ..."

In the afternoon, it was the turn of *Algar Koil*, nearly 12 miles to the east of Madurai. It is the temple of the god *Sundararajan*, very airy, preceded and surrounded by courtyards. First of all, there is a *mandapam* where pilgrims can eat and sleep. It is a portico open in all directions, with benches. Prayers are offered there. The temple, where we could not enter, has a roof completely covered with gold, shining in the sun. Some pretty little monkeys profit from (or abuse) the devotion of the faithful, who regale them with peanuts. Not quite 2 miles from there, higher on the hill, is *a sacred spring*; a well is there for the pilgrims who come to carry out their ritual ablutions below a little sanctuary. We arrived at the same time as the classes of a girls' school. Full of delight, they bathed with their clothes on and splashed each other with great roars of laughter. Never say that Hinduism is cheerless and uncommunicative!

An arduous journey

Friday 4th December. Long bus journey back *from Madurai to Bangalore.* Then, at 10.30 p.m., we went *from Bangalore to Kengeri* in an overcrowded bus. We then had to make our way for more than two miles along a precarious side-path beside a road carrying heavy traffic and in the dazzle of the headlights. These were the most trying hours of the last three weeks. We arrived inside the enclosure of *Asirvanam*, exhausted, on the stroke of midnight.

The return journey

Saturday 5th December. We owed a large debt of gratitude to the Asirvanam community and, in particular, to Father Cletus, who took great care to make our reservations on the bus and plane and was always with us at difficult moments.

We regretted not being better acquainted with botany so as to be able to identify trees, plants and flowers, the vegetation varying so much from the foothills of the Himalayas to the hot plains of the South.

In the course of so much travel at all hours of the day and night, we had been able to observe so many aspects of Indian life on a daily basis, the comings and goings of the humble village population, the noble bearing of the women, the majority of them in saris, poor but as dignified as queens, the joyful sight of boys and girls on their way to school in uniforms or coloured dresses, impeccable in appearance. Yes, it is a very great people.

We finished with a sense of gratitude for these contacts with Tibetan monasticism, of which we knew so little and the heart of which seems so close.

This Saturday, the 5th, having left Asirvanam towards 7 p.m., we boarded the plane at *Bangalore* at 9.50 p.m. It landed at *Bombay* at 11.10 p.m., and a coach took us to the international airport. The formalities of change there are finicking, much slower than anticipated, and we spent a sleepless night at the airport. It was only on 6th December at 6.15 a.m. that the Air India plane took off for Europe via *Delhi*. We experienced several episodes of severe turbulence, air-pockets. Whereas at Bombay the temperature had been 27°, it was only 4° in Paris, where we disembarked at 2.15 p.m. We found ourselves in another world. The one which we left behind remains in our dreams.

A MONASTIC PILGRIMAGE TO TIBET (1994)

The participants

Who would not dream of going to Tibet one day, to survey the beauties of the country and the way its people live, and to venerate the holy places? This was, at any rate, the object of our desires. Having been committed for years to the encounter of this religion, it seemed to us bizarre to have put so much effort into getting to know it without having been able to appreciate the original context in which it was lived. For reasons of poverty, we had earlier declined to join a group of ecumenists who went there in September 1987.[28] Generosity of mind led to our being told on no account to miss the next opportunity. This has just presented itself, in the most favourable terms. We would not be dependant on a commonplace travel agency. This would be a *pilgrimage* to the holy places and to the principal monasteries of Tibet, the organizers being the Lamas of the Tibetan centre of Kagyu-Ling, in Burgundy. The journey would last three weeks, from 8–29 July 1994. The first three days would be occupied by a stay in Kathmandu, as also the last five, when we returned from Lhasa. I prepared with *two weeks of Tibetan at Kagyu-Ling*, a community with whom I have often stayed for language-study[29] and which has welcomed me with great kindness; I have many friends there.

Our group numbered 39. Our guide was *Lama Seunam*, director of the Marpa Institute. He was accompanied by Lama Orgyen, one of the founders of Plaige. On their side, Françoise Croizier, the translator, combined with her knowledge of Tibetan a helpfulness under every trial and a constant smile. The majority of the participants in this pilgrimage came from France, seven from Belgium. *Catholic monasticism* was well represented: three monks, Father Maxime Gimenez from Chevetogne, Father Maximilien Amilon from La Pierre-qui-Vire, Father Bernard de Give from Scourmont – and two Benedictine nuns: Sister Marie-André Houdart from the Abbey of Sainte-Gertrude at Louvain-la-Neuve, and Sister Bruno Marie Colin from the Abbey of Paix Notre-Dame at Liège. Father Maxime was accompanied by four ladies who might be termed his disciples, for they had periodic meetings with him at Chevetogne for spiritual direction. Of the persons already named, several were far from making their first contact with Buddhism, as they had taken part in *spiritual exchanges* which enabled them to stay in *Zen monasteries in Japan*.[30] Others were part of a group which had the experience, in November 1992, of a fruitful encounter with Tibetan monasticism.[31]

What shall I say about our other travelling companions? One does not put one's name down for such a pilgrimage out of pure curiosity. Although their commitment to the Buddhist Dharma and their knowledge of Tibetan Buddhism varied greatly, all considered themselves as Buddhists or Buddhist sympathisers, and each had the remains of Christian origins and openness of mind. Apart from Lama Orgyen,[32] none of the participants had previously seen Tibet.

From Europe to Nepal

Friday 8th July. Along with Sister Marie-André, we met at *Zaventem* airport, where we arrived around 9 a.m.: Claudine Pirotte, mother of a family of six children, who had already been to Japan, Sister Bruno Colin, from Liège and Jean-Paul Cantillon, a Belgian serving with the European Community in Luxembourg. *Departure from Brussels at 10.55 a.m. Arrival at Frankfurt at 12 noon.* There we met with manifold uncertainties and dead ends. Not having received our Frankfurt – Delhi tickets, we did not think we could register our luggage or enter the *Lufthansa* embarkation cubicle. We finally ventured to do so, with only fifteen minutes to spare. Meanwhile, our reservations had been cancelled, other passengers being allocated our places. We were directed to seats left vacant at the rear, and separated from one another. When we were over Budapest, at 2.45 p.m., we were doing over 520 miles an hour, at an altitude of more than 32,800 feet. The exernal temperature was -49°C. Passing above *Istanbul*, we saw the Golden Horn and the Bosphorus. Supper was taken on the plane and the hour was changed according to local time.

IN NEPAL

Kathmandu

Saturday 9th July. We arrived in Delhi at 0.45 a.m., where the temperature was 27°. We were obliged to wait for a long time to recover our luggage since, by an oversight, we were not considered as merely in transit. *Departure from Delhi at 11 a.m,* Delhi – Lucknow – Kathmandu, in a *Royal Nepal Air Lines* plane, *arriving at Kathmandu around 12.20. The Marshyangdi hotel* was luxurious, very clean with great care taken over meals. From that night onwards, I shared the room of *Jean-Paul Cantillon*. As well as a computer specialist at the service of the European Community at Luxembourg, he was a practising Buddhist, directing a Dharma group in that city. Open-minded and kindly, he took part in all the Christian-Buddhist colloquia at Karma-Ling, recording the lectures.

In the evening, we took a walk in the town, through the main thoroughfares. The weather was hot, in Delhi, Nepal and Lhasa alike. As it was Saturday, most of the shops were closed. Those that were open stocked works of art. Many pretty children urged us, or Nepalese women, to let them sell us various works of art, such as necklaces, statuettes or carved daggers. They were ready to bargain, and the prices came down very low. The kindness of all these Nepalese, smiling and pleasant, and the beauty of their faces, brown with lively eyes, was remarkable. The old streets near the centre have houses the carvings of which on doors, beams and balconies we admired. On the other hand, there was no little filth in the streets, fruit and vegetables often being in close proximity to refuse. From the religious point of view, we saw *many little temples*, Hindu or Buddhist, often imbued with syncretism. The consul for Belgium, Keshab Regmi, was kind enough to come and greet us; he is Nepalese. We took our evening meal in a Tibetan restaurant.

Kopan

Sunday 10th July. From the hotel terrace and the fifth-floor restaurant, there was a panoramic view of the city and its neighbourhood, surrounded by mountains. That morning we travelled five miles from Kathmandu to visit an important Gelugpa monastery on the hill of *Kopan*. It was founded by *Lama Thubten Yeshe*, with whom I had excellent relations.[33] I had stayed in this place, which lends itself to meditation, in January 1980.[34] A lady from Vincennes, Chantal Roussel, who was taking part in this pilgrimage remains deeply attached to that spiritual giant and to his lineage. She, as well as Father Maximilien and the two Benedictine nuns, was accompanying us that day. The ascent towards Kopan was at first difficult for the cars, since a storm the previous night filled the gutters and potholes in the earth road with broad puddles. It was the monsoon. We continued on foot up the breathtaking incline. Above, in the shop, were purchased *khata*s (those pretty scarves of silk), and drinks. There had been many changes in the last fourteen years. The former *lhakang* (prayer-hall), grown too narrow and difficult of access, had been demolished and a new one built. The row of little rooms where I had lodged no longer existed, nor the primitive lodge of the Russian Princess Zina, nor the vast tent which used to accommodate the Westerners come from the four corners of the earth for the teaching weeks. They had all been replaced by a fine and more practical, red-brick, two-storey building. In the temple, as a ritual ended, we saw a large number of little monks coming out into the avenue, bordered by brand-new *chortens*. I found again *Lama Lodreu*, with whom I had had such a good exchange. He recognized me at once and clasped my hands with emotion. Chantal wanted, above all, a reunion with *Geshe Kongchok*, whom she had met here in 1989. He is dignified and quiet. She introduced me and, hearing that I was out of sorts, he gave me some blessed pills of his own making.

Bodnath

We then went down to *Bodnath* where, at about 3 p.m., we found the Lamas and the rest of our group of 39–strong. We made a tour of the great *stūpa*, reproduced in so many albums and books on art.[35] The pilgrims entered the stream of circumambulation, turning the numerous prayer-wheels. We made a similar circuit on the roof. While we were up there, the Buddhists said all together the prayer in our blue brochure, then, in response to the request for a Christian prayer, Fr. Maxime recited one which he and the ladies who were his disciples knew by heart. After this, several people went to shop for souvenirs in the little shops surrounding the *stūpa*. The excursion ended with a rather hasty visit to three monasteries in the vicinity of this holy place:

1. That of Beru Khyentse Rinpoche – Kagyupa
2. That of Dilgo Khyentse Rinpoche – Nyingmapa
3. That of Dudjom Rinpoche – Nyingmapa. His mummified body is preserved there.

Monday 11th July. In the morning, a *Christian liturgy* was led by Fr. Maxime Gimenez. This was not the Eucharist, but an arrangement of texts and prayers from the Office of Chevetogne. A small altar bearing icons had been arranged. I attended with Fr. Maxime's disciples and had a beneficent immersion in the atmosphere of the Orthodox liturgy.

Pulahari

We went to visit, by a road made rather trying by the water-filled pot-holes, the *stūpa of Djamgoeun Kongtrul Rinpoche* at *Pulahari*. He died in an accident in 1992, aged 37.[36] The monastery had just been built according to his plans on a plateau overlooking the valley. The view extends into the distance. The air was fresh, far from the pollution of the city. At the entrance, mongooses attract the attention of visitors. The mausoleum stands very high, and the *stūpa* is highly decorated and covered with gold-leaf. The mummified body has contracted somewhat and we prayed with recollection in its presence. There are three statues in the temple: Dorje Chang in the middle, the sixteenth Karmapa and the first Djamgoeun Kongtrul. There is also a portrait of the young seventeenth Karmapa.

ON THE ROOF OF THE WORLD

Tuesday 12th July. At Kathmandu airport, we met the Dalai Lama's translator, Matthieu Ricard. We would see him again on our return. A couple with two little girls were accompanying us on this pilgrimage. The children were named Audrey, 10 years old, and Mikaëla, 8 years old. As we were boarding the plane, the elder said to her mother: "We're going to see the yeti!"

The *China Southwest Airlines* company flew us from Kathmandu to Lhasa in 45 minutes, between 11.15 a.m. and noon. A very light breakfast was served us on the plane. A short while before landing, I drank half a bottle of wine, on the advice of Lama Sherab. I gave one of my three bottles to Chantal, the other to Fr. Maximilien, and we felt all the better for it. I had dreaded the moment when we would suddenly come out at high altitude (Lhasa is at 12,000 feet). In fact *the arrival was the simplest thing in the world*: a gentle, cool breeze was sweeping the plateau. During the flight, we had seen Mount Everest on the left, rising above the neighbouring peaks, a blue sky, little lakes of a deep shade of blue. I did not experience altitude sickness, at least not during those first hours in Tibet. Later, and on subsequent days, like the others on our expedition, I had an occasional headache, breathlessness on climbing stairs, a want of air and tiredness when walking rather quickly, a lack of appetite, great fatigue. Some of the others had migraine, vomiting or insomnia. The temperature was really summer-like at *Lhasa;* on some days 32° or 35°.

Between Gongar airport and Lhasa, there is a road nearly 70 miles long, bordered by sparse vegetation beside a river. We stopped before some frescos of the Buddha on a rock.

Tibet has a surface area of 553,500 square miles. This makes it half the size of India, 2.6 times the size of France, 48 times that of Belgium.

The majority of Tibetans live in the South of the country, in the region irrigated by the *Tsangpo* (known in India as the Brahmaputra) and its tributaries, as also in the Eastern province of Kham. These more hospitable regions, made up of gentle, protected valleys, produce the crops essential to the Tibetans: barley, wheat and a small range of vegetables. Animal husbandry is practised there, too, and cows, goats, pigs and horses are to be found on the farms. The numerous villages, scattered here and there, amount to large farms. A typical large farm is a rectangular enclosure of single-storey whitewashed houses, with an entrance giving onto the courtyard. Around the courtyard are arranged the domestic zone of the peasant and his family, his store-rooms and the stables. Prayer-flags, often torn and dulled by the fury of the winds, fly from the masts erected on the highest point of the roofs. On the flat roofs are stored combustibles such as firewood, brushwood and dried yak dung.[37]

LHASA

The hotel where we were accommodated, the *Himalaya Hotel*, is situated at the south-east of the city, close to the *Tibet University*. It is well run, but not quite as comfortable as the one in Kathmandu.

On the Barkor

As we were feeling in good form, in the afternoon we went to the *Barkor*, a circular avenue, crowded with many people, surrounding the *Jokhang*, which is their cathedral, as it were. The crowd was making the circuit of it, Tibetans of all ages, many having come here on pilgrimage, some of them turning their prayer-wheels. They included a number of little traders. They urged us to buy their knick-knacks, which are often junk: necklaces, bracelets, rosaries, daggers. Many elderly Tibetan women, in particular, had fine faces, and wore coloured dresses, with distinctive regional headdresses on their black plaits. Young boys and girls with smiling faces became particularly attached to us, and they were hard to resist. It was clear that *all foreigners are objects of attraction to them*. Some asked for a photograph of the Dalai Lama and, on receiving it, they gave us a big smile and placed it respectfully on the crown of their heads. The youngest were keen to have a biro. It goes without saying that we were watched. Even before reaching Lhasa, on the way from the airport, we noticed imposing barracks for the *Chinese army*. The soldiers had a fine green uniform with a peaked cap, the officers having more epaulettes and gold braid. Most of the soldiers were young, with a good carriage. The army is omnipresent and does not seem aggressive, but is on alert, ready to face a possible riot. On the Barkor, and particularly in front of the Jokhang, the soldiers in green and the police in blue mingled with the crowd, missing nothing. As the foreigners found themselves rapidly surrounded by friendly Tibetans, the Chinese separated us from them, only to see the same good lady and the small fry rejoin us five minutes later.

My *Trappist habit* frequently attracted attention. It was clear to everyone that it marks out a monk of another religion, and a Christian at that, something clearly very much appreciated by such a devout people. On reflection, I see it as a first, for if, in the past, Tibet witnessed the brief adventures of the Jesuits Antonio De Andrade and his companions, of Father Desideri and the Capuchins at the beginning of the eighteenth century and of two Lazarists in 1846, I can say without fear of error that I am *the first monk to enter Tibet* and walk freely, surrounded by the sympathy of all, on this thoroughfare crowded with Buddhist pilgrims fervently circumambulating the most sacred shrine of their religion.[38] Our two Benedictine Sisters, I think, also realized with emotion that they were the first Christian nuns to make the same circuit, while Fr. Maxime of Chevetogne, in his solemn black robe and black cap, rather like the dress of the Orthodox monks, drew even more attention and respect. He wore his silver pectoral cross in full view. "Otherwise," he said, "they would take me for a Muslim."

The Jokhang

In front of the Jokhang stand four white ovens, from which rose thick smoke, doubtless to avert the malign influence of evil spirits. On the square before the entrance, a large number of pilgrims, both men and women, devoted themselves to multiple *prostrations,* stretched full-length on the ground, protected from the ground by a kind of mattress. The atmosphere was one of complete devotion. The principal *statue* in this temple is the most ancient of their religion, that of *Jowo Shakyamuni,* brought to the king of Tibet, Songtsen Gampo, by his Chinese wife, around the year 630 of our era. Once we had passed through the interior court of the Jokhang, we came upon a rectangular space where about a hundred monks in dark red robes, sitting in the lotus position on cushions, were vigorously giving themselves up to chanting a ritual – all this in a setting of pedestrian traffic both dusty and ardent. The temple has a multiplicity of small chapels. The numerous statues and representations of divinities receive in every corner the homage of devout greetings and the wavering flicker of butter-lamps. It is a blend of smells and feeble lights, of curiosity and faith. Our group from France and Belgium had an advantage in that it included two little girls. The eight-year-old *Mikaëla*, a serious and attractive brunette, attracted particular attention. The old Tibetan women never stop looking lovingly at her. One of them, wishing to show her her affection, took out of her bag a little white cube, a yak cheese, which she offered to the little girl. Not many French girls could boast of having received such a gift.

The Barkor is not only a devotional circuit, it is also *a market*; shops along its whole length offer on the ground, under the sky, a variety of fabrics in vivid colours, clothing, and domestic utensils. This is the heart of Tibet; proof would be redundant. The Chinese are well aware of the fact: policemen in plain clothes watched us out of the corner of their eye. They particularly noticed a young Tibetan nun too eager to chat with our Sisters.

Tour of Lhasa

Lhasa has become a city which is more than half Chinese. All the shops and all the restaurants bear bilingual signs in front of their entrances: above, the elegant characters of the Tibetan language, following them, below, the big Chinese ideograms which are a mystery to us. Most of the shops are run by the Chinese. In the street, the latter appear to be more numerous than the Tibetans, but all that is a rather complicated business. The hotel where we were staying, *Himalaya Hotel,* depends on a Tibetan organization, *Tibetan International Sports Travel,* but it has two restaurants, one Tibetan, the other Chinese, and the staff responsible for meals and rooms are drawn from both nationalities. The attitude of the Chinese women is correct but impersonal, that of the Tibetan women warmer and more smiling; they love to give pleasure.

Wednesday 13th July. Next to our hotel stands *a large barracks* of the Chinese army. From our windows we could see the manoeuvres of the regiment, and sometimes we heard their military music or bugle-calls. At first sight, their discipline seems not rigorous but simple and naive. At dawn, we took a walk beside the river Kyichu, seeing hardly anyone except a few isolated boy- and girl-students, revising their lessons. These were Tibetans, history books in their hands. There were, however, strung out along the river, a small number of fishermen. These were all Chinese, for Tibetans have no right to fish, this being to deprive the fish of life; this being, in any case, a type of food for which they have not the slightest relish.

Drepung

In the afternoon, we went to the monastery of *Drepung*, located about five miles to the west. The name in Tibetan means "heap of rice", due no doubt to the apearance of these buildings on the mountainside. Founded in 1416 by a disciple of Tsong Khapa, that great reformer of the monastic Order, it housed more than 7,000 monks and, all the religions taken together, it could certainly be considered the largest monastery the world has ever known. It was the most important Gelugpa monastery. As a teaching centre, a monastic university, it had, with its two colleges, Loseling and Gomang, a great influence, as far away as Mongolia. Since it was the crucial centre of Gelugpa religious power, the second, third and fourth Dalai Lamas were buried within its walls and from here, too, the fifth Dalai Lama ruled until the completion of the Potala. We became a little breathless from climbing so many flights of stone or wooden stairs, some of them very steep, to move from one building to another. Most of the monastery escaped destruction, so the interior is ancient, though the *thankas* have been stolen. The prayer-hall common to both colleges is really huge. In it we admired the frescoes in vivid colours, down the length of its walls, which the monks are restoring, faithfully preserving the original paintings. Apart from a few of these artists, we saw almost no adult monks nor boy-monks in this famous monastery, though they must be numbered by the hundreds. We had to suppose that they hide from tourists as a security measure. It is, in any case, a prominent site of Tibetan Buddhism which prompts one to what they call prayers of well-wishing. I experienced, nevertheless, a certain disappointment as we descended the hill again. I was received so cordially in their *Karnataka Drepung* in 1983[39] and our Abbey of Scourmont has actually adopted a little boy-monk of Loseling, on account of whom we keep closely in touch. I had been anticipating having the opportunity, here, of saying something about him. In contrast with their Indian monastery, we saw nothing of either abbot or community. This is the price paid for the Chinese occupation.

At a short distance away is the little monastery of *Nechung*, the Dalai Lama's oracle, a medium by means of whom *Dorje Drakden*, the recognized protector of Tibet, advises the Dalai Lama. The goverment never takes an important decision without consulting the oracle.[40] It should be no cause for wonder that the chapel of the protector under both his aspects, peaceable and wrathful, should be dedicated to him. It is common knowledge that the little temple of the current Nechung[41] can be seen at Dharamsala.

Sera

Thursday 14th July. Three miles to the north of Lhasa, occupying the lower part of a hill, is the monastery of *Sera*, one of the most important of the Gelugpa monasteries, the other two being Drepung and Ganden. The building of the monastery was begun by a disciple of Tsong Khapa in 1419. The reputation of this monastic university, with its colleges of Sera-jé and Sera-mé, grew steadily over the centuries. The general effect of the buildings is more coherent than that of Drepung and, while the "heap of rice" is white, the different temples and colleges of Sera stand out against the mountain by virtue of the red of roofs and doorframes. It would be irksome to describe the furnishings of the different chapels belonging to the different colleges, their *thankas* (or icons) their multiplicity of statues, before which votive flames are kept permanently alight. The principal "prayer-hall", where the two colleges reunited hold their combined assemblies, is particularly vast. These different chapels and meeting rooms give off an undeniable atmosphere of devotion simultaneously fervent and a little heavy, in a semi-darkness reminiscent of Hindu temples. To think that bookish men claim that Buddhism is not a religion! Lhasa means "the land of the gods", so this tour of sanctuaries was, for us pilgrims, an occasion for fervent prayers in a place marked by a wonderful past.

However, let us face it, we brought regret away too. I have been to *Sera, in Karnataka* three times.[42] I was on very friendly terms with the monks of Sera-jé, particularly with Lama Thubten Yeshe[43] and, more recently, with the abbot of Sera-mé, Geshe Gosok.[44] To have had no opportunity to utter a word about this to anyone in their monastery of origin is a matter for regret. My regret was shared by a lady from Vincennes, Chantal Roussel, whose relationship with Lama Thubten Yeshe was particularly close. We were able to see the buildings of Sera but practically none of the monks, simply about fifty boy-monks playing merrily on the lawns of one of the colleges, superintended by a soldier, gun on his shoulder. Security obliges.

Life at Lhasa

Lhasa is not as ugly as it is said to be. It has grown a good deal; one sees a good deal of construction under way, and buildings range from white-washed, single-storey houses to high-rise buildings in the most modern style. Some have a certain attraction. There is no suggestion of town-planning. In some streets one might imagine oneself in India, while certain wide avenues no doubt imitate great cities in China. At the major crossroads in one of them, with its red lights, the intersection is seen to support an almost colossal monument: two great yaks apparently covered in gold leaf dominate the vista. Is this the glory of Tibet? It is not edifying for everyone. One of my companions whispered in my ear: "It reminds me of the golden calf."

As a devout Buddhist, my companion John-Paul decided, one fine morning, to go and recite *the pūjā of Chenrezig on the roof of the Jokhang.* Having completed his devotions, he was thinking of nothing but of coming down quietly when he became aware that he was locked in the temple, the doors of which are padlocked at noon. A lama who was taking his little companions to visit the sanctuary was dumbfounded to encounter him at that hour and, fortunately, was willing to open the door for him.

Back at the hotel, we had a two hour meeting in the evening, in Fr. Maxime's room. This was both a fraternal meal and a religious conference, between the Christian monks, the ladies of Chevetogne and our guides on this pilgrimage, Lama Seunam, Lama Orgyen and Françoise the translator. A little altar bearing Christian icons and a statuette of Tara had pride of place at our cordial exchanges, everyone having the opportunity to reveal the riches of his own tradition. After all, we were not tourists and it seemed to us that what we were doing was really *new*: that about ten monks and convinced Christian women should be participating fully in *a Buddhist pilgrimage* in the context of the Tibetan Vajrayāna. This was, it seemed to us, the religious peak of these three weeks, a moving experience for each man and woman amongst us.

Friday 15th July. There were on the streets a great many new cars, the majority Japanese: lorries, vans or private cars, a great number of bicycles, also a kind of tractor with an extended chassis, a little motor at the front, the rear being a transporter van for merchandise, sometimes with people substituted.[45] That morning we visited the *Tibetan Medical Centre (Mentsi khang)*, which is located at the end of the square opposite the Jokhang. The modern building was completed in 1980. It is used, above all, as an outpatients' clinic, and the doctors see up to 600 patients a day. More than 400 qualified Tibetan doctors, half of them women, practise in Lhasa. The school of medicine is housed in a separate building. The third floor has two separate rooms which may be visited. The first is a kind of *sanctuary* honouring the Tibetan medical tradition, including three famous doctors. Another room contains a whole collection of *thankas* relating to medicine. They also show the different plants used in the preparation of medicines. The Tibetan tradition takes astrology into account. We passed through a chamber for acupuncture, which interested several members of our group who were doctors, or abreast with Tibetan medicine.

Saturday 16th July. The group were planning to visit the Potala that afternoon, just when the heat was stifling. However, the Potala being closed, they went to see the *Norbulinka*. I had been unwell yesterday, and was more so today. In the evening I was cared for effectively by Bernadette Pierrard, the mother of the two little girls. She teaches methods borrowed from the Tao and *works on the energies*. The next day on rising, my temperature was almost normal. I recovered gradually in the course of Sunday. However, both from prudence and disinclination, I did not take part in the excursion of the group to *Tsedang* and *Samye*.

Sunday 17th July. Fr. Maximilien remained with me those three days. We wished to visit the *Norbulinka*, but a caretaker at the entrance told us: "Closed on Sunday". Having noticed on the map of Lhasa that there is, some distance away, a *Bompo Ri* (which amounts to no more than a hillock), we located it close to a broad avenue near the Norbulinka. By way of a sandy little path, we skirted this Tibetan enclave in the Chinese town and ended up at a tiny Gelugpa monastery: *Kunde Ling College*. This must be a small monastic school. We were introduced to one young monk after another. The most important knows some words of English. He at once unlocked the padlock of the temple door and explained the statues of the divinities for us. To judge by the limited number of red seats, this college cannot number more than a score of boy-monks. I regret that my very limited knowledge of Tibetan prevented us from prolonging the conversation. We had hardly left the sandy cul-de-sac for the main road when we were intrigued by some harsh, low sounds. These deep rumblings came from the right, the summit of the *Bompo Ri* hillock, from *five long trumpets* emitting deep, jarring vibrations. Five tall monks in red robes were silhouetted against the sky, perhaps not actually Bönpo, but their successors are prolonging their ancestral mystique, right beside the modern avenue.

We did not waste this day. I do not know how much attention either Tibet or China pay to *Sunday* as a day of rest. It seems to us, at any rate, that people worked little, dawdling in the street, and that the ladies and young girls were elegant in their "Sunday best". We kept noticing in Lhasa young girls wearing pink dresses made of floating drapery, rather dated. For our return to the hotel, we hailed the first *rickshaw that passed us;* the driver was Chinese. We were about to board it when up came another *rickshawman* who, with his right hand, violently pushed the Chinese away: "No, not him! Me Tibetan." Having already agreed the fare with the Chinese, we considered it a point of honour not to break our agreement.

The Norbulinka

Monday 18th July. In the afternoon, our visit to the *Norbulinka*. At the entrance, an obsequious Chinese who runs a shop greeted me with a self-seeking "Welcome to Tibet"! This "park of the precious jewel" is a vast enclosure two and a half miles to the west of Lhasa. It was the *summer palace* of the Dalai Lama. The seventh Dalai Lama had the first palace built in around 1750. The bulk of the principal buildings had been built in the course of this century by the thirteenth and fourteenth Dalai Lamas. It was from here that the present Dalai Lama fled Tibet in March 1959. The palaces, badly damaged by the firing of the Chinese artillery in the course of the popular uprising which followed his departure, has been repaired up to a point, but most of their richness has disappeared. We passed through the halls and saw the many frescos and the furniture of the two principal palaces. *The new summer palace*, built as the official summer residence of *the fourteenth Dalai Lama*, was completed in 1956. This opulent and highly decorated building houses the masterpieces of Tibetan art, some very old statues and assorted articles dating from the twentieth century and imported from the West. We passed through the audience chamber of His Holiness, the meditation-hall, his bedroom and the apartments of the mother of the Dalai Lama. Less imposing, but older, is the *palace of the thirteenth Dalai Lama*, which a wealthy layman had built for him in 1922 and which therefore has a patina lacking in the more recent one. These various buildings are widely separated in the vast park, planted with many different kinds of trees, rather badly maintained.

This visit was the occasion of a double encounter. The first was with *an old Tibetan*, whose face showed nobility and goodness; he was moved to notice that, despite my age, I was obviously in better physical condition than he was. More particularly, when we had just left the second palace, we were accosted furtively by a distinguished-looking young man whose English was rudimentary but who was bent on *transmitting a message to us*, the alley being deserted, and shielded from the sight of anyone who might be a threat: "This palace of His Holiness is sacred to us. The Chinese occupy the ground floor and have made it into a shop where they sell cheap junk. Have you already met His Holiness? How fortunate you have been! ... Impossible for us to have a Tibetan education. At college and university, the first language is Chinese, the second (which is very difficult for us) is English. Tibetan comes only third. The result is that the young Tibetans are kept from having any future and maintained in a state of intellectual withering away." He spoke with emotion, not having given up all hope of remedying, however secretively, such a crushing of the Tibetan culture.

On our return to the hotel (the day was cooler due to some welcome rain), we came upon some entertainment which was being offered to a group of tourists: some *popular Tibetan dances*. Three tall male dancers, in black masks and weighed down by multi-coloured costumes partnered three graceful female dancers in the traditional pink dresses; they had sparkling headdresses reminiscent of the hats with symbolic flaps worn by the Bönpo. All to the rhythm of cymbals and a gong.

One thing surprised us. The people of the country, noticing that we were Christians, called out to us: *"Amen! amen!"* by way of an ironic jibe – this happened on several occasions. In reality, they were chanting: "Amin! amin!", and sketching a sign of the cross in the Orthodox manner, which made me think that they had seen on Chinese television a liturgy of the oriental rite. From our windows, every day and almost until midnight, we heard *music*, borrowed from the repertoire of Western countries as often as from that of China.

Ani Sangkhung

Tuesday 19th July. With Fr. Maximilien, we were present at the ritual of the nuns of *Ani Sangkhung*. It is the only convent of nuns in Lhasa which is still active. The foundation having been made in the seventh century, the place is often associated with Songtsen Gampo. At the beginning, the building was actually a men's monastery but, in the fifteenth century, a disciple of Tsong Khapa, Tongten, had it enlarged and changed it into a convent for nuns. The building originally housed more than a hundred nuns but, abandoned during the Cultural Revolution, it began to fall into ruin. Since 1984, it has regained its original purpose. The nuns, who have once more reached the figure of a hundred, are responsible for carrying out the *rituals* of Chenrezig and of Tara. Most of them are very young and did not fail to greet us with their best smiles on seeing two Christian monks entering their prayer-hall. This latter, recently decorated, is very cheerful. To the rear of the convent is a long room, a shrine. It is the place where Songtsen Gampo would have meditated. There is something bewitching about the continuous rhythm of the prayer of these young nuns with clear voices. I was reminded of the constant prayer of our old monks of the Bosphorus.

Chinese television does not suffer at all from comparison with ours. The soap operas inspired by mediaeval China really have style, with the beauty of their costumes and the art of their landscapes.

An expedition: Tsedang, Samye

The evening brought the return from their expedition to *Tsedang* and *Samye* all the members of our group, tolerably excited. They were badly shaken up by the journeys over impossible roads but, on the other hand, delighted with the luxury of their hotel at Tsedang and, in particular, with everything that they saw at Samye. Here I hand over to Sister Marie-André as narrator.

Sunday 17th July. At 9.30 a.m. we boarded our coach to take the road *for Tsedang*, 118 miles from Lhasa in the valley of Yarlung Tsangpo, to the south-east of the capital. My travel guide had shown this as a journey of some three hours. In fact it took a nightmarish journey of more than nine hours to cover the fifty miles still separating us from Tsedang. The reason? The road was being reconstructed over its full length, and work will doubtless continue for several years more, given the almost total absence of mechanisation. In Europe, a temporary, parallel road would have been provided in order not to impede traffic while the work went on, at least for those sections not carved out of the actual mountain. No question of that here! The coach had to run a real obstacle course at an average speed of 3 m.p.h. In fact the mountains are deeply furrowed by torrents which, during snowmelt, could carry the road away. Besides, roughly every 160 feet, a bridge had already been built across crevasses sometimes many feet deep. As the sub-foundation of the road was at various degrees of completion, the said bridges emerged at more or less 16 inches above the level of the road and could not be cleared by vehicles, which were therefore obliged to descend into ravines with deep and muddy ruts and then climb them with great difficulty beyond the bridge. On several occasions, we thought that the coach, leaning perilously first to right and then to left, would not regain its balance or that the track would prove too narrow for its set of wheels. This sport clearly gave rise to a puncture, repaired by our Chinese driver in thirty minutes, after which we had a further halt when a large stone became wedged between the rear wheels and blocked them. The whole body of the coach groaned and our frame suffered dislocation. As clouds of dust were raised by every vehicle we passed or overtook, it was impossible to open the windows. To add further to our discomfort, the exhaust pipe, to prevent damage to it from obstacles on the road, ran above the floorboards all the way to its exit at the rear, giving off heat which would be appreciated in the winter.

However, we felt ourselves privileged when we observed at leisure *the gangs of Tibetans*, men, women and children, *who toiled* in groups of a dozen, under a pitiless sun, and whose camps, most often some tents along the riverbank, lined the road. Lorries were unloading enormous chunks of rock collected at the foot of the mountains nearby; women were carrying four or five of these rocks on their backs, held in place by a plaited cord passed around their brow; others were cutting them in slices with blows from a mallet while men on their knees were arranging them on the site. This work fit for galley slaves, still going full blast at 7 p.m., did not deter the labourers from stopping as we passed, greeting us with large arm gestures and joyful cries of "Tashi deleg!"

In the fields carved out of the alluvia of the river, we noticed peasants busy reaping the millet, rye or winter barley close to the ground with small hand-sickles without handles.

The Tsangpo valley is lined by several peaks more than 18,050 feet high, among them the *Chuwori*. We could see the ruins of the *Gongkar Dzong*, the fortress which guarded the valley, the *Gongkar Chöde Gonpa* and that of *Rawame*, both belonging to the Sakya tradition. We arrived at *Tsedang* at 6.30 p.m. This was formerly the capital of Yarlung and cradle of Tibetan culture. Exhausted by so trying a journey, we appreciated the comfort of the hotel and the Chinese supper provided.

Monday 18th July. We took the road for *Yumbu Lakang*, one of the places in Tibet earliest to be inhabited. Perched on a spur overlooking the valley, it became a small monastery, destroyed by the Chinese; some monks are attempting to rebuild the ruins. We retraced for about nineteen miles the route we had "tested" the day before until we reached the embarkation for the motor boat which was to take us *across the Tsangpo* – something not achieved without difficulty or the risk of grounding. The weather was broiling (over 38°), but we had an amazing view over the valley. Then we underwent a real slalom across a desert of dunes, on an uncovered lorry. Around 3 p.m., we neared a clearing in a willow-wood, where the tents of the encampment awaited us. Visit to the famous monastery of *Samye*, the oldest monastery in Tibet, which was destroyed by the Red Guards in 1966. The great three-storey hall, surmounted by golden roofs, has already been rebuilt, as also two of the four *stūpas* which stand at the four cardinal points. At 8.30 p.m., the Lamas celebrated a *pūjā*, by the light of the full moon; this was followed by a Christian celebration prepared by Fr. Maxime and his group. Inspired by the Eastern rite of the washing of feet, it was too long at the end of such a full day. It nevertheless drew quite a large number of villagers.

Tuesday 19th July. The lorry dropped us at the ford at about 10 a.m. The river-crossing. Visit to the monastery of *Mindroling*, of the Nyingmapa Order. The order and cleanliness which reigned there were striking. Destroyed like so many during the Cultural Revolution, the ruins have, since 1982, been rebuilt by some monks.

On the way back, we were to have visited the *Drölma Lhakhang Temple*, where the goddess Tara is specially honoured. Being tired out, no one protested at the announcement that this visit had been suppressed. Returned to our hotel at 9.30 p.m. (Here ends Sister Marie-André's narrative for these three days).

The Potala

Wednesday 20th July. From the balcony, on the sixth floor of the hotel, there is a magnificent view over the whole town, surrounded by mountains. All the way along the river, one new building follows another, while leaving plenty of free spaces. There are trees everywhere, particularly at the extreme south-east, where we were: eucalyptus trees in green blossom. Visit to the *Potala* in the morning. The building of the present palace began in 1645 under a great man, the fifth Dalai Lama. In 1648, the White Palace was completed. The Red Palace was finished in 1694. The Potala was *the residence of all the Dalai Lamas* from the fifth to the present one, who is the fourteenth. As we gradually became aware of the size and proportions of the Potala, the sensational splendour of this incredible building becomes so tangible and so real that any description seems inadequate. We visited each storey, each of them leading us into numerous chambers, peopled by statues of each ruler and of the divinities. The appartments of the Dalai Lamas, with their chapels and their tombs. Here there are treasures of carved work, in many cases of outstanding workmanship. The atmosphere of spirituality is intense, at times almost stifling. The flights of stairs lead the pilgrims to every floor. From every balcony, there is a splendid view over the city. *A military parade* was taking place below, near a park. Seen from above, these platoons, these square blocks of troops, looked like a children's game with little lead soldiers.

Dogs are numerous throughout Tibet, in the streets, sleeping on monastery staircases, prowling around camps under canvas and making a hullabaloo at night.

Tsurphu prohibited

Thursday 21st July. The morning passed *in fruitless appeals.* The general plan was to go to *Tsurphu*, the seat of the Karmapa. Lama Seunam and his assistants had to endure some bitter arguments, encountering, in one office after another, the opposition of the Chinese officials. The district had been placed under quarantine due to an epidemic spread by dogs.

Ganden

In the afternoon, we went to *Ganden*, a monastery situated 25 miles to the east of Lhasa.[46] This was founded in 1417 by Tsong Khapa, that great monastic reformer, who could not have foreseen the development of his Gelugpa Order, nor the political role it would play. In 1959 this study centre with its two colleges, *Jangtse* and *Shartse*, numbered more than 5,000 monks. These were obliged to disperse under the Chinese occupation and, by the mid-Sixties, the monastery was practically deserted. The final blow was struck by the Cultural Revolution: caught up in the vortex of the fury, the local people found themselves compelled to pull down the buildings. For many years, the site was no more than a collection of ruins. Mao having subsequently reinstated religious freedom, an immense labour of reconstruction was embarked upon after his death. One by one, the buildings emerged out of their ruins while the monks slowly returned. They may number more than 300 today, but we saw only a few of them. There comes to mind the saying of Ecclesiastes (Qoheleth 3.3): *Tempus destruendi et tempus aedificandi*.[47] Never had I felt as on that day the force of the verbs *to destroy* and *to rebuild*. On the hillside, the activity was unbelievable: men and women were giving themselves up to intense labour, moving very heavy stones, while a sawmill cut up the trunks of enormous trees. The cathedrals were built at the price of almost superhuman labour, without the help of modern machinery. Cranes are unknown at Ganden and the scaffolding is precarious.

The destroyers, by I know not what (voluntary?) oversight, had spared *two very holy shrines*: the golden tomb of Tsong Khapa and a great bare room containing a single statue of Shakyamuni in copper and gold, surrounded by a thousand images in clay representing the thousand Buddhas of this era. Having alone survived the vandalism of the destroyers, these remnants of the ruin are all the more precious and arouse intense devotion in pilgrims. While Lhasa is at an altitude of more than 12,000 feet, Ganden is situated at 14,100. We were not specially inconvenienced by this. It must be said that the view over the mountain slopes is superb, as is the extent of the plain.

Our stay in Lhasa was marked by abnormal heat, sometimes 31°. The woollens we brought had hardly been used, and we saw almost no snowy peaks. Lhasa is on a latitude with Cairo, on the same parallel.

We stopped in the morning, not far from Lhasa, at a greengrocer's shop, under a vast tent beside the main road: a good deal of variety, but also of uncleanliness in the meat which they cut up in that way, without any concern about flies, dust and the pollution from smoke.

The fact of not having been able to go to Tsurphu, the seat of the Karmapa, was a heavy blow for the Lamas. To offer to his reincarnation, they had brought long, chased silver trumpets and many other gifts, all of which had to be wrapped up again, but they showed no signs of impatience or disappointment. We learned a great deal from the day's events.

Ascent to the Nunnery of Chouk-seb

Friday 22nd July – A breathtaking expedition

We did not fully realize to what we were committing ourselves. We foresaw a short bus journey, a river-crossing by ferry, then a walk of three quarters of an hour before reaching a monastery of Tibetan nuns: *Chouk-seb*. I set great store by visiting this monastery, about which I had written some years ago.[48] Located in a plantation of junipers, hence its name, it owes its fame to an abbess who was a mystic and who died in 1953 at an advanced age. *Jetsun Lochen*, soon to be known as *Chouk-seb Jetsun*, took up residence on the summit of this mountain, presiding over a community of 300 nuns. This having been totally destroyed by the Chinese after 1959, the nuns have put their strength into rebuilding it.

Contrary to our expectations, getting there was a real adventure. The bus journey took more than an hour and there was no ferry; the coach forded the river, choosing a place where the water was not too deep. On arrival at the foot of the mountain, it put us down, leaving us to continue by our own means. *The ascent on foot was gruelling* and took, for those not used to climbing mountains, almost three hours. We were forced to stop on welcome level areas in order to regain our breath. The monastery is perched at 15,750 feet, the highest altitude we have reached during our stay in Tibet. Our welcome from the elderly nuns was excellent, but the community is largely composed of young, robust nuns. They are daughters of *the mountain*, accustomed to rough work and to carrying heavy loads. Compared with the young nuns in Lhasa, who are more slender and doubtless more intellectual, these are strong women geared to action. The portrait of their foundress, radiating wisdom and goodness, occupies a place of honour in their temple. We hit upon an auspicious day when the ritual, bar one interruption for a meal (taken, in any case, in the shrine) took up the whole day: it was the full moon. Anxious to regain my strength after that trying ascent, I must admit to having given little thought to the superb views over the mountains and valleys. Descending the mountain is child's play. It is all much simpler and quicker, though we had to take care not to slip on the gravel. A woman experienced in mountaineering held my hand during the descent. I am thankful to have been able, given my age, to acquit myself well and without special problems in this sporting trial. This was not the case with one of our female companions, whose heart was not sound. She felt unwell at several points, sprained her ankle and it was a wonder that she did not have to be taken to hospital, considering the anxiety she aroused in us in the course of the journey.

Perhaps this is the right place for us to recall those *pilgrimage rules* laid down by the mystic *Hadewijch* of Antwerp between 1220 and 1240, but easy to transpose into today's context. This is what she said[49]:

> There are nine points to be remembered by the pilgrim on a long road. First of all, to ask his way; then, to choose his companions well; thirdly, to be on his guard against thieves, fourthly, let him avoid eating too much; fifthly, that he wear his clothing short and gird it up firmly; sixthly, that he lean forward on ascents; seventhly, that he stand up straight on descents; eighthly, that he ask the prayers of good people; ninthly that he speak willingly of God.

It seems to me that we have observed these rules quite well.

NEPAL REVISITED

Saturday 23rd July.

Return from *Lhasa to Kathmandu.* Hour of rising 4.15 a.m, breakfast at 5 a.m., departure from Lhasa at 5.30 a.m. It was still dark throughout the valley. The journey from Lhasa to the airport took roughly two hours. We had to wait there a long time for all kinds of formalities. Important observation: on leaving Tibet, it is *impossible to change one's remaining yuans* into any foreign currency (whether dollars or Nepalese rupees) at the airport, the hotel or a bank. A rule which Hadewijch failed to mention: "On leaving Cathay, do not attempt to exchange the currency of that empire."

We left the roof of the world *without having seen many yaks*, unless we had mistaken them for black cows in the fields, for they are shorn at this season. And what about the *yeti*, that abominable snowman?

Duration of flight: 1 hour, 10 minutes, in a plane of the same *China Southwest Airlines.* Passing above the Himalayan chain, we saw *Mount Everest* much more clearly than on the outward journey. Arriving *at Kathmandu* around noon (Peking time), we adjusted to Nepal time (10.20). Even if the temperature was not as high as in Lhasa, about 25°, the damp heat was much more difficult to bear: one enters a Turkish bath, perspiring freely. We came to miss Tibet, where the principal discomfort comes from breathlessness. In the afternoon, we went in a small group to the *Hotel of the Annapūrṇā*, where the Catholic *Mass* began, at 5.30 p.m. on the second floor. It was celebrated by an American Jesuit, professor of physics at the college of Jawalakhel (Patan). His homily on the miracle of the multiplication of the loaves was an original one: he insisted on the balancing, in each of us, between spiritual hunger and the hunger for earthly food. The room was completely full, with about forty faithful, amongst whom the diversity of physical types was striking. It is the Church who has drawn them together out of so many nations! I was moved by this, as I was in the same place, eleven years ago.[50]

When we returned to our hotel, we were informed that a three-day *general strike* had been called by the political parties opposed to the decision taken by the king and his prime minister to dissolve parliament. Tourists were urged not to go out during these three days, or at least to avoid the streets in the centre where a riot might break out. In fact, several of us went to visit *Swayambunath* with its Shaivite temple and its Kagyu monastery.

Sunday 24th July. We went in search of a bookshop. Everywhere in the streets the shops have their metallic shutters lowered to the ground and firmly padlocked. By way of an exception, the bookshop we were looking for was open: this was *The Pilgrims' Book House*, very well stocked with the most worthwhile books on Eastern religions, the history and geography of Nepal and Tibet (magnificent albums), the art and iconography of these countries, travel narratives and biographies.

At 6.30 p.m. in Claudine's room, *Eastern liturgy according to the Vespers of Chevetogne*, with a homily by Father Maxime. There were rather too many of us in that room; the incense made the atmosphere rather oppressive.

Pharping and its temples

Monday 25th July – The strike ended, the prime minister proposing a putting together of the grievances for the 28th. Some distance away from Kathmandu, we went to visit *Yangleucheu*: a grotto and neighbouring lake where Guru Rinpoche stayed. Throughout the journey, we had views over a green valley where the trees and vegetation, fields of rice and maize, are plentiful. This year's monsoon having come late, it rained heavily the previous night. All this contrasted sharply for us with the severe aridity of the mountains of Tibet. We saw, side by side against the hillside, *little Hindu temples (Vishnu temple) and little Tibetan monasteries: Yarenché Gompa* and the *Pharping Ganesh and Sarasvati Temple* which is in reality a temple of Tara (Dreulma) maintained by the Gelugpa. A *Nyingmapa* monastery has a magnificent gilded statue of Guru Rinpoche, full of majesty. This is the residence, when he is not travelling, of an eminent lama, *Trichang Rinpoche.*

On seeing Kathmandu again after eleven days at Lhasa, one has new eyes for it. One had become so accustomed to seeing Chinese men and women, and young soldiers in green uniform, everywhere one looked. Kathmandu is more neglected, despite the pleasant disposition of the Nepalese; it more resembles Indian cities. One also notices the numbers of Western tourists in the streets.

A surprising fact, but confirmed in the experience of all: *books and liturgical objects* of Tibetan Buddhism: *thankas, damarus,* photographic reproductions, albums and traditional clothing, are available at lower prices and are of better quality in Kathmandu than in Lhasa.

Tuesday 26th July. Some of us held a conversation with the General Secretary of the *Nepal-Belgium Friendship Association, Welfare Society – Nepal* on the *situation of the poor* of this country and the means of coming to their help. Everything is a matter of private initiatives. A distinction must be made between the poor population of Kathmandu and the even more wretched condition of the inhabitants of the villages, where the majority of children cannot go to school. It is not simply a matter of giving them money, but of educating them into a clearer view of their potential. Two of our companions, going to and returning from Swayambunath, passed through *poor districts* the wretchedness of which reminded them of certain parts of Calcutta.

Patan, the old capital

In the afternoon, a visit to *Patan*, 3³/4 miles to the east of Kathmandu. The former capital, with its royal palace, two *stūpas* from the time of Aśoka, a golden Buddhist temple, the caretaker of which, a Hindu, became violently indignant on seeing that Lama Orgyen had retained his leather shoes. Several Hindu temples, one of them with five roofs on top of one another (in the Chinese style); several rather small temples dedicated to Shiva; often these buildings have elaborate relief-work on the doors, windows and balconies. In front of the entrance two or four lions, with open jaws and menacing teeth, serve as guardians.[51]

Our group had less appreciation for the visit to two State centres, one for articles in brass, the other for wood-carving. The undertaking is a commercial one, without much concern for artistic value.

Kopan once more

Wednesday 27th July. On Chantal's initiative, a small group returned to *Kopan*. The rain the previous day was heavy. From Bodnath onward, we went on foot and, at the beginning, the journey was made more difficult by the mud encumbering the road, and making it slippery. The climb was less troubled than last time. Visit to *Geshe Kongchok*. We told him the essentials of our stay in Tibet. Chantal spoke to him about her family difficulties and her health worries. He answered wisely on both counts. After the meal, we visited the first floor and saw *the new library*, where we venerated the *chorten* of Lama Thubten Yeshe and admired a *mandala* of Chenrezig. We spoke to the librarian, Thubten Sampel, who was a fifteen-year-old boy-monk here in 1980. There are 170 monks here, almost all of them young, and 86 nuns in the convent below, on the bank of the rice-field. *The majority are Nepalese*, with a minority of Tibetans; most of the Nepalese are Sherpas, as is this young librarian from the neighbourhood of Lawudo.

And Bodnath

Having come back down to *Bodnath*, we went to see the frescoed frontage of the *monastery of Pao Rinpoche*, who lived in Dordogne. Then an excellent visit to a great *Nyingmapa* monastery, that of *Dilgo Khyentse Rinpoche*. Chantal sent for the translator, Matthieu Ricard, who gave us detailed information on the abbess of Chouk-seb and then introduced us on the terrace to the young abbot of this monastery, the 27-year-old *Rabjam Rinpoche*. I had met him when he came with his grandfather, Dilgo Khyentse, to Sherab Ling in 1983.[52] He remembered our conversation from that period. Full of kindness and wisdom as he is, he sets great store by good relations between religions and particularly between monks. At Darjeeling, they have excellent contacts with the Canadian Jesuits. The latter are highly esteemed in Bhutan; their activity in establishing the school system is deeply appreciated by everyone.[53] Next, the Rinpoche led us through the halls of his monastery. The temple is truly beautiful. We took a look at a class composed entirely of very young and tiny monks who are learning, at the tops of their voices, to read.

In the evening, *Lama Seunam* drew for us all a rather positive overview of our pilgrimage. This was, above all else, a *reminder of the fundamental themes of the Dharma*: illusion and impermanence. At this final meeting, the opportunity could have been taken to draw attention to *certain deficiencies* in the organization. It seemed that more importance could have been given to the religious aspect, for example by making a corporate pūjā in this monastery, and allowing time for silent meditation in that holy place. It is true that individual prostrations and offerings were made, but the communal aspect of this pilgrimage was somewhat neglected. As for the relations between *Buddhists and Christians*, they were excellent in my opinion. God knows at what depth, in candour and understanding, some exchanges took place. I certainly had, during those weeks, some of the best conversations of my life.

RETURN VIA DELHI

Thursday 28th July. The *Kathmandu* journey lasted one hour, ten minutes, provided by the *Royal Bhutan Airlines* company (or *Royal*

Druk Air). We arrived at about 11 a.m. and, from 11 to 1 p.m., we hung around the rather chilly airport until we were offered a choice: to stay there or leave for the city. Most preferred to leave. A bus took us to Delhi. It rained in torrents during the morning, and the weather was rather warm and humid, but the cool wind did us good. Throughout the journey, we saw trees, parks and abundant vegetation. At Connaught Place in Delhi, we had an enjoyable meal in a well-run restaurant. Then, in a grassy area, a group of men and young children pressed their services on us. They wanted to polish our shoes, give us massages and sell us garlands of orange-flower. It is a relatively peaceful park, considering that it borders on a crossroad and main thoroughfares with unrestrained traffic. There was an earth tremor at 7.50 p.m. while we were waiting for our bus; I had the distinct impression that the flagstone beneath my feet rocked as though not firmly anchored. Leaving the centre of Delhi at 8 p.m., we were at the airport at 8.45. Formalities for embarkation, once again with *Lufthansa*.

Friday 29th July. Departure from Delhi at 2.45 a.m. We reached *Frankfurt* at 7 a.m., local time. It was rather cold in the plane, which carried 400 passengers. On arrival, the external temperature was 24°. Our group split up, some members having to travel to Paris or Nice. Those bound for Belgium left Frankfurt at 9.20 and reached *Zaventem* at 10.

Conclusion

French Buddhists know *Lama Chokyi Sengue* (François Jacquemart) who, having made the retreat of three years and three months, became director of a centre near Aix-en-Provence, at Huynes. He knows Tibetan rather well, and made a journey to Tibet in 1987. Seeing a Westerner in a monk's robes evidently gave great pleasure to the people on the roof of the world. On his return, he did not wish to give a detailed account of his journey and, when he was asked what had made the deepest impression on him, he spoke neither of the gold of the temples, nor of bare summits, nor of the dazzling blue of the sky, nor of turquoise lakes. He said simply: "What is most striking and most enchanting about Tibet is the Tibetans."[54]

Or, as *Sister Bruno* said, at the end of a lecture about this pilgrimage – she compared a stay in Zen monasteries with this pilgrimage: "In Japan, it was the strictly monastic contact. Here it was the immersion in the faith and ardent devotion of a whole people."

Notes

[1] See our article: Camaldoli–Assisi–Rome, 14–21 September 1989, in the A.I.M. Bulletin of 1991, Nº 47, 102–106, and *Pro Dialogo*, 1990-1, Nº 73, pp. 40–44 and 16–17.

[2] On this *Nunnery*, see above, page 92, note 8, and pages 50–54.

[3] "*Tsampa* is the name of the normal Tibetan food, made from barley flour, mixed with tea and butter; this paste is used for preparing the *tormas* during the ceremonies." TUCCI & HEISSIG: *Les religions du Tibet et de la Mongolie*, Payot, 1973, p. 132, note 1.

[4] Would not the building up of this rice pyramid in levels be a symbolic reconstruction of the universe? And would not the gesture described be an offering and blessing for all sentient beings *(semchen)*?

[5] See BLOFELD: *The Tantric Buddhism of Tibet*. Arkana, 1992. With more details in TUCCI (above, note 3), p. 156.

[6] One might have added something here about their intellectual formation, as part of their day is taken up by classes, to judge from a timetable passed on to us under the title: *Daily Routine of the Nuns*.

[7] See above, pages 48–49 and 177–178.

[8] Encountered at Sherab Ling in 1983; see page 177.

[9] See above, pages 183–184.

[10] See above, pages 180–182.

[11] See above, page 178.

[12] I was able to stay here for two months in 1980, five months in 1983, in order to study Tibetan, as will have been seen above.

[13] On his role, see the work by the Dalai Lama: *Freedom in Exile*, Hodder and Stoughton, 1990, pp. 233–236. We shall see the original *Nechung* in Lhasa in July 1994. See below, page 240 and the corresponding note 40.

[14] See the *A.I.M. Bulletin*, Stanbrook Abbey, 1988, Nº 44, pp. 26–36.

[15] See the fine *Benedictines in India* brochure published in 1990 by the *Indian Benedictine Federation*, 72 pages, illustrated.

[16] Psalm 71.10–11. Offertory of the Epiphany: "The kings of Tarshish and the sea coasts shall pay him tribute. The kings of Sheba and Seba shall bring him gifts. Before him all kings shall fall prostrate, all nations shall serve him."

[17] This lecture is one of the last that Fr. Bede Griffiths gave, a short while before his death. The greater part of it was published in the Buddhist review *Dharma*, Nº 18, autumn 1993, and subsequently in the collection *Convergence du christianisme et du bouddhisme* (*Les dossiers du Dharma*, Éditions Prajna, F – 73110 Arvillard). The same (English) text then appeared in the *A.I.M. Bulletin*, 1993, Nº 55, pp. 122–125. We personally retain the translation of the *full* text, made from a tape-recording. It is remarkable to note that Father

Griffiths thus concluded his career as had Thomas Merton twenty-five years earlier, with the encounter with *Dzogchen*.

[18] See the brochure referred to at note 15, pp. 60–61.
[19] On my visit to this monastery in 1983, see above, page 188.
[20] On this *nunnery*, see above on pp. 92, note 8; 50–54, 208–211.
[21] On the nuns of *Tilokpur*, see pages 49–50.
[22] See above, pages 92, 163, 165, 170–171.
[23] See above, pages 105–109, 151–152, 162–163.
[24] See above, pages 111–112 and note 21.
[25] See above, pages 122–123.
[26] *Immaculate Conception of Mary*, Heverlee, Louvain.
[27] See Guy DELEURY: *Le berceau de Rāma s'enflamme* in *Actualité Religieuse dans le Monde*, N° 107, 15 janvier 1993, pp. 16–17.
[28] Organized by Voyages CLEO of Lyon. The director was Father René Girault.
[29] During the long vacation, each summer, from 1978 to 1988, not to mention other occasions: interreligious dialogue and the inauguration of the temple.
[30] See above, page 137.
[31] See above, pages 204–230.
[32] Lama Orgyen had been there three times in his youth, but he had never seen Lhasa.
[33] See above, pages 105–109, 151–152, 162–163.
[34] See above, pages 151–152.
[35] For example in Toni HAGEN: *Népal. Royaume de l'Himalaya*. Berne, Kümmerly and Frey, 3rd edition, 1975, illustration 45, or in the Guide Arthaud *Népal*, by Robert RIEFFEL, Paris, 1986: detailed description, pp. 256–265 and page 212.
[36] See the *Tendrel* magazine of Dhagpo Kagyu Ling, Saint-Léon-sur-Vézère, N° 29, 1992. The circumstances of this death remain somewhat mysterious. Djamgoeun Kongtrul was one of the four regents of the Karma-Kagyu Order. He had just been appointed a member of the search commission who were to go to Tibet to look for the reincarnation of the Karmapa.
[37] *The Tibet Guide*, by Stephen BATCHELOR, Wisdom Publications, London 1987.
[38] The Portuguese Jesuit *Antonio De Andrade* was the first European to enter Tibet; he was there from 1624 to 1629. A dozen Portuguese Jesuits were there at different dates until 1634 (Documents by G. *Toscano* in the Guimet Museum). The Italian Jesuit *Ippolito Desideri* was in Tibet from 1715 to 1721; see the excellent article concerning him by G. TOSCANO in the *Dictionnaire des religions* under the editorship of Poupard, P.U.F., 3rd edition, 1993, pp. 466–468. The *Capuchins* were present there from 1707 to 1745. Accompanied by P. Gabet, the Lazarist *P. Huc* arrived in Lhasa on 29 January 1846 but was unable to stay for more than a month and a half. As for the Blessed *Maurice Tornay*, a Canon Regular of the Grand-Saint-Bernard, he was assassinated in the Tibetan march-land on a path leading to Lhasa in 1949.
[39] See above, pages 168–170.
[40] On his role, see note 13 above, and the magazine *Notre Histoire*, N° 115, 15 October 1994, pp. 18–22.

41 Visited 20 November 1992; see above, page 217.
42 In 1979, 1983 and 1992, pages 92, 170–171, 225.
43 See above, note 33.
44 See above, page 225.
45 It goes without saying that we see in action, though somewhat less than in India, these famous *rickshaws* or Chinese *pedicabs*, always operated here by muscle-power, rather than the motor-tricycles seen in Indian cities.
46 See above, pages 165–168.
47 "A time to destroy and a time to build."
48 See above, pages 46–47. This monastery, which belongs to the *Nyingmapa* tradition, received help from *Dilgo Khyentse Rinpoche*. See the Dharamsala magazine *Actualités tibétaines,* vol. V, N° 1, May 1994, page 37.
49 In his letter XV: *Lettres Spirituelles,* Claude Martingay, Geneva, 1972, pp. 128–129.
50 Saturday 29 January 1983.
51 After viewing these magnificent sites in Patan in January 1980, I had been dazzled on being invited to climb up to the studio of a sculptor who was also a goldsmith; the glittering of all the statues of Buddha and the divinities ...
52 See above, pages 177–178.
53 See Howard Solverson, *The Jesuit and the Dragon. The Life of Father William Mackey in the Himalayan Kingdom of Bhutan.* Robert Davies Publishing, Montreal-Toronto-Paris, 1995.
54 *Un lama français au Tibet* in *Les cahiers du bouddhisme,* 1986, N° 28, pp. 3–11.

Part Three

Theological Reflections

Chapter IX

Introduction: Divergences and Convergences

> Have your answer ready for people who ask you the reason
> for the hope that is in you.
> (*1 Peter 3.15*)

This warning by St. Peter comes as a reminder. The many encounters reported here would have no meaning if they did not lead us to a doctrinal investigation. The word might sound pretentious, but the return to the interior is essential, as is reflection on what actuates these different spiritual centres, and what is at the source of our own religion. Here we would wish to *avoid two extremes.* One of these would be to imitate certain ivory-tower scholars who, without taking the trouble to enter into contact with people in their particular discipline, try hard to classify doctrines and, rather easily, oppose them. The other would be to immerse oneself in human encounters, with all they contain that is nebulous and pliable, to the extent of losing a critical spirit and of tending to bring everything together, if not of mixing everything together, in a climate lenient towards the New Age. For ourselves, following good examples which are not lacking, we would wish to keep a firm hold on our Christian convictions and attachment to our Church, while at the same time avoiding a certain hardness of heart and intellectual arrogance with respect to those who think differently. We have the desire, if not the claim, to be at once faithful to our roots and disposed towards openness. Besides, is not this the very policy of the commission for Monastic Interreligious Dialogue to which we have the happiness of belonging?

Let us reread a Roman document, one which Pope John Paul II

approved on 10 June 1984 and which remains thoroughly relevant. It is entitled: *The Attitude of the Church towards the Followers of Other Religions.*[1] Paragraph 33 is expressed as follows: "Of particular interest is dialogue at the level of specialists, whether it be to compare, deepen, and enrich their respective religious heritages or to apply something of their expertise to the problems which must be faced by peoples in the course of history. Such a dialogue normally occurs where one's partner already has his own vision of the world and adheres to a religion which inspires him to action. This is more easily accomplished in pluralistic societies where diverse traditions and ideologies coexist and sometimes come into contact."

We appreciate particularly Article 35, where monks will especially see themselves, as also those persons for whom spirituality is the very purpose of their existence:

> At a deeper level, persons rooted in their own religious traditions can share their experiences of prayer, contemplation, faith, and duty, as well as their expressions and ways of searching for the Absolute. This type of dialogue can be a mutual enrichment and fruitful cooperation for promoting and preserving the highest values and spiritual ideals of people. It leads naturally to each partner communicating to the other the reasons for their own faith. The sometimes profound differences between the faiths do not prevent this dialogue. Those differences, rather, must be referred back in humility and confidence in God "who is greater than our heart" (1 John 3. 20). In this way also, the Christian has the opportunity of offering to the other the possibility of experimenting in an existential way with the values of the Gospel.

Besides, the proper course is to avoid an artless irenic which would see nothing anywhere but perfect harmony. The balanced position which commends itself is clearly indicated, it seems to me, when one has recourse to the method which gives this chapter its title: *"Divergences and convergences"*, for discernment is necessary, as is stressed by a more recent document from the Holy See: *Dialogue and Proclamation*, dated 19 May 1991.[2] This states in paragraph 31: "To say that the other religious traditions include elements of grace does not imply that everything in them is the result of grace. For sin has been at work in the world, and so religious traditions, notwithstanding their positive values, reflect the limitations of the human spirit, sometimes inclined to choose evil. An open and positive approach to other religious traditions cannot overlook the contradictions which may exist between them and Christian revelation. It must, where necessary, recognize that there is incompatibility between some fundamental elements of the Christian religion and some aspects of such traditions."

Let us stress this point: the critical spirit must be exercised in both directions. There is no justification for complacency over one's own tradition. It is not "without speck or wrinkle" (Ephesians 5.27). For this reason, the Roman document is frank enough to add (in paragraph 32):

> This means that, while entering with an open mind into dialogue with the followers of other religious traditions, Christians may have also to challenge them in a peaceful spirit with regard to the content of their belief. But Christians too must allow themselves to be questioned. Notwithstanding the fullness of God's revelation in Jesus Christ, the way Christians sometimes understand their religion and practise it may be in need of purification.

"I have not come to abolish but to complete," said Jesus (Matthew 5.17).

When it comes to divergences between the Eastern religions and Christianity, there are a good many of them, and they are weighty ones! However, they should be both brought to light and the effort made, as far as possible, to discover the cultural and philosophical context which explains their origin. A model of its kind, it seems to me, is the project which Dom Bede Griffiths pursued throughout his career. A typical example is to hand in the account which he gave for the BBC in 1989, under the title: *Christianity in the Light of the East,* published in the *A.I.M. Bulletin* in 1991, No. 49, pages 51–58. It is a model of freedom and of insight. He begins each time with the statement of a doctrine of the Eastern religions which appears to us to be contrary to our principles and does his best to show its acceptable side. It goes without saying that the majority of Catholic theologians would be more strict and will say more vigorously that they find themselves before irreconcilable alternatives.

In this connection, and although it could seem audacious to the faithful of a Semitic type of religion, we have appreciated the discerning remarks in an account made by Felix Wilfred during a Colloquium at Pune in 1992 on the uniqueness of Christ[3]: "*Some tentative reflections on the language of Christian uniqueness: an*

Indian Perspective." Taking into account the traditional mentality of India and Asia, this theologian develops ideas which are new to us, but are justified in the context of Eastern religions. He shows also, historically, how this problem of the uniqueness of our religion, as it is posed today, is explained by the fact that it was only in these most recent centuries that the West made its first serious encounter with other religions. India had been accustomed for millennia to coexistence. The author draws attention, above all, to the different epistemologies underlying the discussions: the West opposes and excludes, while the East aspires to unity. The Eastern mentality regards as legitimate, if not welcome, a diversity of paths (*mārga*, path; *pada*, step; *yāna*, vehicle) advancing towards the ultimate mystery of the Divinity.

The perennial importance that the theme of *complementarity*, that *"Marriage of East and West"*, the alliance of the masculine and the feminine, always had for Father Griffiths in the manner of approaching different cultures and religions, is well known.

Besides, a means of understanding is provided for us by the essential distinction between *Mystical Religions and Prophetic Revelations*,[4] rendered standard by Professor R.C. Zaehner, whose courses at Oxford I had the opportunity of following. Ever since then, it has been indispensable.

An account which we liked for its firmness as much as for its openness is that by Father Hans Waldenfels S.J.: *La méditation en Orient et en Occident*.[5] One is aware also of the competence of Father Kadowaki and that of Father Enomiya-Lassalle as regards the encounter with Zen.

For depth of spiritual life, one cannot do otherwise than recommend the works of Father Yves Raguin, who is thoroughly acquainted with Eastern viewpoints.

For the person engaged in dialogue, it is refreshing to listen to such scholars, especially the religious, who recall with distinctness the outlines of the "dogmas" of both sides. One could give their names. When one turns to the Easterners capable of making comparisons, it is easy to notice the incompatible points and the divergences. A recent instance is provided for us by the expositions of the Dalai Lama in the course of his journey across France in November 1993, which were published in the interesting work *Au-delà des dogmes* the following year.[6] I read this book attentively, scrutinizing the places where he compares our two religions. He

Divergences and Convergences

hides behind no smokescreen; he says clearly the things which are incompatible. He accepts neither divine Creator, nor Saviour, nor Last Judgement and rightly sees that the series of reincarnations is not acceptable in Christianity. However, he does not conclude with this statement. He himself searches from time to time for points of similarity. He finds them, in particular, in charity towards one's neighbour and the tradition of the monastic Orders. His visit to the Grande-Chartreuse made a deep impression on him; he refers to it on four occasions.[7] Here are the convergences.

OUR PROGRAMME

What is our programme in the pages which follow? It cannot be to establish theses as a professor of theology would do. It seems to me that at least two areas merit investigation. The first, despite an unpromising philosophical context, lends itself to comparison: that of Mahāyāna compassion with Christian charity. The second is more deeply rooted in the heart of each of our two religions: it is the matter of the person and of *anattā*. Circumstances practically forced me to take a closer look at it, and it seems to me that a comparison on this all-important point would be welcome.

As for a much more delicate topic, which engages not only the reasoning mind but the interior of the Christian faith, we put it forward only with the greatest reserve. One might single it out as an example of the difficulty over the subjects of convergences. It is better, however, to make the effort which might open up possibilities at a later date. We are referring to an eventual relationship between the Christian Trinity and the doctrine, which is fundamental to Buddhism, of the three Bodies of the Buddha or *Trikāya*.

TRINITY AND TRIKĀYA

It all began on the day when, between two conferences, I was attempting to explain briefly to my table-companions, two eminent Buddhists, the Augustinian mode of representing the procession of the divine Persons in the Blessed Trinity. The director of the Karma-Ling centre, Lama Denys, opposite us, was listening. He pointed out to me: "But we have a doctrine of the same type in the

Vajrayāna!" The remark was not completely forgotten; the matter was raised again two years later. It gave rise to a *small group* of Christians and Buddhists who examined the problem in the course of study-meetings at Karma-Ling. To date, we have had three meetings of this kind, not always with the same participants.[8] If we continue to make headway, the results might one day be published, or made the topic of a public Colloquium.[9] For the present, let us simply summarize some remarks, the outcome of those exchanges. A rather short but complex account of them may be read in the magazine *Dharma*.[10] It would be easier, in my opinion, to put side by side the three Bodies of the Buddha and what one might term *the three conditions of the Body of Christ*. We shall say something on this at point 3 below. In order not to put forward anything imprudent, let us first of all simply recall the classical doctrine, both on our side for the Trinity and on the Buddhist side for the *Trikāya*.

1. The Christian Trinity

Let us first of all quote the *Dictionnaire des Religions*,[11] from the article "Trinité" by Father Joseph Doré:

> The principal name in Latin Trinitarian theology is that of Saint Augustine, whose masterly work *De Trinitate* has, in fact, been seminal for all Western reflection. Using a type of explanation which already went back to Tertullian, Augustine drew up what is known as the "psychological theory of the Trinity". This proposes to "understand" the two processions of the intra-divine life according to the analogy of the psychological processes of which the human mind itself is the seat. The generation of the Son-Word is compared with the act of self-knowledge of the human mind: the Word is the Thought which the Father has about himself; as for the Holy Spirit, he is the mutual love which the Father and the Son bear towards each other and which unites them in the closest communion.
>
> It is in a Word which, being his perfect expression, is equal to himself, that the Father knows himself. That this Word may be called Son and that his procession may be called generation, has its foundation in the fact that this is a matter of a being who draws his origin from another being, whom he resembles in every feature and to whom he is bound by an enduring and total community of destiny. Father and Son say to each other a Yes of mutual recognition from which is inferred a new procession. This time, it is a procession of love (generally referred to as "spiration" to differentiate it from the first, which is

generation), from which rises the Holy Spirit as communion in the unity of the Father with the Son and of the Son with the Father.

This stated, a vital point must be grasped: understood simultaneously as acts of proceeding and as the point of arrival of these acts, the processions amount to *purely relational realities*. They are, as such, constituent of *persons*. On the one hand, in fact, the persons have no other reality than that of the divine nature or substance itself, and on the other hand, however, they do not lack all reality.

What must be grasped is that their manner of being real is not that of possessing a proper substance, but of possessing, each in his own way, the single and common substance or nature. They thus appear as three genuinely different modes according to which, by the processions from the Father, the single divine substance relates to itself: first by communicating itself from the source or original position (the Father); then by receiving and giving itself once again to its original source (the Son-Word); finally by being its relationship of union between the generation and the being-engendered (the Holy Spirit), to the effect that this may be the most closely approximating conception that one may reach of the divine "Persons": it is a question of three "subsisting relations" which are three "subsistences" of the single divine substance-nature.

2. The three Bodies of the Buddha

When Lama Denys Teundroup was asked to give an exposition on this essential theme, he wrote the following page, which subsequently appeared in Poupard's *Dictionnaire des religions*.[12] It goes without saying that it calls for an effort of attention from the reader to whom this philosophy is unfamiliar.

> The *Mahāyāna* has developed the prospect of awakening in the three Bodies of the Buddha, which play a very important role in the *tantrayāna*. They are three indivisible and coexistent facets of the realization of emptiness *(shūnyatā)* in its aspect of plenitude. They are:
> – The *dharmakāya*, "absolute Body" or "Body of emptiness": this is the Body-mind of a buddha who, liberated from all conceptual limitation, whether of time, space or any other, is without centre or circumference, past, present or future: omnipresent and eternal, which means for the *Dharma*: timeless. It is essential to notice that emptiness of conceptual limitations has as its corollary the plenitude of awakened qualities, this simultaneity being expressed in the idea of emptiness-plenitude. The Absolute of the *dharmakāya* is not "The Absolute Being", for it is beyond the distinction of being and non-being.

– The *nirmaṇakāya*, "Body of emanation" which, inseparable from the *dharmakāya* and from its awakened experience, the *sambhogakāya*, is the presence, by love and by compassion, of a buddha as it is perpetually manifested in the world, under an appearance perceived by beings as localized and temporal.

– The *sambhogakāya*, "Body of perfect experience", is the constant encounter between the eternal omnipresence of the *dharmakāya* and the historic presence of the *nirmaṇakāya*. It is the perfection of the experience and the non-dualistic expression of a buddha.

3. The three conditions of the Body of Christ and the three Bodies of the Buddha

One could draw a comparison between the three conditions of Christ and these three states of Awakening following this scheme:

– Jesus of Nazareth would correspond to Gautama Shakyamuni, *nirmaṇakāya,*
– the Easter Christ to the *sambhogakāya,*
– the eternal and cosmic Christ to the *dharmakāya*.

To return briefly to each of these conditions, let us recall what has already been said:

The *nirmaṇakāya*, the Body of emanation, is the presence by love and compassion of a buddha as it is perpetually manifested in the world, under an appearance perceived by beings as localized and temporal. Cannot the same be said of the Word made flesh? He lived among us (John 1.14), truly situated in space and time. He went about doing good and curing all those who had fallen into the power of the devil (Acts 10.38).

The *sambhogakāya*, Body of perfect experience, is the constant encounter of the eternal omnipresence of the *dharmakāya* and the historic presence of the *nirmaṇakāya*. It is sometimes known as the Body of rejoicing (or of glory). It will be noticed that it is not perceptible by all; in the same way the risen Christ, on Easter day, was not easily recognized.

As for the glorified Christ, at the right hand of the Father, exalted by the Greek Fathers and, on our side, by Teilhard de Chardin, does he not have these properties of the *dharmakāya*: omnipresent and eternal, liberated from all conceptual limitation, having the plenitude of awakened qualities, which might be expressed as emptiness-plenitude?

The essential Buddhist perspective of the *Trikāya* is that of eternity; certain didactic viewpoints, however, give for the experience of the three Bodies a diachronic presentation which follows the stages of the process of spiritual realization.

In Christianity, the Christological presentation is often made successively. There is, however, for the most profound and mystical authors, a presentation in which simultaneity is highly important.

4. The three divine Persons and the three Bodies of the Buddha

Without casting aside the parallel between the Christological scheme and the *Trikāya*, the comparison which seems the most apposite is that between the *Trikāya* and the Trinity.

We follow the Latin scheme of Saint Augustine, recalled above. For him, the Spirit is the love of the Father and the Son, proceeding from their union. If a comparison is made,

– the Father corresponds to the *dharmakāya*,
– the Son to the *nirmaṇakāya*,
– and the Holy Spirit, who proceeds from them both, to the *sambhogakāya*.

Let us actually recall what has just been said: "The *sambhogakāya*, Body of perfect experience, is the constant encounter between the eternal omnipresence of the *dharmakāya* and the historic presence of the *nirmaṇakāya*."

In Christianity, the divine essence is not to be confused with the three Persons of the Trinity. On their side, too, the Buddhists speak of *svābhāvikakāya*, the essential Body, which seems to us to correspond to the divine essence in Latin Christianity.

5. Some difficult points

The final page of the account of our discussions[13] frankly describes the difficulties raised by our attempt at identification. It will be seen that they are genuine; they are not, however, preclusive. The majority depart from the subject and touch only on secondary issues. To go to the essential, I would say that one important point is that which follows. In the Buddhist perspective, one finds oneself constantly in a psychological atmosphere, as the following paragraph demonstrates[14]:

> The essential perspective of the three Bodies is outside time; nevertheless, in an account relating to the stages of the spiritual path, they can be presented successively: the *nirmaṇakāya* is perceptible when the veil of karma has been removed, the *sambhogakāya* when that of the passions is gone (at the arrival of the state of *arya bodhisattva*) and the *dharmakāya* when all the veils, including that which is an impediment to ultimate knowledge, have been finally destroyed.

A Christian can clearly grasp what it is to which these stages of "deification" correspond. As they stand, he cannot identify them with the three divine Persons, equal in majesty. Christianity has a greater sense of the concrete, and the substantial. Someone did well to ask, at the conclusion of the discussions: "Is the *Trikāya* a simple intellectual construct, or does the triple Body correspond to a spiritual experience?"[15]

If we now turn to the parallel with the conditions of the Body of Christ, it must be admitted that the *nirmaṇakāya* of the Body of Shakyamuni cannot be taken for a real person, since *shūnyatā* or emptiness must also come into play at this level.

I would be sorry to close on a negative note, for, in spite of everything, the comparison described at least retains the value of a programme which merits examination and might contribute to a comparison of the two spiritual paths.

Notes

[1] *Bulletin of the Secretariat for non-Christians*, 1984-2, N° 56, pp. 126–141, *A.I.M. Bulletin*, 1984, N° 37, pp. 111–126.

[2] *Bulletin of the Pontifical Council for Interreligious Dialogue* 1991-2, N° 77, pp. 210–250. *A.I.M. Bulletin*, 1992, N° 52, pp. 122–123. The *Dharma* magazine, from Karma-Ling, N° 18, automne 1993, p. 8. *Documentation catholique*, 20 octobre 1991, p. 879.

[3] *Theological Colloquium, Pune, India, August 1993*, in the *Pro Dialogo* bulletin, 1994-1, n° 85–86, pp. 40–47.

[4] *Inde, Israël, Islam. Religions mystiques et révélations prophétiques*. This is the French translation of *At Sundry Times*, published by Faber & Faber, 1958.

5. Éditions du Seuil, Paris, 1981.
6. Spiritualités Vivantes, Albin Michel, 1994.
7. On pages 90, 111, 159 and 197.
8. From 5–7 September 1992; 16–18 March 1993; 14–15 February 1995.
9. This chapter was written when, soon afterwards, on the premises of Karma-Ling, the *sixth Christian-Buddhist Colloquium*, on the theme *Trinity-Trikāya*, took place, from 15–17 November 1996. There were numerous participants and the high intellectual and spiritual level could be observed. See issue N° 28 of the *Dharma* magazine, février-mai 1997.
10. In n° 18, automne 1993, pp. 65–70, and n° 23, mai-septembre 1995, pp. 62–63.
11. Under the editorship of Paul Poupard, 3e éd., 1993, pp. 2060–2061.
12. In the article *Vajrayāna*, p. 2089. In *Dharma*, N° 18, p. 66.
13. *Dharma* magazine, N° 18, p. 70.
14. *Dharma* magazine, N° 18, p. 66.
15. Letter from François Chenique to Lama Denys, 8 June 1995.

Chapter X
Mahāyāna Compassion and Christian Charity[1]

What is the question in hand?

Obviously, it is essential to define what it is of which one speaks. I have therefore conformed to fashion, and opened the authoritative *Grand Robert*. This is the *Dictionnaire alphabétique et analogique de la langue française*. Here is an English rendering of its definition of compassion: "Feeling which moves to pity and shares the sufferings of others". The first quotation it supplies is taken from the Gospel: "When he saw the crowds, Jesus felt sorry for them because they were harassed and dejected, like sheep without a shepherd (Mt. 9.36).[2] If, on the other hand, we consult the Encyclopaedia *Catholicisme*, Father René Brouillard, S.J., leads us to greater precision, while at the same time reducing the scope of this term:

> *Compassion*. From the Latin *compati*, "to suffer with". In current speech, the word is used to mean "the movement of soul which makes us sensitive to the misfortunes and sufferings of others". In the language of Christian spirituality, it refers in particular to the heartfelt participation of Mary in the Passion and in the redemptive sacrifice of Jesus. It is applied also to the feelings and to the acts of love of all those who, by intention or in fact, follow the example of the sorrowful Virgin and associate themselves with our suffering and dying Saviour. Compassion may be understood in a narrow or broad sense; in the former, it is the properly affective love, sympathy and sorrow experienced before the sufferings of Jesus. In the latter it includes, moreover, the assuagements and reparations which, as a consequence of these feelings, the Christian desires to offer to God, the contribution which our Saviour asks for his Passion and which the believer seeks to give him.
>
> Moreover, since supernatural charity overflows onto all men, Christian compassion is not moved by the sufferings of the Saviour

Mahāyāna Compassion and Christian Charity 275

alone: it holds good also before the afflictions and trials of one's neighbour. Thus, from the compassion, feeling and virtue which first bear us towards Jesus, is born compassion and benevolence towards men. Various devotions support and develop compassion; for example, devotion to the cross, the Passion, to the Sacred Heart, to our Lady of Sorrows, to the Eucharist ...[3]

Mary's Compassion

Since Mary is proposed to us, with good reason, as the prototype of compassion, the priests of my age will recall reading in the breviary, on the Friday before Passion Sunday, on the feast of the seven sorrows of the Virgin, an admirable page of St. Bernard, drawn from the Sermon of the twelve stars: *De duodecim praerogativis Beatae Mariae Virginis:*

> The martyrdom of the Virgin Mary, implicit in Simeon's prophecy, is put before us in the story of our Lord's passion. That venerable old man, Simeon, said of the infant Jesus, "This child is set for a sign that will be contradicted," and to Mary: "A sword will pierce your soul." Blessed Mother, a sword did pierce your soul. For no sword could penetrate your Son's flesh without piercing your soul. After your own Son Jesus gave up his life – he was yours in a special sense though he belongs to all – the cruel lance, which opened his side and would not spare him in death though it could do him no injury, could not touch his soul. But it pierced your soul. His soul was no longer there, but yours could not be set free, and it was pierced by a sword of sorrow. We rightly speak of you as more than a martyr, for the anguish of mind you suffered exceeded all bodily pain. "Mother, behold your son." These words were more painful than a sword thrust, for they pierced your soul and touched the quick where soul is divided from spirit. What an exchange! ... These words must have pierced your loving soul, since just to recall them breaks our hearts, hard and stony though they be ... "Did she then grieve when he was crucified?" Intensely ...[4]

Compassion of the faithful

It is not only the Virgin, but the whole Christian people who can move and be touched by the memory of the sufferings of the Saviour. An ancient and authentic testimony is provided for us by *Egeria*, that noble and pious lady, who probably came from Galicia. Her pilgrimage to the Holy Land took place towards the end of the fourth century.⁵ Here is her description of the ceremonies of *Good Friday in Jerusalem*:

> When the sixth hour is at hand, everyone goes before the Cross ... A chair is placed for the bishop before the Cross, and from the sixth to the ninth hours, nothing else is done except the reading of passages from Scripture. First, whichever Psalms speak of the Passion are read. Next there are readings from the apostles, either from the Epistles of the apostles or the Acts, wherever they speak of the Passion of the Lord. Next, the texts of the Passion from the Gospels are read. Then there are readings from the prophets, where they said that the Lord would suffer; and then they read from the Gospels, where He foretells the Passion. And so, from the sixth to the ninth hour, passages from Scripture are continuously read and hymns are sung ... And so, during those three hours, all the people are taught that nothing happened which was not first prophesied, and that nothing was prophesied which was not completely fulfilled. Prayers are continually interspersed, and the prayers themselves are proper to the day. At each reading and at every prayer, it is astonishing how much emotion and groaning there is from all the people. There is no one, young or old, who on this day does not sob more than can be imagined for the whole three hours because the Lord suffered all this for us.⁶

And in the presence of the Buddha?

In the presence of the Buddha, neither tears nor any such outbreak of popular grief are to be expected. This is because he is, by definition, the Enlightened or, more exactly, the Awakened One, he who had the privilege of revealing the vast illusion of the world and everything in it. That whole mass of Grief to which may be applied the term of *Duḥkha*, whatever is impermanent in the cycle of rebirths called *saṃsāra*, the blessed Buddha is from now onwards freed from it. That which is reflected in his face is an unruffled peace, even profound joy, reflected discreetly by his smile. Each of you has had the opportunity to see some reproduction of him who "has gone beyond", which speaks more eloquently than any theory. The Westerner calls to mind at this point the ideal of *ataraxia*⁷ or of *apatheia*.⁸ One thinks of the *hesychia*⁹ of the Eastern Church. Here we are far removed from the "outraged Christ" of our Flemish primitives, and from the edifying statue which overwhelmed St. Teresa or from the terrible Crucified One from Grünewald in the museum of Colmar. One stands in a quite different contemplation before the serenity of the Buddha in the Indo-Greek style of the statues of Gandhāra.[10] On the one hand we have the beatitude of *Nirvana*,[11] on the other the tragic infinitude of Love.

Let us therefore go straight to the point: the Buddha cannot be in any way an object which arouses compassion.

Buddhist benevolence

If the Buddha has not passed through suffering and an ignominious death that we should feel for him, is he not, on the other hand, the Master who by his teaching has given rise to a vast movement of altruistic feelings across the world? These, moreover, are to be considered alongside the four noble truths: "All is suffering ..."[12] Or, to enter more fully into his standpoint, should one not, rather than fixing one's attention on one suffering person – even Jesus – broaden one's compassion to the extent of the whole world, all the beings of which are plunged into the suffering of *saṃsāra*?

Is one justified in speaking of *Buddhist charity* in the sense that one speaks of Christian charity? This is a question which is frequently raised and which my revered master, Mgr Étienne Lamotte, endeavoured to clarify in a little-known communication which he made in 1952 at the Royal Academy of Belgium.[13] For the time being, we shall merely summarize his study.

Speaking generally, to the question as posed, the majority of the historians of religions answered during the nineteenth century in the affirmative: "I do not hesitate," said Burnouf, "to translate by charity the word *maitrī*[14] which expresses that universal feeling which makes one bear good will towards all men in general and disposed to help them". Since the beginning of the twentieth century, however, several authors have been of a contrary opinion. Oldenberg found nothing in the history of Buddhism analogous to that charity extolled by Saint Paul. Foucher considered Buddhist charity to be "essentially self-centred and solely concerned with personal salvation". Similar opinions are to be found from the pens of Louis de La Vallée Poussin, Keith, Oltramare and Father de Lubac.

The opposition between the points of view expressed is accounted for above all by the diversity of the Buddhist sources to which chance led each of the historians to consult: Buddhist *maitrī* does not appear in the same light in the texts of the Theravāda[15] and the Mahāyāna traditions, from the pen of a Buddhagoṣa[16] and that of a Shāntideva.[17] Authors today, being better acquainted with Buddhist literature as a whole, show more caution. Thus Foucher states: "Crowning the whole, comes *maitrī* or *mettā*, and when it is defined for us as the love borne by a father or mother, even at the cost of their life, for their only child, there is no longer any room for misunderstanding: this love is not the neutral or passive feeling which some take pleasure in claiming it to be."

H. von Glasenapp has emphasised in the preaching of the Buddha the "golden rule" of the Gospels, but expressed in a negative formulation: "Do to no one what you would not have done to yourself."

Lamotte, in his concern for impartiality, takes care above all to recall the fundamental doctrines of this religion. Certain facts become clear. The first is that a monk cannot do much for his brother, each having the obligation to walk the Noble Path on his own account. The second is that the Eightfold Path[18] makes no mention of charity or altruism. For the attainment of *Nirvana*, love of neighbour is not at all essential. Does this mean that Buddhism condemns altruism? Not in the least; on the contrary it recommends it, but does not give this sentiment pride of place and requires, moreover, that it be kept within the limits of a strict impartiality.

The essential role of the layman is to maintain the community of monks with his generous gifts. It is thus that, banned from the convents by the rule and by scruples, fraternal charity reappears in triumph among the pious laypeople and rich benefactors. Care is taken to define all those qualities appropriate to this gift. Even stated at its best, however, generosity, corrupted by belief in "I", cannot lead to more than heavenly pleasures; it does not bring about deliverance.

Monsignor Lamotte's conclusion

We no doubt esteem the exercise of *brahmavihāra* whereby the ascetic, facing in each direction in turn, embraces the whole world in an immense feeling of benevolence, with a broad, developed, limitless mind, free from hatred and ill-nature. He also practises pity towards the unfortunate, and joy for those who rejoice.[19]

However, all things considered, Lamotte ends his very searching analysis with this conclusion: "From the standpoint of the Theravāda, deliverance is conceived of as a state of holiness followed, after death, by entry into *Nirvana*: it is directly brought about by a supermundane wisdom bearing on the transitory, painful and impersonal character of all beings. To attain this wisdom, *maitrī* or benevolence can be helpful but it is not indispensable; it is not, moreover, without danger, since it is not directly oriented towards detachment. The laypeople who support the Community will be rewarded with good rebirths but will not, for all that, attain the end of suffering. The monk, prevented by his state from giving alms, will exercise the gift of that teaching which is the best of all gifts."[20]

All this being justified and difficult to gainsay, this conclusion on the part of Monsignor Lamotte is rigorous, even severe. Other authors, perhaps moved by a certain romanticism, will see compassion as having greater importance at the heart of the Theravāda. Among these is counted E. Franc-Prat, who wrote a fervent article on *Le Bouddhisme, doctrine de miséricorde*.[21]

Father Joseph Masson, S.J. has brought together in two chapters of his book *Le bouddhisme, chemin de libération*, the principal features of Buddhist *altruism*.[22] He provides clarifying quotations from ancient texts. His attention is concentrated on the interior motives for this altruism: self-seeking ones, yes, but also others, which often lead to a supreme detachment and to great sacrifices for the welfare of others. One may have a friendly manner towards others (this is *maitrī*) but also be full of compassion (*karuṇā*), since they all suffer the universal sorrow. Already the *sūtras* of the Theravāda demonstrate a benevolence which radiates outwards to all beings and in all circumstances. One might quote a certain passage from the *Mettā-sutta* on universal love.[23]

Obviously the texts borrowed from the *Mahāyāna* insist more on compassion. One could, even so, distinguish their distance from Christian charity, but the majority of the texts quoted sound the clear note of sincerity and a generous fervour. Many of them are deeply moving.

The openness of the Mahāyāna

The adept of the Theravāda, or *śrāvaka*, aspires to Buddhist sanctity, the state of *arhat,* followed after death by entry into *Nirvana*; the adherent of the Great Vehicle, or Mahāyāna Buddhist, seeks the state of *Buddha*.

The Theravāda had already recognized the emptiness of the individual; there is no one *(an-attā)*.[24] To this emptiness *(shūnyatā)* the Mahāyāna adds the emptiness of things, all devoid of substance. This is not the place for expounding the subtle distinctions made in this connection by the philosopher Nāgārjuna, the principal representative of the *Madhyamaka* school, whose principal work, *the Treatise of the Great Virtue of Wisdom,* is published with a wholly scientific rigour and vast erudition by Monsignor Lamotte.[25] But it is precisely by reason of this philosophical basis of the *Mahāyāna* that one may ask oneself what it is, in the final analysis, to which this great compassion of which so much is made in the texts corresponds. If "persons" are no more than conventional designations and if things have no stability, either, the great compassion has no real object. This is the obvious conclusion for a philosopher and Monsignor Lamotte is not afraid to draw it.[26] However, it goes without saying that he is not insensitive to the ideal which we are about to discuss.

The bodhisattva ideal

Without too many anxieties over these dogmatic subtleties, the popular literature of the *Jātaka*[27] and the *Avadāna*,[28] richly illustrated by decorated figures, abounds in the narratives of previous lives in the course of which the future Buddha Shakyamuni would have accomplished feats of virtue for the service of beings. The wise hare, in order to provide a starving brahmin with a free stew, collects wood, builds a pyre, throws himself into the fire and has himself roasted there. Prince Mahāsattva, seeing a tigress on the point of devouring her cubs, throws himself down from a rock in front of her and makes her a present of his body. The king Sibi buys, at the price of his own flesh, the pigeon being pursued by a hawk and gives his eyes to a blind man. The outlawed and fleeing king Candraprabha, having nothing to give a poor man, gives himself up to the enemy who had put a price on his head.

More examples could be given.[29] UNESCO, in its collection *Connaissance de l'Orient*, has published a *Choix de Jātaka*.[30] It would be a mistake to make fun of these popular narratives. This is the way in which both the uneducated and the learned love to represent for themselves the precepts of morality, and one can see how it is very exalted, here, always based on compassion for the suffering of others which cannot be relieved except at the price of the sacrifice of oneself. Thus a whole troop of monkeys were being pursued by archers who were on the point of killing them. They found their escape barred by a river and one of them (the Bodhisattva), hanging from the branches of both banks, made his body into a bridge over which they all passed. After this, he threw himself into the river where he died from drowning.[31]

It is the same inspiration which governs, in a more solemn and as it were liturgical key, the famous *bodhisattva vow*. The whole perspective of altruistic action, material and spiritual, has culminated in this ideal. A bodhisattva is a man, sometimes a layman but more commonly a monk, who has already gained interior enlightenment and is thus free, breaking the bonds of the body, to disappear into his inaccessible *Nirvana*. He postpones his death, however, in order to consecrate himself to the enlightenment of other beings still immersed in the darkness of ignorance. One does not easily attain to heroism on this path. It is essential first to become aware that "I must do for others what I do for myself. Suffering is common to all beings. Whether it is felt in myself or in others, it is suffering and must be fought against."[32]

The monk who has understood this will at the time of his ordination make the bodhisattva vow:

> I apply to the supreme and perfect enlightenment the root of good resulting from the confession of sins, the triple taking of refuge in the Buddha, his Law, his Community and the production of thoughts of *bodhi* (enlightening wisdom). May I, in a world without refuge, without shelter, without salvation, without island, be the help, refuge, shelter and island. May I convey across all the beings who have not crossed the ocean of existences at all, lead into *Nirvana* – the support of good *dharmas* and freedom from obstacles – those who have not entered there and console the desolate.

This pious wish is one which the bodhisattva may not be content with fulfilling merely by good thoughts, necessary and possessing a genuine force of sanctifying influence on others though they are, nor even by interior and altruistic virtues the merit of which goes to the neighbour; he must show by his actions his devotion to the welfare of creatures by making them all kinds of gifts and particularly the gift of the Law.[33]

Here we are, it seems to me, *at the closest meeting-point between Buddhism and Christianity*. We must realize what is implied by the fact of voluntarily renouncing an immediately accessible, eternal happiness in order to accept remaining indefinitely in the "hellish" cycle of rebirths, and that for the sole purpose of so labouring that not a single being misses liberation. If there is such a thing as an unselfish motivation, it is certainly this:

> In considering that the world is suffering, he suffers, he knows well that this is so, and also how one may escape, and he does not tire of feeling for it.
>
> The sacrifice of his own body as well as of his abundant perfection in moral discipline, patience with regard to feeble beings, absence of consideration for his own body and life, exercise of energy, unwillingness to enjoy mystical absorptions; disinterested wisdom – these are the marvels exercised by contemplatives.

I have just quoted two Mahāyāna texts, but illustrations of this theme are in plentiful supply, and one can feel how close it is to their hearts on reading, for example, the chapter devoted to it by Murielle Moullec in the excellent work *Le Bouddhisme*, published under the editorship of Lilian Silburn.[34] Its foundation can be traced in the philosophical intuition of Emptiness: "When one has come to a state of awareness impartial towards self and others, and one arrives at preferring others to oneself and considering the welfare of others as higher than one's own, then, for the *bodhisattva*, where does the other's good end and where does mine begin?"[35]

A Buddhist without knowing it

A well-known Christian of our own times, the young Carmelite, Thérèse of Lisieux, although she knew nothing of so much as the name of the *Mahāyāna*, came by chance to express her own intimate conviction in terms which squared with Buddhism when she made this burning statement in *Her Last Conversations*:

Mahāyāna Compassion and Christian Charity 283

I feel that I'm about to enter into my rest. But I feel especially that my mission is about to begin, my mission of making God loved as I love Him, of giving my little way to souls. If God answers my desires, my heaven will be spent on earth till the end of the world. Yes, I want to spend my heaven doing good on earth ... I can't make a feast of rejoicing; I can't rest as long as there are souls to be saved. But when the angel will have said: "Time is no more!", then I will take my rest; I'll be able to rejoice because the number of the elect will be complete and because all will have entered into joy and repose.[36]

Jesus, the perfect bodhisattva

We must, however, go a step further. Reflection leads to the thought that if ever someone in the world fulfilled this dream of a person completely given, it is certainly Jesus, sacrificing himself voluntarily for the salvation of all, and this with salvation not only within hand's reach but while he rejoiced by nature in the glory of the Father. As a Jesuit who lived in Japan has written in comparatively recent times, "... the character of the Christian and that of the bodhisattva have, in the final analysis, more in common than might be supposed at first glance. From a Buddhist standpoint, Jesus Christ would be a great boddhisattva, for he is presented to us as the figure of one who, from the starting-point of a total communion with the Father, has turned in mercy towards men ('I feel sorry for all these people', Mk. 8.2), to the point of the annihilation of death ('A man can have no greater love than to lay down his life for his friends', John 15.13)."[37]

Some classic works

1. The book by *Shāntideva* (eighth century): *Bodhisattvachāryāvatara, A Guide to the Boddhisattva's Way of Life*,[38] occupies a unique place in the Mahāyāna. It expounds all its themes in a poetic manner and it is the altruistic movement which provides the atmosphere which pervades it.
2. *Gampopa* (1079–1153), disciple of the great Yogi Milarepa, develops with scholastic precision and firm conviction a doctrine of a similar drift. His *The Jewel Ornament of Liberation* has appeared in English.[39]
3. *Les trente-sept pratiques du bodhisattva*. This is the title of a

Tibetan text composed in the thirteenth century by *Thome-sang-po,* master of Scriptures and logic, who lived in a cave near a Tibetan town. I have had two opportunities to come to know this text. It was commented on for us during a Buddhist retreat at Viviers, in the South of France.[40] Subsequently we translated it word by word from the Tibetan at Kagyu-Ling, in Burgundy.[41] It is a fine Mahāyāna text on which the Dalai Lama loves to give commentaries. In consequence, this commentary has appeared under the title: *L'Enseignement du Dalaï-Lama.*[42] The author proceeds in stanzas, quatrains which always end with the formula: "Such is the practice of the bodhisattvas". It is the most edifying text in the world in terms of advice on the practice of the virtues, above all detachment, self-forgetfulness, patience, compassion, the pardoning of injuries, the love of one's enemies. A Christian will be wide-eyed in amazement on observing, in simple texts of a poignant sincerity, that all the virtues of which he believed himself to have the monopoly exist, and fully alive at that, on the other side.

4. Finally, let us say a few words about the little book which Kagyu-Ling entitled *L'alchimie de la souffrance.*[43] This treatise teaches us, in fact, how to bring about the transmutation of our evil inclinations and of adverse circumstances. They originally gave it the title *L'apprentissage spirituel,* which would have done equally well. It is the work of *Djamgoen Kongtrul,* one of the great Kagyupa masters of the nineteenth century and prime mover of the religious renewal in the East of Tibet. That was an era very different from our own, in which Tibetans, jealous of their independence, shut themselves up in their own country, afraid of any foreign influence. Now, without having set out to do so, intending only to go back to the roots of the *Atisha* tradition (ninth century), the author was able to offer recommendations whose counterparts are found in the Gospels, Saint Paul, Saint Peter and Saint John. The similarities leaped off the page at me, parallel Christian texts coming readily to my mind. It goes without saying that the most striking ones concern altruism, benevolence and compassion.

Besides, the *Mahāyāna iconography* is highly eloquent in this field. In Tibet, the great Bodhisattva Avalokiteśvara becomes Chenrezig, often represented with a thousand arms, eleven faces and a thousand eyes, for he is the Lord of great compassion, longing to help all beings who are suffering. Similarly, the feminine divinity Tara, many of whose features recall devotion to Our Lady, *mater misericordiae*. In Japan you have Kwannon, Amida ...

Then if one is looking for a model, a Mahāyāna "hagiography", it is to be found in *Milarepa* who, initially a magician, was converted, underwent a terrible ascetic training under a lama and became, in the eleventh century, both a great spiritual master and a poet. The ideal of compassion is certainly present in him.

The Buddha actually exhorted the *bhikkus* who were his contemporaries: "You have, monks, neither father nor mother to care for you when you are sick. If you do not care for one another, who will take care of you? Whoever wishes to care for me, let him care for the sick."[44]

Father de Béthune showed us (at the end of 1990) a fine brass medal which the Zen monks had offered at the end of the IVth Spiritual Exchange to the European monks and nuns who had stayed in Japanese Zen monasteries. It bears an inscription in Japanese and English: *"To forget the self and work for the good of others is the highest form of compassion."* Such a sentence is as much Christian as it is Buddhist.

Thomas Merton wrote in the introduction to the Japanese edition of *La nuit privée d'étoiles*: "My monastery is the place where I disappear from the world as an object of interest, in order to be everywhere in the world through my compassion. In order to be present everywhere, I must no longer be anyone."[45]

A double bodhicitta

Mahāyāna Buddhism marks out an *ultimate bodhicitta*, which one aims to reach by various meditation methods; this is to aspire to the final stage of *Emptiness*. An important role, however, is reserved, in *saṃsāra*, for the *relative bodhicitta* which, in practical terms, corresponds to interpersonal relations within Christian charity. Suffice it to recall this recommendation of the Kadampa lineage: "Leave victory to others and take defeat upon yourself." This recommendation is taken up in the little treatise by Djamgoeun Kongtrul (p. 27), referred to above: "I offer profit and victory to the masters, the beings. I embrace loss and defeat."

This is also the recurring theme of the *practice of the lodjong*:

> Gains and victories for others.
> Losses and reproaches for myself.

On the island of Hokkaidō

In conclusion, I quote the testimony of a young Dutchman, *van de Wetering*, who spent eighteen months in a Zen monastery. As he is an eccentric rather than a mystic, describing his adventures with a droll humour, the page which follows has all the more value for that.

It appears that on Hokkaidō, the island situated at the northernmost point of Japan, there exists a little Zen monastery, directed by a master who has never attended school. The son of a peasant, he had arrived at the monastery not knowing how to read or write. However, he had solved his *koans* very well and had attained to understanding.

He was hardly aware that other religions beside Buddhism existed until the day when he heard the monks talking about Christianity. One of them had received a university education and the master asked him to talk to him a little about the Christian religion.

"I am not very familiar with it," said the monk, "but I shall bring you the sacred texts of Christianity."

The master sent the monk to the nearest town, from which he returned with a Bible.

"It is a big book," said the master, "and I cannot read, but read me something from it."

The monk was familiar with the Bible and he read the Sermon on the Mount. The more he read, the more impressed the master became. "It is beautiful," he said constantly, "it is very beautiful." When the monk stopped, the master remained for some time without moving. The silence lasted so long that the monk put down the Bible, took up the lotus position and began to meditate.

"Yes," said the Master, "I do not know who said that but, at any rate, he was either a Buddha or a Bodhisattva. What you have just read is the essence of what I am trying to teach you here."[46]

Notes

1. This is the English text of a lecture which was given in Spanish in the context of the *XIX^a Semana de Estudios Monásticos* at León (27 August–2 September 1982). Its proceedings have been published under the title *Comunidad cristiana y comunidades monásticas* in the *Studia Silensia* of the Abbey of Silos (Burgos), vol. IX, 1983. Our lecture appears on pp. 255–274.
2. Second edition, by Alain Rey, 1987, volume II, pp. 751–752.
3. Letouzey et Ané, volume 2, col. 1417 (1949).
4. *Sancti Bernardi Opera,* ed. J. Leclercq, O.S.B. and H. Rochais, Romae, Editiones Cistercienses, 1968, vol. V, Sermones II, pp. 273–274: *Dominica intra octavam Assumptionis,* N° 14 and 15. English translation: *The Divine Office. The Liturgy of the Hours according to the Roman Rite, as renewed by decree of the Second Vatican Council and promulgated by the authority of Pope Paul VI.* Collins, London and Glasgow, 1974, Vol. III, pp. 262–263.
5. More precisely, according to the best scholars, between 381 and 384. See *Egeria: Diary of a Pilgrimage.* Translated and annoted by George E. Gingras. *Ancient Christian Writers: the Works of the Fathers in Translation,* N° 38, edited by Johannes Quasten, Walter J. Burghardt & Thomas Comerford Lawler, Newman Press, New York, N.Y. & Ramsey, N.J., 1970.
6. Work quoted in note 5, pp. 111–112.
7. Absence of trouble, calmness of mind. A state of mind particularly extolled as the ideal by the Epicureans.
8. State of perfect serenity and mastery of the passions or emotions. A stoic ideal which was taken up by the Fathers of the Christian East.
9. State of complete mental repose, extolled particularly by the Desert Fathers and by the Eastern Christians.
10. Former name of a region covering North-western India, Northern Pakistan and Eastern Afghanistan. Earliest iconographic representations (statues) of the Buddha strongly influenced by Greek art. See É. LAMOTTE: *Histoire du bouddhisme indien. Des origines à l'ère Śaka.* Bibliothèque du Muséon, vol. 43. Louvain, Institut Orientaliste, 2e éd., 1967. On the image of the Buddha, see pp. 479–486.
11. The extinction and abolition of every attachment and bond with the illusory world of appearances. See Dennis GIRA: *Comprendre le bouddhisme,* Éd. du Centurion, 1989, pp. 62–65.
12. On the ancient Buddhist doctrine and the "noble truths" see LAMOTTE, op. cit., pp. 25–52.
13. Under the title *La bienveillance bouddhique.* Classe des Lettres. Bulletin de la Classe des Lettres et des Sciences morales et politiques, 5e série, tome XXXVIII, 1952, pp. 381–403.
14. In Pali *Mettā.* The benevolence which every Buddhist, and particularly every *bodhisattva* must have towards all beings.
15. "Theravāda" is a Pali term meaning the "Teaching of the Elders" and refers to the form of Buddhism in Thailand, Burma and Sri Lanka.
16. Cingalese master. Doubtless the most authoritative interpreter of the ancient Buddhist writings. He represents the fundamental ideas of the Small Vehicle.

17 Master of the monastic university of Nālandā (India), one of the best writers of the Mahāyāna tradition. Best known in the West for his work: the *Bodhisattvacāryāvatara* (= the behaviour of the Bodhisattva)
18 The eight fundamental points of Buddhist ethics: right (or just) thought, right action, right livelihood, etc. It finishes by embracing the whole of life. See D. GIRA, op. cit., at note 11, pp. 66–79.
19 Study referred to at note 13, pp. 388–389, 386.
20 The same study, p. 402.
21 In the *Évangile de la miséricorde. Hommage au Dr Schweitzer*. Presented by Alphonse GOETTMANN, Éd. du Cerf, 1965. The article in question is on pp. 55–76.
22 Museum Lessianum, Desclée de Brouwer, 1975. On altruism, pp. 137–167.
23 *Suttanipāta*, I, 8.
24 *Srāvaka*, hearer (of the teaching), disciple. *Arhat*, the worthy being, able to enter after death into *Nirvana*. *Bodhisattva*, an awakened being, who has made the vow of attaining the supreme enlightenment with a view to helping the beings in the path of salvation. *An-attā*, absence of self, ego, personality.
25 Bibliothèque du Muséon. Institut Orientaliste, Louvain, 5 volumes, 1949–1980. A monumental work.
26 Study referred to in note 13, p. 403.
27 History of one of the previous lives of the Buddha. Very widespead popular literature.
28 Glorious action, act of valour. What we have here are numerous adventures described in the Buddhist *sūtras*.
29 The preceding examples are quoted by LAMOTTE in the study referred to, p. 399.
30 *Choix de Jātaka. Extraits des Vies antérieures du Buddha*. Translated from the Pali by Ginette TERRAL. N.R.F., Gallimard, 1958.
31 In the book referred to in note 30, pp. 166–171: *Mahākapijātaka*.
32 Saint Bernard said: "... semetipsum attendat, et ex propria miseria generalem perpendat", "let (the prophet) consider himself and, starting from his own wretchedness, meditate on that of the whole world" (*De gradibus humilitatis et superbiae*, caput V.16. Édit. Leclercq – Rochais, t. III, p. 28). Earlier: "... exemplo Salvatoris nostri, qui pati voluit ut compati sciret, miser fieri ut misereri discreret", "following the example of our Saviour who was willing to suffer in order to learn compassion, to become wretched in order to learn to have mercy" (op. cit., caput III.6; t. III, p. 21).
33 In all this we are following J. MASSON, *Le Bouddhisme, chemin de libération* (see above, note 22), pp. 147–148. See also the study referred to of LAMOTTE, pp. 395–396. Also, in the *Encyclopédie des Mystiques Orientales* edited by M.-M. DAVY, Robert Laffont, 1975, the account by Guy BUGAULT, pp. 129–130.
34 *Le Bouddhisme*. Texts assembled, translated and introduced by Lilian SILBURN, with the assistance of specialists. Series *Le trésor spirituel de l'humanité*. Fayard, 1977. Chapter IV: *Le bodhisattva*, pp. 133–173. Texts quoted: pp.137 and 139.
35 Quoted by SILBURN, op. cit., p. 138.

36 *St. Thérèse of Lisieux – Her last conversations.* ICS Publications, Institute of Carmelite Studies, Washington, D.C. 1977, p. 102.
37 Hans WALDENFELS, S.J.: *La méditation en Orient et en Occident.* Éd. du Seuil, 1981, p. 88.
38 *A Guide to the Bodhisattva's Way of Life*, translated into English by Stephen BATCHELOR, Library of Tibetan Works and Archives, Dharamsala, H.P., India, 1979. *Vivre en héros pour l'éveil*, translated from Tibetan by Georges DRIESSENS, Seuil, Points-Sagesses, 1993.
39 *The Jewel Ornament of Liberation*, translated and annoted by Herbert V. GUENTHER. The Clear Light Series, Prajña Press, Boulder, Colorado, 1981.
40 See above, pp. 77–79.
41 See above, pp. 75–76.
42 Collection Spiritualités Vivantes. Éd. Albin Michel, Paris, 1976.
43 DJAMGOEN KONGTRUL: *L'alchimie de la souffrance. La voie droite vers l'éveil.* Translation from Tibetan, notes and glossary by Ken McLeod. Éditions Yiga Tcheu Dzinn, Château de Plaige, Toulon-sur-Arroux, 1982.
44 *Mahāvagga*, VIII, 26. Also *Vinaya pitaka*, I, 302.
45 Quoted by Charles DUMONT in *La vocation du Père Thomas Merton* in *Collectanea Cisterciensia*, 1986-1, p. 16.
46 Janwillem van de WETERING: *The Empty Mirror: 18 months in a Zen monastery.* Washington Square Press, 1978.

Chapter XI
The Philosophy of the Person and the No-Self of Christianity

A word of introduction

On the premises of the former Charterhouse of Saint Hugh, in Savoy, now the Karma-Ling Institute, there took place, from 24–26 April 1992, a colloquium between Buddhists of different traditions on the fundamental theme of *anattā*. I was allowed as a kindness to be present. This was an opportunity for me to write a few pages on the subject. It seems to me that this study might take its place in a book concerning the comparison of our two religions.[1]

I. The person in Christianity

Let us first quote the *Vocabulaire technique et critique de la philosophie d'André Lalande*[2] on the word *Personne*: "The usage for this word comes from two sources. On the one hand, the Stoic idea of the role played by man here below *(Prosôpon, persona*; cf. *Manuel d'Épictète*, 17; *Entretiens*, I, 29, etc.), a usage to which the juridical meaning of this word in Latin is attached. On the other hand, the use which has been made of it in theology, notably in the controversies on the Trinity, where it has served to translate *Ypostasis* as opposed to *Physis* (nature) and to *Ousia* (substance). On this opposition, see in particular Boëthius, who gives the definition which remained essential throughout the Middle Ages: '*Persona proprie dicitur naturae rationalis individua substantia*' (individual substance of a rational nature)."

The encyclopaedia *Catholicisme*, in the article *Personne (philosophie et théologie)*, traces the entire evolution of Western thought on this subject. We retain from it only this general consideration: "*Monist* philosophies (stoicism, spinozism, idealism, materialism) are hard put to define the supra-animal individualisation of the human person. They abolish it, thinking that they are enhancing it, by merging it with reason as a whole, or with nature. *Reflective* philosophies, on the contrary, grasp the person in open intimacy and spiritual experience, the experience of freedom, moral experience (Kant, Rauh, Nabert), the experience of value (Le Senne), the experience of total presence (Lavelle), the experience of transcending the world (Pascal), experiences which supply each man with openness to God, the central axis of the definition of the person."[3]

The same encyclopaedia carries an article which is shorter but of greater interest and which I shall follow in this first part.[4] If the strictly philosophical sense of the word "personalism" is of recent origin, the idea to which it refers is ancient, and distant sources for it can already be discerned in the great *Greek tragedians*, Aeschylus and Sophocles who, prior to Pascal, had a very strong feeling for the *wretchedness* of the human condition, united with the exaltation of the *greatness* of man allied with his power to judge this condition. A genuine, implicit personalism, for example, moves Sophocles' *Antigone* and drives her to defy the orders of her uncle Creon in order to show her brothers, Eteocles and Polynices, the respect due to the dead, in full knowledge of the horrible fate which awaits her. Thus she sets over against the written law the unwritten divine law which cannot be effaced from the heart of man.

However, it is only with the *irruption of Christianity* that the status of man as the creation of a God who is essentially Love found its clearest definition. The dignity proper to each human being is founded upon the universal fatherhood of God and the universal brotherhood of Christ. To each soul comes a personal *vocation* and a unique destiny which is not in the least coterminous with life in this world. Created in "the image and likeness" of God, man, every man, is called to "the freedom of the children of God".

The theologians would need only to refine this very concrete presentation of the obligations which result, for every creature, of this position with regard to both God and neighbour. In uncovering in man a reality which is "more interior than what is most inward in him" and "superior to what is highest in him", Saint Augustine, in the lineage founded by Plato and continued by Plotinus, has been the pioneer of modern philosophies of interiority. In the secret of the heart, the transcendent person of God speaks to the person of man and the latter may, in his turn, converse with his Creator, the one and triune God. Out of the debates on the notion of "trinity", already greatly elaborated by the Councils of Nicea and Constantinople, will come a more precise idea of the difference between *nature* and *person*. Thus might one conceive there to be in God three persons and one nature and, in the mystery of the Incarnation, one single person bearing at once a divine and a human nature.

The human person, for *Saint Thomas Aquinas*, is characterised by the capacity to act of itself, that is to say, to own the mastery of its acts: it is actual and subsisting *existence*, vital initiative.

These conclusive explanations would mark the whole development of subsequent reflection on the person and persons. It is in their light that jurists and philosophers would work to constitute the personalism such as we understand it today. The former bent their minds to define the *juridical person* as the human subject in so far as he is the holder of rights and bearer of duties defined by the law. Thus the free man has been progressively recognized as the one who has the power to answer personally for his actions before a court of law. The latter, following *Leibnitz*, have insisted more on the qualities constituting the *moral person*, a substance not only immaterial and indivisible, but moreover indestructible and immortal. In his *Theodicy*, Leibnitz considers that what subsists in man is not only the soul but also the *personality*, that is to say "what makes it the same person, that which keeps its moral qualities in retaining the awareness or the internal reflective feeling of what it is". It is this retention which makes it fit for punishment and reward.

The importance of Kant cannot be minimized. We owe to him, in particular, the recognition of the *respect* which is specifically due to the human person: "Respect refers always and only to persons, never to things or to animals." Besides, his well-known thought: "There are two things that fill my soul with holy reverence and ever-growing wonder: the starry sky above me, the moral law within me", inspires an ethic of the person condensed in the following formula which will be henceforward the charter of all personalism: "Act in such a way as to treat humanity, whether in your own person or in that of others, always at the same time as an *end*, and never use it simply as a *means*."

Philosophical personalism

Philosophical personalism was really founded by *Max Scheler* (1874–1928). He brought to the foreground the theme of *values*. No one insisted more than he on the *axiological essence* of the person. It is called to fulfil the *vocation* which divine love ceaselessly offers it, and which it cannot attain except by uniting itself to others in a movement of sympathy which, at its peak, is a perception of the unique essence of *the other*, seen as a witness to the Absolute. Truly to love another is to love him in God. Consequently, the authentic *community* of persons rests upon the possible encounter of each person with the Person of persons, God himself.

In France, it is to *Emmanuel Mounier* (1905–1950) that the credit belongs for having made of personalism a complete philosophy, entirely centred on the affirmation of the absolute value of the person. A fundamental theme of this doctrine is that of a radical difference between *personalism* and *individualism*, for the former emphasises, as against the latter, "the collective and cosmic integration of the person". The person is closely interdependent with the world and the community of men, whereas the individual is nothing but an abstract entity, a reasonable being arbitrarily cut out from the generality who permit him to live as man. What characterizes the person, according to Mounier, is its capacity to detach itself from itself, to dispossess itself, to set itself aside to become available to others. Consequently, the person is not in opposition to the "we", which constitutes and nurtures it, but to the irresponsible and tyrannical "one", denounced at about that time by Martin Heidegger. The person lives from its faithfulness to that which constitutes it, that is to say, in the ultimate analysis, to God himself, the founding Person of persons and their permanent attraction.

Parallel with the work of Mounier, and followed by the magazine *Esprit*, there developed in France, from 1934 onward, the *Philosophie de l'Esprit* movement, bringing together, around *Louis Lavelle* and *René Le Senne*, those philosophers who were then resolved to vindicate, against every form of scientism, the rights of the person understood as the mind itself at work in knowledge as much as in action. This renewal of spiritualism deliberately placed itself in the posterity of *Maine de Biran*, who had been able to characterise the moral person as self-perceiving in so far as it is the cause of voluntary effort, and of *Bergson*, who had successfully fought against associationism and mechanism.[5]

In a semantic study on *prosôpon* and *persona* in classical antiquity, M. *Nédoncelle* emphasises the evolution of the meaning of the word *persona*. In its usage at the theatre to designate the mask, it evokes as much the interiority of the human individual as the relationship by which another, outside him, may also perceive and indicate him. Thus, this term which would take on so much importance in the Latin world, especially the Christian world, originally retains a double, ambiguous and complementary representation, of both exteriority and interiority. The ambiguity is resolved if the person is considered in a subjective-objective perspective of love and reciprocity. It is doubtless in *Cicero* that the meaning of friendship and of social relationships, but also that of the interiority of the only God, is to be found, meanings which would have granted the accuracy of his idea of person. One grasps it also in the imperial neo-stoicism of *Seneca*, *Epictetus* and *Marcus Aurelius*, the logical connection which unites a great delicacy in inter-human relations in a universal openness, on the one hand, and a very interpersonal meaning for the relationship to God, on the other hand. With the *Christian revelation*, the personality of God is established in the interpersonality of the Father, the Son and the Spirit, that is to say in personalized Love, thus revealed as the very foundation of Being.[6]

No claims to exhaustiveness are made for the foregoing account. Its sole purpose is to to sum up the stages of personalism. Even some important authors, such as Kierkegaard, who would need a more careful study, are not mentioned in it. Moreover, it is clear that many other philosophical schools have disputed for the favours of the West. It is none the less true that this current, deeply Christian in inspiration, may be considered as characteristic of Western reflection in so far as it has its roots in patristic and mediaeval thought. It may be taken as a *competent representative of a traditional way of envisaging the human person in a Christian atmosphere*. Karol Wojtyla is known to have been one of its promotors and his personalist humanism is the ground from which all the teaching of *John Paul II* explicitly drew its sap. Faced by the concepts of Buddhism, therefore, here is a very representative current of Western concepts regarding the human self.

II. Facing the no-self of Buddhism.
  Uncompromising replies: incompatibility

The reader will remember that we have already discussed the *anattā* of Buddhism in our Chapter I – *The subject of religious experience*. He would be well advised to refer to and reread pages 15–18, in which we have not toned down the radicalism of the *Dharma* in this regard. It is a clear and classical doctrine: in this philosophy there is no personal self and the arguments of such contemporary authors as Walpola Rāhula or Chögyam Trungpa are currently well-known. We shall not repeat what we said. The contrast with Christian personalism is obvious. It seems thus, at first glance, that the Western philosophy of the person and Buddhist *anattā* are *incompatible*.

This uncompromising position is found in *Olivier Clément*, who holds, to sum up, to the antithesis between the Eastern loss of self and the rediscovered Christian self, in the conclusion to an article on *Hesychasm*.[7]

Professor *René Habachi*, a Lebanese Catholic who lived for many years in Egypt, is the former director of philosophy at UNESCO. He studied the subject[8] repeatedly and published, in particular, an article in the periodical *Études*[9]: *Réincarnation ou immortalité*. His point of departure is the subject under discussion, which he sums up in two formulas: "fascination with the self" and "obsession by the self". He shows how our West, terribly tired of its "self", seeks to flee it by immersing itself in Eastern experiences of recollection and meditation, in which it hopes to find an end to anguish through interiority. However, there is a fundamental antagonism between two irreconcilable philosophies and, in not a few of our contemporaries, a confusion between the psychic and the spiritual. One fusses around the psychic self, forgetting the timeless value of the metaphysical "I". Only the latter rises beyond impermanence and assures us of immortality. This is a deep study, which deserves the assent of every thinker with a philosophic outlook. This should be so at least in the West for, it seems to me, the author emphasises antitheses and probably has a less sure grasp of specifically Eastern values.

It is into a different atmosphere that we are taken by the recent work of a Hungarian Cistercian, *Gilbert Hardy*, who teaches at the University of Dallas, in Texas: *Monastic Quest and Interreligous*

Dialogue.[10] This is a study of comparative religion referring to two forms of monasticism: the Western represented by Saint Benedict, the Eastern by Dogen, who introduced Soto Zen into Japan in 1227. These two masters differ in many respects; it is for this very reason that the author has chosen them, for they make it clear that, despite many similarities in the ideal of the life and the paths of practice, the two spiritual paths are fundamentally different. Without any misrepresentations, the reader may grasp, after a careful study, that we have before us two approaches: on the one hand, the absolute Quest as a descent *to one's true self*; on the other, the absolute Quest as a return to God. In other words, we are confronted by a dialectic of immanence and transcendence.[11] From the very start, the *stripping of the self* as the condition of the monastic path[12] is clearly indicated.

III. Towards a conciliation

Unless I am mistaken, one of the reasons for the aversion of Westerners to *Nirvana*, is that they imagine it to be *a complete cessation of being*, a notion liable to accusations of *nihilism*. Now only a little familiarity with the texts is needed in order to see that something quite different is involved. First of all, I shall quote our friend *Môhan Wijayaratna*, who in 1980 defended a remarkable thesis: *Le renoncement au monde dans le monachisme bouddhique Theravāda et dans le monachisme du désert* (fourth century). Here is a quotation[13]: "An ascetic named Jambukādaka addressed this question to Sāriputta Thera: 'Friend, what is *nibbāna*?' Sāriputta Thera answered: 'The extinction of desire, the extinction of hatred, the extinction of delusion, there, O friend, is what one calls *nibbāna*' (*Samyutta*, IV). This statement shows the essential meaning of the doctrine of *nibbāna*. It contains the sense of an experimental annihilation such as the extinguishing of a conflagration. *Nibbāna* consitutes a beyond to the path *(magga)* and the fruit *(phala)*; its realization signifies the extinction of the burning fire of thought. 'The world is on fire', says the Buddha *(Samyutta*, I.31). According to him (*Vinaya*, I.34), 'everything is on fire because of the fire kindled by desire, hatred and delusion, as also by birth, decline, death, sorrows, lamentations, grief, despair and suffering. For this reason, the disciples who had attained *nibbāna* used to say that they had extinguished their fire.'"

It should not be supposed that this state is purely negative. *Walpola Rāhula* describes it with a certain lyricism:

> He who has realised the truth, *Nirvana*, is the happiest being in the world. He is free from all "complexes" and obsessions, the worries and troubles that torment others. His mental health is perfect. He does not repent the past, nor does he brood over the future. He lives fully in the present. Therefore he appreciates and enjoys things in the purest sense without self-projections. He is joyful, exultant, enjoying the pure life, his faculties pleased, free from anxiety, serene and peaceful. As he is free from selfish desire, hatred, ignorance, conceit, pride, and all such "defilements", he is pure and gentle, full of universal love, compassion, kindness, sympathy, understanding and tolerance. His service to others is of the purest, for he has no thought of self. He gains nothing, accumulates nothing, not even anything spiritual, because he is free from the illusion of Self, and the "thirst" for becoming.[14]

If Rāhula quotes this fine text, it is to clear Buddhism of the troublesome reputation under which it too often labours: a pessimistic religion ... But should one not see further: a clear presentation of what might justifiably be called a person in the true sense of the word, open and really beaming? This is the very meaning of the word Buddha in Tibetan: *san-gyé*, fully purified.

Some years ago, a rather massive book was published, the reading of which called for great attention: *Le christianisme et les religions du monde. Islam, hindouisme, bouddhisme.*[15] Hans Küng repeatedly confronts the problem of the personal and the apersonal, in connection with either Hinduism or Buddhism, with regard either to the divine Absolute or to the human person. No one could accuse the author of superficiality; the solutions he proposes have depth, as in the article *Understanding of God – personal or apersonal?*[16] On the other hand, his critical examination of Nāgārjuna reaches an extreme of subtle rationality.[17] He deserves to have addressed to him the pertinent remark by *Karl Rahner*: "On reaching the ultimate depth, what man knows best is that his knowledge (or what is usually described by that term) is only a little island in the infinite ocean which may not be crossed, and that the existential question put to the person who wishes to know is this: does he prefer the little island of his presumed knowledge to the sea of infinite mystery?"[18] However, to confine ourselves to the problem in hand, we need to take very seriously the reflections of Hans Küng under the title: *The dignity of the human person*. This is what he wrote on the subject:

> In the context of the doctrine of the mutual dependency of all things (phenomena), Buddhists disagree how the complementary doctrine of selflessness, the no-self *(anātman) of man* is to be understood. Even if this was part of the historical Buddha's teaching, here, at least, it was not yet a metaphysical doctrine (which the Buddha rejected in principle), but an ethical/practical invitation to an experience[19] – a call to turn away in *"selflessness"* from "self-centredness" in this sorrowful, transitory world of appearances, to free oneself from the egocentricity of the empirical self, which does not last and is at bottom "empty" and "futile", and to attain salvation by means of insight into the nothingness of all things (passing through the "great death", as it was later called).
>
> From this ethical perspective, it is evident such ideas are by no means alien to Christianity. Is not Christianity's original concern with the conversion *(metanoia)* of the *whole* person from the egocentricity of his ego to true selfhood? ... Must not the phenomenal, empirical self die – in a Christian sense – in order to come to the real life of the true self? "Whoever loses his life will preserve it" (Luke 17.33) – a key principle, which some Buddhists like to quote in dialogue with Christians.
>
> Christian thinkers, who have long understood "person" in an individualistic sense as a self-contained *individuum*, are trying nowadays to work out a deeper, *relational understanding of the person*, that is, an understanding of the human person as a being that relates. They are reacting to that fatal Western individualism that by invoking the self and self-fulfilment (of the individual, the nation, or the Church) has had a highly destructive impact on communal life. *Paul Knitter* ... has drawn attention to a surprising agreement – after all the misunderstandings – by Christians with the Buddhist doctrine of non-self:
>
> "Eminent Christian representatives recognize that Buddhism provides Christians with an opportunity to know and experience that the true reality of the person does not consist in being an *individuum*, a given entity; rather, the true self is radically, essentially, constantly in relation to other selves and to all reality; its 'being' is constantly one of ongoing 'dependant co-origination'; its being is in relating. Therefore, the true self is a selfless self, constantly losing-finding itself in its relations with others!" The task at hand, then, is to break out of ego consciousness and to experience a non-egoistic, Buddhist awareness of unity, which is expressed in the universal "Buddha nature" of Mahāyāna, but which can also be understood in a new way through biblical symbols and statements ("to be in Christ", "I live, not I, but Christ lives in me", "to be united with God").[20]

It is not only Catholic thinkers who are attempting the envisaging of Buddhist doctrine in a sense acceptable to Christianity. *Lynn A. de Silva*, the director of a Protestant study centre at Colombo (Sri Lanka), published in 1979 an important book on the subject under discussion: *The Problem of the Self in Buddhism and Christianity*.[21] He proceeds in two stages. On the negative side, he finds Buddhist criticism beneficial in its rejection of all concepts of an unchanging and autonomous subject-substance. On the positive side, he brings together the concept of *anattā* (the necessary emptying-out of the false self, or disappropriation) and Saint Paul's *pneuma*: at this level, the spirit gives us a social dimension, of relation to others, necessary to avoid giving *anattā* too individualistic a character.[22] Thus the way is opened up for a Christian anthropology in which the subject finds himself in losing himself, being welcomed by others in a discriminating communion. As Father Jacques *Scheuer* comments[23]: "The positive statements made here certainly go beyond what Buddhism would be willing to endorse, but should satisfy Buddhist requirements with regard to no-self *(anattā)*."

The subject before us is not the sole preserve of philosophers, theologians and specialists in comparative religion. It falls equally within the competence of depth psychology, psychoanalysis and psychotherapy. On these grounds, it has for long had the attention of *Dr. Jean-Pierre Schnetzler*, whose part in establishing Tibetan centres across France is well known. His convictions with regard to Buddhist Dharma have never affected his openness of mind towards other spiritual paths, as *Les Cahiers du bouddhisme* are witness, nor an avowed sympathy for the values of Christianity. Here, for example, is what he wrote under the title *"L'irréalité du moi et la libération"*[24]:

> It is with the perception of a self as a real entity in the ultimate sense as a concept that the denial of the Buddha has to do, with a conception which proposes the self as an ultimate and autonomous entity, existing by itself and having in itself its sufficient reason; it does not refer to the existence of the self considered as something relative and interdependent, of an empirical self such as we shall study it at closer quarters at the level of relative or conventional reality. Such a self, in fact, relating to the existence of others and (conceived of as) the opposition of the self to others, is the practical and dualistic foundation of our everyday existence as we know and live it; it is also the foundation of universal

suffering (p. 40) ... The confusion of these two meanings is pathogenic; it breeds disease and suffering, because it is a passionate attachment to something which has value only as a means, a practical value which is moreover unquestionable, the self being something very precious, but the reality of which is changeable and transient and the drama of which is that it is taken as an absolute. Why is the self overvalued in this way? The reasons have still to be stated precisely, but one may suppose that the attribution to the self of such qualities as solidity, permanence and uniqueness is borrowed from the world of material objects ... with our own body at the forefront (p. 41) ... We need in the first place to have a self which functions well, a strong self, as the psychoanalysts say (p. 46) ... All the mental activity of our self is egocentric, taking itself as the centre of the world: it is egoistical. Its vision of the world is always naively incomplete, biassed; we always absolutize our point of view. By its very way of operating, the vision of the self is always dualistic ... All that must be left behind. "In keeping with the truth you were taught is in Jesus, you must give up your old way of life; you must put aside your old self," says Saint Paul (Ephesians 4.21–22), and he adds: "I live now not with my own life but with the life of Christ who lives in me" (Galatians 2.20). So Christianity teaches the killing of the old Adam, the killing of the self. The symbolism is found in all the traditional doctrines (pp. 46–47).

Anyone who is at all acquainted with the philosophy of the person, particularly in a Christian context, will realize that the Freudian ego is not in any way identical with it. The true human person (as one will remember from the first part of our account) is actually the opposite of this egoistical stronghold closed in on itself, the seat of anguish and obsessions. It is diametrically opposed to it. The Christian person corresponds more to the perfectly liberated one described lyrically by W. Rāhula. This has been clearly seen, not without a certain boldness, by *Father Pierre Massein*, O.S.B., in his Afterword to the book *Buddhadāsa, Un bouddhiste dit le christianisme aux bouddhistes*[25]:

> In my exchanges with Buddhists, what is becoming clearer and clearer is Buddhist apophaticism concerning the person: everything happens as if all the notions susceptible of corrupting this mysterious reality, left unnamed – the person – must be set aside; and in the eyes of Buddhists, the *ātman* – along with the soul or individual phenomenal reality – is one of these notions. The teaching of Buddhadāsa seems to take this form: "No self, in itself, for itself", he repeats unceasingly. What he wishes to exorcise in this way is the temptation to lean on an

autonomous reality, a principle of self-sufficiency ... whereas the law of love is the law of heteronomy. The person is rightly the principle of communion which brings into being a subject in a state of openness to others, and which enables it to transcend the limits of its individuality so as to surmount the temptations of autonomy and of being closed in upon itself. Is not the Buddhist notion of *anattā* closer to the notion of person than is that of *ātman*? When a Buddhist hears this word of the Lord: "Anyone who loses his life for my sake, that man will save it",[26] his heart beats in union with ours; is what we have there not a Christian expression of *anattā*?

This is not the place in which to present the book by the Venerable *Buddhadāsa*; we speak of it elsewhere.[27] We are in the presence of an exceptional being, on every count, for his spiritual influence as much as for his courage and for his openness to Christianity. This is not to say that a Christian would endorse all his arguments. It is inevitable that he has not been able to grasp every one of our values, any more than we would succeed everywhere in understanding Buddhism. His work was published in French on the initiative of Father Massein and thanks to the labours in translation of *Father Edmond Pezet*, priest of the Auxiliary Society of the Missions. The latter lived for years in Thailand and is doubtless among the missionaries best acquainted with the Buddhism of that country. We wish to quote him because he was evidently acquainted with the problem before us, as is witnessed by his recent article: *Les religions ... celles des autres et la nôtre*, which appeared in the *Lettre aux Communautés* of the Mission de France.[28]

> The point on which Buddhism distances itself from Hinduism is its proclaiming "No *ātman*!", that is to say no individual Ātman: no eternal "principle" of the individual, for entering into union-identity with the universal *Brahman*.[29] This is because to speak of an eternal, absolute and ultimate principle of the particular individual would contradict the duality of the particular, which is individualised and manifold. It must also be said that the proclamation "No individual Ātman is not, from the Buddhist standpoint, a negation in the indicative mode 'about what does or does not exist', but an existential order in the subjunctive mode: 'Let there be no attachment to an individual self, taken as an ultimate value!' ... 'No Ātman' is for Buddhists a matter of ethical and practical truth;[30] the speculative (ontological and metaphysical) point of view is without interest to their existential and practical point of view."[31]

The most radical, non-theistic, path of the "No-self", of "Emptiness", which appears to empty out all personal value, aims at "emptying out" only the undue and egocentric attachment to one's own individual particular "self", exalted as an absolute value. The values of what we call the "person" are designated as "No-self". This is not to be understood as the negation or denial of "self", but the conversion of the individual self, his turning round. It is the negation of self-centredness, kenosis, "Emptiness".[32]

That to which Buddhists desire to draw the attention of Christians is that, in their opinion, if they truly wish to enter the spiritual path, they must renounce the desire to safeguard intact their attachment to their particular individuality *(puggala)* to the very end of the Path. Ultimate salvation and particular individuality do not belong to the same order of reality: one is of the Ultimate, the unconditioned absolute of ultimate truth, the other is of empirical experience, of relative and conventional truth.

But then, Christians say, without safeguards for the individuals, ultimate salvation is a fusion of individualities in the great All: this savours of monism or pantheism. This is how they see the fusion mysticism of Hinduism and the Buddhist mysticism of Emptiness, of No-self, of *Nirvana* ("extinction" comes to much the same thing). Now, for Christians, ultimate salvation, communion with God, is "union without confusion", the permanence of personal relationship within communion. God, the Ultimate, is person, tri-personal relationship. Yes, but does the person of whom Christians affirm the permanence, and the particular of empirical experience, which is individualised and multiple, regain the same meaning and value in the spiritual sense? Do Christians claim that God is individual, tri-individual? The designation "individual" has to do only with a material and empirical sense, relative to empirical experience. "Person" refers to a spiritual sense, true to spiritual experience; in a Buddhist perspective: *An-attā*, No-self, emptiness of self.[33]

We cannot enter here into a comparison between *Zen and faith*, which would take us too far, beyond the context of our account. It is clear, however, that Christians who practise *zazen* have had perforce to confront the problem before us. Are they not in quest of an impersonal encounter with Being? Is that compatible with Christian prayer? A preliminary glimpse is to be found in the little book by *Alain Delaye*: "Le Zen et la foi".[34] In it the pioneers of dialogue: Enomiya-Lassalle, Ichiro Okumura, Shigeto Oshida, Thomas Merton, Aelred Graham, Heinrich Dumoulin and William

Johnston are quoted and briefly commented on. J.K. Kadowaki could have been added. It goes without saying that the actual books of these various authors have careful studies on the question.

I believe that Buddhists would appreciate the views of *Tauler* on the *Ground of the soul*. *Chögyam Trungpa* censures "an ongoing flow of mental gossip punctuated by more colorful and intense bursts of emotion". He wants us "cutting through the busyness and speed of discursive thought, the cloud of 'gossip' that fills our minds."[35] "Inspired motivation comes from something beyond thought, something beyond the conceptualized ideas of 'good' and 'bad', 'desirable' and 'undesirable'. Beyond thought there is a kind of intelligence which is our basic nature, our background, an intuitive primordial intelligence ... This kind of motivation is not intellectual: it is intuitive, precise."[36] However, at the point where he descibes this ground, he represents it as an open space, a desert,[37] which corresponds to the philosophy of Emptiness.[38] Let us take care not to see in this a metaphysical entity. It is more of a psychological disposition, a "creative, open way of dealing with situations".[39]

At the heart of the *Mahāyāna* there exists a *Yogācāra* school which resembles the idealism of Fichte. A single grand *I* occupies the metaphysical scene; individual subjects are no more than the empirical manifestations of this eternal Self which thinks itself. This *Mind* is called "self-luminous cognition"; the school is called *citta-mātra* (mind-only).[40]

A brief description of this school is to be found in an excellent little book: *Méditation progressive sur la Vacuité. Enseignement du Khenpo Tsultrim Gyamtso*.[41] More interesting for our purpose is the chapter which he dedicates to the Way of the *Mādhyamika Shentong* or *Vacuité qualifiée*.[42] This is how Lama Denys Teundroup explains this subject in the article on *Vajrayāna* which is given in the *Dictionnaire des Religions* published by Poupard[43]:

> *Tantrayāna* rests upon the *cittamātra* and *madhyamaka* standpoints. Certain of its schools integrate them in the point of view called the *madhyamaka chentong* which, while resting upon the progress of the classic *mādhyamika* then called *madhyamaka rangtong*, literally "empty of proper nature" or "empty of self", develops the qualities inherent in the void. The term *chentong* which characterizes this *madhymaka* approach means literally "empty of other", and is

interpreted as "absolute perfection", "empty of anything other than itself", this being empty of otherness being that of adventitious defilements which are the delusions of dualistic perception. *Shūnyatā*, then, is a plenitude of void or "void-fullness", the emptiness of all illusion being concomitant with the fullness of ultimate reality, or the absolute perfection which, although its nature is absent from all concept, is called in the *vajrayāna*: brightness-emptiness or clear light. Not all the *madhyamaka* schools develop the *madhyamaka chentong* but, for all that, they have very similar standpoints, even if some of the formulas differ.

It will be observed that such a manner of representing the Void to oneself seems less remote than that of *madhymaka rangtong* from a "theistic" concept. Christians who study these matters find real interest in them. This is the case with François Chenique, who dedicated an article to it in *Les Cahiers du bouddhisme*[44] and is preparing an edition of the fundamental text of this school. He gives clear explanations of the controversies which, historically, surround the interpretation of this treatise. In this field, it is impossible to avoid distinctions which seem subtle but are indispensible, given the seriousness of the task. In the vocabulary of the philosophies of India and the scholars of Tibet, we come close to the precious (but too often forgotten) tradition of Christian apophaticism.

IV. The no-self of Christianity

The title of this section is intended neither to be provocative nor to parade an undeserved originality. It is no more than a reminder of fundamental, one might almost say founding, texts of Christian spirituality. The first is the solemn hymn found in the epistle of *Saint Paul to the Philippians* (2.5–11): "In your minds you must be the same as Christ Jesus. His state was divine, yet he did not cling to his equality with God but emptied himself to assume the condition of a slave, and became as men are; and being as all men are, he was humbler yet, even to accepting death, death on a cross! But God raised him high and gave him the name which is above all other names so that all beings in the heavens, on earth and in the underworld should bend the knee at the name of Jesus and that every tongue should acclaim Jesus Christ as Lord, to the glory of God the Father." For our purposes, it has often been noticed how forceful the expressions are which emphasize the abasement of Christ in his incarnation: "He humbled himself, taking the form of a slave". The Greek text is as close as it could possibly be to the Buddhist Void and its *anattā*, when it says: *Alla eauton ekenôsen (he emptied himself) morphên doulou labôn.*

Saint Paul, writing to the *Romans* (12.1) would draw out the consequences of this for us: "Think of God's mercy, my brothers, and worship him in a way that is worthy of thinking beings, by offering your living bodies as a holy sacrifice, truly pleasing to God."

In this, he was by no means an innovator. *Jesus* himself had exhorted his disciples to this. I am quoting here from Saint Mark (8.34–36), but the wording in Matthew and Luke is almost identical: "He called the people and his disciples to him and said, 'If anyone wants to be a follower of mine, *let him renounce himself* and take up his cross and follow me! For anyone who wants to save his life will lose it, but anyone *who loses his life* for my sake, and for the sake of the Gospel, will save it.'"

Among the last public utterances of Jesus is: "I tell you most solemnly, unless a wheat grain falls on the ground and dies, it remains only a single grain; but if it dies, it yields a rich harvest. Anyone who loves his life loses it; anyone who hates his life in this world will keep it for the eternal life" (John 12.24–25).

One might read this fine passage from a Buddhist of high standing, the Thai master *Buddhadāsa*: "From the Buddhist point of view, Jesus triumphed both in his mission and as an individual (now Buddhadāsa knows perfectly well that at first sight the passion and death by crucifixion were a failure). As a person, he was not tied either to the world or to worldly things. In his mission, he succeeded in converting others while putting his life at risk. In other words, he survived all sorts of entanglements, of every kind, in the Buddhist sense of the word. 'O monks', said the Lord Buddha, 'I am now free from every kind of shackles, whether they be divine or human, and all of you, you too have also been freed from all kinds of shackles, whether they be divine or human.' He was aiming at the ultimate victory above all the rest. We might say that one of the most important features of a prophet is that they are all conquerors. We Buddhists regard Jesus as one of the conquerors."[45]

"Go and sell everything you own and follow me", said Jesus to the rich young man (Mark 10.21). Now it is not just a matter of renouncing material goods. One must above all renounce oneself, as we are invited to do by *The Imitation of Christ*: "Fili, relinque te et invenies me."[46] As Saint Paul personified the same truth: "I have been crucified with Christ, and I live now not with my own life but with the life of Christ who lives in me."[47]

Maurice Blondel writes, "Man cannot gain his being except by denying it in some manner in order to refer it to its beginning and to its end. To renounce what one has of one's own and annihilate this nothingness which he is (to annihilate everything which, in us, is nothingness, that is to say everything which is not love) is to receive that fullness of life to which he aspires, but of which one does not have the source in oneself. We have to give all for all."[48]

At this level, we are close, naturally as it were, to the audacious statements of *Master Eckhart* who, with good reason, attracts the attention of our contemporaries. Those of them with some knowledge of Hinduism do not fail to compare him with the acosmism of *Shankara*, "that Buddhist in disguise". And, although important distinctions must be borne in mind, serious studies in this field are not lacking in our times.[49]

Certain books on *Yoga*, while less technical than the preceding, contain judicious comments on the different paths of contemplation, whether rooted in Eastern religions or in Christian mysticism.[50]

On the latter side, *Saint John of the Cross* deserves the interest of specialists in comparative religion. As a remarkable representative of our apophatic tradition, the radicalism of his detachment brings him close to Buddhist *anattā* as generally understood. Clearly the doctrinal basis of revealed religion is not the Four Noble Truths, but if an examination is carried out, within reasonable limits, it is possible to understand the influence of his spirituality on those Buddhists who have discovered him.[51]

A great spiritual man of our times, *Dom Bede Griffiths*, personifying a happy synthesis of Eastern traditions and Christian experiences, clearly had his attention drawn to the problem of the personality. In the evening of his life, a little booklet, *The Universal Christ*,[52] gives us the essentials of his thought. In it one finds, on the one hand, "Teilhardian" formulas on the union of persons in the Mystical Body which embraces humanity (pp. 9, 11, 23 and 60). Moreover, influenced by Hinduism, he is vigorous in his insistence on detachment from the false self, the empirical subject (pp. 37, 38, 43 and 50), in which he is supported by the tripartite division of man in anthropology. Here is an example (p. 38):

> *The true self*
> Fully realized human beings are more than body and soul (psyche). They are body, soul and spirit. This spirit is there within every human being. To relate consciously to the "spirit" is, in the words of Jesus, to find the true self. Without this "self-realization", we live as isolated human beings. We are unfulfilled and fall short of our destiny as human beings. United to our true or transcendental selves, we find our union with Christ. Beyond this we find a true unity or communion with others. All barriers of separation are transcended. Further still, we find a unity with all creation. The unity of mankind can never be attained on the level of body and soul alone. Only when we awaken to the true self can we find that true harmony with others and with the created order.

Catherine of Siena (1347–1380) was certainly not devoid of personality. This simple Italian virgin had sufficient ascendency over Pope Gregory XI, established in Avignon, to induce him to return to Rome in 1337. Her mystical life was frankly nuptial, full of love for her Lord ("think of me and I shall think of you"). She could, nevertheless, write the following lines:

> Man is nothing by himself, he possesses nothing. He exists only in his Creator, from whom he has received everything he possesses. United to this Creator who is infinite Love, eternal Truth, innate Wisdom, this man participates in the qualities of God, within human limitations, of course ... Love of his self, that is to say, of something which, in itself, has no reality, leads to nothingness, it is the pursuit of an object forever fleeing because non-existent. A love so purely selfish is nothing, truth eludes it, its wisdom reveals itself as folly, its justice as injustice and, finally, deceptions and errors will lead it to hell, to the devil, who is deception and sterility.[53]

John Tauler (1300–1361), a Dominican of Strasburg, is, within the lineage of Meister Eckhart, a good representative of Rhineland mysticism. Here is what he wrote on the theme: *How to prepare ourselves to receive the Spirit*:

> The first and principal preparation for receiving the Holy Spirit is

emptiness. The more complete this emptiness, the greater the capacity ... So let yourselves be taken by the Holy Spirit. Let him empty you out, let him prepare you himself, in such a way that you are attached to nothing, that you seem unable to do anything or feel anything, but only to immerse yourself in your pure nothingness. Unless such is your attitude, you will certainly place obstacles before the Holy Spirit, who will be unable to act in you in the fullness of his strength. Alas! No one wishes to enter this path.[54]

No one would suspect the orthodoxy of *Saint Bernard*. As the admirable commentator on the *Song of Songs*, he is one of the most perfect representatives of a personal mysticism. All the same, he could also express views which seem to us not far removed from *Shūnyatā*. Hence in this page of *Traité de l'amour de Dieu*:

"Lord, may your will be done on earth as in heaven." O chaste and holy love! O gentle and sweet affection! O pure and disinterested intention of the will, so much purer and more disinterested for retaining in itself no mixture of its own mind, so much more gentle and sweet for no longer savouring of anything but the divine. A transformed being of this kind has been deified. Just as a little drop of water poured into a great quantity of wine seems completely to lose its own nature and at the same time to take on the flavour and colour of the wine, just as a piece of iron, glowing all over and completely penetrated by fire, deprived of the form that was originally its own, perfectly resembles fire itself, and just, again, as air completely illuminated on all sides by the light of the sun becomes so similar to this very brightness of the light that you would take it for the light itself rather than for air penetrated by light, thus, in the saints, all human affection dissolves itself, as though by necessity, in a manner that is beyond words, and is then totally transformed into the will of God. How otherwise could one say, and with any truth, that God is all in us, if there should rest in man something of man? His substance, it is true, will remain, but under another form, in another glory and with another power.[55]

One might again quote several passages in which *the author of the Imitation of Christ* shows himself extremely close to the Void. He is convinced of his nothingness before God. Thus, in Book III:

– Chap. 14.3: "O quam profunde submittere me debeo sub abyssalibus judiciis tuis, Domine: ubi nihil aliud me esse invenio quam nihil et nihil! ... O pelagus intransnatabile: ubi nihil de me reperio quam in toto nihil!" "Lord, I submit myself in all humility to your unfathomable

judgements: I acknowledge my utter nothingness ... O sea that none can cross! Now I recognize myself as wholly and only nothing!"
– Chap. 31.2: "Et quidquid Deus non est, nihil est, et pro nihilo computari debet." "Whatever is not God is nothing, and is to be accounted nothing."
– Chap. 40.1: "Domine, nihil sum, nihil possum, nihil boni ex me habeo; sed in omnibus deficio, et ad nihil semper tendo." "Lord, I am nothing and I can do nothing. I have no good of myself, but am imperfect in every respect, and always tend to nothing."

Notes

[1] It appeared in *Convergence du christianisme et du bouddhisme. Les Dossiers du Dharma*, 18, Éditions Prajña, Arvillard, 1993, pp. 65–94. Text abridged in the magazine *Dharma*, N° 18, pp. 37–43.

[2] Presses Universitaires de France, 5e éd., 1947, p. 741.

[3] *Catholicisme* Encyclopaedia, Letouzy et Ané, 1988, vol. 11, column 30, by Paul GUILLUY.

[4] *Catholicisme*, vol. 11, col. 22–30, by André DEVAUX.

[5] Article quoted at note 4, col. 23–26.

[6] Article quoted at note 3, col. 34–35, 37–38.

[7] In *Collectanea Cisterciensa*, 1991-1, pp. 18–19.

[8] For example, in the *Revue Teilhard de Chardin*, N° 108–109, septembre-décembre 1987, pp. 37–41: *Recueillement Teilhardien et recueillement asiatique*.

[9] *Études*, novembre 1988, pp. 521–532.

[10] New York, Peter Lang, 1990.

[11] Op. cit., 195–221.

[12] Op. cit., 33–37.

[13] Doctoral Thesis of the third level at the University of Paris – Sorbonne, volume I, page 381.

[14] Walpola RĀHULA: *What the Buddha Taught*. New York, Grove Press, 2nd & enlarged edition 1974, page 43.

[15] H. KÜNG, J. VAN ESS, H. von STIETENCRON, H. BECHERT, Éd. du Seuil, 1986. (The English edition is *Christianity and the World Religions: Paths to Dialogue with Islam, Hinduism and Buddhism* 2nd edition, S.C.M., 1993.)

[16] With regard to Hinduism, pp. 290–292 of the French edition.

[17] Pages 538–541 of the same.

[18] Quoted by H. WALDENFELS, *La méditation en Orient et en Occident*. Éd. du Seuil, 1981, p. 72. Karl Rahner, *Schriften zur Theologie*, IV, p. 79.

[19] "An ethical and practical invitation to an experience". Rather: *therapeutic and liberating*. By the passing beyond illusion, attaining to deliverance from *saṃsāra* (from the ego, duality and the passions which proceed from them). This is a perspective of deliverance.

[20] Book quoted at note 15, pp. 521–522 of the French edition. Note, however,

should be taken of the reaction of *Mrs Shenpen Hookham* to the phrase: "The true self is radically ... in relation to other selves and to all reality." "This is *not* Buddhism," she states, "in spite of what is frequently repeated, for with this one remains in the field of ego and of duality."

[21] Coll. Library of Philosophy and Religion. London, Macmillan Press, 1979.
[22] Quoted and summed up in the magazine *Exchange*, Leiden, N° 18, December 1977, pp. 32–33.
[23] In *Nouvelle Revue Théologique*, t. 103, juillet-août 1981, p. 611.
[24] In *Cahiers du bouddhisme*, N° 15, décembre 1982, pp. 37–50.
[25] Coll. Jésus et Jésus-Christ, Desclée, pp. 197–198.
[26] Luke 9.24 and the parallel texts (Matthew, Mark and John).
[27] Account in *Collectanea Cisterciensia*, 1992, pp. (159)-(160) of the Bulletin of Monastic Spirituality.
[28] Numéro 152, janvier-fevrier 1992, pp. 34–66.
[29] Add "non-dualistic" (Lama Denys Teundroup).
[30] "Ethical and practical truth". Rather: "therapeutic and liberating". The "Buddha-nature" is considered not as a metaphysical position but as a *therapeutic* one; one takes pains to purify it. God is fundamental health, the perfectly *healthy* (Lama Denys).
[31] Article quoted at note 28, p. 46.
[32] Same article, p. 38.
[33] Same article, pp. 56–57.
[34] Éditions du Carmel, La Plesse, Avrillé, 1974.
[35] *Cutting through Spiritual Materialism*, Boulder, Shambhala, 1973, p. 167.
[36] Op. cit., p. 163.
[37] Op. cit., p. 124.
[38] See the chapter entitled *Shūnyatā*, op. cit., pp. 187–206.
[39] Op. cit., p. 163.
[40] Op. cit., pp. 194–196.
[41] Translated by Jérôme EDOU. Kagyu Tekchen Shedra, Institut d'Études Bouddhistes Mahāyāna, Saint-Léon-sur-Vézère, F-24290 Montignac, France. On this school, see pp. 33–42.
[42] Op. cit., pp. 61–65.
[43] P.U.F., 3ᵉ éd., 1993, pp. 2088–2089.
[44] Numéro 15, décembre 1982, pp. 20–36. *L'interprétation du Ratnagotra-Vibhāga* (this is the name given to *rGyud-blama*, absolute continuity). See in particular, pp. 28–31.
[45] *Christianity and Buddhism*, by BHIKKU BUDDHADĀSA INDAPAÑÑO, Thailand, pp. 97–98.
[46] Book III, chap. 37.1: "My son, leave yourself, and you will find me." He says elsewhere: *Non quaero dona tua, sed te.* "It is not your goods that I seek, but yourself."
[47] Galatians 2.19–20.
[48] Quoted by François VARILLON: *Joie de croire, joie de vivre*. Le Centurion, 1981, p. 275.
[49] We point out, in particular: Bernard BARZEL, *Mystique de l'Ineffable dans l'hindouisme et le christianisme. Çankara et Eckhart*, Éd. du Cerf, 1982 and

Doctrine de la non-dualité (advaita-vāda) et christianisme, by A monk of the West (= Père Élie Levée, of La Grande Trappe. He wrote under the pseudonym of Élie Lemoine in *Études traditionnelles*).

50 Thus, *Yoga, contemplation, amour*, by Jean-Michel DUMORTIER, O.C.D. et SWĀMI AMALDAS (an Indian Camaldolese). Éd. du Cerf, 1980.

51 The following book should be recommended, that of a Swāmi of the Ramakrishna Mission: *Pensée indienne et Mystique carmélitaine*, by SWĀMI SIDDHESWARĀNANDA, Centre Védantique Râmakrichna, 77 – Gretz, Armainvilliers, 1974.

52 *The Universal Christ. Daily Readings with Bede Griffiths*. Introduced and edited by Peter Spink, London, Darton, Longman and Todd, 1990.

53 *Catherine de Sienne*, by Sigrid UNDSET, Bruxelles, Biblis, 1953, p. 148.

54 *Œuvres complètes de JEAN TAULER*. Translation by E.-Pierre NOËL, O.P., Paris, Tralin, 1911, vol. III, p. 33. *Deuxième sermon pour la Pentecôte*.

55 *Traité de l'amour de Dieu*, X, 27–28. In *Saint Bernard. Prière et union à Dieu*. Texts selected and presented by Jean Châtillon. Paris, Éditions de l'Orante, 1953, pp. 270–271.

Chapter XII

Prospects for the Future, and What is at Stake

This chapter will perforce be brief, for we are loath to run over well-trodden ground and go over it again for the general public. We cannot close, however, without pointing out both the serious dangers which threaten us at this turn of the millennium, and the promising paths open to those wishing to profit from our spiritual resources.

The wars which are laying waste to several continents often have for motive, or pretext, a difference between religions. That is cause for horror, since the most precious ground for humans, not least on the grounds of variety, should not do otherwise than bring them closer and make them more conciliatory. To engage in dialogue must be a remedy for selfishness, and a new force for peace. Therefore there is a political stake.

There is a great deal of talk in the Church of inculturation. If this is not to be debased into idle chatter, it is time to recognize that cultures are not merely folklore, but often, if not always, the nucleus richest in coverings, the fertile source which nourishes a people's customs, literary unfolding and artistic beauty. To enter into dialogue is to venture to the religious heart of different nations.

As has been rightly said by several pontifical documents, briefly quoted in this book, the dialogue between specialists of religion can advance mutual understanding, but exchanges bearing on religious experience may do so to a greater extent. Here, it is in no way an exaggeration to emphasise the role which monks and nuns, of any tradition, are called upon to play in these approaches, often discreet but how fruitful. There are great possibilities in this field.

None of this is simply the fruit of human action, with its eddies of clumsy efforts and inevitable failures. We believe in the divine Spirit who directs hearts with goodwill and whose work, or rather whose breath, ignores the barriers of language and distance. It should not be imagined, through narrow-mindedness or hypersensitive fear, that none but Christians would be able to understand. Our esteemed partners in interreligious dialogue – Hindu Swāmis, Japanese roshis, Tibetan lamas – would be prepared, it seems to me, to endorse these conclusions. It would doubtless be easier to allow the world of *saṃsāra* to break down and run to its ruin, but the quest for the Absolute is dormant in the ground of human hearts. Is it not worth the trouble to awaken these energies and try to unite them in working for the good of our Humanity?

Around 250 B.C., the Indian emperor *Ashoka* had inscribed on one of his pillars: "One should not honour only one's own religion and condemn the religion of others, but one should honour the religion of others for this or that reason. In this way one helps to exalt one's own religion and one also renders service to those of others."[1]

This was echoed inadvertently by an assembly of Christians in contemporary India: "Other religions are not fortresses which we must attack and destroy. They are dwellings of the Spirit which we have not visited; they are receptacles of the Word of God of which we have chosen to be ignorant."[2]

Notes

[1] The text of this inscription by Ashoka is placed by *Jean Denis* as an epigraph for his fine book: *Les clefs de l'Himalaya,* Éd. du Cerf, 1986.
[2] *L'Église en Inde aujourd'hui*, National Congress, 1969. Quoted by the bulletin of the Brussels Vicariate: *En direct*, n° 98, octobre 1986, p. 9.

Concise Bibliography

John BLOFELD – *The Tantric Buddhism of Tibet*. Arkana, 1992.
Anne-Marie BLONDEAU – "Histoire des Religions", in *Encyclopédie de la Pléiade*, tome III: *Les religions du Tibet*, 1976.
THE DALAI LAMA – *Beyond Dogma, the Challenge of the Modern World*. Souvenir Press, 1996.
Jacques DUPUIS – *Towards a Christian Theology of Religious Pluralism*. Maryknoll, Orbis Books, 1997.
L'Enseignement du Dalaï-Lama. Translated from the Tibetan (= *Les trente-sept pratiques des Bodhisattva*). Coll. Spiritualités Vivantes, Albin Michel, 1976.
Dennis GIRA – *Comprendre le bouddhisme*. Coll. Religions en dialogue, Centurion, 1989.
Bede GRIFFITHS – *The Marriage of East and West*. London, Fount, 1983, Norwich, Canterbury Press, 2003.
Joseph MASSON – *Le bouddhisme, chemin de libération*. Desclée de Brouwer, 1975; 2ᵉ éd. 1992.
Méditation progressive sur la Vacuité d'après les enseignements de Khenpo Tsultrim Gyamtso, translated by Jérôme Edou. Institut d'Études Bouddhistes Mahāyāna. Saint-Léon-sur-Vézère, 24290 Montignac, 1980.
Milarépa. Ses méfaits, ses épreuves, son illumination, translated from the Tibetan with an introduction by Jacques Bacot, Coll. Documents spirituels, Fayard, 1976.
Raymond PANIKKAR – *The Intrareligious Dialogue*. New York, Paulist Press, 1978.
Raymond PANIKKAR – *The Unknown Christ of Hinduism*. London, Darton, Longman & Todd, 1966.
Paul POUPARD (ed.) – *Dictionnaire des religions*, 3ᵉ édition, Presses Universitaires de France, 1993. See the articles on Bön, Buddhism, Christian-Buddhist Dialogue, Mahāyāna and Vajrayāna.

Walpola RĀHULA – *What the Buddha Taught*, 2nd and enlarged edition, Grove Press, New York, 1974.

Robert SAILLEY – *Le bouddhisme tantrique indo-tibétain ou Véhicule de diamant.* Coll. Le Soleil dans le cœur. Éditions Présence, Sisteron, 1980.

SHĀNTIDEVA – *The Bodhicāryāvatara (A Guide to the Bodhisattva's way of Life)*, translated with introduction and notes by Kate CROSBY and Andrew SKILTON, with a general introduction by Paul WILLIAMS, Oxford & New York, Oxford University Press, 1995.

Lilian SILBURN – *Le Bouddhisme.* Texts collected, translated and presented by the above. Fayard, 1977.

CHÖGYAM TRUNGPA – *Cutting through Spiritual Materialism.* Boulder, Shambhala, 1973.

CHÖGYAM TRUNGPA & H.V. GUENTHER – *The Dawn of Tantra.* Shambhala Publications, London, Boston, or Boulder, Colorado, 2001.

Odon VALLET – *Jésus et Bouddha. Destins Croisés du christianisme et du Bouddhisme.* Albin Michel, 1996.

Hans WALDENFELS – *La méditation en Orient et en Occident.* Éd. du Seuil, 1981.

MOHAN WIJAYARATNA – *Les moniales bouddhistes. Naissance et développement du monachisme féminin.* Coll. Patrimoines, Éd. du Cerf, 1991.

R.C. ZAEHNER – *At Sundry Times.* London, Faber and Faber, 1958.

R.C. ZAEHNER – *Hinduism.* Oxford, Oxford University Press, 1966.

Index of Names

Abhishiktānanda (Le Saux, Henri) 19, 35, 87, 91, 142
Akong Rinpoche 115–17, 124, 130
Amchok Rinpoche 154
Amilon, Maximilien 231, 233, 235, 243, 245
Ānanda 42, 44
Anila Rinchen 61
Anila Zangmo 61
Aoyama Sensei 45–6, 138
Avalokiteśvara 177, 284

Bedi, Freda, see Gelongma Karma Khechog Palmo
Bokar Rinpoche 32, 104
Buddhadāsa Indapañño 66, 300–1, 305, 310

Chandana-ji (Sister) 199
Chenique, François 104, 131, 134, 273, 304
Chenrezig 26, 117, 124, 241, 245, 255, 284
Chentse Rinpoche 181
Chöding Trulkou Jampa Khedrup 196
Chogyal Rinpoche 181
Chögyam Trungpa 2, 16–17, 22–3, 38, 115–16, 139, 144, 295, 303, 315
Chö-Kyi Nyima Rinpoche 55, 193
Chö-Kyi Trichen Rinpoche 193
Chouk-seb Jetsun (Dje-tsun) 46, 251

Cletus (Father) 204, 207, 219, 229
Dalai Lama 1–2, 31, 34, 51, 54, 56, 59, 62, 79, 83, 92, 97, 100, 108, 122, 129–30, 136–7, 141, 152–5, 158, 164, 167–9, 171–2, 177, 184–7, 189–91, 195, 209, 217, 225, 235–6, 239–40, 244, 248, 266, 284
De Andrade, Antonio 160, 237, 259
de Béthune, Pierre 133–4, 140, 285
de Dreuille, Mayeul 204–6, 211, 213, 218, 223, 226
de Give, Bernard 1, 119, 133–4, 144, 202, 205, 231
de Lestrange, Augustin 72–4
Desideri, Ippolito 237, 259
Dilgo Khyentse Rinpoche 177, 193, 213, 234, 256, 260
Djamgœun Kongtrul I 34, 127, 144, 235, 284–5, 289
Djamgœun Kongtrul II 213, 234, 259
Dogen 296
Dokan, T.-Y. 26, 29, 37
Dorje Chang 235
Dorje Drakden 240
Dorzong Rinpoche 181
Dreulma, see Tara
D'Silva, Teresita (Sister) 218

Eckhart 11–12, 19–21, 306–7, 310

Index of Names

Gampopa 283
Gelong Sangye Samdrup 65
Gelongma Karma Khechog Palmo 49
Geshe Damcho Yonten 109
Geshe Jampa Tegchok 111, 123
Geshe Kelsang Gyatso 111
Geshe Kongchok 234, 255
Geshe Lobsang Tsultrim 124
Geshe Rabten 33, 95–6, 98, 100
Geshe Tengye 122
Gimenez, Maxime 231, 234, 237, 241, 248, 253
Gosok Rinpoche 225
Griffiths, Bede 91, 96, 209, 218, 221, 223–4, 258–9, 265–6, 306, 311, 314
Guenther, H. V. 33–6, 38, 289, 315
Guru Rinpoche 115, 117, 183–4, 214–15, 223, 254

Habachi, René 295
Houdart, Marie-André (Sister) 52, 205, 207, 211, 218–19, 231, 246, 248
Hozumi Roshi 137

Jacquemart, François 257
Jamyang Lekshe 223

Kalu Rinpoche 32–3, 100, 104, 126–7, 129, 133, 142, 144, 149, 200
Kamtrul Rinpoche 180–1, 215
Karmapa XVI 100, 116, 213
Karmapa 64, 149, 195, 216, 249–50, 259
Khenpo Tsultrim Gyamtso 178, 203, 303, 314
Khensur Pema Gyaltsen 165, 169–70, 202
Kunchok Sithar 187, 196
Kurichianil, John 223

Lama Chokyi Sengue 257
Lama Denys Teundroup 31–2, 39, 130–1, 133–4, 267, 269, 273, 303, 310
Lama Orgyen 231, 241, 255, 259
Lama Seunam 231, 241, 249, 256
Lama Tashi Delek 209–10

Lama Thubten Yeshe 105–9, 111–12, 118, 121–4, 126, 143, 151–2, 158, 163, 173, 187, 203, 225, 233, 241, 255
Lama Zopa Rinpoche 55, 106–7, 143, 163, 173
Lamotte, Étienne 18, 155, 186, 203, 277–80, 287–8
Le Saux, Henri, see Abhishiktānanda)
Leclercq, Jean 67, 139
Ling Rinpoche 51, 171, 187
Lobsang Tsering 225
López-Gay, Jesús 41, 44, 65

Mackenzie, Vicki 111, 143, 201
Mahāvīra 41, 199
Mary (Bl. Virgin) 81, 108, 124, 225, 274–5
Marpa 100, 104
Masson, Joseph 17, 22–3, 279, 288, 314
Merton, Thomas 21, 75, 79, 88–9, 129, 149, 223, 259, 285, 302
Mikkers, Edmond 67, 75, 82
Milarepa 46, 100, 205, 223, 283, 285, 314
Minakshi 227
Monchanin, Jules 87–8, 91
Murugan 228

Nāgārjuna 33, 58, 280, 297
Nambiaparambil, Albert 221, 225
Nechung 240, 258

Ösel 112, 120, 225

Padmasambhava 115, 181, 183, 214
Pajāpatī 42
Paul (Father) of Asirvanam 218
Pema Gyalpo (Mrs.) 184–5

Rabjam Rinpoche 177, 256
Raguin, Yves 9, 20, 87, 266
Rāhula, Walpola 295, 297, 300
Rāmānuja 20
Rancé, Armand-Jean Le Bouthillier de, 71, 74, 77–8, 82
Ricard, Matthieu 65, 235, 256
Roussel, Chantal 233–5, 241, 255–6

Saddhatissa 95, 113–14
St Augustine 3, 268, 271, 291
St Benedict 13, 22, 133, 139, 224, 296
St Bernard 20, 70, 78, 81–2, 168, 288, 308, 311
St John of the Cross 21, 58, 159, 306
St Paul 121, 277, 299–300, 304–6
St Robert de Molesme 67–8
St Teresa of Avila 35, 58, 159, 276
St Thérèse of Lisieux 282, 289
St Thomas Aquinas 17, 292
Samding Dorje Phagmo 46
Sangye Tenzin Jongdong 2, 188
Sarānanda (Sister) 209, 218
Scheuer, Jacques 140, 299
Schnetzler, Jean-Pierre 131, 133–4, 299
Shakyamuni 56, 65, 87, 129, 152, 175, 199, 237, 250, 270, 272, 280
Shangpa Rinpoche 197
Shankara 19–20, 216, 306
Shāntideva 122, 278, 283
Shechen Rabjam Tulku 193
Sherab Gyaldje 196
Shiva 160, 183, 207, 227, 229, 255
Shivānanda 91
Shungsib Jetsun 47
Snellgrove, Daniel 36, 155
Song Rinpoche 105, 107, 121, 167, 202
Songtsen Gampo 47, 237, 245
Soskar Khyentse Rinpoche 216
Sri Ranganathaswāmy 220
Subhādra 18
Sumedho 114
Sundararajan 229
Swāmi Bhavyānanda 95, 112–13
Swāmi Chidānanda 91

Swāmi Chinmāyānanda 92, 179
Swāmi Sadānanda 95
Swāmi Shraddhānanda 96

Tai Situ Rinpoche 48–9, 104, 129–30, 178, 204, 211–13, 217
Tara 117, 124, 173, 209, 216, 242, 245, 248, 254, 285
Tauler, John 10–13, 15, 303, 307, 311
Tendzin Chögyal 191
Tenzin Gyatso 56
Tharling Tulku Lobsang Jamyang 197
Tholens, Cornelius 95, 119, 139
Thomas (Father). 218, 224
Thome-sang-po (Tho-me Zang-po) 34, 284
Thukse Rinpoche 55
Tilopa 49
Tiso, Francis 155, 205, 211, 214, 221, 225–6
Trichang Rinpoche 254
Tsong-kha-pa 33, 168–70, 239–40, 245, 249–50
Tsultrim 212, 215–16

Urgyen Tulku 55

Vishnu 220, 227, 229, 254
Vithayathil, Varkey 211, 213, 218, 223

Weakland, Rembert 88–9, 147
Wijayaratna, Môhan 40, 44, 63, 296, 315

Yangsi Kalu Rinpoche 200
Yelo Rinpoche 154, 187

Zaehner, R. C. 19, 23, 266, 315

Index of Places

Alagar Koil 229
Almora 184
Amritsar 152–3, 159, 174–6, 183, 191, 201
Amsterdam 119
Ani Sangkhung 245
Annapūrṇā 195–6
Antwerp 129
Ardèche 106
Arran 118
Arunāchal Pradesh 172
Arvillard 38, 130, 145, 258, 309
Asirvanam 59, 146, 204, 211, 217–23, 226, 229–30
Assam 165, 170, 190

Baijnāth 48, 207, 214–215
Bangalore 19–20, 23, 89, 93–4, 147, 170, 174–5, 218–19, 222, 226, 229–30
Bangkok 66, 79, 83, 89, 149
Barcelona 116, 124, 144
Barkor 236–8
Belur Math 92
Benares 23
Bengal 87, 148, 213
Béthanie 89–90, 93–4, 140
Bhairawa 192–3
Bhutan 55, 102, 164, 177–8, 180, 185, 193, 256, 260
Bigu Gompa 55
Bihār 63, 175, 197–8
Bihār-Shariff 175, 198

Bīr 177, 180, 185, 216
Biyul Chöling 216
Bodhgaya 62, 152
Bodnath 55, 108, 151, 177, 192–3, 234, 255–6
Bombay 92, 148, 159–60, 165, 175, 179, 228, 230
Bomdila 172
Boulder, Colorado 116, 139
Bourne End Vedānta Centre 112, 140, 143
Brussels 130, 133, 140
Burgundy 2, 100, 126, 191, 230, 284
Burma 44, 287
Buxáduar 165
Bylakuppe 92, 156, 163, 169–71, 177, 185, 192, 220, 225

Calcutta 92
Caldey 109, 143
California 45
Camp of Tashi Ling 197
Cardoner 13
Chamundi Hills 220
Charterhouse of St Hugh 104, 130–6, 139, 290
China 44, 56
China Chok 195
Chithurst 144
Chöling 216
Choukseb 46, 55, 64, 251, 256
Chuwori 247

Cîteaux 67–70, 73–4, 77–8, 82–3
Clairvaux 68, 70
Clerlande 133–4, 140, 146
Cluny 68–9
Conishead Priory 110, 143
Cumbria 110, 123, 143

Dag Shang Kagyu 127
Darghyeling 197
Darjeeling 31, 55, 126, 148–50, 154, 159, 161, 174, 185, 191, 196, 216, 256
Dechen Ling 144
Dehra Dūn 223
Delhi 49, 150, 152, 159, 168, 191–2, 205–8, 217, 219, 230, 232, 256–7
Deoghar 198
Dhagpo Kagyu Ling 212
Dhaola Dhar 154, 201
Dindigul 227–8
Dolanji 2, 188–9, 224
Dordogne 48, 178, 256
Drepung 26, 54, 164–5, 168–70, 176, 201–2, 239–40
Drigung Terdrom 47
Drölma Lhakhang Temple 248
Dzhongkar Chöde Monastery 172
Dzongskar Institute 216

Elephanta 160
Emst 65, 118, 143–4

Ganden 26, 51, 143, 165, 167–70, 176, 187, 202, 240, 249–50
Gandhāra 277
Garchag Thekchen Jangchub Ling 47
Gaya 152
Geden Chöling 53–4, 57, 64, 208, 218, 225
Gelderland 119
Golden Temple 175
Gomang 165, 168, 202, 239
Gongkar Chöde Gonpa 247
Gongkar Dzong 247
Gurpura 172, 182
Gurung Gompa 195
Gyantse 64
Gyari Gompo 47
Gyu-tö 172

Hai Ming Temple 65
Hardwar 97
Higher Institute of Tibetan Studies 187
Himāchal Pradesh 46, 48, 54–5, 79, 92, 163–4, 176, 201, 207, 211, 215
Hokkaido 286
Holland 118
Holy Island 118
Hong Kong 59–60
Huesca 127, 145
Hunsur 163, 170, 172, 182, 189
Huy 128, 141
Huynes 257
Hyangja 197

Institute of Pāli Studies 198

Jammu-Kashmir 207
Jangtse 165–6, 202, 249
Japan 44–5, 75, 119, 137, 141, 152, 231, 258, 285–6, 296
Jokhang 236–8, 241–2
Jullundur 159, 161, 201, 205–7

Kagyu Dechen Ling 125, 144
Kagyu-Ling 2, 34, 37, 61, 64, 100–2, 104, 106, 126, 139, 142, 200, 230–1, 284
Kagyu Samye Ling 144
Kalimpong 159, 174
Kāngra 64–5, 201, 207, 210
Karma Dhubgyu Chhekhor Ling 196
Karma-Ling 2, 31, 38, 61, 126, 130–6, 139, 145, 200, 232, 267–8, 272, 290
Karnataka 54, 143, 159, 162–3, 165, 169, 176, 185, 201–2, 240–1
Kathmandu 151–2, 161, 163, 173–4, 186, 191–5, 197, 231–3, 235–6, 252–6
Kerala 91, 153, 155, 175, 178, 185, 205, 218, 221, 223
Khachö Ghakyil Nunnery 55
Kham 127, 236
Kitong Samten Ling 192
Kolligal 163
Kopan 55, 61, 107, 108, 111, 118,

Index of Places

122, 126, 151, 152, 161, 163, 173, 200, 233, 255
Kotwali 50, 180
Kumbum 26, 202
Kurisumala 91
Kurseong 148, 150, 152
Kushalnagar 171
Kyichu 239

La Pierre-qui-Vire 104, 139–40, 176, 202, 205, 231
La Trappe 71–4, 77, 79, 81–2, 139
La Valsainte 72–3
Labastide Saint-Georges 122, 144
Ladakh 35, 54, 109, 164, 176, 184–5
Lahaul 53
Laos 44, 89
Lavaur 60, 121–2, 141, 144, 225
Lawudo 55, 109, 255
Lhasa 26, 47, 55, 177, 189, 191, 231–2, 235–8, 240–6, 249–54, 258–9
London 113–14
Loppem 89, 93, 140
Loseling 54, 165–6, 168–70, 201–2, 239–40
Lower Dharamsala 50, 201
Lumbinī 193–4

Madrid 124–6
Madurai 226–9
Manange Gompa 196
Mandi 183, 214, 219
Manjushri Institute 37, 61, 110, 123
Marpa Institute 103, 231
Matepani 196
Mathurā 221
McLeod Ganj 50, 54, 58–9, 61, 64, 108, 153–5, 158–9, 161, 164, 172, 177, 180, 184, 186–7, 201, 208, 218
Mentsi khang 242
Michung Ri 47
Mindroling 248
Mont-Pèlerin 98–9
Mundgod 159, 163, 165, 201
Mysore 156, 163, 170, 220

Nāgārjuna Centre 124
Nāgārjuna Institute 126

Nagoya 45
Nagui-Gompa 55
Nālandā 123, 144, 197–8, 288
Nālandā Monastery 60, 122, 225
Nambu Ling 226
Namgyal Monastery 51, 217
Nangchen 47
Nashdom 112, 143
Nechung ri 51, 208
Nepal 2, 48, 55, 60–1, 97, 105, 108, 111, 126, 151, 162–4, 173–5, 177, 191–2, 196, 231–2, 252–3, 259
Netherlands 139
Norbulinka 242–3
North Point 150, 191
Nyingmapa Institute 226

Orval 141, 145

Pāli Institute 199
Palpung 127, 204, 213
Panillo 127
Pātaliputra 174
Patan 174, 253, 255, 260
Pathāncot 49, 153, 177
Patna 174–5, 186, 197–9
Paunar 92
Penrhos 109, 143
Petersham 89–90, 94
Pharping 193, 254
Pilgrims' Book House 253
Plaige 100–1, 103, 121, 149, 191, 200, 231
Pokhara 194–5
Potala 239, 242, 248–9
Powai Hill Park 92, 179
Pradines 46
Praglia 2, 65, 94, 96
Pulahari 234

Rājgir 174–5, 186, 199
Ramoche 47, 172
Rawame 247
Rewālsar 55, 183, 213–14
Rikon 97, 100
Rishikesh 91–2, 95
Rue Capouillet 130
Rumtek 55, 64, 172, 181, 197

Saccidānanda 91

Sainte-Baume 105–8, 142, 167, 202
Saint-Léon-sur-Vézère 212
Saint Xavier's College 160
Sakya Peru 216
Samding 46, 64
Samye 246, 248
Samye Dzong 124, 144
Samye Ling 115–16, 118, 130, 144
Sārnāth 92
School of Dialectics 51, 53–4, 138, 154–5, 161, 187–8, 210, 217–18
Schoten 129
Scotland 115, 118, 124, 130
Sera 26, 92, 109, 111–12, 165, 168, 170–1, 175–6, 187, 192, 202, 225–6, 240–1
Sera-jé 109, 123–4, 170, 202, 225, 240–1
Sera-mé 170, 202, 225, 240–1
Shang Gaden Chökhor Ling 195
Shānti Nilayam 218, 226
Shānti Stūpa 199
Shāntivanam 91, 218
Shartse 165, 167, 202, 249
Shembaganur 175, 228
Sherab Ling 48–9, 177, 185, 193, 206–8, 211–15, 217, 256, 258
Sidhbari 178–9
Sidhpur 52, 178, 182, 185, 201, 217
Sikkim 49, 55, 64, 149, 163–4, 172, 181, 197
Siliguri 148, 151, 213
Sonada 31, 126, 144, 148–9, 161, 200
Spiti 53–4, 215
Sriranapatna 220
Svayambhu 151
Swayambunath 253–4
Switzerland 33, 72, 97–100, 139–41, 146, 164

Taiwan 58–9, 186
Tamié 139
Tantric College 57, 120, 163, 172, 189
Tapovan 179
Tarn 60, 121, 123
Tashi Jong 180, 182, 185, 215
Tashi Kyil 202
Tashi Lhunpo 169, 202

Tashi Phalkhel 197
Temple of the Thousand Buddhas 103
Thailand 287
Tharpa Choeling 37, 98
Theravāda Temple 194
Thirupparankuntram 228
Thubten Chöling 55
Tibet Institute of Performing Arts 219
Tibetan Children's Village 155, 158, 184
Tihange 128, 141
Tilokpur 49–50, 52, 55, 58–9, 65, 177–8, 186, 210, 225, 259
Tsangpo 236, 247–8
Tsedang 246–7
Tsopema 55, 180, 183, 185, 214
Tsuglhakhang 47
Tsurphu 249–50
Tushita 31, 51, 108, 158, 187

Ulverston 61, 110, 123, 143, 171
Uttar Pradesh 184

Vajra Yogīnī 60, 121–3, 141
Valais 72, 131, 141, 150, 200
Vanashram 226
Vārāṇasī 88, 152, 187, 204
Vevey 98–100
Vidyajyoti 150, 191
Vincennes 200
Viraithan 63, 199
Viviers 106–7, 284
Voies de l'Orient Centre 129, 133, 140
Wimbledon Vihāra 114, 143

Yangleucheu 254
Yarenché Gompa 254
Yarlung Tsangpo 246–7
Yeunten Ling 128–9
Yol 154–5, 178, 185, 201, 217
Yumbu Lakang 247

Zangri Karma 47
Zaventem 231, 257
Zongchö Dratsang Monastery 172, 182

www.ingramcontent.com/pod-product-compliance
Lightning Source LLC
Chambersburg PA
CBHW071016240426
43661CB00073B/2323